Out Of The Blue:
The Final Landing

Yet more scary and often funny tales from
the Royal Air Force and Friends

Compiled and edited by
Ian Cowie, Dim Jones & Chris Long

Foreword by
Air Marshal Cliff Spink CB CBE FCMI FRAeS RAF Ret'd

HalldaleGroup

Published by Halldale Group on behalf of "Out of the Blue Foundation"

The Halldale Group
Sentinel House, Harvest Crescent, Fleet, Hampshire, GU51 2UZ, UK.
735 Primera Boulevard, Suite 220, Lake Mary, FL 32746, USA.

www.halldale.com

ISBN 978-0-9570928-3-9

Designed by David Malley, Halldale Group.

Printed and bound by Clays Ltd., Bungay, Suffolk
www.clays.co.uk

Distribution courtesy of Flostream Ltd.,
Slough, Berkshire.
www.flostream.co.uk

The Editors would like to acknowledge the crucial support of their sponsors:

CAE
8585 Cote de Liesse, Montreal, Quebec, Canada H4T 1G6
www.cae.com

&

Halldale Media Inc
735 Primera Blvd, Suite 220, Lake Mary, FL32746,USA.
www.halldale.com

and specifically to thank:

Andy Smith and David Malley of Halldale Group, Elaine Long (Proofreader Extraordinaire),
Neil Long of Womble Bond Dickinson, Andy Weaver of Flostream and Chris Stellwag of CAE,
Glen Greenland, Geoff Lee and Geoff Parselle for images, and all of the Contributors.

The 'Gang of Three' would also like to acknowledge the significant contribution of
Rob Christie, and his colleagues from the former Tay Branch of the Aircrew Association,
who provided many of the stories.

Contributors

Doug Aberdein, Jim Adams, Johnny Baines, Mike Beer, Alan Boxall-Hunt, Rob Christie,
David Clark, Ian Cowie, Brian Cushion, Mike Davies, Sandy Davis, Bill Dobbie, Dickie Duke,
Tom Eeles, David Forsyth, Ken Foster, Norman Gill, Chris Golds, Peter Gooding,
Audrey Greaty, Paddy Grogan, Keith Grumbley, Roy Harper, Jack Harrald, Al Holman,
Mike Holmes, Peter Jeffrey, Dim Jones, Bob Kemp, Pat King, Al LaVoy, David Lewis,
Slim Lloyd-Morrison, Tim Lodge, Chris Long, David Lord, Don Macintosh, John Madgwick,
Bob Marston, Don McClen, Bill Milne, Geoff Murphy, Mark Murphy, Dan Needham,
Gordon Niven, Colin Ogilvie, Phil Owen, Geoff Parselle, Les Phipps, Al Pollock, Colin Pomeroy,
Andy Pooley, Henry Pottle, Hugh Rigg, Clive Roberts, Vince Robertson, Ian Robins,
David Roome, Peter Rosie, Clive Rowley, Rob Sargent, Cliff Spink, Alan Summerside,
Bob Thirde, Graham Thomas, Pushp Vaid, Byron Walters, Dave Waring, David Watkins,
Gary West, Phil Wilkinson, Graham Williams, Tug Wilson, Mike Wood, Chris Wren, Roy Yule.

Cover Image
On exercise in the Middle East.

Rear Cover Image
Tornado GR4 courtesy of Geoff Lee, Planefocus.

4

Foreword

Air Marshal Cliff Spink CB CBE FCMI FRAeS RAF Ret'd

And then there were three! The wonderful, and justified, response that greeted the first two volumes of 'Out of the Blue' were testament to the hard work and imagination of my old friends Ian Cowie, Dim Jones and Chris Long. They have tapped a rich seam of aviation stories from the Royal Air Force, and other aviation organisations, which have provided hours of entertainment for so many people, and not just those of us who have spent most of our lives associated with aeroplanes. More importantly perhaps they have been able to donate the proceeds, which have so far totalled over £60,000, to several Service Charities.

Well, the stories have kept coming and many have pressed the team to produce a final volume – and this is the splendid result. The reader will once again be able to share in the thrills and spills of operational flying where the laws of physics are tested by the unwary – and the later confession is both therapy for the victim and great entertainment for colleagues – and now for us. Importantly, you will gain a great insight into the character of these aviators – hair-raising stories told with great candour and humour. Today, as you read this, new stories are being framed by young men and women of the Royal Air Force where operations have continued almost unabated for the past decades. In time they will have their own stories to tell but as a salute to them, and their predecessors, you should read this book. You cannot fail to be impressed and at times I challenge you not to laugh out loud – I did.

Cliff Spink
Keyston, February 2017

Contents

Featured Aircraft

[1] Argosy [2] Beverley [3] Blenheim [4] Buccaneer [5] Canberra [6] Chinook
[7] Chipmunk [8] F-18 [9] Gannet [10] Grob Astir [11] Halifax [12] Harrier [13] Harvard
[14] Hawk [15] Hercules [16] Hunter [17] Jaguar [18] Jet Provost [19] Jetstream
[20] Lancaster [21] Lightning [22] Lincoln [23] ME-109 [24] Meteor [25] Nimrod
[26] Phantom [27] Sea King [28] Shackleton [29] Starfighter [30] Strikemaster
[31] Swordfish [32] Sycamore [33] Tornado [34] Twin Pioneer [35] Vampire [36] Varsity
[37] VC10 [38] Venom [39] Victor [40] Wessex [41] Whirlwind

Featured Aircraft

[1] Argosy [2] Beverley [3] Blenheim [4] Buccaneer [5] Canberra [6] Chinook
[7] Chipmunk [8] F-18 [9] Gannet [10] Grob Astir [11] Halifax [12] Harrier [13] Harvard
[14] Hawk [15] Hercules [16] Hunter [17] Jaguar [18] Jet Provost [19] Jetstream
[20] Lancaster [21] Lightning [22] Lincoln [23] ME-109 [24] Meteor [25] Nimrod
[26] Phantom [27] Sea King [28] Shackleton [29] Starfighter [30] Strikemaster
[31] Swordfish [32] Sycamore [33] Tornado [34] Twin Pioneer [35] Vampire [36] Varsity
[37] VC10 [38] Venom [39] Victor [40] Wessex [41] Whirlwind

Bagotville Beat-Up

In 1990, I was serving as a Flight Commander on a Tornado F3 squadron which, in June that year, deployed to Goose Bay in Labrador, Canada, for a NATO exercise. Goose Bay is a strange and remote place, with no road links to the outside world, supplied solely by air and, in the summer only, by sea. The surrounding area of tundra provides a fantastic, unrestricted 'playground' for fighter pilots, but off-duty entertainment is hard to come by. We had discovered that, while we were deployed to Goose Bay, there was to be an international air show at Canadian Forces Base (CFB) Trenton, Ontario. This offered the opportunity for a weekend escape for a couple of crews, if the air show could be persuaded to accept a pair of Tornado F3s as static exhibits. In the event, we took three aircraft and six of the squadron's aircrew for what turned out to be an excellent weekend away, with a NATO beer call on the Friday, an excellent air show on the Saturday, and a spectacular hangar party on the Saturday night.

On the Monday morning, with the normal strict instructions not to beat up the airfield ringing in our ears, we strapped into our F3s and fired them up for the return flight to Goose Bay. Well, my aircraft started OK, but the other two both had 'snags' and had to delay their departures. Despite the instructions to depart normally, I took off in combat power, held the Tornado low along the runway, and pulled up into a near vertical climb at the far end, showing that, in its clean state with no underwing tanks, the F3 had some sort of fighter performance. Unfortunately, in its clean state with no underwing tanks, the F3 didn't have that much fuel and, after we levelled off at altitude from the reheat[1] climb, it became apparent that fuel was going to be tight for the long flight back to Goose Bay. A more conservative departure may have been wiser! When we then hit some strong headwinds en-route, the computer indicated that we weren't going to make it back with sufficient reserves of fuel, and we needed a Plan B.

There weren't many options, but CFB Bagotville, in Quebec, was not far off track and seemed to offer the chance of a stop-off for a fuel top-up. When we were close enough, we gave them a call. The Bagotville air traffic controller

---

[1] Reheat: AKA afterburner, produces considerable, additional thrust by injecting fuel near the rear of the engine.

explained that the base was on stand-down for the day – bad news – but that the airfield was open, the tower was manned, and the visiting aircraft section could provide fuel – good news! We duly landed at Bagotville, and were met by a marshaller from the visiting aircraft section, who parked us up on the aircraft pan in front of the air traffic control tower. He was surprised but happy to see us, and called for the fuel bowser. My navigator, a flight lieutenant who went by the nickname 'Spit', offered to go and sort out the flight plan with air traffic, whilst I conducted the refuel and turn-round on the aircraft. This seemed a fair and logical split of duties.

I completed the refuel, the turn-round check of the aircraft and the paperwork, and 'Spit' returned from the control tower, saying that the ATC people were quite pleased to have some trade on what would have been a boring day for them with the base on stand-down, and "THE PRICE OF THE REFUEL IS A FLY-BY"! Now, I have to admit that, although I was a Flight Commander with responsibilities and an example to set, and I was no longer the young 'ripshit' I had been in earlier years, the devil's horns on my head were kept only barely retracted and, given half a chance, they would readily pop out again. A request for a flyby was not something I was going to refuse!

We fired up and taxied out to the runway and, when I called for take-off, I asked for a closed pattern and fly-by, before departing vertically and then as per flight plan. ATC sounded slightly surprised at this, but didn't deny my request. I took off, and we turned downwind, accelerating all the while. A voice from the back cockpit asked exactly what I was planning, and I explained my intention to fly along the aircraft servicing pan, past the control tower, low and fast with the wings fully swept back[2], before pulling up into a vertical reheat climb. 'Spit' seemed content with that plan.

Even if I do say so myself, the 'beat up' was a good one. As I went past the control tower, I was level with the windows of the visual control room, accelerating through Mach 0.9 (about 600 knots) in full reheat, with the wings swept fully back to 67 degrees and with 90 degrees of bank on, to present a top-side to those watching from the tower. I had been aware, when planning this little show

---

[2] Wings fully swept back: The Tornado has the ability to vary the amount of wing sweepback between almost straight, for low speed flight, and fully swept back for high speed.

in my head a few minutes earlier, that the shape of the airfield and its perimeter was such that not far beyond the tower at the end of the 'pan' were some married quarters. Unfortunately, travelling at 1 mile every 6 seconds, by the time I had rolled the wings level and pulled up at +7G to the vertical, I had overrun the airfield and was over the top of said married quarters. The Canadian Air Force residents got the full benefit of the many decibels created by a Tornado F3 in full reheat, as we rocketed vertically up to 28,000 feet. Rolling inverted to level off at the top of the climb, I felt quite pleased with myself, and the voice from the back cockpit said "Nice one, Boss!" We landed back at Goose Bay uneventfully, one hour and ten minutes later.

A couple of hours after my departure from Trenton, one of the other Tornado F3s from our squadron got going and took off, following the same profile that I had done and getting into exactly the same pickle with shortage of fuel, diverting in turn to Bagotville for a refuel. This F3 was crewed by the Australian exchange officer pilot and a Flight Lieutenant navigator, who was on my Flight and, therefore, worked for me. As soon as they landed at Bagotville, the navigator was called to the telephone, to take an extremely irate call from a Canadian Air Force Colonel, who wanted to know who that idiot pilot was who, a couple of hours ago, had flown his Tornado "through my barbeque"! He wanted the pilot's name, rank and number, along with the squadron commander's, as he planned to make a formal complaint. The navigator knew straight away who was responsible and, with commendable quick thinking, told the Colonel that the pilot was "only a young lad on his flight", and that he would deal with him personally when he got back to Goose Bay; there was no need to involve the squadron commander. The Colonel was persistent, but the navigator was more so; his argument won the day, and he was left to deal with the recalcitrant personally.

When this second Tornado F3 landed at Goose Bay, the crew had plenty of 'ammunition' to expend on me, their Flight Commander; this took several days to run out, and cost me many rounds of drinks. During this aftermath, which fortunately for me was nowhere near as serious as it could have been, my navigator 'Spit', who had told me that the Canadians at Bagotville had requested the fly-by, disclosed that actually they had not done so and, in fact, it had all been his idea! How could I have been so gullible?

When Mike Met Victor

When I was nearing the end of my flying training at RAF Topcliffe in 1964, I read an article on the front page of the RAF News, covering the arrival of the first Handley Page Victor B2 Blue Steel[1] at RAF Wittering. The sight of that impressive machine, flying low down the runway in front of welcoming crowds, made up my mind for me - that's what I would like to do. While my wish eventually came true, it could have turned out to be the shortest aircrew tour in history.

I was a 20-year-old Pilot Officer first tourist Air Electronics Operator, arriving at RAF Wittering from the Victor 2 Groundschool at RAF Gaydon, to do my simulator and flying training on Victor Training Flight, before joining 139(Jamaica) Squadron. I had already acquired the trappings of a young officer - a written-off car and an outstanding loan. I now drove a badly-dented 1946 Daimler, bought for £30 in some rugby club. The Daimler was a pig - nothing much worked, and it had a pre-selector gear box. Pre-start checks were difficult; the electrics were shot, so I had to raise the bonnet, set the throttle by jamming a book under the linkage, and swing it on the starting-handle before crewing back in.

On my first day at Wittering, I was scheduled to be in the simulator, down near the Ops Block, some distance from the Officers' Mess. I awoke late (a few too many Norwiches the night before), rushed the niceties of hygiene and into uniform. To get to the simulator quicker, I decided to use the Daimler. I did the pre-starts in the car park, and shot away to the Ops Block. It was a frosty, foggy morning, and the car was iced up. As I approached the Ops Block, I slowed down, looking for a parking spot, and the engine died on me in the middle of the road. My simulator time was not far off, so I left the cab hurriedly, rushed to the bonnet, jammed in the book, and swung the handle. It roared into life; excellent, I thought, until it started off down the road on its own - I had left it in third gear!

In a panic I tried restraining it, hands thrust forward. By the time I worked out that I needed to be in the cab, it was going too fast. The Daimler brushed me

---

[1] Blue Steel: A British, air-launched missile, built to arm the V bomber force.

aside, and off it set, unmanned, with Pilot Officer Beer in hot pursuit on foot, but losing ground. The road ended in a T-junction. Straight on was the airfield, the apron of a hangar and the taxiway. I looked at what lay ahead of the fleeing car... and that's when I first set eyes on a real Victor B2 - XL231. The aircraft had been towed out of the hangar, and parked on the apron. The Daimler set course towards the aircraft, like a dog on heat. 'Bugger,' I thought - my first day at Wittering is shaping up to be my last. The car continued accelerating, reached the T- junction, tore across it, mounted the kerb and roared onto the grass, heading for the apron. A collision between car and Victor undercarriage seemed inevitable. I watched in horror, convinced my third party insurance would need talking up for the impending disaster.

But lo! She began losing speed; could it be that my career was on track again? Yes - the Daimler was definitely running out of puff. She reached the edge of the apron, rolled on to the tarmac, and quietly halted, lovingly close to the B2's port undercarriage. I dashed down the road, and there was my book - the throttle-jammer - lying on the grass, dislodged by the jolt of mounting the kerb, causing the throttle to close and the cold engine to stall. Quickly looking around, and noticing that the debacle had no witnesses due to the fog, I crewed in, gear to neutral, did the pre-starts and drove it back to Ops. I made the simulator slot on time - but my underwear needed changing. On 16 November 1964, I completed my first solo sortie as a Victor 2BS AEO in the same aircraft, XL231. She bore no malice, and I swear she was smiling.

Credit: Flypast-Key Collection

A Tale Of Two Forts

No self-respecting town or village in Arabia can be without a fort and, during my time with 8 Squadron based in Aden, there were two places and two forts which I remember particularly well, because the lively action at these places was closely linked.

What is now South Yemen was previously the British controlled Aden Protectorate. For many years, the aircraft of No 8 Squadron, at Khormaksar, had been helping land forces to keep the peace, in an area of Southern Arabia where tribes were historically hostile to each other and to any governing authority trying to constrain them. In the late 1950s, the Squadron was equipped with the de Havilland Venom, a fine aircraft with a sparkling performance and an impressive operational ground attack capability. Its de Havilland Ghost engine conferred another useful operational advantage: it seemed to be able to chew up the frequently encountered ground-fire and ricochet damage and keep going. One of the troublesome areas often claiming 8 Squadron's attention was Dhala, then one of the small states in the Aden Protectorate.

Heading north out of Aden, on a road often little more than a desert track, you left the desert behind and entered the Radfan hilly area of the Dhala Emirate. The Aden to Mecca route passed through Dhala, but the unrest here was influenced by close proximity to the Yemen border. Yemenis saw Aden and the territories of the Protectorate as theirs; they would frequently mass on the borders, and try to occupy part of the Protectorate. In the late 1950s, after Suez, the powerful voice of Cairo Radio further stirred things up around Dhala. There was a strong British Army and Aden Protectorate Levy (APL) military presence there, holding the lid on a particularly sensitive place. Venoms often found themselves there, lending support during the many actions which seemed to erupt.

The Dhala Emirate was mostly scattered settlements, but behind the main town was a large mountain, the Jebel Jihaf. On top of this mountain was a small garrison and a Government Guard fort. In April 1958, the Yemenis had managed to subvert some of the leading sheiks of the Dhala Emirate; they were given rifles and ammunition from the nearby Yemeni garrison town of Qataba, and began targeting the fort atop the Jebel. While this was happening, on 28th April, the area Assistant Political Adviser, no doubt a fine colonial officer, perhaps un-wisely or perhaps unknowingly went to investigate a complaint of kidnap and murder. This was unfortunate timing; he and his escort were ambushed. They took refuge in the fort, joining the rest of the troops there. Besieged, they all quickly began running short of ammunition and food.

On the evening of 30 April, an aircraft from Khormaksar's resident Valetta squadron dropped supplies to those on top of the Jebel. With plenty of ground fire coming up, this was a potentially scary task and the operation was closely supported by Venoms. In the fading light, I distinctly remember the scene of a circling Valetta, coolly and accurately dispensing the supplies around the fort, whilst we Venoms, in two pairs and directed by a forward air controller, sprayed the dissident area with 20mm cannon, and launched rockets into precise dissi-dent positions when they could be identified. Neither the Valetta nor our aircraft were damaged by ground fire, and afterwards we all went back to the mess bar at Khormaksar, where the Valetta crew, their Squadron compatriots and their highly-regarded Venom friends unwound. It had been a thirsty day and, forti-fied by cold Allsops, a rather fine party developed, where everyone congratulated everybody else on what had been a colourful joint operation. Someone said they should make a film about it. Two days later, Venoms flew an intense programme of sorties, during the final stages of the relief of that particular fort by The King's Shropshire Light Infantry.

But this story concerns two forts, and the second in the tale was just across the border from Dhala - at Qataba in Yemen. As befitted a Yemeni garrison town, the Qataba fort was impressive, a square of four walls with a central quad-rangle. It was as much a barracks as a fort, for Qataba was one of those places on the border where well-armed Yemeni troops would mass and attempt terri-torial takeover. On 6 May, Protectorate Levy troops were attacked by Yemenis, who had crossed and established themselves in sangars (temporary fortified posi-tions). The Venoms called in to attack the rebel positions came under fire from anti-aircraft guns across at Qataba. Now, the place had been out of favour with us for a considerable time, and we long awaited an opportunity to attack such a splendid target. A squadron pilot went up to Dhala airstrip in a Pembroke communications aircraft and, equipped with a powerful telescope, he looked closely across the border at the Yemeni positions, especially the concealed and unfriendly artillery. On the following morning, the Yemenis were presented with some pretext to fire across the border, while Venoms orbited out of earshot. The Yemenis took the bait – and we moved in to start attacks, which continued in a series of sorties throughout the day. Rocket strikes destroyed most of the guns, whilst fuel and ammunition exploded and burst within the building. Early on, before the guns were dealt with, we encountered much enemy fire coming up at us, and several Venoms were damaged but, mercifully, no one was shot down. More sorties were flown on the following day, to complete what was a significant demolition job. We thought it unlikely that a Yemeni would be choosing Qataba for a future posting.

The Dhala area never ever became peaceful; we often found ourselves there again in succeeding months. And, during the Hunter era, when this equally fine aircraft had taken over from the Venom, and when the politics of British involvement in Aden were more newsworthy, the battles of The Radfan would frequently hit the headlines.

Credit: Les Phipps

Cloud-Break

It was a quiet afternoon on 54 FGA[1] Squadron at RAF Waterbeach – a day for 'filling squares' on the training requirements board. I was sent on a low-level cross-country in a Hunter FGA9; the route was to the west over the south of England, north over Wales and back to base. A simple, triangular route, speed 420 knots, height 250 feet AGL[2].

In those days, there were no radio altimeters, and the only navigation equipment was either one ADF[3] or one DME[4]. Navigation was accomplished at low level by thumbing your way along a chinagraph line you had drawn on a carefully-folded 1:500,000 scale map. A mark every 7 miles from an easily-identified starting point denoted each minute flown along the route.

I flew the first leg without incident, then turned north to fly over Wales. I could see that the Brecon Beacons were cloud-covered, so I eased up over the cloud, and reduced the indicated speed slightly, to maintain the groundspeed and keep the timing accurate. After a few minutes, it was getting boring, so I thought "I'll just ease down a bit and skim the clouds". I was enjoying this when WHOOSH, a farmhouse went past! – and it was slightly above me! So I must have been flying past a fairly steep hill – Big Shock, the 'cloud' was about 20 feet thick!

A very chastened young pilot flew back to base. I wonder what it was like for the farmer…

Credit: Elliott Simpson

---

[1] FGA: Fighter Ground Attack.
[2] AGL: Above Ground Level.
[3] ADF: Automatic Direction Finding.
[4] DME: Distance Measuring Equipment.

A Darker Shade Of Blue
(In Several Senses Of The Word "Darker")

Marcel Berthomé, the oldest Maire in France at 94 years of age, winning 9 consecutive elections since 1971, confided to me that if he had been successful in gaining re-election so many times, it was because he had consistently delivered everything he had promised for his Commune, Saint-Seurin-sur-l'Isle, and its 3000 souls. This sprightly nonagenarian, with a full head of hair – albeit a darker shade of black than nature would have it - continues to deliver. A glance at the Commune's Site shows that, under his stewardship, the village has an approach to ecological solutions way in front of most others in France. So what has this got to do with RAF flying I hear you ask? Stick with it and you will see.

Monsieur le Maire Marcel went on to say, "In France, when we need something significant done, we consult. We form a Committee, which takes many months, if not years, to come to a conclusion and to make its recommendations. We then create another Committee to review the findings of the first Committee – and it reports after several more months, if not years. We probably then have an appeal and a counter-appeal and another Committee review." Here his voice tapered off, only to strengthen, "In my Commune, I run things using the principles I learned flying with the RAF from 1943 to 1945. You define your aim and you stay focused on that, not allowing extraneous things to divert you."

So here is the first manifestation of the "Darker Shade of Blue." Marcel flew in the dark blue uniform of the French Air Force with the "Groupes Lourds" – the two French Air Force Halifax Squadrons, integrated within Bomber Command at RAF Elvington, and flying intensively from June 1944 to April 1945, with losses of 41 aircraft and 216 aircrew - about a 50% attrition. These two squadrons had the RAF Squadron numbers 346 and 347, and the French Escadre identities Groupe 2/23 'Guyenne' and Groupe 1/25 'Tunisie' respectively. They moved to Merignac, Bordeaux in October 1945. About a dozen of those who participated remain alive, all well into their nineties. In this story, I do not intend to address details of their training, their incorporation into the RAF, or their operational achievements, which are well documented at the Yorkshire Air Museum at the former RAF Elvington, where their contribution to the Allied

War effort is justly recognised. Several books have covered their activities, and there is a large volume of information in both English and French on the Internet, readily accessible through Google searches.

In painting the backdrop to my second "Darker Shade of Blue" moment, it is worth mentioning, however, an element which will be little known to readers: the tribulations encountered by these young people on arriving in Britain to continue the fight, perspectives which, understandably, are little covered in English documentation, and only sparingly so in French. On arrival in 1943, by boat from North Africa, they were imprisoned in what was, to all intents and purposes, a PoW Camp and interrogation centre at Liverpool Racecourse, as part of the "Filtration" by the British system, aimed at detecting 5th Columnists. This would have been quite a morale-tester when, by opting to come to the UK, they had defied Vichy voices not to trust "Perfidious Albion." The British reader will immediately understand the need for security involving people who had previously been in action against the British in various Vichy theatres in Africa; but it is not too difficult to imagine how they felt about what would seem to them as brutal and unnecessary treatment by their new ally. Not so long before, complying with orders issued by the French National Government in Vichy, they had fought the British as an enemy. Many would have been forgiven for wondering whether they had, after all, made the right choice.

Perhaps the most morale-sapping aspect of all was that most felt unable to tell their families or friends in France where they now were, for fear of reprisals against family members by the German occupiers, or by French "Milice", loyal to Vichy and their German overlords. Many had wives and children in France, but could allow themselves no contact with them for almost two years. They also had to tolerate the political confusion created by those French colleagues who saw General de Gaulle as the French supremo, and those who did not. One anecdote recounts how a refusal to emblazon their Halifaxes with the Free-French "Cross of Lorraine" was only overcome when General Valin, Head of the Free-French Air Force, personally travelled to Elvington to order that the aircraft be painted.

Fortunately, those initial challenges were soon overcome, and the survivors I met were unanimous in their praise of the RAF, recalling how warmly they were treated at Elvington, by RAF colleagues and by the people of York and surrounding areas. They talk affectionately of the farewell address by the Station Commander, and how all the Station personnel assembled to see them off on their permanent return to France. One speaks with undisguised pride at being awarded his RAF Sergeant's stripes, before receiving the French equivalent.

All this is warmly contrasted with the bitterness which remains in their minds to this day, relating to the reception they encountered on returning to France after VE day in 1945. One relates making his way, with considerable "unofficial" help from British and Americans en route, from Elvington to Dover, across the Channel and then to the French Aviation Ministry in Paris. There he was told that he was unwelcome, and that General de Gaulle was "not recognised by us." He found accommodation and food for his time in Paris with British units. Here too, he learned that he and his Squadron friends were labelled "Les Planqués" – probably best translated as the "Hiders" or the "Dodgers".

Worse was to come, as those who had become military only "for the duration", and wanted to return to civilian life, found it impossible to gain discharge, living for many months in a twilight zone - not being accepted within the French Air Force, yet not being able to achieve release from it. Many found the dice stacked against them as "planqués" when they sought to find work – one describing how, in desperation, he had travelled to Algeria to meet the family of a friend, through whose patronage he had subsequently found paid employment.

So there you have it. An episode, little known on either side of the Channel, which involved a group of men and women, many of whose colleagues made the ultimate sacrifice. People whose contact with our predecessors in Royal Air Force blue made a lasting and very positive impact on their lives, and those of the families they went on to raise, but for whom "Out of the Blue" had a very dark side to it.

As a postscript, this additional anecdote may be thought by some readers as "Dark", by some as mere coincidence. One of the nonagenarians describes, in a blog, being driven from Merignac, Bordeaux, after the ceremony in October 2015 to mark the 70th anniversary of the Squadrons' arrival there from Elvington. The plan was to travel right across the middle of France to his home in the east, instead of taking the longer but much faster motorway route. He did so deliberately, planning to stop in a village in the middle of France, whence he recalled one of his Squadron friends had originated. That friend had been killed in a Squadron attack over Germany in 1944.

He stopped beside the village War Memorial to check for his friend's name. On seeing that it was there, he paused for a few minutes in reflection. He became aware of an elderly lady at his elbow. She asked what he was seeking. When he told her, mentioning his friend's name and telling her of his loss with the RAF, she told him that she had been engaged to the young man before the War, that she had been told that he had died, but that, until that chance meeting, she had known nothing of the when, how or where.

Why was she there that day? Why had she talked to the old man at the War Memorial? Both were convinced that their friend and fiancé had "engineered" the meeting. I leave readers to draw their own conclusions.

Credit: RAF

And There We Were ...

As a peacetime warrior (now there's a fetching oxymoron!), my flying career was happily free from unsought excitements, but the incident that evening above Malaysia in 1964 stirred the blood somewhat.

In former times, when the Empire experienced difficulties with fractious folk in distant parts, a gunboat was despatched to impose order and respect. Later, with inevitable military inflation, a batttleship would be sent. But, in the mid-20th century, when the Indonesians were threatening our friends in SE Asia, a flight of V-bombers was deployed to Singapore with the clear message: "Don't mess with us!" So, that was how I found myself commanding a flight of four Victor Mk lAs of No 57 Squadron, detached from our home base of RAF Honington to Tengah, Singapore.

On the night of November 24 1964, I was the navigator, with Flight Lieutenant Terry Filing the pilot and captain, of XH614 on a practice bombing sortie. As we climbed our way North over the Straits of Malacca, to the bombing range near Penang, the weather was fairly normal for the area, with the usual cu-nims[1] bubbling up. While winging our way through the wispy tops of the clouds, without any indication of trouble brewing, there was a flash and a loud bang from the No 2 engine and it wound down. The drill for a major engine failure in the Victor was to switch off its neighbor, as they were embedded in pairs in each wing root. Screaming "Mayday", we turned starboard to come over land while, as a well-trained crew, we sorted out what to do next. Before we could gather our wits, and only about 40 seconds after the first explosion, the No 4 (located on the other wing) also flashed, banged and wound down. This time Terry shrewdly elected not to shut down its companion!

So, with full power on the one remaining engine, No 3, we headed back to Tengah, gradually - but not gradually enough - losing altitude. I peeked aft through the periscope but, apart from being able to confirm reassuringly that the tail still seemed to be firmly attached, I could see no sign of damage. Perhaps, if I had been able to scan the undersurfaces of the aircraft, we would have been more perturbed. Meanwhile Pete, my co-navigator, was thinking about how he

---

[1] Cu-nims: Cumulo Nimbus - cloud type associated with thunderstorms.

could make himself useful as, with the electrics awry, he had lost the use of all his radar gear. Our AEO, Alf, was determinedly trying to restore to the vital equipment such power as he could switch. Meanwhile, Terry and his co-pilot, Tony, were very busy going over all the emergency drills, none of which, of course, had envisaged the novelty of trying to stay airborne on one engine.

In a break in the proceedings, Terry cheerfully remarked "It's all go tonight chaps", and enquired gently of the rear crew members if we wished to bale out. We were unanimous - No! Even in its present messy condition, our Victor was our best parachute. In our review of the situation, we also elected not to jettison our load of practice bombs, lest they harm people on the ground. Terry decided that, if he could restart No 1 engine, he would have a crack at landing back at base. After several attempts to restart the No l, in the rarefied air at our altitude, the engine could not be persuaded to kick in.

Readers may be wondering, at this juncture, what it was that caused the embarrassing failure of the two engines, which had gone a long way to spoiling our entire evening. In a phrase, "Centre-line closure". The Mk 1 Victor was powered by the Rolls Royce Sapphire, a normally reliable and efficient engine. The only other RAF aircraft powered by it was the Javelin, of which several had been lost during the preceding few years, mostly as a result of engine failures in the tropics. A modification had been introduced and, although some modified engines had been installed in Victors, no one had read across from the Javelins to our type of aircraft.

The Sapphire's axial-flow compressor[4] case was built as a clamshell, the two semi-cylindrical casings being held together by a row of nuts and bolts along each side. The bolts passed through flanges that were thicker than the rest of the casings. In high cirrus clouds, as experienced in the top of tropical cu-nims, the compressor centrifuged the ice crystals to the inside of the casing. There they melted but, because of the differential thickness of the casing, it shrank non-uniformly, becoming oval instead of circular in section. The stators[2] along the minor axis of the oval closed on to the centre-line, and impinged on the rotating part of the compressor; you can work out the result! Incidentally, the modification devised to solve the problem was to fix abrasive strips between the

---

[2] Stators: Fixed, non-rotating blades that form part of an axial-flow compressor.

rotor blades, so that they ground down intruding stators. All of this we were to learn later.

Back to my tale and RAF Tengah, where the tannoy was going incandescent, pleading: "The 57 Squadron Detachment Commander is to report to the tower immediately!" I wish, but I was otherwise engaged. On its one functioning engine, our Victor gently drifted down as we approached the welcoming lights of Singapore, and Terry again attempted a relight of No 1. This time, in the denser air, it bit - we were back in business! Our Victor was very heavy for landing, but the circumstances were less than ideal for hanging about to lighten it by burning off fuel. Terry lined up for the long, fast approach at Tengah. An overshoot was out of the question and, as an undershoot was also best avoided, Terry's options were limited. He put XH614 down firmly at the end of the 8000-ft runway, and equally firmly applied the brakes. The Victor was a hot ship for its time, and a braking parachute was usually deployed to slow it on landing. Just occasionally, the 'chute, instead of deploying, just fell off. Sod's Law ensured that this was such an occasion! The 'chute left us when we needed it most. Terry stood on the brakes, but they burned out and, although the aircraft was retarded, it still went off the end of the runway with its crew bracing like crazy. It rolled gently to a stop in the overshoot area and, after a pause for sighs of relief, we realized that there was still the matter of the burnt-out brakes to address.

So, with a torch and a fire extinguisher, I lowered myself out of the door and examined the undercarriage. It was crackling and smoking, but there was no sign of fire - to the apparent disappointment of the crash crews, who roared up to do their heroic thing. While my fellow crew members were tidying up indoors, I examined the exterior of XH614, to see if there was anything to indicate the cause of our undignified early return. The 10 x 4-ft panel under the No 2 engine was gone, leaving the entrails of the engine exposed. The flaps aft of the engine were buckled and heavily scorched, as was the port side of the rear fuselage. It was all too clear that, if the rear crew members had elected, or been forced to, bale out of the door on the port side of the cabin, we might well have been shredded.

The remainder of our eventful evening was spent in compiling and sending off the usual accident report. It caused quite a stir at HQ Far East Air Force, and back home at Honington and HQ Bomber Command. Despite a quarter of our aircraft being out of action, the operational mission of our detachment had to be maintained. The reason for the engine failures was soon established, along with the fact that, fortuitously, between them, our remaining three Victors happened to have six modified engines. Our engine fitters were put to work and swapped engines around, so that each of the aircraft had two good engines. In a few days, a replacement Victor was flown out from Honington, along with more modified engines. Our detachment was back to full strength after a commendably short time.

Best of all, Terry Filing was awarded an immediate Air Force Cross.

Postscript:

The subsequent detailed inspection of XH614 revealed a hole in the bulkhead, between the Nos 1 and 2 engines, where a piece of the disintegrating No 2 had penetrated. The drill in the event of a major engine failure, to close down the adjacent engine, was soundly based.

XH614 was parked in a corner at Tengah, and was robbed blind for spares for months afterwards. Then, a repair team from the UK worked on it for several weeks. With the runway closed for unrelated repairs, a No 55 Squadron crew flew it off from the perimeter track and staged it all the way back to the UK, where it behaved itself for years as a bomber and then as a tanker.

At the end of 1965, the Filing crew finished its tour, and we went our separate ways, Terry to a course to learn Chinese! He retired in the late 1980s as a Group Captain, Director of Intelligence and Security of the RAAF. Now settled in Perth, Western Australia, he has not given up trying to improve his golf handicap.

Credit: Arpingstone/Wikipedia

Manual Labour

The Hunter Pilots' Notes described the aircraft's handling in words to the effect of: "The controls are light throughout the speed range." This was true when in powered control, with functioning hydraulics. However, the system reverted to direct mechanical links to the control surfaces, either on loss of hydraulic pressure, or at the flick of a couple of switches on either side of the cockpit. In manual control, the stick forces to counter the 300- or 400-knot aerodynamic loads on the control surfaces were substantial. Hard manoeuvring, like aerobatics, required physical strength and determination.

This adventure in the T7 (two-seat variant) probably started in a crew-room or bar, sometime before the incident. The T7s were often used to give airborne experience to students on Forward Air Controller (FAC) courses; the trainees were predominantly from the army. We were at Sharjah, and I was flying one such, an Army Air Corps (AAC) helicopter pilot who could, therefore, take a fuller part in handling the aircraft than your standard infantry or gunner officer. One of the older Squadron shags set about a wind-up with his description of a wizard jape. He assured one and all that the victim would be incredulous at Hunter pilots' extraordinary strength and muscle power.

We took off and headed for the exercise area, with my passenger, as was normal, in the right-hand seat. We took the opportunity for some general handling, and to view some sights. One of these was an AAC campsite on the floor of a large wadi (dried-up river bed). Some time previously, the whole camp, including 2 choppers, had been washed away one night; a flash flood swept away the tents, vehicles and kit, following thunderstorms in the mountains many miles away to the east. An RAF Wessex later hauled the choppers out of the wadi, some distance downstream. My passenger had not been involved in that debacle, but he told me about it. As we tooled along at about 2,000 feet enjoying the views, 'shag's' words came back to me: "throw the old Hunter around a bit, recover to straight and level, and call the passenger to look at something on the right hand horizon. Then flick the powered controls into manual, and hand him the controls with the instruction to do some similar hard manoeuvres." This I did, and was immediately subjected to 6G, as my passenger wound in full nose-up trim on his trim switch (a powerful electric motor drove the trimmer, and the right hand, passenger's/instructor's, stick-top switch overrode the left). I hurriedly reselected the powered flying controls back on! By the time I managed take back and regain control we were pointing vertically downwards, deep in heavy buffet at about 3,000 feet, and over 6G recorded.

It was a hard school out there, and much learning like this was of the on-the-job kind. I never established for sure that I hadn't been the victim of this particular jape!

Credit: Arpingstone/Wikipedia

How Deep A Hole?

In late 1948, I joined the RAF and was sent to Rhodesia for my pilot training. This was great; I had been afraid that I might end up in one of the Flying Training Schools in the UK, and so would miss the chance of getting into the middle of Africa. I had been all round the coast of that continent more than once, as an apprentice in the Merchant Navy, but one of my great aims had always been to get right into the centre and see the real Africa. Southern Rhodesia is now Zimbabwe, but I shall always think of the country that I went to as Rhodesia. It was then a modern, forward-looking, Crown Colony, with Dominion status in the offing. To me, it was a wonderful land, and I took full advantage of the RAF's travel service, exploring as much of it as I could in the wreck of an old pre-war Hillman car, which I had bought for twenty pounds. When that could no longer cope with the bush travel I imposed on it, and so gave up the ghost, an ancient 1920s Model A Ford took its place.

No 4 Flying Training School later came home from its traditional overseas bases, and settled at RAF Valley in Anglesey, remaining there for many years, but in 1949 it was based at RAF Heany, about twenty miles outside Bulawayo in Southern Rhodesia. At the same time, there was a navigator school at Gwelo, another RAF station further to the north in the Colony. Together with fifty-nine other cadet pilots, I arrived in Bulawayo very early one morning, after a three-day train journey from Cape Town. The Union Castle liner, RMS Edinburgh Castle, had happily put us ashore there after the voyage from Southampton. They were glad to see the back of us. The First Mate who, on such a ship as this, was called the First Officer, told me so personally in no uncertain terms! Well, I had had an ongoing battle with most of the First Mates that I had sailed with during the previous two and three quarter years, so that was no problem. The three day train journey took us up through the Karroo to Mafeking, and then into Bechuanaland, which is now Botswana, before crossing into Rhodesia at Plumtree, and was one long fascination for me. I was seeing this great brown land just as I had always wanted to see it, and it thrilled me.

RAF flying training, up until the point at which a student was awarded his coveted wings, lasted for about eighteen months in those days. It was divided into three parts, which went under various different names at different times and at different flying schools. At Heany, each period was programmed through about six months, and the first one that we had to face was the Initial Training phase, the next Basic and the last Applied. Initial consisted of nothing but groundschool, months of it, which really tested our patience. All the time, there were Tiger Moths and Harvards, landing and taking off over our classrooms, whilst we had to listen to dull lectures on Meteorology, Navigation and such like. In an attempt to get airborne, I joined the flying club at Kumalo, the Bulawayo airport, and, after getting my licence validated for Rhodesia, had a couple of hours in their Cessna 120. But the powers that be got wind of it, and banned RAF student pilots from civil flying. However, I survived all that, and started flying on the Basic phase, where we flew forty hours on Tiger Moths, then converted to Harvards for another thirty. I had great respect for the Harvard. It stood huge, ugly and businesslike, powered with what seemed to me at the time, to be a vast great radial engine. A few years later, I was posted back onto Harvards, and flew them operationally as a light ground attack aircraft. In my eyes, they then become just a very slow, small aircraft and easy to fly, but not so during training; Oh, no!

The final six months of the course was taken up with the Applied phase. Here, if we did not get scrubbed (removed from the course), we learnt a little bit about how to use an aircraft for the exercises that would be our normal flying when we actually managed to get onto a squadron. We learnt such things as how to fly in formation, how to dive bomb, and how to do the basic air-to-air cine-gun exercises. All this was a marvellous experience for anyone such as me. Before joining the RAF, while learning to fly at a civil club, I had realised that flying, in some way or another, was the only life for me, and now I was on the road to becoming a professional pilot. I was even getting a little pay, and a sum considerably greater than my previous wage as a Merchant Navy apprentice. But the RAF discipline was something that I found very difficult to cope with, to say the least. At Heany, it was in fact nearly non-existent compared with modern military training. You can't really have powerful discipline, when the uniform that is worn most of the time consists of grubby old khaki shorts and a shirt. However, I was continually in trouble, for behaving in a manner that was considered not to be the way that a cadet should behave in the best interests of the Service. I was not popular with the authorities.

Also, I had no wish to return to England; Rhodesia was wonderful, and I found that I would have little trouble in getting a flying job there as soon as I had the necessary hours, and could obtain a 'B' Licence. I wanted to leave the RAF and stay there. If I was scrubbed from the course, then I would achieve that aim with little difficulty. But, nevertheless, I just could not face the ignominy of the 'Scrub'. I learnt just how far I could step over the mark, but often made life difficult for myself. In fact, I think the real reason why I was not chucked out was because I played rugger for the station. Sports were very important in the RAF, and rugger especially so. Also, just as in South Africa, the rugger culture was very strong in Rhodesia, with its large Afrikaans population. There were numerous clubs in Bulawayo, all with their own grounds, and we were part of the local league, playing once or twice each week during the dry season. The RAF did reasonably well in this league, so the team members, of which I was one, got good marks against their names. I needed such marks!

This, then, was the scenario when I was about half way through the Applied stage, and 4 FTS was visited by the trappers (examiners) from the Central Flying School. Trappers were generally disliked throughout the RAF. Their job was to make sure that flying standards remained extremely high, and that techniques remained standardised. They would pick ordinary line pilots from the units that they visited, and give them a thorough test flight; very nasty, not popular at all. We were told that cadets would have to fly with these people so, in this instance, for once we were on the same side as our instructors, who would also be made to suffer. I dreaded the prospect of being picked as one of the victims of such a test flight. At about that time, my left thigh was scratched badly by some thorns whilst I was walking out in the bush. The scratches soon became septic, and turned to ulcers. My leg swelled up and was very painful so, after a couple of weeks, when my own doctoring had had no effect, I reported sick. The Medical Officer grounded me at once, which annoyed me. I hated the thought of staying on the ground and getting behind the syllabus.

I limped back down to the flights and saw, there on the notice board, my name down to fly with the trappers next day. Oh no, how could I cope with that one? Now, if I went to the flight commander, and told him that I had been grounded by the Doc, that would be 'sissy', and look as if I was 'chicken' when it came to difficult situations. It would be seen as just running away when nasty situations arose. I was sure that, after such a performance, I would be looked upon as someone with no guts; someone like the 'vibrators', who we were always told about; those whose engines always 'ran rough' during the flight out on a wartime operation, and who turned back short of the target. My way of thinking in those days could never allow that to happen, but I've grown more sensible with age. I did my trip with the trapper.

For some reason, that trip went very well, though the trapper never said so to me; all he did was grunt - they had a typical way of grunting. I was called for by the squadron commander, and went into his office, shaking in trepidation, apart from being in considerable pain from my leg. My instructor was with him, which boded ill, but I was amazed. He congratulated me, and told me that I had helped to show that the unit worked to excellent standards.

'Well done Holmes', he said. Gosh! I had never been in authority's good books like that before. It was a very odd feeling. There and then, I should have told him that I was grounded, but no, I didn't. The flight commander called for me and continued the line of praise. The feeling got even odder. The flight commander said, 'Go and have an hour's solo, don't bother about exercises, just enjoy yourself, do some aerobatics'. This was certainly a briefing that I had never been given before, but I should have told him that the Doc had grounded me. I didn't; I went off solo and enjoyed myself.

It was the hot season at that time in Rhodesia. Great thunderstorms build up over the veldt, and torrents of rain often fall. It's the way that life comes to Africa, but flying conditions can get rather uncomfortable and very bumpy. We never flew near those storms and, if they approached the airfield, all aircraft were called back in. Then, as the storms got close, landing conditions could get nasty. There would be sudden, gusty changes of wind direction, with crosswinds which were not easy to anticipate. Now, a Harvard's tail was always prone to swing on the landing roll, if you did not use the rudder correctly. It was all part of life in flying Harvards, something that you knew all about and dealt with as necessary. If you didn't, the swing would quickly develop into a ground loop, which you could do nothing about. In order to correct the swing and keep straight, your legs and feet worked automatically on the rudder pedals. You had to understand it all and were taught to do so. If you did not, you broke the aircraft, which was a heinous crime and could lead to The Scrub. The sudden gusty crosswinds, which might come from any direction round an approaching storm, were just the things to start such a situation, so that afternoon, as soon as I noticed a thunderstorm looming up near Heany, I came straight back. My leg was proving to be a bit painful, and I would be glad to land.

It happened; just as the tail was easing down to touch the ground, a nasty little crosswind gust caught me. A bit too late, I had seen the dust devil starting to rise ahead, and a little way off to the side. It should have been easy to deal with - just a bit of quick rudder work, with possibly a go-around, but my injured leg did not react and cooperate as it should have done. It did not quickly push my foot on the rudder pedals, in time to stop the swing, as was needed. The tail came round to chase the engine, and we came to an abrupt halt, pointing in the direction from which we had come, off to the side of the runway. What should have been an easily corrected swing had turned into a ground loop. The left wing was pointing up at an odd angle and the right wing down towards the ground. I had bent the undercarriage; I had broken an aeroplane.

I found that it would taxi all right, so I headed on in and parked. My little problem had been noticed! There was a reception committee consisting of, amongst others, my flight commander and my instructor. Numerous other cadets, together with ground crew members of the flight, had also come out to view the scene. I felt ghastly; this was surely the end for me. There was no ceremony. I was told to go straight into the squadron commander's office; he also had witnessed the episode, through his window. These people always watched what went on, and noticed the least misdemeanour. I stood to attention on the mat. I had been on mats before, but they had been admin or ground school mats, never flying mats. Now I was in a complete mental flap; a ghastly quandary. What could I say? Should I tell this all-powerful man that I was grounded, roll up my long, floppy shorts, show him my swollen thigh, explaining that this was the reason for my terrible lack of flying ability, or should I just see it out. A Medical Officer's word was law when it came to situations like this, so I would be guilty of directly disobeying such a powerful order. That could really mean bad trouble for me. On the other hand, damaging an aircraft like this could surely hold the prospect of the 'Scrub'. What an awful situation to have dropped myself into. I decided to stick it out. If they did scrub me, I could then admit to having been grounded, and would so be able to leave with a certain amount of honour, at least in the eyes of my fellow cadets, I hoped.

The strip that was torn off, was long, powerful and never to be forgotten. It caused my placing, in the final course order on graduation, to be much lower than it would have been otherwise. I dug the garden, outside the squadron commander's office, every day during all my time off for the next two weeks. It was not really a garden, just hard bare ground, solid Central African rocky ground, and in the hot season it just seemed harder and rockier than ever, never raining when needed, in order to soften it all up a little for me. Funny – I hadn't had any trouble digging a hole for myself!

Credit: Leo zal/Wikipedia

ETPS In A Spin

One of the most enjoyable parts of my time as a pilot instructor on the staff of the Phantom Operational Conversion Unit (OCU) in the late 1970s was the chance to do something different, and there was nothing more different than the experience I had one November. The Empire Test Pilot School, based at RAF Boscombe Down, has the motto 'Learn to Test, Test to Learn' and, as part of their course to produce a fixed-wing test pilot, they send a small group of 3 students to evaluate a type of aircraft with which they are unfamiliar. Their task is to approach the aircraft as if they are prospective customers: they must find out what is good and what is bad, what is acceptable and what is not. They then return to Boscombe Down, and put their assessment together for the tutors.

In 1977, the three students who came to Coningsby, all experienced pilots in their own rights, were: a Lt Cdr of the United States Navy, very experienced in carrier fighters although not, of course, the Phantom; a Dutch Air Force Lieutenant, who flew F-16s; and a Harrier pilot of the RAF. They had 10 hours of flying allocated to them for the Preview, as it was termed, and I was to be their pilot for each of the flights, for they could not complete any type of conversion in the short time. All flights would be made in one of our dual-control Phantoms, and I would be the captain in the back seat. For the flights, they would each carry a kneepad tape recorder, on which they would record their findings for the eventual written report. Obviously, the short flying time available meant that much was to be compressed into each sortie, and they arrived with a set of aims and requirements. Together, we fitted these into sortie profiles, and the majority went without a hitch. However, one of the Preview aims was to evaluate air-to-air refuelling, and so we booked a slot in the North Sea with one of the RAF Victors from Marham.

It would have been logical for this sortie to be flown by the US Navy pilot, very used to the probe-and-drogue method of refuelling used by both the RAF and USN, whereas the Dutchman had only been exposed to the boom system employed by the USAF, and the Harrier pilot had refuelled only rarely, albeit off RAF tankers. However, it was not long since a Buccaneer aircraft had collided with a Victor tanker, resulting in the loss of both aircraft, and also of the three rear crew of the Victor, who had no ejection seats. An edict had been issued which said that no pilot was to 'tank' from a Victor without having completed the one-day 'receivers' course, held at RAF Marham, to ensure that the procedures were known thoroughly, and the receiver pilot could be assumed to be safe. There was no time for our American to do this course, so the RAF Harrier pilot was the only option, and he and I duly took off one morning to conduct a series of exercises for the Preview report.

We went first to the tanker, flying his 'towline' off the Yorkshire coast, and uneventfully made several 'dry' contacts using the centre hose, before the Victor transferred the allocated 6,000lb of fuel; this left our Phantom close to full fuel, and we departed to complete the remainder of the sortie. The next task on our list was to measure the 'Stick Force per 'g' at certain speeds, and so we found ourselves at 30,000ft, flying at Mach 0.9[1], and ready for the assessment, which was to find the pressure required to maintain a turn at 4g. To do this, the front seat pilot had an instrument akin to a tuning fork and, by placing it in front of the control column, the pressure of his hand on the 'stick' could be measured. It was agreed that I would fly the aircraft into this turn and, once established, the front-seater would take control and carry out the measurement. However, one of the vagaries of the Phantom now became apparent. The fuel tanks in the fuselage were divided into cells, with No 1 just behind the rear cockpit and the last, No 7, just forward of the fin. On all but two airframes, the fuel fed from 7 tank only when the total fuel state had reached a critically low level and so, in general, this cell was isolated by pulling the 'A' and 'F' buttons in the starboard wheel-well. However, the delivery pressure of fuel from a tanker, particularly when fed from the centre hose, which could transfer fuel at 5,000lb/minute, was sufficient to overcome the valves and No 7 tank had now been filled as we had taken on our 6,000lb. This placed the aircraft's centre of gravity well aft; I rapidly became aware of this through the lightness of the stick (7 tank fuel was not gauged) and, at 4G, the aircraft was on a knife edge, close to pitching up.

I told the front-seater of the problem, and suggested that we looked at a different speed or G, but he was adamant that this would be an excellent example of a Phantom handling problem (of which there were many waiting to catch the unwary or inexperienced pilot). He assured me that he could cope with this, and

---

[1] Mach 0.9: Just less than (90% of) the speed of sound.

so I handed control to him and released the stick, although I cupped my hands behind the control column, but NOT FIRMLY ENOUGH!

With no warning, the stick moved rapidly aft and the aircraft nose pitched very rapidly up to about 40°, before a massive nose slice in both roll and yaw took place, through the inverted and back to upright. Although it was the first time (and the last) that I experienced a spin in the Phantom, it didn't take much to recognise it and, as I grabbed the stick again and planted it firmly in the centre, the thought that flitted through my mind was that the 30,000ft entry altitude would give me a fair time to recover before reaching 15,000ft when, if not recovered, the rules said we would have to abandon the aircraft. I was also aware of falsetto swearing from the front seat: his kneepad tape recorder had flown into the top of the canopy and beaten itself to death, dispensing batteries as it went. He was nevertheless receptive enough to act on my instruction to cancel the reheats and NOT to deploy the brake chute, a last ditch recovery option. As part of conversion to type, all OCU students had watched the famous USAF film on spinning the F-4, sitting mesmerised as the commentator intoned the words "There is no known recovery from the flat spin" and watched, from both internal and external cameras, a Phantom descending in a flat spin, with the brake chute (an extra-large anti-spin chute fitted for the trial) deployed vertically above the doomed aircraft and having absolutely no effect whatsoever. The crew duly ejected, and the aircraft reduced itself to its component parts in the desert.

I had no intention of doing this and, since we were not in a flat spin (the nose was pitching up and down with each rotation), I went on with the recovery technique and, as soon as I applied in-spin aileron the aircraft started to respond, the rotation slowed and the nose fell to hold a steep dive. We recovered to level flight at around 18,000ft, and I set heading for base. On the way back, the ETPS student became quite unhappy when I said that I would be telling the engineers and the Ops Desk what had happened. He felt that we could just say nothing and 'keep quiet', but I wanted the aircraft checked for a possible overstress. Furthermore, although I was cleared to authorise my own flights when conducting OCU syllabus sorties, the unusual nature of the ETPS Preview required authorisation by OC 228 OCU, a Wing Commander. When I told him what had occurred, this fine gentleman, who I later had the great privilege of working under in later appointments, said "Did you have to deploy the 'chute" and, when I said that it had not been necessary, simply said "Well done. On Friday's ground training you, as the most current pilot in Phantom spinning, can tell us all what it was like."

The final piece of humour was that the ETPS student, who no doubt thought that his falsetto swearing at the spin entry had not been recorded as his own recorder had stopped, had forgotten that the Phantom had its own Cockpit Voice Recorder; this had worked throughout, and the other two students used it to produce the Preview Report. At the end of their time at Coningsby, they kindly put on some beer in the Crewroom, and the replay of this voice-recorder tape provided considerable fun for all – except one ex-Harrier pilot!

Credit: Mike Freer

On Half A Wing And A Prayer

Reproduced from his book 'On A Wing And A Prayer', by kind permission
of the author, Roy Yule, and DB Publishing Ltd.

The Ruhr Valley, affectionately known as Happy Valley, was, in fact, hated and feared by bomber crews. The ferocity of its defences, most especially the wall of flak and light surrounding Essen and the great Krupp works, made some bomber pilots have the urge to flinch and turn aside before reaching the aiming point. On October 23rd 1944, we were briefed for a night raid on Essen, and were to have very close contact with one of those 'Fringe Merchants', as they were called.

On the operations board in the briefing room, twenty Lancasters were listed in alphabetical order. Sgt Yule was chalked against S-Sugar 2. I was unique; all the other captains were officers. Tonight's operation would change that. Bad weather had held up operations for the last three days, and today there was no improvement, with low cloudbase and thick cloud up to over twenty thousand feet, but Met had predicted that the high cloud would clear over Essen. That was enough for Butch Harris[1], who was anxious to get on with the battle of the Ruhr. This was another thousand-bomber raid and, in normal visibility, the sky over Lincolnshire was a throbbing mass of bombers on a maximum effort like this. Climbing through thick cloud, you knew they were all there, but you could not see them. Occasionally, a black shape loomed out of the mist, which necessitated quick avoiding action. The tension eased slightly when you stopped circling and steadied onto the first course.

Sugar 2 climbed steadily - ten thousand feet, fifteen, then eighteen, our allotted bombing altitude. Still we were in cloud. I continued climbing to twenty-two thousand feet, hoping to get in the clear, but it was not to be. With a 13,000lb bomb load, we had reached our ceiling. I then gradually dropped back to eighteen thousand feet. Approaching Essen on a northerly heading, we were still in cloud after nearly three hours, when suddenly we burst into clear air. Far below us 10/10ths cloud nullified the searchlights, but the flak barrage ten miles ahead, above the green dripping sky markers, seemed to fill every inch of sky.

---

[1] Butch Harris: Nickname for Air Marshal (later Marshal of the Royal Air Force) Sir Arthur Harris.

Stan had asked for bomb doors open, when Greg suddenly screamed "Down Jock!" The wireless operator was required to keep watch in the astrodome while in the target area. He had just popped his head up, and was horrified to see another Lancaster, directly above, disgorge its bomb load. I swung the control wheel to port and rammed it forward, at the same time kicking on full rudder. Don looked out to see a 4,000lb bomb smash through the starboard wing, slicing off 28ft of the trailing edge and carrying away the aileron2. Fortunately, the bomb had not had sufficient time to fuse, or we would just have been scraps of skin floating over Essen.

The impact of the bomb had straightened up Sugar's dive to port, but I still had to keep on full left rudder and full remaining aileron just to stay level. The

Lancaster was vibrating badly, as Stan dropped our bomb load on the green target indicators. Closing the bomb doors, we had to turn west to get on to a homeward heading. This was achieved with great difficulty. I found that, if I stretched my left foot hard on the rudder pedal and yanked the control wheel over as hard as possible, Sugar 2 would just crab slowly to port. It seemed to take ages, but we threaded through the flak bursts and got on to the required course. Leaving the barrage behind, we were soon back in cloud.

The situation was grim, vibration was so bad the instruments were barely readable, and I had to steady the sprung instrument panel with my right hand to get an approximate idea of the aircraft's attitude. The gyrocompass was useless, but I could just read the master compass repeater if steadied. I was twisted in my seat, keeping on hard left rudder and the control wheel turned fully to the left. If I had let go of either, the Lancaster would have done a continuous roll to starboard, becoming uncontrollable.

With nearly three hours still to go, what I had dreaded happened. A bomber ahead of us in the cloud crossed in front, and his slipstream twisted us starboard. With our wings nearly vertical, we lost altitude fast. I could only strain for the extra half-inch on the rudder and remaining aileron and wait. Slowly, so slowly, Sugar 2 righted herself, but we had dropped 4,000 feet. Both starboard engines were now running rough, as I pondered what to do when we got back to RAF Wickenby.

Should I bale the crew out over the airfield, before heading the Lancaster out to sea and attempting to bale out myself? The circuit would be thick with returning bombers, and we would have no chance if we hit slipstream at low altitude.

Tubby piped up from the rear turret, "Hey Jock, the shit's being shook out of me back here!" I told him in no uncertain terms to shut up, although I realised it was no fun being dragged backwards in a goldfish bowl and being rattled to bits. I informed the crew that I was going to attempt a landing at base, but that any of them could bale out if they wished. Each, in turn, said they would stay with me. Nearing base, I called up Wickenby Control, informed them of the damage, and stressed that a clear circuit was essential. We were at 10,000 feet, and still in thick cloud. Control informed me that cloud base was still only 800 feet, and that they would call me when all the other aircraft had landed and it was safe for us to descend. Unbeknown to us then, Air Vice Marshal Sir Edward Rice, Commander of No 1 Group was following the drama in the Wickenby Control Tower.

At this point, our navigator was proving his worth. He was in complete command of our navigational aids, and knew our position at all times. I still had the agonisingly slow struggle to turn on to each course, and all turns had to be to port. I gave Gus instructions where, in relation to the runway in use, I wanted to be when we broke cloud. As we listened on the R/T to the forty-plus Lancasters from the two squadrons landing, we had another problem to think about. With the delayed landing time, and the greatly increased drag on its airframe, Sugar 2 had burned up far more petrol than normal, and our fuel was running very low. All the outer tanks were empty, and Don estimated that what was left in the No 1 tanks would give us only fifteen minutes flying time left.

At last clearance to land was given. On the descent, I asked Don to lower 20 degrees of flap and the undercarriage. I had to know how Sugar 2 would react at landing speed with wheels down. I still had enough height to recover if she dropped the starboard wing and, if so, then we would have to land with our wheels retracted, on our belly. The test went all right, Don raised our wheels again, and we continued our descent. We broke cloud at exactly 800 ft, in the position I wanted. What a relief to see outside again, and not have to strain to read the vibrating green luminous instrument needles. There was one more heart- stopping moment when, on the final approach and with the undercart down, the starboard wing did drop slightly due to normal turbulence. The Lancaster slipped off a few hundred feet rapidly before levelling up and the wheels screeching on the tarmac. Taxying into dispersal, Don and I shut down the engines. Then, as the crew went out to look at the shattered wing, I undid my straps, stretched out, put my head back and relaxed. What bliss!

Next day, Wg Cdr Molesworth told me to put on my 'best blue', as Air Vice Marshal Rice wanted to see me. I was driven over to No 1 Group Headquarters at Bawtry, about thirty miles from Wickenby. Rice was not a Group Leader as charismatic as Cochrane of 5 Group, or Bennett with the Pathfinders, but he was a man who did the job Harris wanted doing - making sure that every serviceable aircraft bombed Germany at every possible opportunity. He visited airfields regularly, but was not known to chat with air or ground crews; he would stick with the Station and Squadron Commanders. AVM Rice was No 1 Group Commander for two years, and it was during this period that 1 Group rose to its pre-eminence in Bomber Command, probably due to his insistence on heavier bomb loads. There were times when the maximum all-up weight of the Lancasters (bombs and fuel) was exceeded by as much as 2,000 lbs.

Arriving at Bawtry Hall, a magnificent building standing in its own parklands, I wondered what exactly the Chief wanted to see me about. Molesworth had told me that Rice had seen for himself the extent of the damage on Sugar 2's wing. When ushered into his office, I gave him the best salute I could muster. He beckoned me to sit down in a chair facing his desk. He was a man about fifty years old, very military looking, with a double row of first-world-war ribbons on his chest. He immediately put me at ease by smiling and asking various questions. When he found out that we were still five miles from the aiming point when the bomb hit us, his smile vanished and he exploded with "The bastard!" I found it difficult not to smile. After a few more searching questions about the control of the aircraft, he shook my hand and said, "Good show, Yule, I'm putting you up for an immediate Commission."

Upon returning to Wickenby, I checked the Flight notice board and found that we were listed on a battle order, and that the briefing was early morning next day...

Editorial Note: Not only that but the DFC too!

Ocean Safari

Exercise Ocean Safari 1985 was a NATO exercise involving ships and aircraft from various countries, and including a battlegroup from the USA. I was a young navigator on 100 Squadron, equipped with an antique fleet of various marks of English Electric Canberra bombers, long past their sell-by date as bombers, but used for various target tasks. In this instance, we were designated "Orange" forces, with orders to attack Ocean Safari shipping and test their air defence systems. Without a Radar Warning Receiver, we had no idea of the effectiveness of the ships' defences, but we could still rush around as low and as fast as possible, for as long as we had the fuel to stay on station. At 420 knots and 50 feet, it was just unbridled, fabulous fun!

It was the last day of the exercise and, of course, the opportunity to leave a lasting, or at least temporary, mark on the naval shipping. For this purpose, the Canberra still had a functional bomb bay, soon to be loaded with our munitions of war – toilet rolls! The idea was that, as the rolls released, they would stream and, if jettisoned along the decking of a ship, would produce a visually pleasing, if bland, decorative effect: "Christmas Tree-ing the Fleet!" That morning, Kendo and I were leading a pair from Stornoway and, after visually acquiring the fleet, we singled out a straggling pair of ships which had cut across each other's bows, in what I concluded was a vain attempt to confuse our attack. No such luck for them; we went for the ship to our right, while our partner took the left one. It was a perfect run, straight down the deck with bomb doors open, me watching my colleague's Christmas Tree efforts, and enjoying the sight of the toilet rolls deploying perfectly. Elated, we returned to Stornoway, where I was met by the ashen-faced navigator from our two-ship partner:

"What's up?" I enquired.

"Did you see what you were bombing; the colour of its decks?"

"No, I was too busy watching you," I answered.

"They were RED!"

That stopped me dead! We had just committed an act of war by overflying a Soviet Naval vessel with our bomb doors open; the Soviets (in a Krivak-II frigate) had had every right to shoot us down. Fortunately, of course, the ships in our straggling pair were far too busy "playing" with each other to be bothered about a couple of buzzing gnats with only toilet rolls for weaponry – thank goodness!

Rescue 51

What follows is not really special; I suspect that most people with a couple of tours on a maritime squadron could tell a similar kind of story. It was just one aspect of the multi-faceted maritime role. We took it for granted that well-trained crews, be they ship, helicopter or fixed- wing, would always operate effectively together.

On the morning of 3rd January 1979, I reported for Search and Rescue (SAR) at RAF St Mawgan, as the 'guest' First Pilot with a crew other than my normal one. I had watched the weather forecast the night before, and listened to the Shipping Forecast before arriving at work; things didn't sound too good, with a deep low-pressure area tracking towards the South West Approaches (SWAPPS), bringing gale-force winds and heavy precipitation, possibly falling as snow. The Met Officer at St Mawgan provided some further detail: snow was expected to affect most airfields in the UK at some time in the next 24 hours. A conference with the Duty Commander Flying (DCF) took place, and the problem was put to the Operations Controllers at Northwood that, if we remained at St Mawgan, it was probable that we would be unable to maintain cover for a significant portion of the next 24 hours. Under normal circumstances, the SAR task would have been passed to RAF Kinloss on a temporary basis but, as there was a significant threat of snow there as well, this was not really an option. Therefore, it was decided that we would deploy to Prestwick, one of the very few airfields with a snow-free forecast, and hold SAR cover from there for at least the next 24 hours. We got our kit together and, after the aircraft had been de-fuelled in order that we would be below maximum landing weight at Prestwick, we were on our way.

Prestwick in those days was almost a ghost airport. Transatlantic flights had long since ceased to make refuelling stops, and there were no other scheduled services to speak of. The runway was clear and dry, but it was very cold. On landing, we were advised that the taxiways and apron were "passable with care due to icy patches." It was quickly apparent that there were more "icy patches" than taxiway, and "care" quickly gave way to extreme caution. Having parked and refuelled, we declared ourselves 'on state', and then turned our attention to the accommodation arrangements. We had been booked into the Towans Hotel, very close to the airport terminal. The Towans dated from the 19th century; its glory days, like those of Prestwick, had passed, and it was now in something of a very faded time warp. The notice in reception, inviting guests to book breakfast if they had an early flight, was almost completely redundant.

At this point, one of life's bizarre little events occurred: the OC MT Flight from St Mawgan suddenly arrived in an RAF Land Rover! What he was doing at Prestwick I never did find out, but he had seen our Nimrod arrive and set about locating the crew. By the time he came to see us, he had already arranged call-out transport for us with the RN establishment, HMS Gannet, on the other side of the airfield. That was another little task that we didn't have to worry about. By now it was mid-afternoon, and the crew settled down to bridge, Uckers (a particularly vicious form of Ludo), or catching up on sleep. With only 3 channels on the communal television, and no daytime TV anyway, there was little else in the way of diversion. Although we were the only guests at the Towans, we were accommodated not in the main building but in a rather spartan block with paper thin walls called The Annex. By about 2230, we had all drifted off to our rooms, anticipating a chilly night's sleep.

Not long after I had turned in, I heard the sound of someone hastily traversing the icy courtyard. The Annex door opened and the hotel night porter's voice called out: "Captain, there's a telephone call for you!"

The captain was in the room adjacent to mine and he asked: "Who's calling?"

The swift response was, "I dinna ken sir, but he said something aboot Scramble!"

Twelve pairs of feet hit the floor simultaneously. Training and procedures now took over; on the crew coach, there was a very short outline brief: the search datum was in the vicinity of the Channel Islands, a merchant ship in trouble; collect a met and NOTAM[1] pack; wind up the aircraft (which had been left in a quick-reaction condition); and get on our way Southbound as Rescue 51. All this was accomplished in a little under 30 minutes and, once airborne, the radio operator opened up with Southern Rescue Coordination Centre (Plymouth Rescue) and obtained the latest situation report.

---

[1] NOTAM: Notice to Airmen – a notice filed with an aviation authority to alert aircraft pilots of potential hazards along their planned route.

Once we reached cruising altitude, we were able to conduct a more detailed crew brief. A Greek merchant ship, the Cantonad, had capsized off Guernsey. Sea King helicopters from RNAS Culdrose were en route to the search area, and the Guernsey Lifeboat had been launched. To complicate matters, the reason we had deployed to Prestwick was now all too apparent. The weather in the SWAPPS was truly awful. There was a deep low-pressure area centred just west of the Channel Islands, with tightly spaced isobars around it, resulting in surface winds of over 40 knots. To add to the fun, we could expect severe icing and turbulence at all altitudes, and precipitation falling (well, being blown horizontally) as snow. These were all the things that, as an aviator, one sought to avoid, but we were going to take ourselves right into the middle of it. As Scottish Radar gave us a radio frequency change to London and wished us good luck, I quietly reflected that tonight we might need it.

Our transit to the search area took a little over an hour and, as we started our descent, we were able to establish contact with the Sea Kings. The Guernsey Lifeboat had almost miraculously plucked one survivor from the mountainous seas, and the Sea Kings were searching for others. It was quickly agreed that we would be best employed using our load of 12.5 inch parachute flares to illuminate the search area, thus increasing the chance of finding more survivors. This was a fairly complicated procedure, as we had to drop the flares ahead of the helicopters and at 90° to their search axis. The timing had to be such that the flares hit the water ahead of the helicopters, and the next stick was in the air and alight before the previous one extinguished. All of this had to be accomplished in the dark, at an altitude of 4,000 feet, in severe turbulence, with winds of 60 knots or more.

We had set up our drop pattern, and put down a few sticks of flares, when we received an urgent message from Plymouth Rescue: they had a higher-priority task for us; we were to proceed to a position approximately 100 miles west of Guernsey, where a German merchant ship, the Mira, had reported sighting a distress flare. Our task was to locate the origin of the flare, and try and identify the vessel in need of assistance. So, with a brief explanation and an "I Go Now" to the Sea Kings, we were on our way westwards. Locating and identifying the Mira presented its own problem. There were three radar contacts in the vicinity of the datum position, approximately 45 miles south of The Lizard - but which one was our ship? Due to the usual "Who will pay?" wrangle, the marine-band radio (VHF-FM), used by civilian vessels, had not been specified as part of the Nimrod communications fit. Military ships and aircraft had VHF-AM and, as communicating with civilian vessels was deemed to be of very low priority, VHF-FM had not been provided. Experience in service had shown that this was a mistake, particularly when we became involved in fishery protection under Operation Tapestry. Thus, a programme of equipping the Nimrod fleet with marine-band radios had been instituted, but this was proceeding very slowly and, of course, tonight when we really could have done with it, we didn't have it. So, a classic maritime solution was adopted: we spoke to Plymouth Rescue on High Frequency (HF) radio; they phoned Land's End Coastguard, who had an open line to Lisbon Radio; Lisbon Radio was working the Mira on HF, and they asked the ship to fire flares in order that we could identify them. It was a lash-up, but it worked. The Mira fired the flares and we saw them first time, so we were now able to commence a search down the approximate bearing on which she had sighted the distress signal.

At this point, it is probably worth saying a little about the Nimrod MR1. It was a highly capable aircraft with state-of-the-art navigation aids and a digital tactical data system, albeit with, by today's standards, a miniscule memory of 128 Kilobytes! However, the sensors that we relied upon had a distinctly steam-driven feel to them. Nowhere was this more true than with the ASV21D search radar. ASV21 had been developed for use on the Shackleton in the 1950s, but its origins could easily be traced to the H2S radar carried by Bomber Command aircraft in World War 2. Unlike modern digitally processed radars, ASV21 had no clever features to de-clutter the display or remove spurious returns, neither could you lock it on to a target and leave the navigation system to guide the aircraft there automatically. Its effective use relied upon skilled operation and interpretation by a well-trained operator, and well-practised crew procedures to home the aircraft to the chosen target. That night it was fortunate that we had an experienced and first-class radar operator.

The weather conditions off Guernsey had been atrocious, but here they now became truly awful. It had been very uncomfortable being bounced around by the turbulence whilst dropping flares, but we now had to descend to between 300 and 500 feet in the pitch black, in the roughest piece of sky I ever had the misfortune to have to fly in. We overflew the Mira, and set off on the bearing on which she had reported seeing the flare at an estimated range of 5 miles. Our intention was that we would commence a cloverleaf search based upon that position, in the hope that the vessel in distress would see us and fire another flare. In the pitch dark, with intermittent heavy showers and a high sea state, this represented the only realistic chance we had of locating what we now thought to be a small boat. But then, as we approached our datum, one of the beam lookouts reported a brief flash of light very close by. Against all the odds, we had achieved a visual sighting of something, but we now had to mark its position accurately, and try to ascertain what it was. We therefore tried to gain radar contact on the vessel, to enable us to home on to it more accurately. We positioned the aircraft to get the best possible aspect on the datum and, for the second time tonight, our luck was in. Through the clutter and sea returns, the radar operator discerned a small intermittent contact which 'painted' just frequently enough to enable him to recognise it. We commenced a homing under his direction, in an attempt to identify it. At a mile and a half from the target, I triggered the steerable searchlight in the starboard wing; the glare revealed a maelstrom of mountainous waves, and a sea almost completely white with flying foam and spray. We failed to see anything as we passed the target but, as we turned away for a further attempt, both I and one of the beam lookouts again saw a dim flash of light. The next run was more successful; in spite of being buffeted around as we homed-in, we caught a very brief glimpse of a small yacht in the glare of the searchlight. Immediately the visual contact was called, the Tactical Navigator released an 8-hour-life, frequency channel 15 (CH15) sonobuoy, to mark the survivors; CH15 was the standard channel used by NATO maritime aircraft to mark the position of survivors. If, for any reason, we had to depart without handing over, the oncoming aircraft would automatically search for a CH15 buoy to locate them.

However, reinforcements were on their way, in the shape of a Sea King from Culdrose. If conditions for us in a large aircraft were very uncomfortable, I shudder to think what they were like in that helicopter. As the Sea King approached, we passed a situation report, and continued to orbit the yacht, whilst they started an approach to the vessel. On the first two attempts, they had to break off because of the conditions. On the third, they were able to confirm the sighting and establish that there were two people on board but, because of the mountainous seas, any attempt to rescue them was out of the question, neither would the Mira be any better placed to attempt a rescue until the sea state subsided. With the helicopter on its way back to Culdrose, it seemed that all we could do was to continue to orbit the yacht, to show that at least they had not been abandoned. Plymouth Rescue had other plans for us though: we were told that we would shortly be relieved by a French Navy Neptune patrol aircraft and that, after effecting the handover, we were to return to the scene of the original incident. We had been tasked, re-tasked and re-tasked again - flexibility of air power at its best. For the first time, I noticed the time: it was now 0330, and I could barely remember the passing of the last 5 hours.

As the Neptune arrived, we re-marked the yacht with another 8-hour-life sonobuoy and a Marker Marine (a long duration buoyant flare), gave them a situation report, and agreed separation for their arrival and our departure. There's no Air Traffic Control to help you in these situations, you have to arrange it yourself. A little over 20 minutes later, we were back off Guernsey to pick up where we had left off. All the original players were still there, and the weather, if anything, was worse. The bad news was that no more survivors had been found. We started flare-dropping again but, after a night of extreme conditions, the helicopters were getting low on both fuel and physical endurance. It was decided to withdraw them, as there now seemed no hope of finding anyone else alive, and to keep them there could have endangered the crews themselves. With the helicopters going off task, we were also released, leaving only the Guernsey Lifeboat to continue searching in the approaching dawn.

Throughout the night we had been monitoring the St Mawgan weather. The forecast had been grim, and the actual weather showed it was depressingly accurate. The wind was well outside our crosswind limit, and it was snowing. Landing back at base was out of the question and, with poor conditions affecting most of the southern UK airfields, we had to look further north. Thus, an hour after departing Guernsey, we landed in almost unnaturally calm conditions, but still in the dark, at RAF Valley on Anglesey. Before we could get some rest, there was a long list of things to be done: after flight checks on the aircraft, including making safe what remained of our load of flares in the bomb bay; collecting the mountain of classified documents and equipment that we carried, and taking it to secure storage; completing the Form R (Search and Rescue post flight signal); and liaising with base, regarding their intentions for us and the aircraft. We also spent time on that essential part of maritime post flight activity, waiting for transport. Everywhere you went or were going, you always had to wait for the crew transport. By the time all this was complete, and crew members had been allocated rooms in their respective messes, most of us had been on the go for over 24 hours with little or no sleep, the previous 8 hours having been filled with intense activity in appalling conditions. I remember nothing of the remainder of that day, as I slept for a straight 16 hours.

The events of the 4th January 1979 involved military fixed wing aircraft and helicopters, warships and merchant vessels, and an RNLI Lifeboat. Everything worked because well-trained aircrew and seamen, thoroughly versed in search-and-rescue procedures, were able to put them into practice in the most adverse conditions. We were there that night because we were professionals doing our jobs. There was, however, one notable qualification: the lifeboat men were professional, but they were also volunteers. We returned to St Mawgan the following day and, after packing up, went home to our families. The squadron had phoned my wife to let her know I was spending another night away, but given her no details of what we had been doing.

"Why did they keep you at Prestwick?"

"They didn't, we were called out and ended up at Valley afterwards. It was a yacht off the Lizard. Was there anything about it on the TV news?"

"I think there was a short piece last night, two women rescued by helicopter. A man with them had been lost overboard. No mention of a Nimrod though."

"OK."

When I look back I remember those early hours of 4th January 1979 as being the worst night I had the misfortune to be awake through, let alone flying. But it almost immediately became history. Back then, there was no TV catch-up facility, in fact not even home video recorders. By the time I thought that there might have been a report in the Western Morning News, it was too late, and getting a back copy was too laborious. Anyway, it was back into the busy routine of a cold war Nimrod squadron. My logbook for the remainder of January shows that: I flew on a Passex (tracking exercise against a friendly submarine in transit); completed two flight deck simulator exercises, and a Maritime Crew Trainer

(MCT) exercise; flew a Survop (surveillance operation), probably against a Soviet submarine, landing at RAF Kinloss on completion of the sortie; flew two sorties on Exercise Rubble, a weapons training exercise; and flew a Casex (Combined Aircraft Submarine Exercise), against a friendly submarine tasked to act as a training target. Then, in February, we went out to the Pacific, to Hawaii and Tahiti, to participate in Operation Nereus, an oceanographic research project. But that, as they say, is another story entirely.

Postscripts:

Lt Vernon Munday and Leading Aircrewman Raymond Walters were awarded the Queen's Commendation for Valuable Service in the Air for their part in the dangerous rescue of the survivor from the Cantonad.

The 30ft yacht 'Peacock' had departed Salcombe on Tuesday 2nd January, bound for Peros Gurec in Brittany with a crew of three, one man and two women. The man had been lost overboard the following day. The flare sighted by the Mira was the last one that the two women had; the light seen from the boat came from a small hand torch. When the weather abated the following morning, they were rescued by a Sea King helicopter from RNAS Culdrose. Neither woman suffered serious physical injury.

The Towans Hotel was awarded Grade 2 Listed Building Status in 1995, but was destroyed by fire a year later.

The Guernsey Lifeboat recovered the bodies of 2 crew of the MV Cantonad, in addition to the sole survivor; 15 lives were lost in the sinking. Press reports at the time state that the lifeboat remained at sea for 12 hours, in a gale that reached Hurricane Force 12. It was the first time in 25 years that it had snowed in the Channel Islands. For his actions that night, Coxswain John Petit was awarded a third bar to his Royal National Lifeboat Institute (RNLI) Bronze Medal. The RNLI is a charitable organisation, dedicated to providing rescue at sea and supported entirely by donations from the public. Nearly all of its crews are volunteers, prepared to respond immediately to a call for assistance.

The entry for the month of January 1979 in the 42 Squadron Operational Record Book, now held in The National Archive, makes no reference to the events of 4th January. The crew's efforts went unrecorded.

Not You Again!

Aficionados of Out of the Blue Vol 1 may recall the saga of the blundering hero in his Jaguar jousting with a Tornado off the North Norfolk coast (One More Take-Off Than Landing). Mid-air collisions are, thankfully, rare (since, even if not fatal, they are expensive and generally injurious to the career prospects). Random mid-air collisions (ie between aircraft not of the same formation, and not even operating together) are even more rare. Random, head-on, mid-air collisions are definitely best avoided – if that is not oxymoronic. To misquote Lady Bracknell (now there's a rum coincidence), one such event is definitely a misfortune; two is – yes, I am forced to admit it – careless.

The date was 9th January 1990, and I was part-way through an idyllic tour as commander of Britain's premier fighter squadron. The sortie was simple enough – I was the No 2 in a pairs Simulated Attack Profile (SAP), as part of a newly-arrived pilot's combat-ready work-up. The route took us north from RAF Coltishall to targets in the north of England and south of Scotland, and we had a third aircraft in company, who would act as an aggressor (bounce). At least, that was the plan. All was going swimmingly well – we had both hit the first target and beaten off the bounce – until we approached the 'Hexham Gap'. This was a relatively narrow corridor across the Tyne Valley, between the restricted airspace of Spadeadam EW[1] Training Range to the west, and Newcastle Airport and the built-up areas of Tyneside to the east. Transit of this corridor was not below 500 feet, and the town of Hexham itself was to be avoided. No tactical manoeuvring was allowed, so our friendly bounce was shadowing us on our left and high, ready to have at us again once we got clear of the gap.

With no threat to contend with, my trusty wingy and I were free to concentrate our lookout in the area ahead of us. As we crossed the Tyne Valley, I became aware of something grey, which flashed past my port wing – or almost past. At the same time, I felt a thump, and the aircraft started to roll left, but not uncontrollably. I called to the rest of the formation that I had hit something, suspecting a birdstrike. "It's just crashed behind you," came the laconic reply from Brian, the bounce. Some seagull, I thought! A glance at the left wingtip

---

[1] EW: Electronic Warfare.

revealed that all was not as Messrs Sepecat had designed it, and there were some eye-catching protrusions from where the outer control surfaces should have been. At the same time, several lights illuminated on the warning panel. However, it became apparent that an immediate departure was not required, and that there might be a sporting chance of getting the thing back on the ground. Brian made a relay Mayday call for me, and I considered the options. Newcastle was the closest, but had no stopping aids, no military expertise and possible civilian traffic. Leeming had the first two and not the third, so the decision made itself, really. Brian despatched our erstwhile leader to make his own arrangements for returning to base, and joined up with me.

I'd like you to know that the next few minutes were an exemplary demonstration of aircraft handling, airmanship and rational decision making – I really would! The truth, however, is somewhat more prosaic, although no less exciting. I recall having great difficulty in concentrating on one thing at a time. It became clear that most of the lights on the warning panel had to do with fuel and hydraulics, and it didn't take the brains of an archbishop to figure out that this might be because of the fluids – hydraulic and fuel – which were leaking out of the hole at the end of the wing, and which both constituted a fire risk. I cannot honestly remember whether I deliberately shut the left engine down or whether it quit on its own, but the net result was the same. The one really sensible decision I made was not to touch the flaps, since I had no way of knowing whether the port flaps had been damaged, and the last thing I needed was an asymmetric flap extension.

So there I was, committed to a single-engined, flapless landing. The cognoscenti will tell you that either constitutes an emergency in a Jaguar, and that a combination of the two is decidedly undesirable. On the other hand, the rest of the world will tell you that, since the Jag has no thrust and no wing, the loss of half of one and some of the other is really nothing to worry about. Throughout the recovery, Brian did a sterling job of keeping a very well-meaning Air Traffic off my back, and providing sage advice only when requested. An academic low-speed handling check, while highly desirable, was also highly impractical, and so I carried out a practical one during the approach, to try and determine at what speed the lack of wing and control surface might make itself apparent. The good news was that it manifested itself as a progressive roll; the bad news was that it started the wrong side of 200 knots.

In terms of stopping aids, I had - in chronological order - the drag-bag, the brakes, the departure- end wire (the Jag was not cleared for the approach end, and I didn't need any more bits dropping off the aircraft) and the barrier. The limiting speed on the chute was, I recall, 150 knots. However, if I waited for this to occur, I would probably be somewhere south of Doncaster when it deployed, so I resolved to fling it out on touchdown and trust to luck and the other three options. By this time, of course, I had quite an audience in the tower and on the airfield, and I am told that it was worth watching. My rocket-powered roller skate came over the hedge at some exorbitant warp-factor, and smote the runway in approximately the right place. At this point, fortune favoured me: the chute came out and stayed on, the excellent Jag brakes worked a treat, and I never even made it to the departure-end wire, let alone the barrier. What an anti-climax!

While I was in the line hut, attempting to complete some makeshift paper-work, the phone rang, and I was told it was for me, and that it was the Inspector of Flight Safety himself. On picking it up, I heard the immortal words: "Not you again!" In fairness, the Inspector had been my Station Commander at the time of the previous epic, so his lack of sympathy was probably understandable. From there, it was a quick trip to the Doc (who pronounced my body functioning, although he probably couldn't vouch for my brain), and thence to the bar where, sad to say, I fell among thieves – and one particular thief of long acquaintance, who prevailed upon me to accompany him to his quarter, there to sample all of his impressive array of malt whiskies. My log book records that I flew home in the back of a T-bird[2] the next morning; I shudder at the thought.

There are 2 postscripts to this story, one slightly serious and one extremely amusing. The Cause section of the Military Air Accident Summary (MAAS) for this event states that '…many factors had combined to produce a situation whereby none of the crew members could have reasonably been expected to have seen the other aircraft'. The MAAS for the previous disaster stated that 'it was considered that the accident happened because neither pilot saw the other aircraft in time to prevent a collision' (no s**t, Sherlock!). In essence however, both happened because the aircraft were masked from each other at the critical

---

[2] T-bird: Slang for the two-seater, training variant.

point and, crucially, maintained the same relative angle (as most things will do if they are going to hit you), thus exceeding the detection limits of the human eye. This evidence was given in both enquiries, so why did the first culminate in a pounding of the Wilton, hats on, no coffee, and the second with a grudging acknowledgement that 'these things happen'? What changed in those six years? An answer may be found, I believe, in that, in the intervening period, a similar accident had occurred in Germany, in which a Harrier had collided with a German F104. However, there were 2 crucial differences: firstly, sad to say, there was a fatality in the Harrier whereas, in the other two accidents, everyone had emerged, if not unscathed at least alive, to answer for their crimes; secondly, there were 2 nations involved, and a different low-flying system. The MAAS for the Harrier/F104 accident states that: 'The importance which relative motion has on the ability of the human eye to detect conflicting objects is well documented…' In 1984, it was probably politically unacceptable to tell Joe Public that the UK 'see-and-avoid' system had its limitations. By 1990, this acknowledgement was probably inescapable. An element of 'realpolitik', then? To quote the admirable Francis Urquhart: "You might very well think that; I couldn't possibly comment."

The second footnote is a cracker. I have not mentioned that my nemesis on this occasion was a Tornado GR1 from Laarbruch, and I was told that it was the first to be fully fitted with all the recce gear to bring it to GR1a standard; Mr Popular again! The crew had ejected at very low level following the collision, and had still been swinging in their parachutes when they hit the ground; indeed had they not been above a downward-sloping field, the results might have been much worse. As it was, they sustained severe leg injuries – I think three broken legs between the two of them. Ten years later, in the course of my duties in the MODSAP team in Riyadh, I was visiting the RAF Team Representatives and seconded aircrew at Khamis Mushayt. This clearly needed to be done over a weekend, and Wednesday evening saw us descending the escarpment to the beach below, ready for some diving and snorkelling the following day. One of our number was detained, and he and his family arrived after it was dark. Tent-erection in the pitch-black is not easy, so the rest of us turned out to assist, not least by bringing some light – but not that much - to bear on the proceedings. During this evolution, one of the kids noticed signs of previous injury on the tent-owner's legs, and politely enquired what had caused them. At this point, there was a loud fit of coughing from our diving team leader, himself a former squadron colleague on the Jag force. There was a terse response from the tent-owner, the gist of which was that some blind b*****d in a Jaguar had appeared from nowhere, while they were minding their own business, and lopped off their tail.

"Hi, Neil!" I said.

Credit: MoD

My First Solo

The first solo must rank as one of the most momentous experiences in a pilot's life. I am no different, although I have to confess that, while much of the detail has been long forgotten (eg the weather conditions prevailing, runway in use, which I think was 17 - in those days before the earth moved round a bit and it was re-classified), other facts about my first venture into the skies on my own are indelibly etched on my memory, and I remember them as if they happened yesterday.

It was Easter Camp for which, in those far off days of the late 50s, we had the airfield largely to ourselves, the 4 or 5 daily movements of the BEA Dakota being the only other air traffic. There was the usual buzz in the crewroom, as we pre-solo students approached our first solos and there was, inevitably, some rivalry and banter amongst us. One such exchange was rudely interrupted by the grey, wavy-haired head of my instructor, Jack, poking round the door and uttering the well-known invitation to partake in aviation. "Getchikiton!" This expression had originally come from one of the other Qualified Flying Instructors, the laconic Geoff, but had quickly been adopted by his fellow instructors. Stories about Jack were legion, and much embroidered. A skillful, articulate and much-admired instructor, he didn't suffer fools - or students – gladly, and Lord help you if you got on the wrong side of him, particularly if he had been 'enjoying himself' the night before. He had flown Hurricanes in the Second World War, I believe, and there were numerous tales of his flying and other exploits - but that is for another time.

Pre-flight briefing was minimal: we were to do circuits, and the sortie was a continuation of yesterday's trip. I went out to the Chipmunk assigned to us, and carried out the pre-flight checks, awaited the arrival of the instructor and, once he was aboard, fired up the engine. Here's where my memory lapses, as I don't remember very much about the early circuits we conducted. However, I do remember quite distinctly, just after getting airborne from Runway 17, that the throttle was pulled from my grasp and closed at about 300-400ft, over the city suburb which I now thought would be my final destination. I quickly rammed the throttle fully open again, whereupon it was just as quickly closed. "We'll crash!' I exclaimed over the R/T. "Well"', said the instructor, "what are you going to do about it?" I aimed the Chipmunk at a nearby school playing field, stating, "Land there, Sir!" "Good," came the reply from the back cockpit, and full power was restored. Such was my introduction to the EFATO (Engine Failure After Take-Off). We completed the circuit, and taxied to somewhere around where the main airport terminal is today, although in those days it was just a taxiway surrounded by grass.

We braked to a halt, and Jack pulled the sliding canopy back, uttering the finest words of encouragement befitting the occasion. "Well, you can bloody-well go and kill yourself, but I'm damned if you're bloody-well going to kill me!" With that, he got out of the cockpit, fumbled with the straps, hoisted his parachute over his shoulder and, without a backward glance, set off on the half-mile walk back to the crewroom. Left to my own devices, I taxied to the holding point, completed my pre-take-off checks, and took off. Somewhat surprisingly, I remember very little of the actual flight, craning round once airborne, and seeing the straps tied up in the empty rear cockpit, being one of my sobering recollections. I also remember being downwind at 1250ft, (accurately flown, naturally) and thinking "I've now got to get this thing down, and there's no-one to help me." Again, I don't remember the landing, but it must have been 'reasonable', and I taxied into the dispersal to park the aircraft. At the same time, Jack had arrived back after his morning stroll, and we met as I arrived outside the crewroom (had he done this before, I wondered?) "What the hell happened to you?" he enquired, and I racked my brains to think of which of the myriad of faults lying in wait for the would-be pilot I had committed. I failed to think of any, and replied, "Nothing, Sir." "Good!" he replied, "you owe me a beer." And with that, he disappeared into the Instructors' hidey-hole, and I was left to contemplate my future as a pilot.

Editorial Note: He made it to B2 and B(I)8 Canberras!

Anyone For The Beach?

The following story originally appeared in Aviation News magazine in February 1987. It appears here, slightly updated, by kind permission of the author, David Watkins. Thanks also to the HMS Belfast Association for photography and additional information.

In late 1947, a joint RAF/De Havilland unit was set up to examine the feasibility of jet operations in the tropics. A ground party and two Vampire F3s were despatched to Singapore by sea and, by March 1948, one aircraft had been air-tested and was ready for the arduous test and flying display programme. The tactical trials were completed by May, when Flight Lieutenant George "Kiwi" Francis DFC AFC* took over command of the unit - an excellent choice. Kiwi had joined the RNZAF in 1940, before moving to England, where he flew Hurricanes, Tempests and latterly Meteors at Lubeck on 616 Squadron, the RAF's first jet fighter squadron.

By the end of 1948, the unit had completed several demonstration tours, covering the Malay States, Indo-China and Thailand. The jets generated huge crowds, interest and excitement wherever they went. One particularly effective aerobatic display was at Kota Bahru, Kelantan State, for the Sultan, four wives and the heir apparent. In Kiwi's words, he "gave them the full treatment". By early 1949, it was time to head north. As Kiwi took off from Tengah on 11 January, on the first leg of the Hong Kong and Pacific tour, little did he know what excitement lay in store. His log book records:

11 January VG703 Tengah – Saigon 2.00
11 January VG703 Saigon – Hong Kong 3.10
15 January VG703 Air Test .20

The flight to Saigon was uneventful. Later the same day, he took off for Hong Kong with Hanoi as his diversion. The weather forecast from Tan Son Nhut was good for both fields, although there was a tropical storm in the South China Sea. This soon made itself felt, as both airfields closed down with thick cloud. The storm degraded radio communications, so Kiwi's dead reckoning navigation skills were put to the test. Arriving at what he thought was overhead Hong Kong, he managed to get a back-bearing out of Kai Tak Air Traffic Control (ATC). Desperately short of fuel, he turned the Vampire about and headed back for Hong Kong but, after a few minutes flying, the engine cut out when the fuel tanks emptied. Spiralling down through more than 30,000 feet of cloud, Kiwi broke through over the sea, and was astonished to see a small sandy beach which he judged suitable for a forced landing. He "dead-sticked" the Vampire, bringing the aircraft safely to a halt before he ran out of beach. The aircraft was undamaged, apart from a dented drop tank, resulting from impact with a protruding rock. Kiwi had steered the Vampire to put the rock, only just, between the main undercarriage wheel and the drop tank.

The landing had been made on a strip of sand on Bias Bay (Ta-ya Wan) in the South China Sea, a traditional haunt of China's pirates, in particular 'Madam Wong'. The beautiful and mysterious Madam Wong, alias Chung Lo-Yu, used Bias Bay as her operational base, because of its proximity to Hong Kong and protection afforded by surrounding rugged hills. In six years of attacks, boardings and kidnappings, Madam Wong, with her substantial fleet of pirate ships, terrorised the crowded waters between Hong Kong and Portuguese Macao. Only a year previously, pirates had seized the Dutch ship *Van Heutz*, and robbed its 1600 passengers of at least £250,000, rifled the cargo and held the first-class passengers to ransom. Bias Bay was clearly an unhealthy spot for Kiwi Francis to force-land what was a potentially valuable prize for Madam Wong.

Kiwi managed to make radio relay contact with Hong Kong Air Traffic Control via another aircraft. ATC was quick to inform an 88 Squadron Sunderland from Kai Tak, captained by Flight Lieutenant Letford, who was on patrol in the area. An immediate search was commenced by Letford and his crew to the north-east of Kai Tak, and the stranded Vampire was soon located. Earlier in the day, Flight Lieutenant Letford had been engaged in naval exercises with the cruiser *HMS Belfast*, and he passed the aircraft's position to the ship, which was still in the vicinity. Whilst Belfast proceeded at full speed to the area, the Sunderland alighted in Bias Bay and moored offshore, to provide protection against the Chinese pirates, who were already gathering in some strength. Whilst Kiwi was pre-occupied with his radio, a group of bandits had indeed surrounded the aircraft; Kiwi noted them with some surprise. However, they seemed friendly enough, and he managed to indicate that they should help him manhandle the jet above the high-water tide mark. Their main concern seemed to be the lack of a propeller. At some point, a Chinese lady, presumably Madam Wong herself, showed up, and she seemed to be very much in charge.

Once *HMS Belfast* had moored a couple of miles offshore, a Royal Marines landing party disembarked to secure the aircraft. This was not welcomed by the bandits, who had to be called off by Madam Wong, with whom Kiwi was in conversation. The cruiser's covering firepower reinforced her decision. Kiwi decided that it would be impossible to refuel the Vampire in situ, let alone achieve a successful take-off from the soft, sandy beach. The only alternative was to hoist the aircraft aboard *HMS Belfast*, and the Royal Army Service Corps duly supplied a ramp landing-craft and a pinnace. A detachment of the Royal East Kent (The Buffs) was detailed to provide landing cover, and additional security against a surprise attack from the pirates, who had, by this time, infiltrated the undergrowth on the foreshore.

On the following day, Squadron Leader Gall and Flying Officer Dulieu from No 88 Squadron flew a party of technicians and equipment to Bias Bay in another Sunderland, to assist in the removal of the Vampire from the beach. During the afternoon, Kiwi received a signal from his boss. It was short and to the point: "Burn and Return". Darkness had fallen by the time the aircraft had been manhandled on to the landing craft and floated away from the shore, towards the waiting ship. Eventually, and only with tremendous difficulty, the Vampire was subsequently hoisted aboard using one of Belfast's cranes. Remarkably, the aircraft remained intact and undamaged throughout its ordeal, an undoubted tribute to the magnificent teamwork and co-operation from all the Services involved, and despite that afternoon's signal.

On arrival at Hong Kong, the Vampire proved to be heavier than the crane supplied to lift it up to the runway, so, to prevent it tipping over onto the deck, a crowd of people provided counter-balance weight on its rear end. The Vampire was overhauled and, less than 48 hours after being unloaded from *HMS Belfast*, was airborne again with Kiwi Francis at the controls. He laid on an impromptu display, as a token of gratitude to everyone involved in its recovery, and in thwarting the efforts of Madam Wong.

Credit: David Watkins   Credit: Peter Davis, HMS Belfast Association

Flight Lieutenant George "Kiwi" Francis DFC AFC* died on 10 July 2006. He joined the RNZAF in 1940, and completed his flying training at Ohakea on Hawker Hinds. After operational training on Hurricanes, he joined No 32 Squadron, which was engaged on night-fighter sweeps over France. He flew Hurricanes and Spitfires in North Africa, and Tempests with No 486 (NZ) Squadron. Later, he flew Meteors with No 616 squadron at Lubeck and No 263 squadron at RAF Acklington. Prior to posting to the Vampire Trials Unit, he was on the Air Fighting Development Unit. In the 1950 Birthday Honours List, he was awarded a bar to his AFC. Later he converted to helicopters, and joined the first Dragonfly squadron, No 194, at Kuala Lumpur. In 2 years, he flew over 1,200 hours in Dragonflies and Sycamores against communist guerrillas, and was awarded the DFC for his Malayan exploits. In 1956, he joined No 275 (ASR) squadron at Thornaby, and formed "E" Flight at Chivenor the following year. He became a Fighter Controller in 1959, and served in the UK, Germany and Aden before his final tour at Uxbridge, where he was one of the first to operate the computerised Air Defence of Great Britain radar system. He finally retired from the RAF in 1974, after a truly varied and outstanding career. His wife Mollie pre-deceased him in 2004, and they were survived by their 2 daughters.

Credit: David Watkins

A French Bird

When 'Jet Noise was very much the Sound of Freedom' and, more importantly, the adage 'Speed is Life' had real meaning, I was lucky enough to be stationed on a Canadian Defence Force base on the banks of the River Rhine in Southern Germany. I was a pilot on 439 (Tiger) Squadron, flying the single-seat CF-104 Starfighter - or 'The Widow Maker' – a nickname that clearly didn't amuse my wife at all!

Starfighter pilots loved the aeroplane for its simplicity and raw power. Designed by Lockheed as a high-level interceptor for the United States Air Force in the 1950s, certain design features were quite revolutionary for that time. For instance, it had a downward pilot ejection system, to reduce the time the pilot would spend in the extreme cold after a high level ejection. Its small supersonic wings, its big jet engine, long fuselage and T-tail made it look unique! The best turning performance for the aircraft was achieved at 540kts, which meant the cruising speed was kept high at 450kts - faster than other strike/attack aircraft of the time. Because the wings were so thin, no fuel could be carried in them, just in fuselage tanks and tip tanks; underwing pylon tanks could be carried for ferry flights. The 104 didn't possess a Radar Altimeter or Moving Map Display but, in the mid-1980s, it did have a third-generation Inertial Nav/Attack System fitted. Although the ground-mapping radar and autopilot could both be used to good effect at low level, the aircraft's very high performance, combined with short range, made it challenging to operate single-handed, particularly in that environment. A 6-barrelled 20mm Gatling Gun was fitted internally. The Stick-Pusher System (kicker) protected against possible loss of control following overly aggressive pitching manoeuvres, in which the fuselage might mask the tail-plane. Therefore, because in hard turns it could automatically bunt the aircraft unexpectedly if the pilot was overly aggressive, at low-level this system was always switched off - for obvious reasons! Likewise, the original Starfighter downward-ejection option mentioned before had long since been over-ridden by the engineers - phew!

Early one morning, as the sun rose over the Black Forest, I was fortunate enough to be detailed to fly a low-level navigation sortie in France. The calm, clear conditions were ideal for low flying. As many will know, planning was both quick and easy, for these dedicated pre-planned routes were already in booklet form; this was made possible because they had been approved in advance by the French authorities in Paris. So, with Diplomatic Clearance in place and flight plan filed, I was soon out-briefing[1]. I then walked to the Hardened Aircraft Shelter with route book in hand. I knew that 2 other Starfighters were to follow me at 5 minute intervals. Once airborne and at 450kts, I headed west at 500ft, almost immediately entering French airspace. My route took me north of Strasbourg, past the military airfields at Nancy and St. Dizier, and then south, passing the source of the River Seine, and onwards towards Dijon. Turning south of the town onto a north-easterly heading, the return route was a straight line across the Vosges Mountains, back into German airspace on the Rhine close to Lahr, another Canadian air base, prior to recovery to Baden.

My efforts to look out for other aircraft kept me aroused, as I fully expected one of the other squadron pilots to cut the corner and sneak up on me unseen, probably from below – the RAF Exchange Officer was always fair game! For most of the trip, the countryside was stunningly beautiful and, under clear sky, life felt good! However, it was not to last, as there was some low cloud on the western side of the Vosges Mountains, which would adversely affect my return route, and my attempt to find a valley to 'sneak' through failed. Instead I had to pull up; fortunately there was no controlled airspace to worry me above my track. Full reheat, onto instruments, 300 pitch, check heading and think about calling Colmar for a radar service. The moment I settled into the 400+kt climb, there was a massive bang!

Incredible noise, foul stench, excruciating pain in my hand and shoulder. Bird remains and windscreen glass from the quarter-light had hit me so hard it cut my hands. Luckily it missed my face and eyes. By the time I had composed myself, I was in clear air above 4,000ft. The engine seemed to be behaving well – how lucky! I considered my options. Colmar (a Mirage 2000 base) was just 20 miles away, and Bremgarten in Germany was a little further off - but it had a nuclear power plant close by. As low-level overflight of nuclear facilities had to be avoided at all costs, I felt it unwise to go that way in a damaged aircraft.

---

[1] Out-briefing: the final pre-flight brief for crews and supervisors

Therefore, I reduced speed to a comfortable 360kt and flew an orbit, while trying to raise the first Starfighter following me on the radio. The wind noise hindered clear communication, but we managed to join up, and he checked me over while I conducted a low speed handling check. We then 'chopped' to the Colmar approach frequency, and he made a MAYDAY-relay call on my behalf. It was only then that I found out that Colmar was on Exercise – in fact TACEVAL[2] – they were practising for war; I then really wished I'd chosen to go to Bremgarten instead!

My colleague escorted me in for my landing and saw me touch down, before heading home. I cleared the runway, and taxied behind the follow-me truck to parking. I was met by a group of armed guards in full Nuclear, Biological and Chemical protective clothing, wearing helmets and gas masks; they promptly arrested me. I could see that they were clearly 'very pissed-off.' The Base had been put on Air Raid Warning RED as a consequence of my unexpected visit/intrusion and, as a result, they were treating me as a 'Defector'! Because of the language barrier, it took several unpleasant minutes before I could convince the gas-mask-wearing guard commander that I was a genuine, friendly NATO pilot who had had a real emergency and needed medical help. The smashed window, blood on my hands and glass in my boots sort of did the trick – eventually – and I was released!

After the "All Clear" was given from air attack, the medics kindly stitched me up and then, about an hour later, the RAF Exchange Officer at Colmar appeared (someone I had last seen over 10 years before during flying training). After contacting my Squadron back at Baden, he took me for a very civilized lunch in a very empty Officers' Mess. Several hours later, a Canadian Forces Huey helicopter arrived to pick me up and fly the 60 miles home. At Base, the helicopter flew past the side of the primary school where, with the side door open, I was able to pick out my son and daughter playing at break-time - which led to much family excitement that evening, as they had seen me waving with my bandaged hands!

At the compulsory Friday late-night Beer Call the following evening, I was able to dine out on the tale and, as my hands were bandaged for some time, I

---

2 TACEVAL: Tactical evaluation of NATO declared units by NATO staff.

did this for several more weeks! For obvious reasons, the Boss told me a number of times how glad he was that the outcome hadn't been any worse! My scars still remind me of those happy, heady days, now some 35 years ago – when, of course, I still had hair! I was told later that I had hit a buzzard-type bird. As such, I have always thought it fortunate that my eyes/face escaped the impact, and that the Pratt and Whitney J79 engine coped with the pieces of glass and bird parts which it had ingested, without any complaint. Perhaps it's not surprising that the aircraft took over 2 months to fix.

Credit: Rob Sargent

In Charge Of A Shackleton!

It was in the spring of 1970 when I arrived at RAF Wittering, as a newly qualified Photographic Interpreter (PI), posted to the Reconnaissance Intelligence Centre to support the Harrier. Proud of my 'invisible mending' Pilot Officer's rank stripe, I was given the responsibility of liaison with 233 Operational Conversion Unit, to help in the recce phase of training new pilots on the Harrier. Needless to say, having flown gliders, and holding a Private Pilot's Licence, I was desperate to get a ride in this iconic and exciting aircraft. I found some sympathy for my ambition from the commander of the OCU, Wg Cdr Baker, who agreed to let me go to North Luffenham, to get fitted out with the Harrier flying kit, which would enable me to fly as a passenger. I made best use of this opportunity and, over the three years at RAF Wittering, 'hogged' every back seat ride that was available.

At the start of the Harrier operational capability, it was decided that the aircraft would be used from deployed field sites, and that the first testing of this ability would take place at RAF Milltown, a relief landing ground for RAF Kinloss in Scotland. As there was going to be a recce element to the deployment, I was to accompany the detachment. Needless to say, I bagged a seat in the Harrier T4 to fly there. For some reason which now escapes my memory (possibly a station exercise), four Harrier pilots and I were recalled to base at Wittering, and it was agreed that we should cadge a lift on a Kinloss-based Shackleton that was going down south on exercise.

We duly arrived in the Shackleton crewroom, and fitted out in immersion suits, as the Shackleton was due to carry out some training over the North Sea. In the anonymous green suit, there was, of course, no way of distinguishing a pilot from a lowly PI and - when the captain of the Shackleton announced that, when we were over the North Sea, he would let the FIVE Harrier pilots have a go at flying the Shackleton - I kept shtum! The Shackleton impressed me; a hamburger was produced for us before we got out of the circuit! I was also impressed when there was much discussion, in preparing for the dropping of a flare, whether it should be dropped to the port or starboard of a buoy; in the event, we hit it!

After droning around for an hour or two over the sea at 250ft, the Harrier pilots and I were invited up to fly the aircraft. My turn came, and I flew the aircraft. From my vast experience of a Cessna 150 and Auster, its handling was rather more 'solid' than I was used to - you had to use rudder and it was heavy on the ailerons. The captain said to me after about 15 minutes: "You OK? - Just keep it on that heading – I will get the next Harrier guy up!" He left his seat and, a couple of minutes later, one of the Harrier pilots took my place, giving me a rather quizzical look!

So that was it: a Pilot Officer PI, in sole charge of one of Her Majesty's aircraft. Not a word was ever said between me and the Harrier pilots – but I suppose, after 45 years, the tale can now be told.

Credit: US DoD

A Diplomatic Incident

In the story 'Terramoto', on page 168 of the book 'Out of the Blue', the author says that an aircraft on 543 Sqn's first detachment in Peru in 1968 caused a diplomatic incident by landing in Chile. It wasn't Chile, it was Argentina – I know because I was the Navigator Radar in that Victor crew. I thought I'd set down my recollection of the incident to put the record straight. So there we were, the right way up, with 45,000 feet on the clock, in a perfectly serviceable aeroplane, just coming into the overhead of the airfield at which we intended to land. The only snag was that it was 0300 on a Sunday morning, the airfield wasn't operating, and we were over a foreign country for which we didn't have diplomatic clearance. This is the story of how we got ourselves into that position, and how we – more or less – got out of it.

It had all started in the early summer of 1968, when I was coming towards the end of my first tour as a Navigator Radar on the Victor SR2s of No 543 Squadron at RAF Wyton. We were warned to prepare for a detachment lasting several months in a hot climate. It emerged that we were going to be monitoring the forthcoming French nuclear test series, due to take place in the South Pacific. Four crews were selected and, within days, we found ourselves at RAF Marham, doing a much abbreviated air-to-air refuelling (AAR) course, as it seemed likely that the closest we were going to be able to get to the South Pacific was Jamaica. However, after three or four exciting AAR sorties, we heard that we were going to be based at Jorge Chavez International Airport at Lima, Peru, and so in-flight refuelling would not be necessary.

The detachment was due to leave on 12th June, which was a bit worrying as my wife was expecting our first child on the 10th! However, as my Navigator Plotter was also required to stay at Wyton – a long story involving a misplaced secret document and a Board of Inquiry – my captain, who was the detachment commander, took another complete nav team, and my Plotter and I eventually went out in the first replacement Victor, when my daughter was six weeks old. By the time we arrived in Lima, the detachment was already well-established, both operationally and socially. The other crews had already flown monitoring sorties after the first test in the series, and had made friends with the English-speaking community of Lima. In between the French tests, the only flying was familiarisation for newly-arrived crews, and background radiation checks, so we had a fair amount of time off. The second test took place in early August. On Saturday 10th, I was relaxing in the hotel after a day out in Lima, when I was summoned to the airport to fly with another crew whose Nav Rad had gone sick. I quickly changed into flying kit and went through the briefing with the rest of the crew, who – unlike me – were well rested after their night-flying stand-down. It appeared that, because of the upper winds, the debris cloud was going to be a long way south of Lima.

Just as we boarded the crew bus to go out to the aircraft, Nobby, my captain for the sortie, went into a huddle with the detachment commander, who had gained the appropriately Spanish nickname of 'El Commandante', and a United States Air Force (USAF) officer from their detachment in Lima. He came back with a mysterious smile on his face and said: "I'll tell you about it once we're airborne." We took off into the night, and the sortie went smoothly. We found the cloud off the coast of Chile, and began to fly a W-shaped pattern to find the hottest spot. After an hour or so, it became obvious that we would soon have to leave the task if we were to have enough fuel to return to Lima. However, Nobby announced: "El Commandante told me that if we needed to stay on task, we could divert to Mendoza in Argentina. There's a USAF detachment there, who will turn us round and send us off to Lima in time for breakfast."

Reassured by this, we continued 'sniffing' the cloud. We ended up at 54,000 feet, and so far south that I could see the distinctive curve of the Golfo San Jorge, on the Atlantic coast of Argentina, on my radar. Eventually we turned north, and flew up to Mendoza, which is in the foothills of the Andes, some 500 miles west of Buenos Aires. As we approached the overhead at Flight Level 450, the pilots could see only a dark patch where we expected to see the airfield lights. Undeterred, they called up on the approach frequency, and after some delay, a rather sleepy voice answered in Spanish. None of us spoke Spanish, but Nobby at least had bought himself a 'Teach Yourself Spanish' book before he left the UK, and somehow was able to get across that we'd like to speak to someone American. Our Spanish friend said the equivalent of "Stand by", and we started a long racetrack pattern, still at FL450, over the airfield. Our options began to reduce in line with the fuel gauges. Soon we no longer had enough to make it to Buenos Aires, and Santiago - which was nearer but on the other side of the

Andes, surrounded by mountains, and without approach lighting - was distinctly unattractive. However, Nobby kept reassuring us that everything would be all right, and, after what seemed a lifetime, but was probably only an hour, an American voice came up on the radio.

Shortly afterwards, the runway lighting was switched on – there was no approach lighting here, either – and we began our descent. "We need to make a quick turn-round here," said Nobby, "so I won't stream the brake chute and then we won't have to repack it". That seemed fair enough, and we all settled down to monitoring the approach and trying to work out what height we should be at using QNH[1] at an airfield 2,300 feet above sea level. We touched down after 7 hours in the air, braked hard, and followed the guide truck to a parking spot. As soon as we had shut down the engines and opened the door, an American head popped up and said: "Hi, guys. We'll turn you round as quickly as we can, and get you on your way". Our sense of relief didn't last long, as our American disappeared and was replaced by an Argentinian conscript with a gun. We were invited to leave the aeroplane, and taken to a crew room where we were given coffee. The Argentinians treated us with suspicion, and who could blame them? We were foreign military aircrew who had turned up in the middle of the night, without prior warning or clearance, flying a reconnaissance aircraft over their territory.

My memory of the next few hours is a bit hazy, but I think there were numerous attempts to get in touch with the British Embassy in Buenos Aires. Of course, as it was a weekend, the Air Attaché was off playing golf somewhere up-country, and couldn't be contacted. We hung around in the crew room, drinking more coffee. While we didn't seem to be actually under arrest, we were nevertheless followed to the loo by a guard. Eventually, we were taken to the Officers' Club and given lunch. By this time, I'd been awake for well over 24 hours, and the lack of sleep was catching up with me. I couldn't eat a thing and needed to lie down, so they put me in a bedroom in the Club, where I had some much-needed sleep. When I caught up with the rest of the crew later in the afternoon, they had all been interrogated by the Station Intelligence Officer. I was left out

---

[1] QNH: A pressure setting that causes the altimeter to read altitude above mean sea level (as opposed to QFE, normally used at RAF airfields which gives altitude above the airfield).

because he didn't like to wake me up! "They asked if we'd been flying over some offshore islands called the Malvinas," said John, the Navigator Plotter, to me. "I've never heard of them. Have you?" I hadn't heard of them either; fourteen years later the whole world would know of them!

We stayed overnight in the Officers' Club. On the Monday morning, the Air Attaché arrived by air from Buenos Aires, and straightened out any "misunderstanding". After that, the Argentinians were very friendly (which was nice of them, considering that we were still in our smelly flying suits), and one of the pilots from the advanced training school on the base was detailed to look after us. When we went back to the aircraft, we found a hydraulic leak in the main undercarriage – possibly caused by the unusually heavy braking - which would have to be fixed before we could fly again. The S Eng O[2] and a technician flew down from Lima by civil airlines to repair it, but it meant that we were stuck in Mendoza for three days. Our host did his best to keep us entertained. He took us into the city of Mendoza to visit the monument to General San Martin, one of the great liberators of South America, but unfortunately the trip was reported in the local press, so the Base Commander put a stop to any further jollies off base. However, the Mendoza area produces some of Argentina's best wine, so being confined to the bar wasn't too unpleasant. The American detachment, flying RB57s[3] from Mendoza in the same air-sampling role as us, were a little put out by our arrival, as the full story of what we were doing had appeared in the Peruvian press, while they were ostensibly researching high-altitude winds over the Andes. Cover story blown!

Our Victor generated a lot of interest on the base, as it dwarfed the local advanced trainers. I was showing an Argentinian pilot round the outside of the aircraft, when he reached up to the air-sampling kit on the front of the port drop-tank and said "What's this?" We had been given stern advice not to touch the outside of the aircraft after it had flown into the post-test cloud, so I said the first thing that came into my head: "Don't touch, it's fragile". He didn't question it, but how he imagined that something that could withstand Mach 0.85[4] at

---

[2] S Eng O: Senior Engineering Officer.
[3] RB57: The US reconnaissance version of the Canberra.
[4] Mach 0.85: A measurement of velocity where Mach 1 is the speed of sound.

50,000 feet could be too fragile to touch, I don't know. When at last the aircraft was repaired, we winched down the pannier we were carrying in the bomb bay, and loaded the engineers' tool kits and spares into it. I was a little too eager to help, and managed to trap my little finger between the pannier and the aircraft as it was being winched up. It was incredibly painful, but I decided I could manage the four-hour flight back to Lima. Once we got back into Lima, I sought out the detachment medical orderly, who took me along to the local doctor, employed by the British Embassy to look after us. The doctor looked about 90 years old, and his X-ray equipment wasn't much younger. He and his nurse put on leather-lined aprons and set up the X-ray machine, which was pointing not only at the finger, but also at some personal assets that I was rather keen to preserve. Anyway, I'm pleased to report that the X-ray showed that the finger wasn't actually broken, and that, later on, I successfully fathered two more children.

Credit: Flypast-Key Collection

Harrier Field Ops

Anyone who has been a part of the Harrier force will, without doubt, have some very fond memories. It was quite a unique world to be part of, operating an aircraft that was a fighter and a helicopter rolled into one - well almost!

The most enjoyable times were to be had when Deploying to the Field or, on some rather soggy occasions, Mud-Moving. I was lucky enough to be around in the early days, when we deployed up to 6 times a year; this frequency was reduced in later years, as the preparation for such events was quite involved. Nonetheless, sometimes when the Station hooter sounded, maybe for a station exercise or a NATO tactical evaluation, we would deploy the whole shebang with no prior preparation. I remember on one occasion, just slicing the joint of

beef, when that loud haunting sound became apparent. As it was a Sunday, I said to my wife that it would just be a call-out, and I should be home again in a couple of hours. How wrong could I be; several days later, having deployed to a field site, and having moved location, we finally arrived back at camp somewhat weary. I rushed home to find the garden full of wives, who were clearly making the most of their time without us!

A field deployment involved a myriad of personnel, and I am not sure I could list them all, as it involved so many. The Army engineers were needed to lay the metal strips, if they were required, and to lay the MEXE metal landing pad. In addition, they installed the rubber fuel storage tanks. The RAF Regiment were our field defence unit. We needed engineers of all trades, photo-reconnaissance interpreters, and Army liaison personnel, headed by the Ground Liaison Officer (GLO), who were responsible for tasking the aircraft. We needed personnel for spares, refuelling, cooks, medics, signals and more. And, of course, we needed the pilots to fly the missions. In charge of all this was the site commander, a squadron flight commander.

Aircraft were generally landed vertically on metal pads, and then taxied to the camouflaged "hides." These were often on the edges of woods, sometimes inside the wood, and sometimes hidden amongst buildings, particularly in disused villages in and around the training areas. Tasking was often carried out using a telebrief system, which connected the pilot by phone cable with operations, the GLO, and with other aircraft if a multi-aircraft mission was being planned. Each site would normally have 4 to 6 aircraft to operate. Briefings between pilots were mostly carried out whilst in the cockpit, as was planning. Trying to plot a route on a map, whilst in the rather restricted confines of a Harrier cockpit, was not easy. Once ready, the jets would be taxied to the take-off area, which was normally a grass field but sometimes a road.

Missions varied, and included single-aircraft reconnaissance tasks, using either the built-in port camera, or the centrally-attached 5-camera reconnaissance pod. The pilot might be searching for troops and equipment in an area, on a road or at a known point. It might be a mission to report on the serviceability of bridges, masts, barracks etc. There was often more than one target, which had to be found, photographed and a detailed report compiled for radio transmission to the in-flight reporting post. After landing, the film would be rapidly downloaded, and taken to the Reconnaissance Intelligence Centre (RIC) for processing. How much easier it would have been if digital cameras had been available then! The pilot would be connected by telebrief to the GLO for a debrief, and then to the RIC to debrief with the Intelligence Officer.

Other missions flown would be singletons, pairs or even larger formations: "Mud-Moving" missions to seek out and destroy such varied targets as bridges, barracks, missile sites and moving targets, known to be along certain routes of advance or in certain areas. The targets had to be located, and then attacked with the weapon of choice. Of course, in peace time, it would have been rather unsporting to fire live ordnance, so the attack was recorded on the head-up-display camera. This was later assessed, to ascertain whether the attack had been successful. Once again, an in-flight report was needed on the way home and, after landing, the pilots debriefed by telebrief, with the GLO and amongst themselves. All of these missions were normally around 40-45 minutes from take-off to landing, so one can imagine how intense the workload could be. Added pressure was often introduced by other NATO aircraft being tasked to intercept and try to destroy, or at least foil, any target runs. It was all a great challenge and great fun.

After flying around 5 or 6 sorties, a pilot would give up his warm and sweaty seat to another for his battering. Each aircraft would normally fly 10 to 12 sorties per day although, on one occasion, due to some terrible weather, we only had one aircraft on the site for a few days. This had to operate solely from the MEXE pad, taking off and landing vertically. Flight time was limited to 15-25 minutes, and the site managed to launch the jet 20 times in a single day. At the end of each day, the personnel relaxed in the comfort of their 12x12 tents, often playing cards to pass the time. The highlight of the evening was the meal, which gave everyone on the site the opportunity to chat about the day's events, amongst other things. Electricity was often in short supply, so early nights were the norm as were early mornings. There was always a rush for the limited supply of hot water and most, including myself, would find themselves abluting in very cold water. Personal hygiene was not the best! Morale was always high, even though at times conditions were not the most ideal. I remember many periods of wind, rain and occasionally snow, but morale was never dashed. At the end of a deployment, site personnel often put on a concert, using a 10-ton truck as the stage. There were some cracking acts from all ranks and trades.

As my experience level grew, I became the deputy site commander, taking charge of the operation when my Flight Commander took his turn in the cockpit. We also took it in turn to set up the site, and to dismantle it at the end of the deployment. On one occasion, and I can't remember the name of the site, it was my turn to wrap up the operation, and my Flight Commander's turn to lead the formation back to base; my Flight Commander at the time was a dear, departed ex-Red Arrows pilot. It was normal practice for the departing aircraft to do a farewell flypast over the site before heading off. On this occasion, the take-off was on a field, which had a row of trees at each end of the take-off run. I placed myself about halfway down the take-off field to watch the departure.

The aircraft departed normally and, some minutes later, they performed a beautiful flypast in box formation, and then headed in the direction of base. I slowly walked back along the strip, enjoying the lovely sunshine. It wasn't long before the sound of a Harrier could be heard in the distance, but then the sound disappeared, and I thought that it might be another aircraft from a different site. At the departure end of the strip, there was a gap in the trees, just about big enough for a Harrier to fit through. Yes, you know what's coming next! Out of the blue, and silently, came my Flight Commander in his Harrier, pulling hard and with about 90 degrees of bank on. He passed through the gap and then aimed for me. I am not sure what happened in the subsequent few seconds, but my next view was of a Harrier disappearing fast and low, heading home.

The story continues as, for the next field deployment, we were using a site, Geseke I think, which was based around a disused village. The aircraft were deployed around the buildings and, for take-off, we had to taxy across a local German road and onto the field strip. As one can imagine, the operations did not go unnoticed by the civilian population, and the normal quiet road became quite busy with "spotters." Our police had a busy job controlling the numbers of civilian cars which, of course, were perfectly entitled to use their road. At the end of the deployment, it was my turn to lead the flock base to base and, as was the norm, we carried out a formation flypast of the site. As usual, the site commander placed himself part-way along the strip to watch proceedings. After the formation flypast, I split from the group and, having previously scoped the layout, decided to fly through a large gap in the trees which paralleled the take-off strip. If I timed it right, I would pass right over the site commander, planning to give him a squirt of fuel. For those that don't know, the fuel jettison switches were on the right side of the stick, so it needed a quick change of hands to operate them. Having always flown with my right hand, it was not easy, at low level, to change hands, look for the jettison switches, operate them and then change hands again. As many, including myself, have since experienced, the change to flying with the left hand is really easy to make, only taking a matter of minutes for one to feel comfortable.

I concentrated now on passing overhead my Flight Commander, who was striding down the strip towards the road crossing. In a matter of seconds I had passed him, and I quickly switched hands to turn off the fuel jettison. My next recollection is of a large number of German civilian cars passing directly under the aircraft, and I still had not managed to operate the jettison switches. Oops! It was not a good error to make. I pulled up and away, finally managed to turn off the fuel jettison switches, and rushed back to base wondering what news would be waiting for my return. For weeks I waited for the Boss to call me into his office, but that call never came - at least not for this event!

Nearly Lost Your R(H)AG

The Phantom was a great beast to fly, and RAF Leuchars a great airfield to fly it from. This was especially true in the good old days, when the RAF had just the one Phantom air defence squadron. Sure, it felt more like a Jet Provost than the light and nimble Lightning, but four eyes are better than two, and eight missiles much better than two, to say nothing about loads more fuel; well, most of the time. Having started life as a US Navy carrier jet, it was also equipped with a sodding great tailhook, which saved many airframes from an ignominious fate.

Of course, to use the hook, you needed an arrester cable, but every fast-jet airfield (we had quite a few in those days) had two of these, one for aborted take-offs or to prevent overruns on landing, and one to land into (à la Fleet Air Arm), if you anticipated problems on landing. At the time we are talking about, though, the easterly installation at Leuchars, which was the approach-end cable for Runway 27, had been unserviceable for nearly 2 months. A Lossiemouth Jaguar had engaged it heavy and fast and the time being taken to repair it had become an issue for the station 'wheels.'

On the morning of 13 February 1975 - it's OK, it was a Thursday – the approach-end cable was at long last declared serviceable. That afternoon, I took off as No 2 of a pair to do routine interceptions over the North Sea. The plan on recovery was to do a pairs GCA[1] and landing. As we were closing in on the leader to join in close formation, we suffered an unusual electrical problem; among other things, the right hand generator had failed. I deployed the Ram Air Turbine (RAT), but this just made matters worse, as it induced a total electrics failure! The FG1 that we were flying did not have a battery - the Royal Navy saw no need for one, as there was always plenty of power to plug into on board a carrier. The RAT was rapidly retracted, which restored a modicum of power, though there were still some weird indications that didn't fit any 'standard' failure condition known to me or my even-more-tech-savvy back-seater.

We advised the lead aircraft that we had a problem, declared a PAN[2] to

---

[1] GCA: Ground Controlled Approach using ground-based radar
[2] PAN: A transmission indicating that a state of urgency exists but that there is no immediate danger.

Leuchars Director, and took stock of the situation. We had meanwhile slowed down to below gear limiting speed, so decided to lower the wheels and see what happened. The undercarriage came down as advertised, though there was no indication that we had nosewheel steering. We agreed as a crew that 'three wheels on our wagon' was all we needed for a safe landing, so decided to leave well alone and not try lowering any flap. Because of the uncertainty about nosewheel steering, we further agreed that we should engage the approach-end cable. This information was duly relayed to all who needed to know, and the ensuing approach, landing and pull-out of the cable was something of an anti-climax. We left the jet in the cable, and in the tender care of the crash crew and groundcrew. As we were enjoying a swift drag, standing on the grass at the side of the runway, an Austin 1800, sporting a flag on the bonnet, appeared at a great rate of knots, with clouds of pipe smoke emerging from the open driver's window. "I hope you haven't broken my RHAG!" said the group captain, as he came to a halt. I didn't stop to think that this remark might have been made tongue-in-cheek, and replied in a tone of voice not normally used by flight lieutenants to their elders and very-much-betters, that the F4 seemed to be in one piece, as were me and my nav, and that I couldn't give two hoots for his cable. He blew a couple of smoke rings and said very quietly that he saw my point.

Credit: Anthony Noble

It Doesn't Pay To Curtsey

I volunteered for the Support Helicopter Force after 2 fixed-wing tours, and three-and-a-half years as a professional child-frightener at the Officer Cadet Training Unit. On arrival at RAF Odiham, as a relatively senior Flight Lieutenant, I met the boss of Standards Flt - a Squadron Leader a couple of years older than me - and we seemed to hit it off quite well. He later became my Squadron Commander and, as such, was a guest at our wedding, for which he authorised a 3-ship flypast, in exchange for large volumes of beer for the crews involved. Imagine that happening nowadays...

He then out-accelerated me to reach Air Rank and pick up a knighthood, whilst I stumbled up to Specialist Aircrew Squadron Leader. I wrote him a letter of congratulation when his elevation to the peerage was announced, and promised to curtsey the next time we met. His response was one of gratitude for my felicitations and a statement: "If you curtsey to me, you little shit, I'll knee you in the nuts!"

The next time we met was at a Families' Day type of event - me in flying suit, and he in No 1 Home Dress. I duly curtseyed, whereupon he knee-d me in the nuts, and we fell to the grass for a brief struggle. We then dusted ourselves down and retired for a beer, leaving a very perplexed-looking Station Commander, wondering what on earth it was he had just witnessed, and probably thankful he did not have to do anything about it!

Sink The Tirpitz - Part 1

The Russian Connection

Reproduced from his book 'Bomber Pilot', by kind permission of the author,
Don Macintosh, and Browsebooks Publishing Ltd.

In the main hall of the manor house at Woodhall Spa, home of the Dambusters,
two WAAFs stood ready to lift a grey dust-sheet from a large table. At the door
of the room stood an RAF sergeant with a .32 Webley strapped to his blanco'd
belt. On one side, apart from the beribboned pilots and navigators, stood the Air
Marshal, conspicuous by his thick blue rings and gold laurel leaves and, round
him, his senior officers. Ralph Cochrane, direct descendant of Thomas Earl of
Dundonald, the Sea Wolf - Almirante of Brazil, Chile and Greece, who escaped
from a debtor's prison to become the scourge of Spain and a companion of San
Martin.

The Air Marshal nodded to the Intelligence Officer, and the WAAFs whisked
the dust-sheet off. "It's the Tirpitz!" someone exclaimed. Sitting on a relief map
of fjords and mountains, lay a squat, grey model of a battleship. "That's what
you'll see, gentlemen," intoned the Intelligence Officer. "Sister ship of the Bismarck - 15 inch guns and just a shade under 60,000 tons. You probably know
that just about everyone has had a go at her - the Navy with midget subs, and
we've bombed her without any noticeable success. You all know what happened
when the Bismarck got out and sank merchant ships like turkeys at a shoot.
Even now, she is tying up naval ships desperately needed elsewhere. As the season of mists and darkness approaches, she can come out with a few destroyers
and, with her big guns and radar, pick off a dozen of our merchant ships like
herons in a goldfish pond, and slip back to the safety of her lair in Norway.

"You will fly to an airfield in Russia and either bomb on the way, or from
there, depending on the weather. You'll get your detailed briefing from the various leaders; this is just a general briefing. In that context, gentlemen, are there
any questions?"

"What about fighters?" asked Carey, a New Zealand pilot. The smile left
the IO's face. "There are two squadrons of Focke-Wulf 190s at Bardufoss, some

distance away," he said apologetically, lowering his eyes and not looking at the airmen. Bloody silly question. What does Carey think he's going to say, "Anybody who doesn't like fighters and thinks it's dangerous, apply for leave?" "Any chance of Russian fighters meeting us and escorting us over the target?" asked Alec Jones, a pleasant but slightly dim Aussie. "It's possible," said the IO, "but I don't think it's very likely." "I hope he isn't going to ask about long range Mustangs escorting us, or some such horseshit," Nigel whispered.

We climbed into the squadron buses and got back to our base at Bardney. The bar was working overtime, and I was glad to be out of the rarefied air of Woodhall Spa. Duggie, a solidly-built pilot from Carlisle, handed me a pint of beer, his eyes alight. "What do you think of it, Mac? The Navy lads will be furious with Butch Harris if we pull it off." "A touch of the Kamikazes in it, don't you think?" Nigel chipped in. "Bloody right, Nigel, if the lads in the Focke-Wulfs catch us over Norway. Churchill's mad keen on it. It's personal with him - he wants to see the last of their big ships bite the dust. I bet there's been a bit of arm-twisting going on, high up." "If you don't like it you shouldn't have joined!" a cry went up from the small circle around us.

Next day I rested as much as I could in the tin Nissen hut, and, after lunch, cycled out to have a good look round our aircraft, 'C' Charlie, spending some time cleaning the 'greenhouse' windows - making sure there were no spots on them that I might mistake for fighters and get frightened unnecessarily. With most of the preparations already completed, we assembled for final briefing. We were all in high spirits at doing something out of the ordinary, and landing in an unknown country. I didn't pay too much attention to the met briefing, and anyway it would be daylight when we got there. I seem to remember something being said about the cloudbase 'lifting.'

On the crew bus out to dispersal, Jeff said, "I wonder what Russia's like?" "Bloody awful, from what my uncle Bob tells me," I said. "He's an admiral's quartermaster on the Arctic convoys, Robert MacFarlane, and he says they're a difficult bunch and wouldn't give you a drink of water. Guards all over the place. He said they were treated more like enemies than sailors risking their lives to bring food and weapons." "That's if we get there!" said Jock. Nigel ignored this remark. "I've got all the gen on communications for landing in Russia, Mac," said Phil. "It's a funny old system of broadcasting the letters of the alphabet, and then identifying which sector you're in. A Liberator will take off ahead of us to set up a radio control station at the Russian airfield, to help us in."

We piled out of the crew bus, and I climbed into our Lanc through the little door near the tail, to be greeted by the familiar smell of pee, hydraulic oil and high octane fuel. The Lanc had only one set of controls, since it carried only one pilot, but could be jury-rigged for dual training. If the pilot got himself shot, the bomb-aimer had his chance to become a self-taught bomber pilot - a bit like 'failed MD, London,' since almost all had failed flying tests at an early stage. However, behind my seat was a comforting half-inch of armour plate, which increased my chances of survival if shot at from the rear, and reduced his chances of instant glory.

The aircraft were, unusually, parked nose-to-tail on the taxiway leading to the take-off position. Bob, my Flight Engineer, called: "They want to know if you'd like topping up with fuel after the run-up, Skipper?" "No, Bob," I told him. "It's only a few gallons, and there's always the chance of the caps being left undone." In the belly of the Lanc was what looked like a pillar-box with a parachute attached - the Johnnie Walker, a marine bomb with gas propellant, so called since, once in the water, it kept on going. It was supposed to bob up and down, moving slowly forward, until it hit the ship on the water-line. We all thought it was a crazy idea. The majority carried one single six-ton bomb, bulging the bomb doors. "Five minutes to start time, Mac" Nigel called from his desk.

I started up the Merlins, and taxied slowly towards the end of the runway, behind the other squadron Lancs. I watched the one immediately in front take off, and lined up. An Aldis lamp flashed a green from the chequered caravan. All checks complete, I pushed the outer throttle well forward ahead of the others, to counteract the prop rotation. Go. Three tons over weight, and a Christmas cracker in the belly, the four Rolls Royce Merlins roared and strained forward. If we lose an engine, there won't be anything to worry about – permanently! Right at the end of the runway, I heave back and we beat our way into the twilight.

In an hour, welcoming darkness enveloped us, and I attended to the small autopilot wheel on my left constantly, keeping our height between 800 and 1200 feet, my fingers touching the release lever. In the event of engine failure, only 10 or 20 seconds, in which to take corrective action, separated us from the sea. We flew on into the pitch black night, hour after hour, the Merlins purring steadily. My world became the disembodied instruments, glowing luminously in front of me. Each of us was wrapped in his own thoughts, the quiet hum broken occasionally when I called the gunners on intercom. For the moment, we were safe from attack.

"Better start your climb soon, Mac," called Nigel. "We'll be at the Norwegian coast in half an hour. Climb initially to 12000 feet. They'll see us on radar, but we'll be over Sweden soon, and I don't think they'll bother us." "Stick the revs up to 2650 for the climb, Bob," I called. "Skipper!" Jock came up on the intercom. "A helluva lot of sparks came from the engines when you opened up just now." "Don't worry, Jock," I told him, "It's only the flues being cleaned out from the carbon deposits after the very low revs." We carried on our climb for the next twenty minutes, pulling back the revs at the top of the climb. I didn't think there would be any night fighters over Norway but, since I wasn't a close confidante of the Luftwaffe, I kept the gunners on their toes, searching, while Bob and I peered into the night ahead.

After an hour, Nigel said we should soon be over Sweden, although we hadn't asked permission, and an hour later, Peter called, "Someone's catching it, away over on our right." I peered hard into the night, and saw a faint glow in the sky. Nigel came out to have a look. "Yeah. That's Stockholm," he said." Away to the South. The Swedes must be firing at one of the Lancs that took off ahead of us. The wind has gone round and blown us towards the city." A Swedish Bofors gun was firing clips of three red tracer shells straight up into the sky. They soared lazily and burst harmlessly. "They're preserving their neutrality, but they know who's winning the war today. I'll see if I can get an astro fix. Try not to alter course, and let me know if you see the coast." Conversation died as Nigel reached for his Mark 9 clockwork sextant. The mystery of getting navigational help from distant suns at infinite distances stunned us all into silence. When we flew over the Reich, Nigel would bash his Gee Radar box for navigation, occasionally telling me that he had lost the signal for a bit. Now, he was a being set apart - a being in communication with the stars. "I think I've got a fix," he said after some time. "It's not a terribly good one, but it ties in with my reckoning. Did you see the coast?" "Sorry, Nigel, It's thick cloud underneath now." "Oh well, no matter; I'll try and get another one. Meanwhile, you do know that Finland is still at

war with us, and will fire at us, not up, like the Swedes?" "O.K. Nige, fine," I
said. "Jeff, are you wide awake? There could be night-fighters over Finland, I just
don't know, but keep your eyes peeled. What's it like in the turret?" "Bloody
cold!" he replied. "I've got my electric suit turned full up, and I'm keeping a
lookout. I'll just give my turret a spin, to see it's all working." The Lanc yawed
as the heavy turret swung on full traverse. Flying east, into the dawn ahead, the
sky was crystal clear, and underneath was a solid carpet of layered cloud.

"That last fix was OK, Mac. It puts us pretty well on track, but I'm afraid
it's DR (dead reckoning) from here on. Any chance of a pinpoint, Peter?" "Not a
hope, Nigel. How long to go to Archangel now?" "Just over half an hour," Nigel
told him. Keep your topo maps handy, in case it clears." "I've got them here in
the hatch, Nige. They're pretty ropey, large scale of the tundra, with dotted lines
of the rivers wandering all over the place. I don't expect the Russians would give
us any recent maps, I'm sure these date back to the Tsar!"

A red sun appeared ahead. I could see Bob clearly, as he crouched by his fuel
panel on the catwalk on my right. "How much fuel is left, Bob?" "Hang on a jiff,
Skip, I'm just working it out." "Start descending soon, Skipper. I estimate about
25 minutes to go. We don't want to overshoot Archangel," Nigel called. "165
gallons left. About an hour's flying to dry tanks. That's allowing for throttling
back on the descent." "Phil, any luck on the radio? Have you spoken to anyone?" "No, Skipper. I can't understand it. Everything's working OK, but I can't
raise anyone, and the Russian directional beacon doesn't make sense. Would you
switch your VHF set to channel 'C' and I'll listen out on that as well?"

It was now full daylight, and a thick solid carpet of white cloud extended
beneath us to the horizon. We were flying just above it at 2000 feet, exhilarated
by the sensation of speed as we skimmed over it and, with more fuel, it could
have been fun. A sense of imminent danger gnawed inside me. No control. No
weather report. No altimeter setting; after 10 hours flying and two thousand
miles, it could easily be 500 feet in error. Then, for the first time, I heard voices
on the short-range radio. "I've only 15 minutes fuel left. Are you going down
now? Have you raised anyone? What's happened to the Liberator? What setting are you using?" Ahead, I could see half a dozen Lancasters circling, and
anxiously calling each other, like crows disturbed from a tree. One voice rose in
alarm. Bob's face was showing dismay. I reached over to the radio box on my

left, carefully switched it off, and all the noise stopped. "OK, everyone, I'm going through this lot. We're obviously over Archangel. The airfield's only 10 miles from the town. I'm going to let down over the sea. Bob, reset your altimeter when we break cloud, estimating our height above the water." I pushed forward, throttled back and, with misgiving, entered cloud.

The clear bright, sunny world above changed to a dark tunnel, as I watched the height unwind. 700 - 600 - at 500 feet, I saw whitecaps about to come in the cockpit window. I checked hastily as we skimmed over the waves of a cold, grey sea, and immediately we shot back into cloud again. I re-set my altimeter to Bob's. "Nigel, I'm turning back to Archangel, and going down again." Through the tunnel again, down, 500 - 300, at 200 feet I gritted my teeth and, at 150 feet, caught glimpses of the sea through the ragged ceiling. "Jock, watch the wings in the turn. Yell out when you get frightened." It was 50 feet from my seat to the wingtip. Nigel and Peter came up together on the intercom. "There's a tall chimney ahead, that must be Archangel." Relief. After my initial fright, I became adjusted to flying on the deck. My last low flying had been on an AT6a in Florida. Peter called: "OK Mac, I can see where we are, I'll take you along this river, which will lead us to the airfield at Yagodnik."

I was feeling much happier, now we had found the bloody place and got underneath the clag. Bob handled the throttles, while I looked expectantly for a runway to appear ahead. Silence. "Mac" Nigel called in an anxious voice, "We must have passed it by now. Turn back for Archangel." I turned back over the tundra - grass, swamp and clumps of pine. In a few minutes, we were back over the town. "Let's have another go," I said, "We should see the runways this time." Once more we swung over the familiar chimney and headed south. Bob kept glancing anxiously at his gauges, now just above zero. "Time's up!" Nigel called from his desk. As I turned back for Archangel, icy fear gripped me. If we crash land, it's even money that firecracker in the bomb bay will explode. The boys with the Tallboy bombs are OK. My mind raced. The second hand on the stopwatch in front seemed to slow down. "Nigel, Pete. This is it. This is our last run before I put her down. I want an accurate time and distance run from the centre of the town. Jeff, give Nigel a drift from your turret. Nigel, after we set course and start the watches, get down with Pete in the front and check with the maps."

"Better put some flap down, Mac" Bob called. "Right, Bob. That'll slow

us up and give us more time to look around." "Ten degrees left, Skipper,"
Nigel called. "There are two very similar rivers. This ties in more with our T
& D heading." The second hand moved sluggishly round the dial. "Time's
up!" Nigel called. We flew on, suspended in time and space, for two more
minutes, when a cry of "Lancs!" went up, and I glimpsed the familiar wings as
we thundered across the grass field. I spun the Lanc around in a near vertical
turn, not daring to lose sight of the field. One shot. I saw a river underneath as
I banked, opened the throttles, then called, "Gear down. Landing flap." There
was no approach. I cut the engines as we crossed a fence, swerved to avoid red
flags round a hole and braked quickly to a halt.

Relief, surge of spirit and reaction set in. Outside, near a hut, were a group
of Russians with tram-drivers' hats, blowing brass instruments, and holding
a long red banner aloft, bearing the legend: 'Welcome the Glorious Flyers of
the Royal Air Force.' We had arrived. Alice in Wonderland! A grass island on
the Dvina, no radio contact, impossible weather and a bloody brass band! In
aviation, expect the unexpected. I congratulated Nigel on getting us there, but
he seemed a trifle embarrassed. "Welcome, one very frightened glorious flyer,"
Phil laughed nervously.

A Jeep came up with a WingCo from the Military Mission, accompanied
by a Russian officer wearing large red epaulettes and displaying three brass
stars. "Morning, chaps, glad you got here," the WingCo called loudly. "Don't
stray about the field, where all the Russian planes are parked. They tend to
shoot first and enquire afterwards. Half an hour later, a truck pulled up, a
Model 'T' Ford, and dropped me off at my billet - a paddle steamer moored to
a wooden jetty in the river, near the huts of the Russian camp. A Russian soldier lounged near the gangway. I climbed aboard, and saw an oval brass plaque
below the bridge – BUILT BY BARCLAY CURLE LTD. RENFREW 1899.

Duggie Tweedie, a pilot with whom I shared a hut at Bardney, came in,
bubbling with news. "Mac. You got here! What a shambles! The Lib with all
the radio gear lost an engine shortly after take-off and turned back. Bloody
marvellous! Apparently the Russkys sent a signal to 5 Group Command, after
we left Lossie, saying, 'For God's sake don't come, it's absolutely clamped,' and
gave the weather as ten-tenths at 100 feet, visibility 800 yards with fog patches.
You wouldn't send a dog here in that. Command did sod all. Apparently, some

clown at Met HQ bent the isobars on his chart, and said it would clear for our arrival. Bloody idiot, contradicting the local boys from 2,000 miles away. I can guess the hand that twisted his arm. All these merchants at HQ, flying their mahogany bombers."

"So that's what happened, Duggie, I got foxed looking for runways." "Runways? Mac, that's a laugh! This is a training airfield, where they stash away American planes brought here at great expense. They're either unserviceable, or they don't know how to fly them." "They never told us anything about grass before leaving Bardney," I said. "I don't think they knew, Mac. Whatdya have left?" Duggie asked. "About ten minutes," I said. "That's a bit fine. We were lucky, we hit it first time. We passed over the field without seeing it when George, my rear gunner, saw aeroplanes on our left disappearing into the murk. I frightened myself doing a vertical turn, in case we lost it again. They're all up there in the main hut with Russian interpreters, McMullen, Tait, Bazin and the rest, biting their nails. A dozen of the lads are missing, including Georgie Camsell and Stan Laws from our squadron. They're down somewhere; nobody can have any gas left now." "Poor bastards," I said, "At least it's flat round here. It's all a bit different from what I expected, Duggie." "Yes, Mac. Napoleon warned his Marshals against making pictures in their minds and then trying to make reality fit the picture instead of the other way round."

The news filtered through - miraculously, all the crews were safe, although many had crashed - Georgie Camsell in the tundra. Later, he told me of his astonishment at hearing a rumbling sound, and watching his bomb break its moorings to trundle ahead of his plane as he belly-landed. Dickie Howard, the only American, had landed with ten feet of pine tree sticking out in front. The Russians had sent a Catalina flying boat to try and guide in anyone they could find. Dickie saw them and followed. Unfortunately, the Cat could only do 100 knots flat out. Flying at treetop height, Dickie was concentrating on following the Russians, and congratulating himself on his luck, when his plane dropped in a partial stall. He instantly opened the taps, but not before a large chunk of pine went through the bombing position in the nose. Fortunately, the bomb-aimer had climbed out after they started following the Catalina.

Stan Laws landed on a wooden runway of logs sunk in mud, but it was short and wet, and he went off the end. Miraculously, eight aircraft in all, fully armed, had crashed without anyone being injured. The Russians parachuted doctors and medical staff to the sites of the crashes, expecting to find dead and wounded. The flat wet marshes and lack of fuel helped. The rest was the pilots' skill and God.

Credit: The National Archives UK

Credit: MoD

Sink The Tirpitz - Part 2

From Russia With Bombs

Reproduced from his book 'Bomber Pilot', by kind permission of the author, Don Macintosh, and Browsebooks Publishing Ltd.

Next day, the reconnaissance Mosquito aircraft came back and reported that the fjord was under a blanket of cloud which looked set, and that any attack on the ship was unlikely for a day or two. Back at the mess for an extended dinner, Alec sat beside me. "Mac," he said, "We've just checked some of the aircraft and they have terrific mag drops. We're busy changing all the spark plugs, and yours will be done tomorrow. This flying at very low revs is all very well for fuel economy, but it leads up the plugs to hell. You have to put them up to climb power every half hour to burn all the soot off." "So that's what it was; Jock said he saw sparks coming out when we climbed."

Next morning, Bob and I went out to 'C' Charlie. On the wing, a Russian mechanic had one of the cowlings off, while another sat with a hammer in one hand and a chisel in the other. Bob rushed towards them shouting "No, no. Nyet!", shaking his head. They stopped, still grinning, and left without any hard feelings when we indicated that their services were not required. Bob stayed, in case any other aviation experts decided to ad-lib on our engines. I went off and told Alec what was happening. "I know, Don," he said, "It's all a bit wild. They're great at improvising and, whatever you ask them to do, there's no arguments. They have a stab at it. They issue orders down the line, saying - do it - even if it's impossible. They have to show they're as good as we are, or else. But it's got a bit out of hand; we only have half-a-dozen mechanics of our own to service both squadrons. The Russians were adamant that they could service us easily, and our chaps flying the big mahoganies back at HQ believed them. None of them have been here, and they thought it was the same as Waddington or Bardney, with Russians instead of Brits. Six planes are complete write-offs, four more are unserviceable, and one's lost its bomb. It was a mistake to come here."

On each of the next two days, the Mosquito returned from the fjord, reporting that it was covered in cloud, with no chance of seeing the ship. We sat around, bored, fed up with inaction and discomfort, now that the novelty of being in Russia had worn off. "Look at Tait," said Duggie, "See what he's reading - Suvarov. I've heard on the grapevine that, if we sink the ship, he's going to be flown to Moscow and personally decorated by Stalin with the Order of Suvarov. Look at the senior blokes at the high table; they don't look very happy. Six aircraft complete write-offs, and two crack squadrons sitting on their bums here, falling apart. That's before we start. You can't tell me that you can fly nearly forty planes over occupied Norway and Sweden, lousy with Krauts, and they don't know exactly where we are. If I were a Focke-Wulf pilot at Bardufoss, I would be licking my chops and oiling my guns, waiting for the massacre of the innocents. Unescorted Lancs. In broad daylight!"

Later in the evening, we heard a rumour that the weather at the target was improving, and that there was the chance of an attack next day. On the strength of it, I turned in early. Next morning, when we were called, it was still dark, and Nigel and I went to the briefing hut together. We climbed down the wooden steps past the guard, and ducked through the low entrance to the building, which was half buried and covered in turf. Inside, it smelled like a cigar box, from the rough cut cedar logs lining the walls. Two oil lamps standing on a table lit the inside, and cast huge shadows and a warm golden glow on the fresh-faced Russian officer facing us, in his long greatcoat and red-striped trousers, his brass buttons displaying the hammer and sickle. Nigel, opposite him, in shabby blue, wearing his bulky yellow life-jacket, a gold crown over the eagle. Soldiers of two empires.

The Russian interpreter came over, and Nigel addressed him, nodding at the officer across the map-covered table. "Ask him if he knows the position of the guns round the target, and does he have the colours of the day for identification with your own fighters on the way back?" A rapid exchange in Russian followed. "No, he doesn't know about the guns," the interpreter said. "He said there is no need to worry about identification, since his people know where you will be." "Danke," said Nigel. "Tell him, thanks for his help," and turned to me. "Waste of time, Skipper, they're playing dim. They couldn't care less." "What do you expect? Nige. We're on our own, but it was worth a try. Let's go!"

With great relief, we flew north-west in a clear sky. Flying low over the tundra in loose formation, the familiar sight of the Lancasters around me was comforting. The Tirpitz drew us on like a magnet. "I hope we get a shot at it after all this trouble," Peter called from his bombing hatch, "Wouldn't like to land in this lot." Outside, the desolate landscape was grim and stark. Nobody lived there; we wouldn't either, if we crash-landed - not for long anyway. Apart from nagging worry over the Focke-Wulfs that might be lying in wait, I felt extremely cheerful. By a bit of luck, we had got to Russia in one piece, with a serviceable aircraft. We had no fuel worries, and at least we knew what the airfield was like for our return. Above all, it was clear underneath and, if our luck held for an hour or two, we would get the ship at anchor in our bombsight for half a minute, and justify all the time and effort we had spent. I could see, ahead of us, the rear turrets of the Lancasters as the gunners swung their guns. Nigel came forward with a map in his hand. "That's Lake Inari ahead, Skipper. I suggest you start your climb very soon. You can see the hills rising ahead of you in the distance. Our bombing height is 11,000 feet."

"Going down to the bombing hatch now," Peter called. "Oxygen on, everybody," I called, and heard the replies moments later, and the steady hiss and puff of my own supply. Glancing at me, with his hand on the throttles, Bob watched the hills ahead anxiously. "Alright, Bob. Push them up now." The Merlins gave a deep-throated growl, accompanied by a drum-like vibration as he poured on the power; in the cold air we seemed to go up like a lift and shortly, beyond the hills, we saw in the distance the icy blue outline of the mountains. The bomber pack narrowed to a thin line as we approached the target area. I pulled my thick goggles down, in case of any splinters, and started to concentrate on the instruments in front of me. A short time later, at our bombing height, I saw over the mountains to the fjord ahead. "There she is!" Peter shouted over the intercom, "I'm starting my run-in now. Come 10 degrees to starboard. Left, left. Steady."

Ahead, amongst the leading Lancasters of 617 Squadron, I could see flower-like bursts of flak as they ploughed steadily on, as the guns in the hills opened up first. "Bomb doors open. Right two degrees." I held the controls lightly, the machine trimmed hands-off to give Peter his best chance. There was a lot more flak bursting, this time from the ship, as I kept glued to my compass and altimeter. "Shit! She's disappearing into the smoke," Peter called. "I can just see the masts. Steady, I'm going to bomb anyway." Seconds later, he shouted, "Bombs gone!" The plane, relieved of its load, immediately leapt up 700 feet. Other Lancs were now milling about as we turned for home, and the fire from the ship slackened, probably because she could no longer see us. I banked sharply, and stuck the nose down. "Let's get the hell out of here! Jeff, watch out for the 190s, they'll be here any time now." The Lanc vibrated, as I poured on power and saw the airspeed wind up. Peter came out of his hatch in the nose. "They'll be bloody lucky if anybody hit

her," he said. "Some of the boys were just dropping their bombs in the smoke. It's incredible how fast the Krauts got their smoke going. I wouldn't have believed it unless I had seen it." "Pete, get back in the turret. We've stirred the buggers up, and they're probably lying in wait for us."

We left the mountains behind and flew low over the hills, and an hour later crossed the lake on the way back, safe now from the fighters. No one had been in any doubt that, if the Focke-Wulfs caught us, we'd be lucky if half of us got back. We saw Archangel in the distance, and this time it was clear and sunny, with the now familiar island in the river. Everyone was a bit depressed at failure after all the effort, and being so tantalizingly close to success. I can't say I was; I was glad to be alive, but couldn't understand why we hadn't been attacked. After we landed, the Russians went off us pretty rapidly. They too felt that they had gone to tremendous trouble and effort for a non-event, which they hadn't believed in in the first place. They looked on us as a bunch of amateurs whose behaviour confirmed their low opinion of our flying abilities. We all wanted to get back to base. The feeling was mutual. Our plane was fully serviceable, and I offered to be amongst the first off. Some of the rest stayed to talk and lick their wounds.

Next evening, at last light, we took off for Lossiemouth in Scotland. The weather had set fine, and there were still a few days before the winter mists set in. Ten minutes into the climb, all four engines started surging. Bob looked at his panel. "That's not very healthy; look at that." He pointed to the oil pressure gauges dancing up and down. "What the hell is it, Bob? I can't understand why all four should be affected." We climbed on and, as we levelled off at 10,000 feet, the port outer cut momentarily, then oversped, followed by a violent surge on the starboard inner. Nigel appeared, silently, on the catwalk beside Bob. Peter also appeared, and said: "I don't fancy our chances of another ten hours of this, Mac, across the sea." "I know, Pete," I said, "It's a long way back to Lossie, but it's bloody shaky turning back. You know what these bastards are like - a plane coming from the west in the dark, no aids or communication - they're more than likely to open fire on us; to say nothing of how we are going to land. I don't think they're geared for night flying."

I flew on westwards, but the engines weren't getting any better. Another wild burst of desynchronisation followed, as all four engines surged and oversped. I looked to my right where Bob, Pete and Nigel watched me expectantly. "OK, you're right Peter, there's no way we'll make Lossie in this condition. Something will break and we'll wind up in the sea. Give me a course back to Archangel, Nige. Jeff, keep a lookout. Anything that comes snooping behind us, let him have it." "Turn left onto zero eight six, Mac. I think we got a bit north. Jeff's given me some drifts, and we should be just able to see the coastline."

The whole thing was a shambles from end to end. I thought we were practically home and dry, and now, here we were, out on a very long limb. At least we have plenty of fuel and the weather's clear. Perhaps we can get down somehow, but we're using up our ration of luck awful fast. Dead ahead in the distance, a searchlight sliced through the darkness, pointing vertically in the sky. "Jesus, searchlights!" Pete called out. They're waiting for us." We didn't like searchlights. Over the Reich they coned you and, in the glare, one lost all perspective. "It's not moving," Nigel spoke. "I reckon that's where the airfield at Yagodnik should be, and he's put on his light to help us in." That was a relief. The engines were still surging and banging away, but giving power. Maybe we can wriggle out of this one. All we have to do now is to get down, and at least it's flat. "Bob, get yourself ready for jettisoning if I ask for it. I don't fancy crash-landing with all this fuel aboard, and I'll want the landing lights. Make sure you know where they are." We had never used them before for landing, since it was forbidden in England, where they could attract unwelcome attention.

As we approached the airfield, the searchlight waggled, then continued pointing straight up in the sky. Nearer still, the beam was lowered horizontally, illuminating a long strip of grass and some huts at the far end. No flare path, no approach lighting - nothing. I didn't hang about, not knowing when one or even two engines might cut for good, putting us really up the creek. I swung across onto the final approach knowing that at least the altimeter setting for landing would be accurate, having been set only an hour before. I assumed the searchlight was near the airfield boundary, but I wasn't sure. On the approach, before I reached the light, a very large black hole confronted me, with no clues to gauge our distance or what our height should be. I called for Bob to lower the gear and flaps, and let down nervously to 300 feet. When the searchlight disappeared under the nose, I carried on along the beam, chopped the throttles and hoped for the best, uncomfortably aware of the lack of visual reference. I saw the solid green below change to separate blades of grass, brilliantly lit and shadowed from behind, and pulled sharply and hard back on the controls. Almost immediately we touched down softly and rumbled across the grass on three points.

After we had stopped, I crawled over the main spar to the rear, where Phil and the gunners were waiting inside the open door. Outside at the entrance stood Group Captain McMullen and, behind him, two elderly Russian soldiers, holding rifles with long fixed bayonets, accompanied by a Russian officer. "Don't move," he called. "The soldiers have orders to shoot at anything suspicious, on sight. I've got to count you and give the OK to the officer, then we'll march back and he will give the password to the camp guard. I was afraid that some of you might have dashed out to inspect the aircraft, and got shot at." "Thanks, sir," Phil said. It wasn't often we were welcomed back by the CO, that is unless one put up some terrific black like getting lost, or bombing our own troops. He always was a thoughtful old boy, and felt personally responsible for everybody, as well as being a bit religious, unusual for an Aussie!

Next morning at breakfast on the steamer, I saw Alec and asked him: "What the hell was wrong with our aircraft last night? I've never seen anything like it before." "You're not going to believe this, Don, but before the Russians got to your 'C' Charlie, which happened to be the last to be refuelled, they told us they were running short of 100 octane. We told them that, in an emergency, they could give you a mix of one-third 90 octane and two-thirds 100 which, with what you had in the tanks would be only slightly down on the normal rating. Something got lost in translation by the time the instructions reached the guys at the pump, and you were filled with a mixture consisting mainly of 80 octane. Great to run your car on, but definitely not recommended for Merlins. They're busy draining the tanks now; it'll take them all day. One of our blokes is watching them, and you should be ready to go back tonight."

Next night, we took off in fine conditions. Nigel told us that Finland had arranged a cease¬fire with the Soviets the day before, and probably wouldn't fire at us. We flew down the Gulf of Bothnia, looking enviously at Stockholm with all its lights winking, watched the man firing his duty clip of shells in the air, over the Norwegian hills, and back across the North Sea, home to Scotland and Bardney, without incident. Over the next few weeks, we practised at the bombing range, and this time I didn't cheat. We carried out a few daylight raids, which were becoming fashionable and were a lot safer, since we were escorted variously by Spits, Mosquitos and Mustangs. We attacked a dam in the Ruhr, and saw American B17s in formation above us and a mile or so ahead, in a running battle with German fighters. The 190s appeared to have a special hatred for the Fortresses, zooming in on them as they ploughed steadily eastwards. I saw a Fortress on the outside of the formation trailing black smoke and slowly leave the formation, losing height. Parachutes blossomed as the crew left the crippled bomber, bringing home the realisation of a deadly battle in progress.

Rumours about the ship abounded, but we all hoped that, after the shambles in Russia, the plan had been abandoned and, with the coming of winter, safely forgotten. We all thought it a death trap. We had been lucky last time, next time it could be the turn of the F-W boys to get lucky.

Sink The Tirpitz – Part 3

Job Done

Reproduced from his book 'Bomber Pilot', by kind permission of the author, Don Macintosh, and Browsebooks Publishing Ltd.

Outside the mess at RAF Bardney, the tall corn, planted right up to the windows, was being cut and stacked. Duggie sat beside me at lunch. "Have you heard the latest, Mac? The ship's back on again. The Jerries have moved her south because of the advancing Russians, and our lads are taking out the mid-upper turret and fitting extra tanks inside to mount an attack direct from Lossie." "You're joking! Tell me they're taking out the rear turret as well, and issuing us with hand¬held Vickers!" "I'm not Mac," he said, "You'll find out soon enough."

The mess was subdued. No jokes. We had no illusions. It had become a grim duel between us and the ship. Sink it, before our luck runs out and we get hacked to pieces by the F-Ws. Jock wished us goodbye and good luck before we left Bardney. He was quite happy not to be going, and I didn't blame him. I wouldn't have wanted to be a spectator on our last trip to Russia, with all the antics we got up to. Next day, we flew to RAF Lossiemouth. When we had completed our preparations, I returned to the Officers' Mess, where a party of very drunken officers were singing round a piano, celebrating. I left the Mess quietly for my Lancaster 'C' Charlie, doubly sober. I climbed in through the little door near the tail, and was greeted once again by the familiar smell of pee, oil and high octane gas. As I squeezed past Phil's radio position, lugging my chute on the way to the cockpit, I tapped him on the shoulder and shouted in his ear, "For God's sake don't touch your key, Phil. We're absolutely awash in fuel, one spark and we'll find ourselves in Inverness!"

Nigel called out 'start minus five', pulled his curtain aside, and looked out. "Bloody awful night. Jesus! Look at that Lanc!" In the rain and wild wind, we saw a Lanc halfway down the runway, lit by his own exhaust flames, swing sharply left, almost leave the runway, recover, and then just clear the sea wall at the end. "I bet that put the shits up them," Bob chuckled, "that was one of 617 Squadron's lot. I know what happened; they have this peculiar thing of opening all the throttles and only then pulling the override tit. If it doesn't go in on one of the outer engines, you get a bloody great swing." Bob, a dark-haired, country boy, the tallest on the crew and a refugee from farm tractors, thought practically everything was funny. Highly efficient, the only time I ever corrected him was on our first night trip, when he kept putting his light on to see his log. I asked him: "Bob, which would you prefer – cremation, clutching a beautifully made-out log, or a bollocking from the Engineer Leader? Keep your light out, or we'll get a fighter up our rear!"

We taxied slowly towards the take-off position. I did my TFPFFSOB mnemonic for cockpit checks. A foul night, and a howling cross-wind from the left. Open up, stick on the dashboard. 100 - 105 - 110 knots. The sea wall was coming up fast. At 125kts, I pulled back hard on the controls, astonished at the weight. Slowly we lifted, immediately crabbing into the crosswind. "Gear up!" I could pick out the stones in the sea wall, in the glow of the exhausts. Just below eye level, long rows of whitecaps appeared to reach up to the windows. The altimeter rose slowly, 150 - 200 feet. "Better get some of the boost off," Bob yelled. "Temps are right on max." "OK," I told him, "come slowly back to 9 lbs and take the revs back to 2850." At 300 feet, we levelled and the airspeed improved. "Inch some flap in." It took five minutes to get to 1000 feet and clean up. "Bob, set me up at 1800 rpm and whatever boost that gives." Peter came forward from his take-off position in the rear. "Crikey, that looked bloody dangerous," he said, "I reckon that 617 bod used up all his luck." "Let me reassure you, Peter, it's actually a lot more dangerous than it looks." "Gee thanks, Mac," he said, and slid forward into the bubble in the nose. We headed north, passing over Unst in the Shetland Islands, where Jeff said he could see ponies sheltering on the hillside as we swept low across the island.

It was now the end of October, and probably our last chance that year of a successful attack. We were better organized; Bob had two large flasks of coffee and a stack of sandwiches aboard. On our trips over the Reich, we hadn't bothered much about food and drink, since the flights were shorter, and we were generally too occupied. We had come through our initial baptism of fire and weather - the time when most crews perished, before their learning curve started climbing. To survive, one had to be both efficient and lucky. The efficiency was that of the crew; there was little time for temperament, and none for dishonesty in covering up errors. We had lots of spirited discussions, and even rows, on the ground, but not in the air - although we heard some crews had heated arguments in the air. Nigel and I sometimes had terse exchanges, during which he quickly produced urgent persuasive arguments for a course of action which made the choice self-evident. As before, we flew at 1000 feet above the sea, on our pressure altimeter. Unfortunately, it became progressively less accurate without recent information for resetting it, which we didn't have. Many unwary crews had perished in the mountains and the sea by trusting it completely.

We had been on course for under an hour when there was a loud hiss, and 'C' Charlie started a gentle descending turn. I put my cup of coffee down and flew manually. I called Bob to check the air pressure which fed the autopilot, and he gave me the bad news that the pipe had fractured and there was no way of fixing it. Bugger! Twelve hours flying by hand, without leaving the seat. I should be very good at flying a Lanc after this. Bob will have to take my beer bottle back to the Elsan a few times; no fancy relief tubes on the Lanc. Even the bloody single-engined AT6a in the States had a relief tube. Sod the Brits! I suppose the chaps at the drawing-board had a picture of the Captain sitting on the Elsan at the back, reading the Times in his best blue, and saying brightly, "Do let me know, chaps, if you sight the enemy."

Like a proscenium curtain rising slowly on a stage, Homer's rosy-fingered dawn revealed the snowcapped mountains of Norway, as we climbed towards them. As if a blindfold had been removed after the pitch black night, we saw the gnat-like dot of another Lanc in the distance, and became aware of our insignificance on the face of God's magnificent and beautiful creation. Our planet, Earth. We crossed into Sweden, flying north-east. Below us, all was ice and snow. Cruel and beautiful. "Not much chance if we crash-land on that lot," Peter called from the front, where he had a panoramic view. "Yeah, we'd be safer baling out, Pete," I said. "I thought you always wanted to catch a reindeer." Ahead, in the distance, we saw the toy Lancs milling and circling around. "That's the lake," Nigel pointed. "Don't worry, Mac, they're early. You've got a few minutes yet to catch them up." I nodded to Bob to shove the revs up. I didn't fancy doing a solo run over the 'Tirpitz' but, as we arrived at the lake, a yellow flare, followed by a trail of blue smoke, arced from the lead plane as he set course to the North. "That's Tait," said Nigel, and we followed like geese in a loose gaggle.

Approaching the target area, I saw ominous low cloud filling many of the fjords. At briefing, we had been told that our bomb was rare and difficult to manufacture, and that we should bring it back if we didn't get a clear view of the target, and a reasonable chance of hitting it. This was all very well in theory, but failed to recognise that this trip pushed the planes right up to the limit of their endurance in fuel - to say nothing of luck. It took no account of wind or weather changes, or of minor differences in fuel consumption between aircraft. Carrying six tons of bomb back could make the difference between landing with a sparse margin of 100 gallons - 25 gallons per engine - and ditching off Scotland. Since Archangel, I had formed a rooted aversion to flying around with fuel gauges touching zero. Peter shared my feelings. Dark clouds, pushed by a strong wind, raced at the fjord. As we ran in on the bombing run Peter called in dismay, as he caught a fleeting glimpse of the ship disappearing into the murk. "Bombs gone!" he yelled, as we leapt upwards. "Bomb doors closed. Shit! We nearly had her there; why the hell didn't we leave half an hour earlier? There's a lot of smoke down there, but I don't reckon anybody's hit her."

The ship was lucky again, and so were we. I stuffed the nose down, till the needle of the airspeed covered the red line, and the Lanc vibrated like a living thing as we sped down towards the sea and safety; away from the trap, death, and towards Scotland, home and safety. I skimmed over the waves, enjoying myself, until Nigel called and said if I wanted to get back to Lossiemouth, I'd better climb up to 8000 now we were out of range of the fighters. He said that fuel consumption and winds were best at that height. We climbed up on the long drag back to Lossie and, eventually, Nigel asked me to lift the nose high so that the radar aerials underneath would give him his first Gee Radar fix. Anxious to know where we were and our fuel state, I made a special effort, dived to increase airspeed and slowly hauled the nose up high, until the needle dropped back towards stalling speed. I pushed the controls hard forward and, as I did so, all four engines cut for a few seconds. Nigel appeared, white-faced. "What was that?" "Negative G, Nigel. A weakness of the SU carburettors, they're not designed for it. The float chambers shut off fuel. Well, gee, Nigel, how's your Gee going?" "I don't think that's very funny, Mac. I was in the middle of my fix and I thought we'd had it. Please don't do that again." "Don't worry," I said. "I won't. It frightened me too for a fraction of a second, until I recognised what it was."

Lossie was clear and, as we passed the white lighthouse on the green meadow, the colours showed vividly in the shafting sun, in contrast to the grey of the sea. By this time, the Lancaster had become an extension of myself, and I greased it in to a beautiful touch-down, glad of our safe return. In the bar, we had a drink with Bazin, our WingCo. He was complaining bitterly about being baulked just as he was about to land. Apparently Keegan, an Aussie, had dutifully brought his bomb back, arriving with his gauges touching zero. He came in shouting that he had to land, and didn't have enough fuel for an overshoot, and cut Jimmy Bazin out. Jimmy said he didn't have all that much fuel himself, and none to spare on idiots. We flew back to Lincolnshire the following day, and found ourselves on the battle order four days in succession. On the first day, we plastered a German night-fighter base in Holland, which gave us great pleasure. We could see the whole airfield riddled with bomb craters. That would make the bastards' eyes water and keep them busy, filling in holes, for a day or two.

Next day we went to Brest and I saw Marchant die. The anti-aircraft gunners in Brest were the best in Europe. Since it was a major naval base, Grand Admiral Raeder had the batteries manned by naval gunners who were in daily practice. Over the Reich, fighters were the main line of defence, and the batteries were manned by boys and any old odds and sods that the Wermacht could scrape up. They hurled their shells up in a barrage, and our losses from flak were small. Once again, we were bombing a ship, a blockship being prepared to close the harbour. As we ran up loosely in line astern, the patchwork fields of Brittany lay beneath. Fifteen planes; four ahead of me. Whup, whup, whup. Three shells burst exactly at our height, staining the blue sky. I heard them burst, and got a whiff of cordite as we flew through the brown smoke. Seconds later, another clip of 88mm burst, closer this time. I saw the man ahead of me rock his wings in the blast. I heard the chain noise as bits of shrapnel hit the skin of the Lanc. Another burst, and the aircraft ahead and to my left lost his front. Like sleight of hand: one second he was flying along, and the next the whole fragile nose disappeared, and became a gaping black hole as he sustained a direct hit. For a few seconds the unmanned machine flew on, then, slowly at first, it dived with increasing speed and spiralled towards the earth. No white chutes blossomed from it as it disappeared from view.

We were sent back the next day. We had never worried about guns before, but the gunners at Brest were something new. At night, at least if you were awake, you could try and dodge a fighter attack and hide. We now had a great respect, tinged with professional admiration, for the sailors firing at us. I recognised the same French village that we had flown over near the target and, almost unconsciously, recited the first verse of 'Connais-tu mon bon village' I had learned at school. Back again at Brest in daylight, the gunners were in good practice, and this time I saw Georgie Camsell's port wing suddenly bend up six feet from the tip as a shell burst beneath it. When we got back to Bardney, I learned that Bill Forsyth, three behind me, had bought it. They hit him right amidships, and his fuel tanks exploded, enveloping his plane in a ball of fire. Only the rear gunner got out. The sailors were red hot. One a day. We were the pheasants going over the butts. We forgot about the Tirpitz. It was late in the year, early winter, and soon the Arctic night would descend and cover her till the Spring. However, the poker players sitting with their stack of thirty chips hadn't forgotten, and were itching to go for the big one. There wasn't a great deal of excitement in the Mess, only resignation. The big ship seemed to be invulnerable, and to lead a charmed life. No-one believed that, with winter setting in and worsening weather conditions, there was any real chance. Maybe the Krauts were right, perhaps she was unsinkable; after all, it took practically the whole of the Royal Navy to sink the Bismarck.

Duggie came up to me, a half-pint of beer in his hand. "Well, Mac, the boys at HQ in their mahogany bombers are really out for glory. They're still determined to dish the Navy. Harris is getting a lot of stick over his bombing policy, and wants to pull one out of the bag. It's on again." "I hope they've sent the usual postcards to Norway, via the Swedish embassy, to say we're coming," I said. "You can say that again, Mac. Everybody and his little brother knows now we're going." A dark, intelligent looking, Welsh pilot came up to us unbidden. "My sinus is really bad," he said, looking concerned. "I went to see the Doc this morning, and he's grounded me. He says I won't be fit for a week or so. I'm going home for a spot of leave." "Sorry to hear that, Taff," I said, looking at Duggie, who maintained a discreet silence. No-one now mentioned the Focke-Wulfs at Bardufoss, ten minutes flying time away. Brest was bad enough; this was looking more and more like the charge of the Light Brigade, with the difference that, this time, there was no misunderstanding, and the charge was being led gallantly from a thousand miles away. Not ours to reason why.

Jock was there to see us off, looking pleased and shaking hands with the crew, wishing us good luck and saying, "Sink it this time!" I ignored his handshake; I was in no mood for false pleasantries. I'd get that bloody ship, so we wouldn't have to go back again. If the fighters came, I'd make one of the bastards pay for it before they got us. I was no longer afraid, only angry and determined.

On a grey November day, we flew up over the misty Scottish hills to Lossiemouth, our second home. Again, we took off and flew the long night low over the sea. As dawn broke, and we approached the Norwegian coast, I became concerned at not being able to see any other Lancs. I had complete confidence in Nigel, but we should be seeing other people about. I had a moment of panic that perhaps we had missed a recall message or got the time wrong. I called Nigel, who looked out, and went back to check his chart. All three of us, Peter, Nigel and myself, agreed on our position from a visual pinpoint on the coast. Partly reassured, I altered course to the North and, in a little while, I saw a black spot in the distance, and soon a number of planes began converging ahead of us. This time we carried the single six-ton bomb, and were designated windfinders. Correct wind at the target was paramount for accurate bombing, and consisted of flying a race¬track pattern of five minutes, near the target. The navigator then plotted his air position and the difference between that and his ground position gave him a wind strength and direction. As we approached, I picked out a landmark, carried out my orbit and transmitted the result to the lead aircraft. I turned in for our own bombing run and, a minute later, for the first time, I saw our quarry. There, squat, grey and massive, even at twelve miles out, sat the Tirpitz, just like the model we had seen months ago at Woodhall Spa. Not a cloud, not a ripple on the water, and no smoke. I watched, fascinated, and saw the long sheets of flame as she fired her main armament of fifteen inch guns towards us. A gallant gesture, but I didn't even see them burst. Sporadic flak, both from the ship and the hills, burst ahead, as the leading planes approached their aiming point.

"Christ! This bomb sight's gone u/s (unserviceable)," an anguished cry came from Peter. "Wha-at?" I answered. "A bloody fine time to find out! Jesus!" Nigel interrupted me; "Peter, give me your readings and I'll work it out for you to bomb manually. I haven't done it before, but I'll have it ready in a few minutes.

Mac, I suggest you orbit, and try to come back on this heading." I turned off, distinctly unhappy. Why the hell couldn't he have found out before? We'll get a terrific pasting, going over the ship on our own, apart from these bloody fighters having me all to themselves. Where, seconds before, I had been enjoying the spectacle, now I was extremely alarmed, and felt very lonely and exposed.

"Bomb doors open," Peter called. "Right, left, left a fraction, steady, steady." Everyone else had gone. The sky was thick with brown smoke, where flak had been thrown up, but the fire had slackened. Thanks, God, I don't know how you did it, but thanks, and I promise to go to church next Sunday. The ship now disappeared under the nose of the Lanc, as a few shells burst around us, but nothing like I had expected. "Bombs gone!" Peter shouted, and again we leapt in the air as the huge bomb dropped towards its target. "Bomb doors closed." I pulled the black lever on my left, stopping the loud swish of air as the bomb doors closed. I nodded to Bob, and two large hands grabbed the throttles and pitch levers, pushing them to full power.

"She's turning over!" Jeff cried excitedly from the rear turret, where he had a grandstand view. "What a sight! It's terrific! You should see it, there's mud all over the place!" "Jeff," I called him, "That's as maybe, there's always mud after bombing. Never mind that; you're supposed to be watching out for fighters. Stop looking at the ground and get searching. Can you see any yet?" "No, but I can see another Lanc stooging about." "That'll be the film Lanc," I said, "He's got three movie cameras and doesn't carry any bombs. It's an Aussie crew, and they're flying back direct to Waddington in Lincolnshire."

I watched the airspeed needle creep over the red maximum line and read 300 knots, as I dived for the sea, home and safety, and did a quick mental calculation. A fighter would still have an overtake of 150 knots, but in ten minutes I'll be out to sea. He'll have to spot us in the next five minutes to follow and overtake us; after that he's lost us. "Keep searching, Jeff," I called, and watched the minute hand on the clock move slowly over the dial. As we reached the comforting wave tops, five minutes were up and I breathed more easily. I could hardly believe it! We got away again! I wonder why the firing slackened as we ran up. I don't believe Jeff. Means well, but gunners are a bit romantic. I wonder where did the fighters get to? Perhaps there is something in that business of the Lutwaffe and the Navy not speaking to each other. Sounds incredible!

We flew steadily on, hour after hour. Phil called, "Want to listen to the One O'clock News? I'll switch on the Marconi, and every one can hear." The pips came on, followed by the measured tone of the BBC announcer. "A force of Lancasters from Bomber Command today attacked the German battleship Tirpitz at her anchorage in Northern Norway... etc." No mention of sinking it. Weird that, hearing about an attack on the news, and still airborne. Hours later we saw the first seabirds underneath, indicating, as they did for Noah, that land was near. It was still a novelty, flying over vast tracts of sea in daylight. Lonely.

As we neared Lossiemouth, cloud thickened up, and we could no longer see the water below. Phil came up with a signal that the weather was poor at Lossie, and suggesting that we divert to Fraserburgh along the coast. Nigel checked his chart, and said it was almost as quick to have a stab at Lossie and that all our gear was there. He said he could bring us in on Gee Radar and find the white lighthouse, which practically lined us up with the runway. I called Lossiemouth, got a pressure setting, and broke cloud low over the sea, skimming over the whitecaps. The cloud lifted a little as we approached land and, quite suddenly through the rain, the lighthouse appeared on my left. I turned towards it, the black ribbon of runway stretching ahead. A quick S-turn, with gear and flaps dropping, and a burst of throttle brought us floating over the threshold for a fast landing. We were home.

It was now teatime, and I went to my temporary billet to wash, and change into the one shirt I had brought with me. I took a long walk in the biting wind, refreshing after twelve hours cooped up, unable to move, in a cramped cockpit. By the time I got to the Mess, it was early evening. The bar had been kept open, some crews having gone straight there after landing. Conversation was still in the medium decibel range, and I noticed there was a lot of heavy braid about. I joined Duggie, Nigel and Peter, all with large glass mugs of beer in their hands. Duggie passed me a pint and said, quietly, "Did you hear she's sunk?" I took a long draught before answering. "Who says that, a gunner?" "No, Mac. It's supposed to be gen. It's not official yet, but the senior intelligence officer seems pretty sure." "Well, I hope he's right, Duggie," I said, "I'll believe it when I see a good clear picture of the masts sticking out of the water."

Jock had got himself a lift up from Bardney, and came up to me excitedly and said, "Groupie McMullen's ordered drinks all round!" He dashed off and came back with four glasses of whisky and, by this time, about a hundred people were crowding the bar, taking up the offer of free drinks. I began to believe that perhaps we really had sunk her, after all. I didn't feel any elation, only relief. It had been too serious for jubilation. We had kept pushing, till somebody's luck gave out. It was a straight roll of the dice and, by blind chance, the Tirpitz's luck gave out first. I was glad we wouldn't have to go back - ever. "Mac," Nigel said, "You know you were worried about not seeing anybody over Norway? Well, half the chaps didn't take off. There was hard frost during the night, and Bazin told the ground engineer to de-ice all the aircraft, but he decided he knew better and thought it wouldn't be necessary. He was last seen walking towards the sea," he said with a grin.

At a dance that evening, there were lots of WAAFs about. Everything felt normal again, and the girls who danced with us, warily, never asked us or seemed to be interested in what we had been doing. Next day, fairly hungover, we flew back to familiar Bardney, wondering where we would go next. We heard that, minutes after the sinking, a Norwegian patriot, overlooking the anchorage, risked death to tap out a detailed report back to London and, the same evening, Winston Churchill watched a film of the sinking, flown in by the camera plane, over his brandy and cigars. Why the Focke-Wulfs didn't catch us was lost in the fog of war. Even a pair of fighters, with their heavily- armed cannon, would have wrought havoc and spoiled the attack, probably saving the Tirpitz. The field

 was ten minutes away, and the Luftwaffe had at least an hour's warning. Half an hour before the attack, a number of them took off and were reported over

the ship - ten minutes after the sinking. The leader disappeared in the flames and smoke which engulfed the end of the Third Reich. No-one will ever know what went on in his mind, or where the fighters were during that vital half hour, and it will forever remain shrouded in mystery.

Postscript:

Recently de-classified papers reveal that there was an anti-Nazi sympathiser among the air traffic controllers at Bardufoss who managed to delay the "scramble" of the FW190s for the crucial ten minutes...

The Night London Airport Was Mine

I was coming to the end of my 3-year tour with the Blind Landing Experimental Unit (BLEU) at Royal Aircraft Establishment, Bedford, where I had been posted to carry out the automatic landing trials on the Vulcan. These trials had been initiated after it was realised that, in the event of a nuclear attack upon the British Isles, there would be a need to disperse the V-Force Vulcans to designated airfields around the country. Since this would have to be carried out regardless of the prevailing weather conditions, there was clearly a requirement for an all-weather landing system. Automatic landing was the obvious choice.

The main test aircraft at BLEU were Varsitys; these sturdy 'twins' were used in all manner of tests, apart from Automatic Landing. They were pleasant to fly, and could carry an immense amount of test equipment, plus 'boffins.' In addition to the Varsity, Auto-Land was installed very successfully in Vulcan, Comet 4, Canberra and the American airliner, the DC-7. When flying the latter, we always had the aircraft's American captain on board and, oddly enough, we had to obtain a Private Pilot's Licence, validated for that aircraft. We flew in all weather conditions as a matter of course and, indeed, sought out airfields we knew were closed due to bad weather, to assess the available approach lighting facilities. Occasionally, Mr Calvert, the Grand Master of Visual Aid Studies, flew with us, and it was he who declared that the Varsity was the perfect vehicle in which to carry out these tests in relative safety. Many of these airfields were American, and I often wondered what their aircrews thought when they heard a solitary aircraft doing circuits and bumps in fog, when they could hardly see to drive their cars.

The validity of these tests is self-evident. There can be few pilots who enjoy the prospect of a long instrument approach, the transition from instruments to visual, through an uncertain cloud-base and variable ground conditions, such as, rain, snow, mist or fog. The inputs imposed upon a pilot in the latter stages of an instrument approach are enormous. I recall a senior line pilot saying, during a lecture on this subject..." At 100 feet, when you have yet to see the runway following an instrument descent, you reach the threshold of PAIN." He was so right.

All our automatic landing tests were carried out using a single-channel system: that is to say, one of each piece of equipment, autopilot, radio-altimeter, ILS (Instrument Landing System), etc. The proposed civilian versions (such as in the Trident) would have three of everything as a safety, belt-and-braces measure. The whole process, apart from some switch-pulling, was automatically controlled: height and heading; ILS and glide path acquisition; and one of my favourite items, automatic throttle control - dial your speed. What more could one ask for? It meant that the pilot could literally sit 'hands-off' with confidence, until the point of touchdown. In the event of any crosswind, the drift angle was automatically kicked off just before this point; naturally, in fog, one does not anticipate strong wind.

We had a long-standing contingency plan that, if London Airport was ever closed because of fog, we would go in and carry out circuits and landings to demonstrate the system. On 4th December 1962, my colleague 'Pinky' Stark went there to do just that but, unfortunately, his aircraft lacked a vital piece of test equipment, which was to have given him directional guidance after the automatic pilot had been disengaged on landing. He was thus restricted to doing touch-and-go landings. If the fog had been less dense, and he could have seen at least two centreline lights, he would, of course, have carried out full-stop landings. On 5th December 1962, having flown the Comet in the morning, I was told to be ready to take a Varsity to London Airport that night, to complete the demonstrations. On this occasion, I would have the aircraft equipped with the new 'Runway Guidance Indicator.' This was in 'breadboard' state - not yet built into the instrument panel. It consisted of a tube passing over my right shoulder, projecting a Sperry Zero-Reader Instrument Landing System (ILS) signal onto a 'Head Up Display,' on a glass prism, mounted on the instrument panel coaming. This piece of equipment was essential in the exceptional conditions which prevailed. The actual Runway Visual Range (RVR) on this night was 45 feet. To put that into perspective, runway centre-line lights are spaced at 100 feet; thus, only one centreline light could be seen at any one time. Another interesting observation would be that, in this visibility, an observer standing at the edge of the runway would be unable to see a fully-lit Vulcan, stationary on the centreline! I had never before experienced fog as dense as this.

We took off from Bedford at dusk, and carried out two circuits and full-stop landings to test the new 'Runway Guidance' equipment. It was working efficiently, so we left Bedford and were soon circling London Airport. The conditions were most unusual: above 300 feet the sky was clear, but in the London basin lay this dense 'pea soup' with no signs of lights beneath. London was at a complete stand-still - no buses, no trains. We would later learn that none of the VIPs scheduled to join us for the demonstration could get to the airport. However, we were there, plunging into the 'soup' on 'Auto's', and using the standard ILS for azimuth and glide path indication. Soon after we entered the fog, we heard the clatter of ice be-ing thrown off the props onto the fuselage. De-icers on...we were already locked-on to the glidepath and, quite soon, the Inner Marker audio beeped. There was no sign of approach lights, although we knew they were on... Touch-down, still no lights, but we were on the centreline, as I could feel from the centreline light pods touching our nose wheel. Throttles and auto-land were switched off, and I kept straight manually using our new toy - Runway Guidance - very gingerly on the brakes, lest they cause a swing.... and so to a full stop. Now, not being able to see any lights at all, how was I going to turn around and return to the take-off point? LAP Airfield Radar came to our aid, and was able to navigate us through 180 degrees and direct us back to the take-off position for a further circuit.

We were supposed to gather up a number of VIPs at this point but, as I have said, the fog was such that they were unable to get to LAP. We did, however, man-age to pick up Captain Poole, the BEA training pilot. He was brought out in a van, also navigated by the splendid ground radar... I'm sure they could see a ferret cross the runway. We carried out four circuits and landings, and returned to Bedford. I have often wondered what the authorities would have said had they known that my Instrument Rating had expired some days before!!!!!

Credit: Ruth AS/Wikipedia

A Cock-Up In The Bullpen

It was the late spring of 1977. The runway at RAF Wattisham was up for resurfacing, and the two resident F4 squadrons were deployed to RAF Wethersfield, near Braintree in Essex. Wethersfield's last permanently-based aircraft had been the F-100 Super Sabres of the 20th Tactical Fighter Wing, which had departed for Upper Heyford in 1969, and the base was, in 1977, a satellite of Alconbury, home to some Engineer outfits, and also being used for storage. However, the airfield was still useable, most of the surfaces were in good order and, with the addition of a couple of mobile arrester cables, it was deemed fit for F4 operations. The forced detachment, however, also involved the most appalling cross-country drive, by way of the country lanes and cart-tracks of Suffolk and Essex – of which more later.

56 Squadron had been allocated an enclosed area called the Bullpen (we, in our ignorance, did not know that this is, in US sporting parlance, an area where the pitchers in baseball - aka bowlers in rounders - warm up and hone their skills). It had a couple of small servicing hangars, and some pretty rudimentary technical and ops accommodation but, in the time-honoured fashion of the deployable squadrons of the day, we pretty soon made it quite cosy. Google Earth shows me that the Bullpen has not changed all that much since. During our deployment, we were subject to the normal round of exercises, dreamed up and sponsored by people with nothing better to do. One of these was Exercise Highfield, and the evening of 26th May found me, and my trusty nav, Ian, on Readiness 10 – required to get airborne in 10 minutes from a scramble order. We had been allocated an aircraft, XV480, which was on the end of the line, and we had dutifully gone out to it, checked it over, signed for it, arranged the switches in an eye-catching fashion, and declared it "On State." This meant that no-one could touch it without our say-so. We then retired to the crewroom to play Uckers[1], or some such.

It was a slow old evening, with not much happening; the odd aircraft was launched, but the action could not be described as hot – probably a lack of suitable targets. When the time came to retire, we calculated the odds of being required

---

[1] Uckers: A two or four-player board game, a vicious military adaptation of Ludo, traditionally played in the Royal Navy, that subsequently spread to other Services.

to aviate, and elected to doff our goon-suits[2] and sack out in whatever we were wearing underneath. I suspended my goon-suit artistically from the hook on the back of the door, such that I could dive into it feet-first (at least, that was the theory), and then hit the sack. On QRA[3], such rash actions would be a sure-fire precursor to a practice scramble hooter, but here the odds of a peaceful night seemed quite good. It was not to be. At about 0400, the Ops phone rang. Jock, our ancient (or so he seemed to us young blades) Ops Officer, answered it: "56, Master Nav Lee.......OK.........copied". The ringing of the perishing tellingbone had, of course, woken most of us up; eventually, one of our number could stand the suspense no longer. "Who was that, Jock?" he enquired. "Wing Ops" came the reply. "What did they want, Jock?" "Survival Scramble." "When, Jock?" "Now." **"WHAAAAT!"**

All hell broke loose. A Survival Scramble indicated enemy bombers or missiles imminently inbound, and was the signal for everyone who had a serviceable air-craft to get airborne in the minimum time, whatever their notional readiness state had been, rush to a predetermined Combat Air Patrol (CAP) position, and await developments. Suddenly, the crewroom was full of half-awake bodies, charging in all directions. Sadly for my carefully-laid plans, those inky-fingered swots who had eschewed doffing their goonsuits were charging through the door on which mine was hung. I eventually made it out in a clatter of bits, clutching helmet and torso-harness while trying to do up the goon-suit zip, and headed for my aircraft. I clambered into the front seat, threw a few switches and started strapping in. It gradually became apparent to me that something was missing – to wit, the friendly groundcrew to help me, the reassuring roar of the Houchin ground power unit, and the tell-tale flashing green lights to tell me that Vasco de Gama in the back was aligning the INAS[4], without which we weren't going anywhere. A glance over my shoulder solved at least one of the mysteries – the back seat was horribly vacant. Another glance to my Right 3 o'clock solved the remaining conundra; there was Ian in the rear cockpit of the next jet, there was a Houchin with 2 nice green lights

---

[2] Goon-suits: Slang for the immersion suit worn by aircrew when cold sea temperatures demanded additional protection in the event of having to bale out.
[3] QRA: Quick Reaction Alert - refers to aircraft and crews that are held at a high state of readiness.
[4] INAS: Inertial Navigation/Attack System.

on top, and a groundcrewman on the front steps scratching his head and looking expectantly towards the crewroom door, whence he expected the clown of a pilot to emerge any week now.

He was quite surprised to see me arrive from a totally different direction, but got on with helping me strap in – again. Ian said nothing more than "Where have you been?" before getting on with more urgent business. The INAS, the alignment cycle of which was normally the limiting factor in a scramble, was cooking nicely and making all the right signs and noises, and a podge of 2 engine start switches transformed what had threatened to be an ocean-going shambles into quite a tidy departure – and we made our 10-minute state, thanks to the duty runway being quite close to the Bullpen exit! The cause of this minor fiasco – for those of you who have not yet twigged - was that, unbeknownst to me and in the middle of the night, the b*****d engineers had towed another aircraft out and plonked it on the end of the line. Which is where I'd gone; Ian, being of sounder mind, had headed for the aircraft with 'XV480' written on it. The new aircraft had not yet been signed off and allocated to a crew, so there was little competition for the cockpits. My log book recalls that we found a tanker over the North Sea – despite trying to avoid it – and that we watched the sun come up in the East before throwing ourselves back on the ground 3½ hours later. It was small recompense that I was flying with Ian, rather than my alter-nav, Robbie, who had this tendency to cheat at 'Battleships' while on CAP. By the time we got back to the crewroom, Jock had gone off shift, which was probably just as well.

Credit: Author

You may recall my mention of the drive between Wattisham and Wethersfield. Our sister squadron, 23, found that they had one more serviceable aircraft than available crew and, following the prescribed procedure, scrambled the necessary pilot from his bed, expecting the all-clear to sound long before he arrived. This gentleman had a large and noisy motorbike. Discretion prevents me saying how long it took him to go from asleep in Stowmarket to airborne at Wethersfield, but his transit time bore little resemblance to the 59 minutes my AA Routefinder says it should take…

A Hairy Moment

As a member of a well-known University Air Squadron in 1954, I attended the summer camp in Norfolk where, on one occasion, I went up with the CO, who would from time to time fly with the students, to assess both their skills and character. After demonstrating my ability to stay aloft, I was asked to dive the Chipmunk steeply (almost vertically, it seemed) and only pull out when told. As the altimeter unwound rapidly, suddenly the CO spoke, and I immediately pulled back on the stick. "Not yet" he said, and I pushed the stick forward. When eventually I pulled out of the dive (at the very last moment, it seemed), I caught sight of an astonished train-driver's face, as we flew over his cab! Back on the ground, I was told with a chuckle that the point of the exercise was to test my moral fibre and intestinal fortitude!

A few weeks later, back at our home base, I went up again with the CO, to demonstrate my loops and barrel rolls, after which he introduced me to the slow roll. On landing, I was told to go back up and do loops and barrel rolls, and if "brave enough" attempt slow rolls. Consequently, feeling that my "moral fibre" was again under scrutiny, there was no doubt what I had to do! Climbing to height, I performed a series of brilliantly-executed loops and barrel rolls (well, I am writing this!), and then got up the necessary speed, raised the nose above the horizon and rolled to the left. All went well until upside down, when I fell out of my seat and hit my head on the canopy! With only the stick to hold on to, I pulled back and went into a screaming "pull through".

Suddenly, I was looking straight down, with nothing but the green of a farmer's field filling my view. I, as a geology student, thought I was about to be literally and deeply embedded in my subject matter! Out of the corner of my eye, I saw the RPM running off the clock, despite the closed throttle, and the airspeed had reached the "never exceed" of 173 knots, and looked like going past it. At that point, my "moral fibre" started to unravel, my intestinal fortitude came under strain, and I blacked out (or rather I think I simply closed my eyes). When my vision returned (i.e. I opened my eyes), the windscreen was filled with glorious blue, and an immense feeling of euphoria replaced the panic. I flew around to let my moral fibre restore itself, and noted that the wings were not swept back, neither were any rivets popped, nor control surfaces shredded.

Happily, my intestines had retained their fortitude, as no body fluids of any description were expelled!

At least one lesson was learned. Thereafter, I did all the pre-aerobatic checks, including making sure my harness was secure and tight. Obviously, I came to the conclusion that, whatever way I had tightened my harness, it was wrong. From then on, I had to make sure my lap-straps were absolutely tight first, then the shoulder harness, and lastly a final tug on the lap- straps, to make absolutely sure that there could be no vertical movement.

Credit: Arpingstone/Wikipedia

A Kriegie In Stalag IVB

STALAG IVB, Muhlberg-on-Elbe, was situated in Lower Saxony, 89 miles south of Berlin, 20 miles north of Leipzig, and 25 miles northwest of Dresden. The countryside all around the camp was very flat, and all the buildings were single-storey, with the exception of the guard towers; one had a good view in all directions. The nearest airfield was at Falkenberg, a village about 2½ miles across the fields to the northwest. This was used by Junkers 52 transport planes, up to the last two weeks of the war, when the Yanks flattened the village and the airfield with about fifty B26 Marauders. The other airfield we could see was at Lowewitz, about 8 miles away. Sometimes, when the wind was blowing from that direction, we could hear the engines being run up and the noise of take-offs. This was a night-fighter base, at which the crews were all trained on Junkers 88s. Looking out from the camp, we could see the little black dots making their approach for landing behind a wood in the distance.

In the early spring of 1944, we had a visit from one of the 88s from Lowe-witz, late one afternoon. Word must have got out that, in the Stalag, there was a compound with about 1800 RAF prisoners. Every other day, at least one Ju88 beat up the camp; the RAF barracks greeted the low flying aircraft as a break in the monotony of prison life. As soon as we heard the approaching planes, hundreds of bods would rush out of the huts and line the compound, gesticulating with all sorts of signs for the aircraft to get down a bit lower, in the hope that one would crash into a watch-tower, or better still, the German barracks at the main gate.

However, it all finished not quite as we had hoped. One evening, after a low-level run across the camp, a Ju88 did a climbing turn and dived down again towards the compound. The pilot came in much too fast, and at an angle that was much too steep. Although he pulled the nose up, the tail kept coming down; the aircraft hit the middle of the exercise compound in a cloud of dust, and we thought it would explode. Then, with a burst of power, he rose almost vertically over the double-barbed-wire main fence, narrowly missing the guard tower with his port wing, and taking with him, wrapped round his tail wheel, some of the wire and the cable for the searchlights. Sadly, when he hit the compound, he killed a Canadian pilot and shattered the leg of his pal. Picture to yourself a brave Canadian, having been shot down by a night fighter, probably a Ju88, and having escaped with his life, then being killed in a POW camp by another 88, while taking a walk. That really was a cruel fate. Some of the boys saw the plane make its landing approach at Lowewitz. It was rumoured that the pilot had been court-martialled for damaging the aircraft and bits of Stalag IVB, and sent to the Russian front. That put an end to low flying over the camp for some time. The next visit we had from the sky involved the crew of a Flying Fortress, who baled out over the Stalag. One of the crew actually landed in the middle of the camp; he was literally a prisoner before he hit the deck!

During the last few months of the war, nothing could really move during daylight, without being shot up. No food could be brought into the camp until after dusk. One afternoon, a Focke-Wulf 190 crossed the camp at rooftop height, with a Mustang on his tail. The Mustang pilot opened up his guns over the huts, and the 190 crashed behind trees about a mile away. Some of the Mustang's shells went through the roofs of some of the barracks; never have so many bods hit the deck at the same time. Some threw themselves five feet down from the top bunks, only to land on their mates from the lower bunks, who were already on the floor.

There was a daily 'wood fatigue' that went out into the woods to collect fuel for the cookhouse. At this stage of the war, there were between 30,000 and 40,000 POWs in Stalag IVB. The fatigue consisted of two teams, often men who pulled two high-sided carts that were supposed to be horse-drawn; two German guards went with the carts. As the fatigue was coming back into the camp one day, it was strafed by two Mustangs, killing five prisoners and a guard. Some of the huts were also hit, killing another prisoner and wounding several more. Previously, the only threat had been a jettisoned bomb load. Had this been a stick of bombs rather than a burst of cannon fire, it would have been plain bad luck. Now, all those Mustangs, Lightnings and Thunderbolts, being flown around by pilots with itchy fingers, constituted a real menace. Happily, the Germans agreed to our request to mark the Stalag; so, we put whitewashed bricks on two compounds to read POW, and they came in useful a few days later.

About 400 yards from the end of the camp furthest from the main gate ran the railway from Leipzig to Berlin, and it was from a siding near the camp that the cattle-trucks were unloaded when they brought prisoners to IVB. The railway siding was partially hidden from the air by fir trees and, one morning, a locomotive with a long line of trucks stopped there at first light. In the afternoon, the train was spotted by four Thunderbolts and a couple of Lightnings, which swept down and strafed the whole train. As they turned at the end of each run, they crossed the camp and waggled their wings at thousands of POWs cheering like mad. One Jerry flak gunner fired away from one of the trucks, but he stopped after a few minutes. He had a big heart, for the whole train was full of ammunition. The first truck to go up broke most of the windows in the nearest huts. From the compound, the blazing pine trees and the long line of burning trucks were a fantastic sight. Every few minutes, another truck would explode, and wheels and rolling stock would be hurled all over the place. We sat around in dark huts, listening to the trucks still exploding at 9 o'clock at night. Someone would shout, "That's the last one!" Then, everyone would jump when another one went up; it was almost a week before the electricity supply was restored.

Then, three days later, we were liberated by Russian Cossacks at 6 o'clock in the morning.

Credit: SA-kuva

Chute And Shoot

The early days of the new University Air Squadrons (UAS) were not without incident. At that time, in 1941, there were two cohorts at entry. One comprised the university's undergraduates, and the other was a Direct Entry provided by the UASs, and populated mainly by senior schoolboys, who had volunteered for flying in the RAF and would soon be on their way to the "front." One of the first members of the Direct Entry cohort, who became an operational Typhoon pilot in Belgium in WW2, subsequently returning to the same UAS as Chief Flying Instructor, before becoming OC No 4 Flying Training School, relates the following story of his first days in the UAS.

A few weeks after taking command, the first CO of the Aberdeen UAS, a Wing Commander, and up to that point CO of one of the four Blenheim squadrons then operating from RAF Dyce, managed to borrow a Blenheim from his former squadron to give some of the new members of AUAS some air experience. This was achieved three at a time, in the crew positions of the aircraft. Although generally friendly and popular with the members of the new Squadron, as well as his old one, the CO was not all that happy to be rested from operations, and occasionally became a little fractious.

On the day in question, he had just landed from one of these "jollies", the last sortie of the day, and taxied to park on the apron. It did not help matters that, as the students left the cockpit, one of them accidentally picked his parachute up by the ripcord handle, deploying the canopy, which then billowed all over the cockpit, pinning the Boss to his seat. The students and ground crew pulled the parachute out through the crew entrance, accompanied by a stream of invective from the Boss, who realised that, once the story got out, he would be the butt of jokes by his former Blenheim squadron colleagues.

With mounting irritation, he supervised the gathering up of the parachute canopy, then - to help him to get out of his seat - put his hand on the control column and accidentally pressed the gun button, sending forty rounds from the Blenheim's forward-firing gun over the heads of the good burghers of the local village and the startled ground crew!

He later insisted that the wiring must have been faulty, and an armourer was disciplined! The air experience jollies in the Blenheim also ceased with immediate effect!

Into The Black

It all happened very quickly. A harmless-looking situation soon became life-threatening, but I survived to re-learn the lesson that danger often bites when you are most relaxed.

After several tours as a single-seat, fast-jet, ground attack pilot, I took on a secondary duty as chairman of the station gliding club. I had never flown gliders, so felt that I should learn how to do so. I enjoyed the training, and soon gained sufficient experience to lull me into a false sense of security.

It was, I think, March, with the winter weather just giving way to signs of spring. I was airborne in a single-seat glider, when I saw a darkening cloud approaching the airfield. Knowing that the growing cumulus indicated vertical air movement, and being quite used to flying in weather in my day job, I decided to have a closer look, seeking a bit of lift to prolong my flight. Sure enough, as I approached the cloud, I started to climb. Then it all went horribly wrong. The power of nature was much greater than that of my aircraft's controls, and I was instantly sucked up into the cloud. I had audio indication of rapid ascent, and the altimeter showed how high I was going. Unfortunately, little other information was available. With no attitude or turn-and-slip indicator, my first instinct was to try to maintain wings-level, and to unload to avoid stalling. The turbulence made such efforts difficult. Even the piece of string taped to the canopy, usually used to indicate sideslip, was useless, as the cloud's snowy interior froze it in place. Next, the noise indicated, and the ASI confirmed, that I was accelerating and descending. This led me to pull back to avoid an excessively high speed. Shortly after that, I exited the cloud. That was good. Unfortunately, it was not so good that I was flying very fast, pointing nearly vertically down, and not far from the surface. My planned landing area was visible, and I managed to get there safely.

In the now steady snow, I sat in the aircraft and gathered my thoughts. No one approached. More experienced glider pilots had seen my entry into the cloud, then heard my high-speed manoeuvres, and feared the worst. When I re-appeared and landed, they felt that I might be best left to regain my composure. The whole episode had lasted just seconds, but I came as close to disaster as at any time in my flying career. I didn't have time to consider abandoning the aircraft, which might have been a sensible option. Fortunately, the glider was tough enough to tolerate such abuse so no harm was done.

Nylon And Farnborough

Among the agreements drawn up by the Allied Powers at the end of the Second World War was the establishment of three air corridors connecting West Germany to Berlin, and the setting up of the Berlin Control Zone over the city. The Zone was a circle, 20 nautical miles in radius, centred on the Berlin Air Safety Centre, a quadripartite organisation overseeing air traffic movements within the Zone, and located in the centre of West Berlin. Allied aircraft were free to travel to and from West Berlin along the corridors and within the Zone, provided they were unarmed and had no offensive capability. Thus, the majority of movements were civilian aircraft, operating into and out of the main Berlin airports of Tegel and Tempelhof, while the RAF used Gatow, located at the western edge of the British Sector, hard up against the Berlin Wall. These corridors and airfields were thoroughly exploited during the Berlin Airlift of 1948-49. Within the Berlin Control Zone, which extended several miles beyond the built-up area of the city, were numerous Soviet military installations – barracks to accommodate the several thousand troops stationed around the city, tank and other armoured vehicle installations, extensive training grounds and two operational airfields.

The RAF had two Chipmunk aircraft based at Gatow, the story being that they were there to allow pilots on ground duties in Berlin to 'keep their hand in', by carrying out training flights from time to time. The Chipmunk, a long-standing and valued training aircraft, had been around from about 1950, serving in Flying Training Schools in the UK, and as the standard trainer for the University Air Squadrons from the mid-50s to 1973. It was a basic, no-nonsense, no-frills machine, highly manoeuvrable, aerobatic and with a cruising speed of 90 knots. It had an endurance of about 2 hours. Navigation aids consisted of a World War 2 style 'P' compass, the pilots relying on maps and the Mark One eyeball. The aircraft were maintained by a small but dedicated team of engineers at Gatow, and enjoyed a superb serviceability record. I don't recall any major serviceability incidents occurring during my time flying from Gatow.

It was quickly realised that aircraft flying from Gatow could be used for aerial reconnaissance, exercising the right to fly freely within the Zone, and cover the activities of the Soviet forces. This had been practised over several years before I arrived in Berlin in the mid-70s. Pilots and navigators serving with the British

Commanders in Chief Mission (Brixmis) carried out the flights, with occasional help from Gatow, and had adopted a well-oiled routine, honed by experience. No fixed cameras were mounted on the aircraft, they were hand-held for photography. The worthy and sturdy Nikon F2 camera was used in my time, and 2 or 3 bodies were carried, along with a selection of lenses from 50 to 500mm. Ilford HP4 black-and-white film was used, as this gave the sharpness and definition required for photographic interpretation; this was long before the days of digital photography! We would carry around 20 rolls of film on each sortie and, with practice, a film could be changed in around 30 secs (longer in turbulent conditions). The tandem-seating arrangement of the Chipmunk suited the task admirably, with the camera operator occupying the front seat and the pilot in the rear. Shots were normally taken from the left hand side, with the sliding canopy opened about 9 inches or so. With 2 pilots flying, each took it in turn on alternative sorties to fly or be cameraman; when a navigator was carried, he always occupied the front seat as cameraman. Sorties were flown anywhere between 250ft and 1500ft, depending on circumstances; for instance, you would not want to fly at 250ft over a Soviet deployment on a training ground, with live firing taking place! The agility of the Chipmunk made it simple to manoeuvre for the best camera shots. The pilot would line up the aircraft with the target slightly on the left, the camera operator would have the camera with the appropriate lens at the ready, and bank was applied just as the target disappeared behind the left wing. This gave the camera operator a direct view of the target down the wing. Angles of bank could be quite large, sometimes as much as 60 degrees being used on occasion, although the 'g' forces involved at this angle of bank made severe demands on cameraman-ship!

So what did we cover on these ventures? Occasionally, we were given a briefing by our Army colleagues in the Mission, outlining any special activity or equipment to look out for. For the most part, however, crews quickly became familiar with the layout of the various targets in the area, and sorties usually consisted of a circular tour of the Zone, taking in most of the likely installations and training grounds. Thus, in the main, it was a freelance operation, relying on the skill, experience and knowledge of the crews, with occasional inputs from the Army. Sorties were normally flown either in the morning or afternoon of the working week, and very occasionally at the weekend, since Soviet forces worked on Saturdays. For a trip, the crew would travel, from Mission Headquarters in the old Olympic buildings near the city centre to RAF Gatow, in an Austin Allegro. On arrival, the crew would proceed to the hangar, change into flying kit, and place the cameras and lenses in a green cloth bag, supposedly to hide the contents. They would then proceed downstairs to the Chipmunk, and the camera operator would get in and arrange his equipment as best he could in the cramped cockpit, while the pilot would complete the pre-flight checks and climb aboard. When all was ready, and with the engine primed, the hangar doors would be opened and the aircraft wheeled out for starting to carry out the missions, variously code named Nylon and Farnborough. As mentioned earlier, Gatow was close to the Berlin Wall, which ran down the western edge of the airfield boundary, on the far side of which was the Soviet army barracks of Krampnitz. Undoubtedly, the scene outside the hangar was carefully monitored by Soviet personnel, hence the need for secrecy during the starting process.

Gatow, during the Cold War, was a little-used airfield, and there were never any traffic hold- ups. Departure, therefore, was swift and, almost immediately after take-off, we were on the 'other side'. On my first few sorties, I was almost overcome with amazement at what I was seeing and what I was doing – flying a light aircraft brazenly over Soviet-occupied installations and training areas, and taking photographs! Whether we went clockwise or anticlockwise round the Zone depended on circumstances and any specific targets to be covered. Trips would last around 2 hours, sometimes more, with both fuel gauges registering zero on return – not a comfortable experience, but one dictated by circumstance. The Chipmunk had no 'mod-cons', and there was no heater. Flying entailed dressing up in bulky flying clothing in winter, further restricting movement in the confined environment of the cockpit. Light chamois flying gloves, necessary for camera operation, guaranteed frozen fingers when taking shots through the open canopy. Opening the canopy for photography had a further penalty; whereas the windscreen protected the front seat occupant from the majority of the wind, the pilot in the rear seat had no such good fortune, enduring an icy blast each time the canopy was opened. After 2 hours of this, the crew would be thoroughly frozen on return to Gatow. Summer produced its own brand of hazards. In addition to the turbulence, which made photography and accurate flying difficult, the cockpit could become uncomfortably hot. This time, the breeze from the open canopy was most welcome for the pilot in the back, although flying with the canopy open usually raised the noise level unacceptably, hindering communication. Taking photographs from a manoeuvring aircraft is a nauseating, disorientating business at the best of times. Even the stoutest stomachs are severely tested; turbulence merely adds to the discomfort. I remember coming close to vomiting on several occasions, but never actually did so; the sick bag was never far away however.

Not far from Gatow was the large Soviet installation and training area of Dallgow Doeberitz, where you could usually find something going on - deployments of troops and equipment, including T64 and T72 tanks, BMP armoured vehicles and a host of other hardware. Sometimes surface-to-air missile deployments were seen, and always numerous troops. What never ceased to amaze me was the sheer enormity of it all – the vast array of arms, the large number of troops, and the hundreds upon hundreds of vehicles. For example, in the north of the Zone lay the Soviet airfield of Oranienburg, a large helicopter base with almost as many helicopters deployed as we had in the RAF! Flying over these installations, one could usually see rank upon rank of tanks, armoured personnel carriers, trucks, guns and so on – thrilling but, at the same time, somewhat unsettling. At Werneuchen, in the extreme east of the Zone, was a Soviet fighter base, equipped with Mig 25 Foxbat aircraft, then a state-of-the-art fighter. By a quirk of geography, the Berlin Zone boundary bisected the airfield, so it was a legitimate target, or rather, half of it was! I once caught a Foxbat outside its hardened aircraft shelter with the canopy open. This was too good an opportunity to miss, so we dropped down and completed an orbit of the aircraft shooting all the time. Meanwhile one of groundcrew rushed to close the lid. Too late! We had our shots, and quickly departed the scene. Incidentally, this was not some stupid mindless act by some hooligan aircrew; we carefully checked for any activity in the air and on the ground before going in. However, as with much of the operation, it was a case of an opportunity presenting itself and being quickly exploited. Clearly you got no second chances.

The 'shopping list' of items to be photographed came from various Intelligence agencies, and was so long as to be rather meaningless. We adopted the attitude of 'if it looks interesting, unusual, unique or new, take a picture – film is cheap!' Their requests were often outrageous, eg what is the thickness of the armour on the glacis plate of the T72 main battle tank? However, very occasionally we were able to put a piece of the giant intelligence jigsaw in place. A longstanding request was to determine the thickness of the cables connecting the radar dish to the main body of the Long Track SAM tracked vehicle. One day at Glau, south of Gatow, we came across just such a vehicle, bathed in bright sunlight with all its hatches open. We descended and completed an orbit, as the missile crew vainly struggled to close the lids before we could shoot. Again, we completed the orbit and photography, and departed rapidly from the area. Some time later, we learned that the photography revealed a lot of detail of what lay under the hatches but, more importantly, the sunlight illuminated the cables connecting the dish to the body, allowing accurate measurement. From this measurement, the current being passed could be estimated, and thus the range of the radar – quite a 'scoop!' Generally, however, it was a case of monitoring an ever-changing scene, looking for possible targets and recording 'no change since the last visit'.

On returning to Gatow, the Chipmunk would be stopped outside the hangar, the doors were opened, the aircraft pushed inside and the doors closed. We would then get out, change out of our flying kit, and return to Mission headquarters, where the rolls of film would be handed in for processing. A debrief with Army specialists followed, and a brief report compiled highlighting any significant sightings. A fuller report was written next day, after the photographs had been processed and studied.

Was it frightening? Were we scared? After overcoming my initial astonishment at what I was doing, a certain routine emerged in carrying out the sorties. As aircrew, we became accustomed to the rigours of the operation, the discomfort and, yes, the potential dangers. However, I do not recall feeling scared at any time, although occasionally apprehensive. In a single-engined machine, there is always the problem of engine failure when the only way is down, this time into hostile territory. Although I was not aware of any specific scheme to rescue us from a downed Chipmunk, we had our own plan to throw the cameras and equipment overboard before impact hoping they would not be discovered too quickly. We were led to believe that the Mission would arrange for our swift repatriation, although the fate of the US pilot Gary Powers, shot down on a U2 flight over the Soviet Union, caused us to reflect on the possibilities from time to time. There were odd moments which caused an increase in pulse rate, like when a Foxbat flew deliberately close to us at high speed, rocking the aircraft in its turbulence. On another occasion, when operating at the extreme east of the Zone and thus farthest away from Gatow, the engine coughed - just once - but it was a heart-stopping moment, which caused us to return post-haste to Gatow, over, rather than round, the city as was the custom. While I was not aware of ever being shot at, I several times saw Soviet troops use us as a target, pointing anti-aircraft guns and other weapons at us, and tracking us with radar dishes. However, some years before my arrival on the Mission, a Chipmunk returned with a bullet hole in the spinner! Thus, we may have been fired at, and were just lucky that the troops were such lousy shots!

In the final analysis, was it all worth it? I certainly derived great satisfaction from the task and the results. We made a great contribution to the overall 'take' of the Mission, and were able to provide a more accurate picture of what lay behind the walls of the Soviet installations which our Army colleagues on the ground were unable to see. True, we didn't have first-hand contact with either troops or equipment, but our interpretation of the overall picture and the photographs provided valuable intelligence. I can look back on my Chipmunk flying with great satisfaction and considerable pride.

One final thought on the Chipmunk. In 1978, I think, I went across to Boscombe Down, accompanied by one of the Mission navigators, to try out photography using the Bulldog as a platform. This was at my instigation, as I was well aware of the increasing age of the Chippie, and the international ramifications of engine failure over Soviet territory and subsequent forced landing. The trial was successful, and I duly presented my report to the 'powers that be', after which I heard absolutely nothing - a situation which didn't change during my time there, and no-one mentioned it thereafter. This episode seems lost to history, but now two of us know about it!

Credit: Alan Wilson

Runway Sweeper

In the mid-1970s, RAF Laarbruch, just west of the German-Dutch border, was the home of two Buccaneer squadrons, poised to take on the Red Forces from the East. One July morning, two Buccaneers, of which I was the leader, were tasked for a simulated attack, as part of a NATO exercise in the Schleswig Holstein area up near Denmark. This required a take-off at 0745, and we arranged for the airfield to be open early for us, although the station didn't really come to life before 0800, and the first take-off was virtually never before 0900.

Unusually for July, as we drove to work in the breaking dawn, it was obvious that the whole airfield was in really thick fog, which we found was forecast to clear once the summer sun got to work. However, we could not delay our exercise "slot time". We briefed the sortie, noting that the weather states everywhere east of the Rhine, and at our diversion, had clear skies and excellent visibility. I decided that we would taxy out along the parallel taxiway, enabling me to assess the thickness of the fog for our take-off, and leaving a final decision till lined up on the runway, for a stream take-off, using the centreline white markings for guidance. At that time, RVR[1] had not been invented, and the rules simply required the ability to keep straight on the runway.

As we entered the runway, we received take-off clearance from air traffic and, with freshly painted centreline markings, I decided that we just had adequate forward visibility to go. After all, we were only doing what we demonstrated on every IRT[2]. I was about to advance the throttles when ATC asked us to hold, as they were unable to locate a runway sweeper on its regular early morning tour of the airfield. Just then, out of the white mass a few metres ahead, exactly on the runway centreline, emerged a grey shape moving towards us – you've guessed it – the large 3-ton runway sweeper.

After a few seconds, while the sweeper, as surprised as us, moved out of the way, and with a confirmation that the runway was now clear, we took off uneventfully, and I still remember the exhilaration as, at only about 300 feet, we emerged into wonderful sunshine and blue sky over a solid white blanket. Meanwhile, the other aircrew were still groping their way to morning briefing. The rest of the sortie went as planned and, when we returned to Laarbruch two hours later, the visibility was unlimited! I was pleased to buy the ATC controller a beer at the next Friday happy hour, but he deserved more than that!

---

[1] RVR: Runway Visual Range - a means of measuring local visibility.
[2] IRT: Instrument Rating Test - to determine a pilot's ability to fly on instruments without visual reference.

Majunga Memories

Readers of OOTB2 may recall a story about loading a Hercules in Majunga, Madagascar. For those who have not yet enjoyed that literary masterpiece, I painted the backcloth of why the RAF was in Madagascar in the late 60s/early 70s – an episode little known to the Great British Public. In retaliation against the Ian Smith regime, and his Unilateral Declaration of Independence for Rhodesia, PM Harold Wilson persuaded the UN to impose sanctions; one facet was attempting to stop blockade runners sailing goods into Lourenco Marques. This was achieved by each Royal Navy ship on its way to or from the Far East loitering in the Beira Straits for a month, working with Royal Air Force Shackletons which overflew the Straits each couple of days, detecting blockade runners and reporting details to the RN ship, which then stopped the blockade runner. Views are mixed on how successful it all was. But, a stay in Madagascar provided a most unusual interlude in RAF careers for the relatively small number who spent time there, and generated many stories, some of which are printable. Here are four more.

Solidarity In The Face Of Thieves

In Majunga, the Adjutant/Interpreter, the Administration Officer and the Supply and Movements Officer shared a three-bedroom flat a few floors above the Detachment's Headquarters, known as the Bureau. The flat had its own Malgache "boy", Joseph, to keep house, and a Comorien cook, Miradgee (the reason for including this apparently unnecessary detail will become clear). Each bedroom was sparsely but adequately furnished, with a single bed inside an all-enveloping mosquito net, a bedside table with light, a wardrobe, a chest of drawers, a table/bureau and a couple of chairs. Each bedroom also had two doors: one off the central corridor, and a sliding door leading onto a balcony, which ran the full extent of the flat.

One night, during my first week there, lying on my front, I began to dream that there was someone under my bed - but then I realized that dreaming I was not. I lashed out at the figure, only for my fist to be caught up in the mosquito net. The figure leapt up, and exited the room onto the balcony, dropping things as it went. With me shouting in pursuit, half aggrieved, half scared, the figure ran round the balcony to the lounge, out the front door and down the stairs.

I soon gave up the pursuit – at about the time I realised the figure was small, black, naked and covered in oil (I later learned this was to make it more difficult for a pursuer to maintain a hold if the thief was caught). After I had collected what the thief had jettisoned, the sum of my losses was a toothbrush and some toothpaste. I also realised that, on hearing my shouts and the commotion, my two flat-mates had leapt to their feet in their rooms – and locked their doors from the inside. So much for solidarity - clearly more of that amongst thieves than in the face of them. Miffed I certainly was.

Fast-forward a few weeks, and a changeover for another of the flat-dwellers. After his first night, he awoke to find he had been robbed, and had not heard anything. And we found the front door open. Then I had a Eureka moment – who would know that there was a new person in the flat, and how was access being gained to this fourth floor flat? Suspecting "inside" participation – the cook and housekeeper each had a key – I took Joseph to the balcony, and made it clear that, if we were burgled again, Joseph would be taking the short route to the ground…over the rails of the balcony.

Why Joseph? He was much the smaller of the two. Bluff of course, but it worked. The next incomer to the flat was not burgled.

Canute, I Ain't

To better appreciate this tale, you need to understand that, prior to my RAF service, I worked as a ghillie on a grouse moor in Scotland, and had had lots of experience of driving Land Rovers over very difficult off-road conditions. I was pretty good at it and, worst of all, I knew it! As a "permanent staff" officer, on taking up post, I had the luxury of my own assigned Land Rover – status indeed for a fresh-faced Flying Officer. In the UK, one would normally be a Wing Commander, in command, to merit one's own vehicle.

After a few days, I decided to explore on my own in my trusty Landie. I left the airport and followed a sandy track along the coast, through the area known as Amborovy. This was then a pretty-much-deserted area during the week, although there were beach houses dotted around, which no doubt would be used at weekends and holidays. I saw, on one house, half a dozen native Malgaches working on a roof. After a few kilometres, I saw, beside the track, a little gap which gave onto a steep, vehicle-wide path, sloping down the cliff to the beach. After driving down that for 30 or so metres, I was on a beautiful beach with nary a soul to be seen in either direction. Out with newly acquired lamba, a thin, multi-coloured cotton cloth about the size of a large beach towel, spread it on the sand and down onto it for a planned 10-minute kip in the sun - to change my white, January legs into browner versions which would not betray one's recent arrival.

I awoke about an hour later to see things had changed dramatically. Black sky, thunder and lightning, with heavy, tropical rain pattering down and growing in intensity. And the tide was coming in! My Land Rover was now just a few yards from the incoming sea. Ah well, no sweat. Press the knob to engage 4-wheel-drive, and up the slope we'd go. But - disaster. Half way up, there was a total loss of traction on what was now a wet, slippery track, formed of that red clay from which Madagascar had earned its alternative name of the Red Island.

Reverse, slide back down to the bottom, and engage the Low Ratio crawler gearbox! Surely that would get us out of trouble? After all, I had driven Land Rovers out of peat bogs in Angus when other, lesser mortals had got theirs firmly stuck. But, no better. Half way up, we lost traction again, and slid back down to what was now a very narrow strip of beach, as the tide was still coming in. And it was getting narrower with each incoming wave! Several attempts met the same fate. Oh sh.. - how was I going to explain a flooded Land Rover in my first week? Would I be on the next flight back to the UK, with my tail between my legs, to participate on the wrong side of a Court Martial for losing the Queen's Land Rover?

Then I remembered the workers on the house. Breaking the Malgache speed record, I sprinted up the slope and along the track. With much gesturing and encouragement, I persuaded these worthies to follow me. They were bare-footed, and in torn shorts and T-shirts. Back to the Land Rover, load 2 in the back, 2 on the bonnet to add weight to both the rear and front wheels (a trick from the peat bogs which now seemed light years away) and 2 pushing. In a great spray of red mud, we managed, just, to reach the top of the slope. My relief was palpable. I emptied the contents of my wallet, probably about £10 worth of FMG (Francs Malgaches known irreverently as French Machine Guns), with much repetition of "Merci, merci" from them and from me. Off I sped to the middle of town, and our flat above the "Bureau". Ten pounds had been a small sum for me to pay to rescue my career from a potentially unpromising start, and would have seemed a fortune to those natives of one of the poorest countries in the world.

Next day, I shared my scary experience with Chief Tech Williams, the MT Maintenance chief, who, like me, had just arrived. He said the vehicle needed an overhaul anyway, and took it off to the Vehicle Servicing area. Later in the day, he came to see me with a wide smile. In his delightful singsong Welsh tones, he said something like, "No bloody wonder you could not get her up that cliff. The prop-shaft to the front wheels is missing, so no front-wheel drive ... oh, and by the way, where there should be springs in the brake-drums, somebody has put string – strong string mind you!" It was then that I discovered that Majunga, supposedly a short-lived organisation, was the dumping ground for vehicles which were becoming surplus to requirements in the Middle and Far East, as bases were closing, and of course they got rid of their rubbish first.

No doubt, my adventure caused considerable mirth, with much re-telling in two different places with very different cultures at the same time: in the flat, which acted as the Sergeants' Mess, and in half a dozen "Shacks" in Shanty Town, Mahabibo. In the latter, at least, the money which resulted from my stupidity would have had a beneficial effect.

A Pukka Officer

Off one of the fortnightly resupply Hercules C130 flights from the UK stepped a Squadron Leader, dressed in a well-fitting, khaki drill uniform. Moreover, the uniform was impeccably pressed, remarkable after 14 hours in the Hercules and its uncomfortable, canvas, parachute seats which were never designed for luxury. Even more remarkable, this officer was wearing highly polished Oxford-pattern black shoes, so highly-polished that one could have used them as a substitute for a mirror whilst shaving. This was a technique known as "Bulling," requiring much spit and polish, and usually reserved for training schools for recruits, or for parades.

It transpired that said Squadron Leader, from a Headquarters formation, had come to conduct an "inspection" of the administration functions, Personnel and Accounts – in modern parlance, we would call it an "audit." By definition, these are trying times for those involved in the administration team, as their processes and efforts are subject to detailed scrutiny, in the knowledge that auditors, military or otherwise, invariably need to identify a few things which need correction or improvement, in order to justify their time and, in our case, travel and attendant costs. The "swallowing of the pill" associated with such audits and their subsequent reports, will generally be made easier if the team being inspected can remain philosophical, and if the auditor approaches his task in relaxed, if effective, manner.

In this case, 'twas not to be. The Flight Lieutenant running the administration team was, by nature, prickly, abrasive and difficult – and, as "Clothes maketh the man," the auditor was formal, officious and remote; an unfortunate mix, and difficulties soon surfaced. The remoteness of the Island in those pre-computerised days, with communication to the UK via letter exchanges each two weeks on the fortnightly flights, or Morse code links to and from the UK via the Royal Navy in Mauritius, with frequent errors in transcription, meant it was easy for policy changes from UK to go unexecuted, or errors in process to go undetected. So, our auditor found much to criticize, and revelled in the opportunity. The auditor was there for two weeks, until the next fortnightly flight. He dined each evening with the "permanent" officers, in a fairly cold, if courteous, atmosphere, before retiring to press his uniform and polish his shoes. Until his last evening, that is. He had accepted an invitation from the Non-Commissioned Officers in the administration team to spend his last evening with them…

Very early next morning, the Hercules had to take off at about 0600, whilst it was still cool enough to achieve take-off on the short-ish runway, still carrying the maximum amount of fuel required to assure the 14-hour flight to Muharraq in the Arabian Gulf. Our auditor appeared at the airport, as required, at 0500, brought by his new friends, the NCOs. He looked distinctly green around the gills, and the immaculate uniform looked rather crumpled. He confessed to having had rather more Trois Chevaux beers and local rums than were good for one, but claimed he could not really recall which watering-hole he had frequented. But there was a clear give-away; he had undoubtedly availed himself of the services of one or more of the hostesses at the Town's bordello, run by Madame Chabaud. How did we know? The beautifully bulled toecaps on his shoes were worn down to show the grey leather under the black polish. One could only conjecture that his "audit" of the recreational facilities there had involved some horizontal activity.

Methinks the administration NCOs had wrought vengeance in a manner which their Flight Lieutenant superior could never have achieved!

A Less Than Elegant Tale

There were but two passengers on the Hercules which was taking me home after several months in Madagascar: a Motor Transport (MT) Driver, who was being sent home in disgrace for various reasons, one of which was that he had caught one of those social diseases for which Madagascar was known; and yours truly. As an aside, this airman had come to my attention twice before.

It transpired that we had arrived on the same Flight in January 1971. Why had I noticed him, particularly amongst the 80 or so arriving passengers? The Detachment Commander had given himself a mission, to hold an arrival briefing for all incoming personnel within one hour of arrival – one key theme of which was to 'keep it in your trousers,' as VD was rife. The combination of his boring delivery, the unaccustomed heat, and the fatigue of the 36 hour trip from the UK, had combined to make my eyelids very heavy. Suddenly, the monotone delivery changed gear. "That man there – wake up!" came his piercing shout, accompanied by a finger pointing in my direction. With immeasurable relief, I quickly realised I was not being singled out – it was the airman sitting immediately in front of me. His card was marked.

Next occasion. As a "Permanent" member of staff, on call 24/7, I was not required to be Station Duty Officer (SDO), a pleasure reserved for the two Shackleton crews who did only 8 weeks on rotation in Majunga. Just prior to departure of one set of crews back to Ballykelly, I generously agreed to be SDO, so that all of the crew could enjoy their farewell thrash. Not so generous really, as SDOs never had anything to do. Wrong! It was monsoon season. At about 2am, I took a phone call: the Detachment Minibus had been in a road accident. You could not make it up. The Minibus, with local "working" girls on board, and the Land Rover of 'Joe the Doe' (the Department Of Environment representative, who was responsible for maintaining the buildings we rented) had collided. Fortunately, no one was hurt, but there were questions around authorisation, drivers who had been drinking, inappropriate passengers and so on – all in the monsoon deluge.

You have guessed correctly; it was "that" MT Driver again. I submitted verbal evidence to the Inquiry that, whilst the driver had clearly had a drink, he was not drunk. The DoE man, on the other hand, could scarcely stand, having had so much. However, our man's card having been marked, it was easier for justice to find him guilty of causing the collision than the DoE man who belonged to another Ministry, and over whom the Detachment Commander had no jurisdiction.

And, of course, our man had committed other "crimes." The Unit Inquiry took a few weeks to reach its conclusions, and our marked man was to be repatriated in disgrace. In the meantime, it also became clear that he had caught the disease which dare not speak its name.

Roll forward to that return flight. A Herc took about 14 hours to reach Muharraq from Majunga. My co-passenger was poured onto the aircraft by his mates, much the worse for wear, at 5am. Such was his state that he should probably not have flown – but the boss wanted him out of his hair. As stated earlier, he was my only fellow-passenger. Within minutes of take-off, our hero was on the tail ramp using the Elsan chemical toilet - curtain-less, such was his need. Decorum was abandoned, if even thought of – and I swear both ends were operating at the same time, creating an unbelievably bad odour. He was to repeat these performances, albeit with reducing frequency and volume, several times during the 14 hours, each time he awoke and, with unerring accuracy, propelled himself to the ramp. That was to be the only aspect of his performance in which he demonstrated accuracy – you get my meaning. I quickly made a mental note on no account to use that Elsan – irrational perhaps, but you never knew what you might catch.

I was somewhat miffed that, apart from the Loadmaster checking the cargo restraints periodically, and, after a few hours, each crew-member using the Elsan at least once during the interminable, noisy and uncomfortable 14 hours, the crew paid no attention to us. I had thought they would invite me to the flight-deck, and the comfortable bunk with which the Herc flight-deck was blessed – but no.

On arrival at Muharraq for a short stop, whence a new crew was to take the aircraft on to Akrotiri and Lyneham, the Duty Movements Officer, who met the aircraft, was a great chum. Rich took me to a bar for a liquid refreshment or two. Who should be at the bar but the crew who had just brought me in? Clearly unrecognised by the disinterested crew, I took great delight in asking innocently: "Did you guys just come in from Majunga?" "Yes," came the reply. "I was down the back. Did you know that airman on board was being casevac'd home because of VD, and he used the Elsan you all sat on quite a few times?"

The anxious huddle which formed, the anguished discussions, and the looks of concern, almost made up for my 14 hours of purgatory, some of which they could have relieved – no pun intended.

Showing Off In A Stringbag

A Naval Airman's Alphabet ...with apologies to W H Auden (The Orators)

S is for Stringbag: Biplane of Bygones
and Bane of the Bismarck
and Toast of Taranto...

I qualified as a Naval helicopter pilot in 1977, and enjoyed a varied flying career, including operational tours in Northern Ireland, in 846 Squadron during the 1982 Falklands War, on exchange with the United States Coast Guard in Miami, and two years in Naval Flying Standards Flight and the Central Flying School External Exam Wing. I subsequently completed a fixed-wing conversion in 1989, and flew Jetstreams at Culdrose and Yeovilton, before re-joining the Commando helicopter world. As Senior Pilot 845 Squadron, I deployed to the Former Yugoslavia where the squadron flew its Mk4 Sea Kings, in the all-white livery of the UN, at the start of the Balkans conflict. Then something quite amazing happened. In 1993, just before taking command of 707 Squadron, I received an invitation to join the Royal Navy's Historic Flight (RNHF) and become a Swordfish pilot.

To be selected for RNHF was the highlight of my flying career; it was a humbling experience to join a small band of "Stringbag" pilots, whose senior fraternity had flown throughout WW2 with all the daring and resilience that open-cockpit warfare demanded. I felt privileged to be entrusted with such an aeronautical treasure, an icon of the Royal Naval Air Service. Throughout my conversion training, and subsequent two years displaying the Swordfish, I was very aware that RNHF pilots represented the whole Fleet Air Arm, and that our branch of the Senior Service expected the utmost professionalism and resolve from those 'on display.' I had two full display seasons (1994 and 1995), clocked up almost 80 Swordfish flying hours, and I think I got away with it...but not without some interesting moments.

The Swordfish is a big, rugged aircraft, weighing almost 4 tons, and the pilot's eyeline is more than 10 feet above the deck. First flown in 1934, it was regarded as obsolete by 1939, yet remained in front-line service until the very end of WW2, during which it sank a third of a million tons of enemy shipping, more than any other aircraft in the war. Swordfish battle honours include the Battle of the Atlantic, the attack on the Italian Fleet at Taranto in November 1940, the operation to seek, pursue and destroy the German Battleship Bismarck in May 1941, and the ill-fated operation against the German Battlecruisers Scharnhorst, Gneisenau and Heavy Cruiser Prinz Eugen, as they made their famous 'Channel Dash' in February 1942. Above all, the Swordfish carved its name in the history books by its exploits in protecting convoys; from August 1942, they also sailed on the Russian convoys. On one such convoy, Swordfish, embarked in the escort carriers HMS Vindex and HMS Striker, flew 1,000 hours on anti-submarine patrol in the space of 10 days and, in September 1944, Vindex's Swordfish sank four U-Boats in a single voyage. Such feats were accomplished despite appalling weather conditions, often at night, and with all the additional arctic hazards of snow and ice on the decks. I once asked a veteran Swordfish pilot what clothes he had worn on Arctic convoy flights; he replied "…er, all of them, actually."

The Swordfish is a joyously simple aircraft to fly (providing you remember to switch to the main fuel tank after take-off), and positively spellbinding, an entrapment cast over all who fly and maintain it. It is a true Naval 'work-maid,' the original TSR (Torpedo, Spotter, Reconnaissance), and the wartime chariot of many very brave men. My two years in RNHF coincided with celebrations to commemorate the 50th Anniversaries of D-Day, VE Day and VJ Day, and I was fortunate to participate in some grand aviation spectaculars which marked our remembrance of the 'Closing of the Ring.' My Swordfish partner was CO RNHF, Hugh Deuxberry, a soft-spoken, pipe-smoking Irishman of gentle humour and a gifted pair of hands – he trusted me to formate closely on him, and I like to think he suffered not too many grey hairs as a consequence.

There were two airworthy Swordfish in the RNHF 'orbat' in 1993 (and since they were built by Blackburn rather than Fairey, the original manufacturer, they were unofficially known as "Blackfish"). The first and longest serving member of RNHF was LS326, a 1943 Swordfish Mark II, Battle of the Atlantic convoy veteran (836 Squadron) and star of the film 'Sink the Bismarck.' Although she had a few capricious moments during my tour in RNHF, LS326 tended to be very reliable, and rarely missed a display slot in those two years. And then there was the Mark I[1]

---

[1] Mark 1s had all canvas-covered wings; the lower wings on Mark IIs were metal-sheathed to allow them to fire rockets.

newcomer to RNHF, W5856, the world's oldest surviving Swordfish . She first flew on Trafalgar Day (October 21) 1941, an auspicious beginning to eight decades of flight. W5856's career began with a year in the Mediterranean Fleet; she was then refurbished and used for advanced flying training and trials, at home and in Canada, before being placed into storage. She was eventually purchased by the Strathallan Collection and then, in 1990, by British Aerospace for presentation to the Swordfish Heritage Trust. The partly-restored airframe went to BAe Brough for a complete restoration to flying condition, and her engine was 'zero-houred' by Rolls Royce at Filton. She made her first public appearance on 22nd May 1993, so she and I were air display novices together. When I flew W5856 in the 1990s, she was painted in the pre-war colours of Ark Royal's 810 Squadron, with side-letters A2A.

Royal Rendezvous
On the 50th Anniversary of D-Day in June 1994, the Swordfish pair was privileged to lead the massed flypast salute to Her Majesty the Queen and 12 other Heads of State, in commemoration of all Allied D-Day combatants. These included my own uncle, later killed at Arnhem, who piloted a Dakota of 271 Sqn RAF on the eve of D-Day 1944, dropping members of the 3rd Parachute Brigade into Normandy; his aircraft was damaged by enemy gunfire, but managed to return safely. By comparison, the Swordfish task in 1994 was simple: be on time, at the right altitude, on the right track to intercept HMY Britannia as she passed abeam the Southsea Common War Memorial. We were to lead an armada of aircraft drawn from the Royal Navy, the Army Air Corps, the Royal Air Force, US and other NATO nations, plus a large contingent of vintage aircraft that had flown during WW2, and Concorde too! All of them flew faster than a Swordfish, so the master plan was for them to converge on us from astern as we ran in to the rendezvous. In W5856, my rear crew included Commodore Terry Taylor, Chief of Staff and Deputy Flag Officer Naval Aviation (and a former RNHF Swordfish pilot), plus a mailbag full of commemorative 'Flown in a Swordfish' First Day Covers. The stage was set for a grand day's flying. Start-up, taxi-out, and take-off from Lee-on-Solent went smoothly, and we were soon orbiting our Initial Point near Fareham. At the appointed moment, I settled into close formation on my leader's wingtip, and we began our run-in from the north-west. Snug in the cockpit and trimmed out, I had time for brief glances, to locate the Royal Yacht heading towards the entrance to Portsmouth Harbour, and to take in the grandeur

of the occasion. There was also the massive presence of the American carrier USS George Washington, at anchor in Stokes Bay, the flotilla of pleasure craft and warships ...and then, with less than three minutes to 'On Top', the engine missed a beat, then a few more, then it began to grumble and vibrate followed by a misfire. I moved a wingspan away from Hugh in LS326, and checked the instruments; the oil pressure and temperature were fine but, by now, the engine was making a noise similar to a cement mixer churning a couple of house bricks. And then, just to the right of our track, was the welcoming sight of the runways at HMS Daedalus, the Naval Air Station at Lee-on-Solent. I had no intention of ditching alongside the Royal Yacht and so, with expectations of my role in a grand flypast thoroughly dislocated, I peeled away from Hugh, put out a PAN[2] call to Solent ATC, briefed my One-Star passenger that we were breaking off from the fly-past, and set up for a glide approach to the easterly runway at Daedalus. At idle RPM the engine continued to falter, and I was glad to have some height in hand. Astern of us, the aerial vanguard filled the sky and began a flawless flypast, led by LS326, leaving me dismayed at the cruel fate of a misbehaving engine just moments before our Royal rendezvous. Once sure of getting in, I side-slipped to lose height, straightened up and touched down... and as I trundled down the runway and turned off into dispersal, the engine picked up and began ticking over smoothly. With the wheels chocked and the ground crew hanging on to the tail, I gave a gentle burst of throttle, the engine revved normally, ran sweetly and ticked over steadily at idle revs. A subsequent detailed inspection revealed no faults, the engine was 100% fit! Gremlins, HT leads, mixture and carburettor blues, I had no idea what had caused the engine to utter its previous protests, but it had been a resilience-building five minutes. Commodore Taylor accepted our precautionary landing with grace and good humour, commenting that the fates had been against us, but at least we had been there and there would be other days in the sky. On reflection, I realised that few in the crowd and amongst the dignitaries had been aware of our plight, nor was that act of commemoration lessened by our forced absence. And life is not always unkind - a year later, I was granted two moments in a single afternoon that made up for my D-Day + 50 disappointment.

---

[2] PAN: A transmission indicating that a state of urgency exists.

Hot Foot

In June 1995, both Swordfish were booked to display at British Aerospace Woodford's Air Day, one of the best airshows in the calendar. Just for a change, Hugh Deuxberry and I swapped mounts, he took W5856 and I flew LS326. It was a grand day, the weather gods smiled as Hugh and I flew down the display line, wingtip to wingtip, and pulled up for a synchronised wingover at the start of our pairs routine. At that point, nose skywards and airspeed unwinding gently, I realised that all was not well around my right flying boot… it had become 'acutely warm', and waves of gaseous heat were flooding around the cockpit. In the Swordfish, sandwiched between the instrument panel and the engine, sits a 167 gallon fuel tank. I couldn't see flames, but I could smell and feel uncontained combustion in the rudder-pedal footwell. Several things happened – I completed the wingover, closed the throttle, and warned my rear cockpit crew (LACMN Andy Gillett) that I suspected we might be on fire, we were going to land immediately, and that he should get out as soon we stopped. I put out a PAN call to Air Traffic, telling them I had a suspected fire in the cockpit, touched down on the runway, steered onto the grass adjacent to the Fire Station, and shut down. As briefed, my rear cockpit crew had vanished by the time I had unstrapped and climbed out. The smell and the heat had also gone, my flying boot no longer appeared to be on the point of spontaneous combustion, and the Swordfish looked unscathed. In fact it looked pristine. The Fire Service chief and his red fire trucks nosed up to LS326, eager to douse non-existent flames. Smiling quizzically, the Fire Chief remarked that '… in his entire career in the Fire Service it was the first time an aircraft had come to the Fire Station to have a fire put out!' I smiled back, but I had this sinking feeling – had I imagined it? My right foot told me otherwise. At that point, the groundcrew called me over; the culprit had been found. Just aft of the exhaust pipe outlet, on the right side of the Swordfish fuselage, there sits a hinged inspection panel, secured with two Dzus fasteners; these had sprung undone at the start of the wingover, the airflow had popped the panel open like a scoop, deflecting the Pegasus hot exhaust gas neatly onto my foot. When I landed and stopped the engine, the flap had sprung shut, no more BTUs[3] in the cockpit and around the fuel tank. End of mystery. And what of my pairs partner in W5856, last seen at the

---

[3] BTUs: British Thermal Units – a measurement of heat.

top of a wingover? Hugh Deuxberry never missed a beat, even as I had broadcast my PAN call and peeled off to land, he completed a solo display (and even bought me a beer afterwards). It had been, he said, lighting his pipe, a good airshow, the crowd loved it, the fire crew had had a bit of a run out, and both 'Fish lived to fly another day. Exactly.

Dogfight With A Mustang

During the late May Bank Holiday weekend in 1994, I had departed an otherwise silent Yeovilton in W5856, on my way to Torquay for its annual air show. It was a wonderful day, clear skies, a light breeze and almost unlimited visibility. My track towards the English Riviera took me along the A303 and across the Blackdown Hills. Beyond Ilminster, as the terrain began climbing, I did too, and at that point I noticed the engine oil pressure had begun to fall. Clearly all was not well in the Pegasus lubrication system. I turned for home, told my crew what was going on, and briefed the solitary tower/approach controller on watch at Yeovilton. As I reversed course, the airfield at Merryfield hove into sight. This former WW2 field is Yeovilton's relief landing ground, used for decades by Jungly, Wasp and Lynx helicopter pilots. On a Bank Holiday, it should be quiet and the Tower unmanned, so I made a beeline for Runway 09. After I turned finals, I realised that, far from being deserted, the circuit was alive with fixed wing aircraft; lots of them, all fairly small, all at low level and all moving really fast. Umm. I'd trained pilots at Merryfield for years, and I had never seen anything like this. Well, they would just have to get out of my way, because I was set on landing 5856 without delay. On short finals, I finally twigged that the aircraft in the circuit were large radio-controlled models... and then suddenly, with a flash of silvered wings and glinting perspex canopy, a yellow-nosed Mustang P51D pulled up right in front of me, perhaps 100 feet ahead. If 5856's forward-firing Vickers machine gun had been armed, I could have got a no-deflection shot on target... the Mustang filled my windscreen for a brief moment, before flipping inverted and crashing into the runway undershoot - my first and only kill. I continued my approach, touched down, slowed to a walking pace, sidled off the runway onto a taxiway and stopped. I had barely clambered out when a gentleman, clutching the remains of a large and once beautiful model P51D, came jogging up to the aircraft. His pride and joy had parted company with both wings and its tail in the post-dogfight crash. I expected a torrent of reproach and accusation; instead he smiled, apologised for not getting his aircraft out of the way sooner and said in a broad Somerset burr, "I seen 'ee coming in to land, and I thought, whoa, what bloody scale is 'ee built to?" The RC modellers at Merryfield that day were immensely kind, readily forgiving my intrusion, and delighted to have a close look-see at the Swordfish. The RNHF 'downbird' crew arrived whilst I was having a cup of tea with the Mustang flyer's wife and family (she had actually built the model, and said it would be fairly simple to rebuild, so perhaps I should claim just half a kill). And the oil pressure glitch proved to be a faulty instrument feed line, soon fixed, and we were airborne again.

In Two Places At Once

The VE Day 50th Anniversary celebrations in May 1995 included two headline aviation events – the Buckingham Palace Flypast and the Duxford Airshow. I went to the latter in 5856, whilst Hugh led the former in LS326. The Duxford show featured a tremendous gathering of vintage warbirds and, that afternoon, whilst waiting for the Flying Display Director's safety brief to get underway, we pilots followed the BBC TV live coverage of the other big event, the commemorative flypast in London. We watched as the lone Swordfish, LS326, tracked up the Mall, with a procession of aircraft in her wake (just as she had led the D-Day plus 50 flypast in 1994 (see above), and heard the commentator announce, "…and the Naval Swordfish leading the formation is being flown by Lieutenant Commander David Lord, Commanding Officer of 848 Naval Air Squadron…" The pilots at Duxford turned to look at me and there were cries of "Oh no it isn't, oh yes it is" etc. I told the assembled aircrew that with a surname like mine many things are possible. And I am sorry Hugh but, if the BBC said I was leading the Flypast, I was and that's all there is to it.

After my display at Duxford that afternoon, I flew home at low level – I didn't mean to, but gravity seemed to be exceptionally strong that day, and 5856 just would not climb much above a few hundred feet. All the way to Yeovilton, I wound my way home in an open-cockpit biplane, waggling my wings at the many villages along the way that were bedecked with Union Flags and bunting, and celebrating with VE-Day street parties – lots of people waved, and we waved right back, it was almost as if they had been expecting us. After landing at Yeovilton, tired but exhilarated after the best cross-country flight I have ever enjoyed, I thought I might be on the receiving end of a few low flying complaints - but none ever materialised and, yes, I solemnly swear that I will never do it again…

Many of my colleagues in RNHF have similar tales to tell, and the few vignettes described here are mere threads of a greater tale that is the Swordfish. A quarter of a century since I last flew a Swordfish, the RNHF pair continue to soldier on, icons of Britain at war and the spirit of 'they don't make 'em like that any more.' No, they don't!

This brief tale is dedicated to all past, present and future RNHF aviators, maintainers and supporters, and especially to those air display pilots and crews of my era, to whom fate dealt a bitter hand, including Hoof Proudfoot (P-38), Norman Lees (Spitfire), Kevin Moorhouse and Steve Watson (Mosquito), Billy Murton and Neil Rix (Firefly). Their fortune was not as good as mine.

To help keep the Swordfish aloft, please show
your support at www.navywings.org.uk

"Don't Crash Or Nuttin'"

I remember the day I became the most hated man in the Royal Air Force. I was sitting in the 74 Squadron crewroom at RAF Valley, where I was a TI[1] and QFI[2], when the Station Commander rang to tell me I had been selected for the F18 Exchange with the US Marine Corps. Fast-jet exchanges were highly coveted, and I had applied every year since my first tour on the Phantom - and this time I had hit the jackpot. The F18 Hornet was cutting edge at the time, and the tour was to be at Miramar in California – like I said, the most hated man in the Air Force.

Flying the Hornet was a dream - the best dogfighting aircraft in the world at the time, and I had just spent the last 3 years teaching Air Combat on the Hawk. I couldn't have been happier. The first half of my tour was on VMFA 121 Sqn, flying the F18D twin-seat version, with a Weapons Systems Operator in the back. Our CO, XO and OPSO had all been on the F4 previously, with the XO having done an exchange tour with the RAF at Leuchars. As soon as he found out I had been teaching at the Tactical Weapons Unit, he wanted to get my Air Combat Training (ACT) done as quickly as possible, and get me qualified as an ACT Instructor (ACTI).

My first work-up trip against him was a hoot right from the word go. He was supposed to teach me the finer points of fighting the Hornet but, 5 minutes into the brief, he said, in his broad New York accent, "Aaaah, I don' need to tell ya how to do this stuff. Just do wad ya like. I mean don' get me wrong…don't crash or nuttin'." So that was the brief. My WSO (another ACTI) was horrified, but got over it quickly when we started the first fight. I could do things with this aeroplane that I could only have dreamed of in others. Unlimited Angle of Attack; carefree engine handling; a soft wing system that let you point the aircraft in any direction. What more could you want as a fighter pilot?

The Marine Corps was a little rigid in the way it taught airborne exercises so, with my previous training and a bit of lateral thinking, I was able to carve out a decent reputation, and quickly became an ACTI. This meant I could now work up new pilots and WSOs on the Squadron - and the XO's words came

---

[1] TI: Tactics Instructor.
[2] QFI: Qualified Flying Instructor

back to haunt me on one such trip. The pilot I was working up was struggling a little, and we were trying to coach him through dealing with unusual situations. When things went to plan he was fine, but he had trouble reacting to changing situations – something I recognised in myself when I was a young pilot in training. In order to help him out, I came up with a plan on one particular exercise – a Guns Defence or Guns D as it was known. The set up was that I would be out front by about a mile and enter a 4g turn. He would close to a guns position, and then I would enter a pre-planned manoeuvre that consisted of a 7.5g break towards him, and an overbank to 1350 in full burner into a spiral.

The plan is for him to come nose-off and not be greedy for the shot. Let it develop, and then keep me under pressure until he can get the shot. As it is a pre-planned exercise, and he knows what I will do, he copes with it perfectly. Now let's shake him up a bit. I brief my WSO that this time, when he closes, I will close the throttles to idle to build up the closure, pretend we can't see him, so he thinks he can get the guns kill and, as he gets really close, I will slam full burner, reverse the turn and flush him out in front. It will be a salient lesson to him that, even in pre-planned exercises, things can change. Great plan and what a brilliant learning experience that will be for him.

So, we pretend to lose 'tally'[3] and I can hear the excitement in his voice as he knows he is going to gun me. Throttles to idle, and he's approaching like a steam train. Just as he goes nose-on for the kill, I slam the throttles to burner and kick full left rudder with full left stick to tightly roll around him. It was at that point that the left hand engine surged. A huge flame came forwards out of the engine intake. I remember, from years ago, my lessons on jet engine theory. The phrase that stuck in my mind was this: "Flame out the back, very good. Flame out the front, very bad!"

The lack of thrust from the left side, together with burner on the right and the violence of the manoeuvre, yaw the jet to the left, and we depart controlled flight into a tumble. The 'g' is horrific, and my vision goes black for a while. I remember that, 3 exchange pilots ago, the RAF guy had departed a Hornet and ended up ejecting, having tried every spin recovery from every aircraft he had ever flown. I just let go of the controls, and put both throttles to idle and wait

---

[3] Tally: Abbreviation of "tally ho."

for a few seconds. They are the longest few seconds of my life, and all I can hear is the XO's voice saying, "Don't crash or nuttin'!"

I think the jet sensed that the Chimp-Fingered Baboon had let go of the controls, and decided to come out of the departure all by itself. As the 'g' subsided, I got my vision back, in time to see my wingman float aimlessly out in front of me. I selected the Sidewinder, got a seeker lock and pulled the trigger. Well…a kill is a kill after all. I cleared the surge in the engine, and we headed back to Miramar in relative silence.

What was supposed to be a valuable learning experience for the other pilot became a huge one for me. Before that trip, I was pretty sure I could have done anything with that aeroplane – afterwards…not so much. However, when looking at the other pilot's film of the event, the manoeuvre we ended up in was pretty much impossible to track with the gun, and the flame coming out of the intake was such a distraction he was unable to stop himself floating out in front of us. I don't think my guns jink made it into the Marine Corps tactics manual, as it was a bit of a one-off, but I like to think that the "Tug Wilson Holy Crap Last Ditch Memorial Move," is still the only fool-proof way of defending against a gun attack.

Credit: US Navy

Is This A Sim Ride Or What?

For my second tour, I was posted from the Victor SR2, a powerful performer, to the somewhat less impressive Victor K1A, an aircraft fitted out as an air-to-air refuelling platform. There were a lot of similarities, however, so the change from the Right Hand Seat (co-pilot) to the Left Hand Seat (Captain) was not particularly traumatic. After the usual 3 months Ground School, we started on the flying phase and, by that time, we had self-selected a crew to fly together during the course. We spent a lot of time in the simulator, which was, by modern standards, a very modest, fixed-base device, but the time in it was pretty intense, as it was the period when the training philosophy was, once the basics had been covered, to keep loading more and more complicated multiple emergencies, to stretch the crews to their limit. It was not unusual to come out of a sim session drenched in sweat – indeed, we thought that it was the specific aim of those whom we saw as a bunch of sadistic instructors. In fact, it was also a requirement to push the crew to the point when they would have to step over the side (abandon the aircraft) - a difficult decision, and one that had to be learnt. However, it was all very much in the spirit of, "if you can't take a joke you shouldn't have joined!" and, without any doubt at all, it did prepare you for the real world, where things aren't always "fair" or predictable.

After 3 flights with an instructor, we were sent off for our first crew "solo" - an undemanding navigation up the North Sea and back. With me at the front was a straight-out-of-training co-pilot (as I had once been) and, observing us, a Staff Navigator from the Operational Conversion Unit (OCU). Given that, at that point in the course, I had not been given the training for the Instrument Rating Test required to fly in bad weather, it was planned that we would be launched in good visual flying weather conditions. We were given an old bomber version of the aircraft, which had not been converted to a tanker fit, and which had been sitting out on the ramp and only rarely used.

No worries, then, really. Well, of course, the "not fair" Gremlin pitched up to bite us on the bum. We were suddenly given a weather recall, as our base, RAF Marham in Norfolk, was starting to go out in deteriorating, but not yet bad, weather. As we set off back down the North Sea, the Number 2 Engine oil pressure started fluctuating and gently reducing. Following the procedures, we hauled out the checklist and, eventually, the situation became such that we had to shut it down. Not a big deal - we had three more! Next up - when we lowered the undercarriage, we only had two greens (only two of the three elements of the undercarriage were showing as safely "Down"). Not good, but we couldn't land until we had done some more checks.

As we set off down the glide path in the heavy rain, my windscreen wiper (yes, we had those) packed up, so that I could see nothing out of the front by which to judge the landing. The co-pilot had only landed the aircraft 3 times before, and had not landed on a wet (contaminated) runway; in any case, with a red warning light for one of the main undercarriage legs, I had no choice but to do a go-around. Again, not a big deal, but generally not planned when asymmetric (with one or more engines out) and the undercarriage at least partly down. No doubt with a big grin, the Gremlin then decided to make all our radios unserviceable (it subsequently turned out that the rain had got into the avionics in the cockpit via a perished windscreen seal).

Back to the checklist, and happily the standby radio decided to help us out, so we re-established contact with Air Traffic Control, and, even better, the undercarriage finally showed 3 green lights. The next radar-guided approach and landing were entirely uneventful but, on arrival at the squadron ramp, a very agitated Wing Commander, the Boss of the OCU, came charging into the cockpit, suspecting us (well, I suppose, me) of concocting a completely unnecessary drama. I was immensely relieved that a very calm Staff Navigator (Tommy Thompson, for those who might remember him) tapped him on the shoulder, gently explained the whole story, and the temperature very rapidly cooled back to normal.

The lesson? Be grateful that the Sim Instructors had given you such a hard time - it really was the way the flying was going to be - they had done a great job.

Credit: Mike Freer

Tornados Over Kosovo

Fighting From Home Base

In 1999, international pressure was building towards further intervention in the Balkans. Once more, Serbia was demonstrating its predilection for ethnic cleansing, this time against the ethnic Albanian population in Kosovo. SACEUR (Supreme Allied Commander Europe) was directed by NATO to mount air operations aimed at forcing the Serbs to cease their aggression. And so, on 24 March 1999, an air campaign began, commanded by 5 ATAF (Allied Tactical Air Force) in Naples. It was known to NATO as Operation Allied Force, to the Brits as Operation Engadine, with the bulk of the RAF attack contribution coming from RAF Brüggen's 3 Tornado GR1 Squadrons. 14 Squadron was tasked as the lead, with each squadron contributing sufficient crews to fly two 6-ships. A pool of eighteen aircraft and associated engineers was assembled from across the Wing, and the aim was to have six aircraft plus spares available each night.

What would make this Operation stand out was that it was to be mounted from our home base in Germany. Flying live ops into a hostile theatre and returning home to our families at the end of each mission was something the RAF had probably not done since the Suez Crisis. What effect this was likely to have on the aircrews, ground crew, Station personnel, and, most significantly, the families, was an unknown quantity. I genuinely do not know why this decision was taken; perhaps it was simply for economy of effort, as operating from home base gives instant access to the whole Station support network, which could never be fully replicated once deployed. It may also have been the speed with which the Op developed, precluding the necessary planning for the deployment of 18 aircraft, tons of equipment and hundreds of personnel. So, home base it was, and each Squadron began working up its selected 6-ship crews, which would operate pretty much autonomously. In parallel, the engineers began the process of generating the aircraft, whilst integrating 3 squadrons'-worth of personnel, plus station 2nd line staff into one team - quite a task in itself.

The aircraft fit was a TIALD[1] laser designator pod, BOZ chaff and flare dispenser, Skyshadow ECM[2] pod, two AIM-9L Sidewinders[3] and two 2,250

---

[1] TIALD: Thermal Imaging Airborne Laser Designator.
[2] ECM: Electronic Counter Measure.
[3] Sidewinder: A type of air-to-air missile.

litre fuel tanks. Our attack weaponry would be either Paveway II or Paveway III laser-guided bombs. In addition to a bigger bang, PWIII provided a greater stand-off range and a 'bunker-busting' capability; gone for good the area bombing of earlier campaigns. Sorted? Not quite! Other factors would still affect our ability to prosecute attacks, as we were about to find out. Three VC10 tankers completed the package. A typical mission would see the VC10s launch into German skies a little before midnight, followed by the Tornados. A pair of Tornados would shadow each tanker, through France and out over the Mediterranean, with refuelling being completed prior to the Italian coast. Once over the Adriatic, the VC10s would orbit, awaiting our return.

My first mission was conducted in clear skies. No moon, so completely dark, but not a cloud in sight from Brüggen to Kosovo and back. Our target was a buried fuel depot, our weapon PWIII. My first-night nerves proved to be unnecessary, as we encountered no resistance whatsoever, no AAA[4], no SAMs[5], no fighters - nothing! However, the mission was a complete failure, with no weapons on target from four drops (the first lesson was unfolding, with the Wing's other missions producing the same result). Disappointed and relieved in equal measure, and nearly 7 hours after taking off, we eased our way down through the dawn sky, to be met by an anxious Station Commander. Apart from the all-important attack, all had gone like clockwork.

PWIII had only recently been brought into service, and its wide range of employment options was still being evaluated by the weapons instructors. It transpired that the weapon release parameters in the Tornado computer did not match the look angle of the weapon's seeker head; the bomb would not 'see' the target and was therefore never guided. The Wing's lack of success was reflected, embarrassingly, in a tabloid cartoon, where two crusty old pilots propped up the bar, medals spread across their chests. One was pointing out a medal pinned to his knee saying, "I got this one for Kosovo." Harsh, but fair; the weapon was temporarily removed from our inventory, pending further investigation. During debriefing, the question was raised as to how we would cope if we encountered heavy weather en route; we didn't have to wait long to find out.

---

[4] AAA: Anti-Aircraft Artillery.
[5] SAM: Surface to Air Missile.

Our next target was a radio station on a mountain top — as straightforward as it gets. Shortly after take-off, though, the weather began to deteriorate. Rather than the expected loose formation on our VC10, we had to fly very close to maintain visual contact. Try to imagine driving in very thick fog, your only frame of reference the side of an articulated lorry — and doing it for two hours. On top of that, add heavy turbulence, so now the articulated lorry also appears to be on a roller- coaster, randomly rising and falling. As we approached the refuelling bracket, the tanker trailed the hoses from the two wing pods. Now, in addition to the tanker's oscillations, we had to contend with a very angry, gyrating fifty foot python — the refuelling hose and basket. Red lights turned to amber, clear to refuel — gulp, you must be joking! During refuelling, man-in-front (pilot) is not supposed to look at the basket, into which he is aiming to insert the probe. He adopts a set position, using various references in his field of view. Any small adjustments of position prior to moving forward are 'recommended' by man-in-back: "up a smidge"; "right a tad"; and so on. My man-in-front selected the position but, with the turbulence and the gyrations of the python, it was impossible for him to adopt anything other than a best guess. Providing any meaningful assistance from the back was impossible, and making contact with the basket was completely in the lap of the gods. We missed; we missed again. Refuelling should have been completed over the sea, but time wore on and the Italian coast was looming. If the turbulence was bad here, what would it be like over the mountains? Eventually, we made contact, as had our leader on the other wing hose. But it was horrendous, easily the worst conditions I had ever flown in.

Not normally averse to cracking the odd witticism whilst airborne, I tried to think of something appropriate to say to take the tension out of things. However, I recognised that this was one time when I should keep 'shtum', and let boy wonder 'do some of that pilot s**t.' Eventually though, as conditions deteriorated, I felt we needed to get clear of the tanker. My man-in-front replied that all he was trying to do was avoid hitting it! Looking to my right, it appeared that our leader was doing the self-same thing. Impact with the tanker would almost certainly have necessitated us 'stepping over the side', and enduring a very uncertain parachute descent. It would also, probably, have resulted in the total loss of the tanker crew — no Martin Baker ejection option for them, poor sods. In the end, nature took a hand, and both Tornados were unceremoniously dumped off their respective hoses, with no damage done, apart from to our nerves. However, we had survived the pummelling and, more importantly, taken on enough fuel to allow us to continue the mission.

Thankfully, the weather cleared over the Adriatic, so we formed into our two 3-ship trail, and headed off into bad-lands. We made ready for the attack: weapon package selected (two PWII); height channel updated to correct for us flying flight levels on 1013 millibars; check that the laser code being fired matched

Credit: US DoD

the one set on the weapons; Skyshadow and BOZ set. We also updated the navigation kit. From height, it was possible to mark radar-significant features, but not with any great accuracy (plus or minus a few hundred metres at best). Had we been in GR4s (we were in the process of converting), it would have been a different matter. They came with leather seats, alloy wheels and GPS as standard, so we would have been all right, but there were no such luxuries on the GR1. As a temporary measure, we were given a £70 GPS, which we strapped with Velcro to the top of one of the two-shades-of-green TV displays. At an appropriate moment, the man-in-back would simultaneously select 'fix' on the aircraft system and 'freeze' on the GPS. The GPS position was entered onto the TV tab, and an error was displayed which, if sensible, was accepted, to update the aircraft position. As Heath Robinson as you like, but effective — and in the best innovative traditions of the RAF!

So, fix/attack, stab, TIALD uncaged, let's find that target and get the job done. But nothing happened. Reselect — a few flashes on the screen, but still nothing. In an electric aeroplane, if you have a system fault, often a quick recycle through 'Off' sorts out the problem. Fix/attack, stab, uncage, a few more flashes, maybe a vague view of the ground, maybe not. It was the same across the formation, as we all reported "no drop." Not a single TIALD operational, no weapons released. Three hours flying, through the worst weather most of us had ever experienced, only to be denied by a system that was never designed to be flown at altitude, never mind in icing conditions. Worst of all, we still had to negotiate the weather front again on the way home! Thankfully though, we were able to take on enough fuel for our return while still over the Adriatic, arriving back in Bruggen after almost seven hours. It had become the norm to meet the VC10 crews in the bar for breakfast after an op. This time, they undoubtedly knew it had been hairy, but I think they could tell from our drawn faces that it was probably much worse than they had imagined. Astonishingly, the guys who had flown in Gulf War One said it had been like that on most nights! So, there we were — two sorties, no targets hit, no combat mission completed, and the biggest threat we had faced to date was not enemy action but the weather.

As I mentioned, conducting an air campaign from home base is not something the RAF has done in recent times. However, we soon settled into a set routine: plan night one, fly night two, squadron duties and routine training days three and four, a couple of days off in between. In an attempt to retain some normality, the Mess continued with its social calendar. So, there I would be, quaffing a jar of Wobbly and troughing on bratwurst and chips, with the sound of that night's wave getting airborne, quite surreal! On those occasions, I would spare a thought for the crews; as I headed home to bed, they would be preparing to engage their targets. On one occasion, the Station Padre, whom I knew well, sidled up and asked if everything was OK. He didn't mention any names, but someone had suggested I was showing signs of strain. Was I OK? My mind went back to 1990 in Bahrain, and my part in the build up to the Gulf War. I recalled a few occasions when I had to find a quiet place, to settle myself and control some very unsettling feelings: nerves; panic; worse? I took a moment to reflect; I am surrounded by the norm, the familiar, time off ops to do routine stuff and, most of all, my family. Coming home to my wife and children was a great comfort, and quite a contrast to deployed ops, especially in the Middle East, where there is often no 'downtown' to speak of. Assessing that I was fine, and reassured that, in the background, the support staffs were looking out for us, I concluded that all was, indeed, OK.

Family life, too, was a little unusual. There can't be many professions where families could see Dad go off to work, dreading that, over the next few hours, he would be getting shot at! This was made especially poignant as my two eldest were, like many others, attending boarding school. As it happened, they were home with us for the Easter holidays. With them being away for a large portion of the year, we always made the most of our time together. So it was quite odd to fly a combat mission, then set off with the family to a theme park, or cycle round the station on our way to the pool or bowling alley. After one sortie, I got back in time to join the family on an early morning riding lesson. Our instructor chivvied me, saying I was riding as if I had been up all night. If only she had known!

During my earlier deployment to Bahrain, in the build up to the first Gulf War, my eldest was about six years old. When asked where Daddy was, he had replied, "at the golf." Oh the innocence of childhood! Now, in his teens, he was clearly able to comprehend what was going on. On one occasion, along with a few other families, my wife took our children through the trees at the edge of the married patch, in order to watch the Dads get airborne. Thus, he was more readily able to relate to the news on the TV. Having asked him recently, my eldest's only real recollection of the period was that I seemed to sleep a lot! His younger siblings just remember the bright blue flame of the reheat, as we trundled down the runway and into the night sky. My wife has never really said much about it. Her only real gripe was the endless stream of VIPs they had to 'glad-hand' with, from politicians to Senior Officers (plus wives!) and Royalty alike. The only person she felt showed any empathy with them was George Robertson, the then Defence Secretary. The person she disliked the most was our Prime Minister who showed no sign of being even vaguely interested!

The Op continued apace. Our target for mission three was a factory complex in the middle of a town in southern Kosovo. Our attack run was down a convenient stretch of open ground, running from the countryside to the target in the town centre. We flew south of the target and boxed round to the left, ending up on an attack heading of roughly south-west. Minimising collateral damage to non-combatant civilians and facilities was our absolute first priority. This routing also gave me the opportunity to sneak a look at the target as we headed east — and there it glowed, right under my TIALD cursor. All looked good, and so it transpired; two PWII right through the roof. Relief, I felt I'd finally lost my combat cherry! The return leg was as quiet as the way out; all in all, it was rather a strange experience to have delivered 2,000 pounds of high explosive ordnance, with no reaction from the ground.

I had read a couple of accounts from guys who had flown in Gulf War One.

A few of them had commented on how emotional the experience had been. What?, I'd thought, shedding a tear? Really? Well, on this occasion, after the customary debrief and viewing and validation of the TIALD video, I chose to return home to the family. Not the bar for 'breakfast' that day. My wife could sense something was different. I arrived home quietly, made myself a coffee, and retired alone to the back garden. I sat there for quite some time, reflecting on what had just transpired. Tears? Maybe, moist eyes certainly. It was quite an unsettling reaction. Whatever else was going on down on the ground, they were still human beings. There can't be many other professions on the planet where 'proving you can do the job' results in devastation for your opponents. As I write this and read it back, I still get a shiver down my spine. My wife's support was as ever, spot on.

Next up, it's fair to say that my one sortie in the vicinity of Belgrade exposed me to the most spectacular firework display I will ever witness, with AAA tracer everywhere. Almost certainly, there would have been volleys of SAMs, but so far I hadn't seen any (my man-in-front did later refer to me as 'Blind Pew', when he was dined off the squadron — not quite sure why!) We lined up in trail, the target a storage site. Soon, our leader was calling 'chaff/flare', the action call for defensive measures to be deployed. Then 'tanks.' Again, an action call for the man-in-back to jettison the almost-full fuel tanks and bomb load, thus shedding a great deal of weight and permitting greater manoeuvre. They were only a minute ahead of us, but seemed to be getting all the attention; to be honest, I was quite happy with that. You could hear the tension in Lead's voice as he made the calls.

Hey, ho. A good look out around us before concentrating on our attack. We did have No 3 behind us, whose job was to watch our tail. It was more of a psychological boost, as quite how they would spot a missile heading our way in the gloom is anyone's guess. So we pressed on. Again, I had a very good mark on the target, followed by weapon release and splash[6]. Exactly what was stored in those buildings was not known to us. However, there was an almighty explosion, and a fireball that blanked my screen for a time, then a pall of smoke and flame rising rapidly into the air; job done. Time to head home for tea and medals — pronto.

---

[6] Splash: Code word used to indicate that the target has been successfully hit.

As a result of our leader's experience, he elected to cancel the attack of the three-ship behind us. After all, as we weren't in a fight to the death for the freedom of the West, there was no point in taking excessive risks. The decision was not challenged, but it will always be a fine line to walk.

In May, Milosevic capitulated, and withdrew his forces from Kosovo. It had been quite an experience for us on a variety of levels. Whatever the military value of the targets we hit, the 'war' had been won. Conducting the campaign as a Wing reflected HQ's desire to spread the workload, but it had the effect of 'stinting' the experience from an individual viewpoint. I'm sure 14 Squadron could have completed the task with a minimum of augmentation, but I'm nevertheless 'glad' that things had been done as they were. Although I only flew six sorties over a six-week period, I now had the combat experience I had so long felt the need for. Not for the glory of battle, nor any feeling of supremacy or power, but just for the simple human desire to see if I was up to the task. You just had to trust that your political masters had done their homework! For the families too, it was back to normal. Although, other than Dads and husbands keeping rather unusual hours, and maybe looking a bit distracted, were they really aware of what we had just been through? I doubt it.

As a post script, just prior to retiring from the RAF, I embarked on a one-week course to obtain my Day Skipper sailing ticket at the Joint Services' Centre in Gosport. Over the course of the week, we cruised up and down the Solent, calling into the various ports and pubs; simply marvellous, even though it was November. In the course of this, we inevitably regaled each other with our service experiences. The army type mentioned that he had led the first NATO troops across the border from FYROM into Kosovo. He commented that he could see the effects of the bombing campaign all around. There was one scene in particular that had stuck in his mind. It was a small town in the south of the country, untouched by the war bar for a factory right in its centre. He said it was amazing to witness; the factory had been totally destroyed, without any buildings around it being damaged (barring a few broken windows, no doubt). I mentioned the name of a town — and he confirmed it was one and the same. He was even more amazed when I said that it was my sortie that had been responsible. So I got a very satisfactory battle damage assessment — a little late but still very welcome.

The Earl Of Portsmouth

In January 1951, the RAF had launched a new recruiting drive to bolster the shortfall of aircrew. At the end of our initial training at RAF Jurby (Isle of Man), prior to a posting to RAF Thornhill (Southern Rhodesia) for flying training, we were hurriedly kitted out with new uniforms to suit our new status as "Acting Pilot Officers." Ours was the first course to pass out with a commission on probation; all previous courses had passed out as SNCO Cadet Pilots. On arrival at the Flying Training School, we were regarded by the substantive officers and many non-commissioned ranks with suspicion. We were not popular with the senior course of NCO cadet pilots, who had passed out ahead of us at Jurby (where only the top student would earn a commission after gaining his Wings). However, it was not our choice and we were stuck with it; after about a month, the situation eased and everyone got on with the job of learning to fly.

Three weeks before the end of the course at Jurby, a tailor from London had arrived to measure up seventy Cadet Pilots for Nos. 1, 2, 5 and 6 uniforms. A well-known, and generally well-respected London firm had apparently won the contract, and we were soon to realize why; with only two days to go before our embarkation leave, the new uniforms arrived. None of them fitted. Patch pockets had been sewn on at different levels, sleeves cut too short or too long, jackets and trousers too loose or too tight. We thought that perhaps they had been tailored by the night porter, or bought in as a job lot from a theatrical warehouse.

The apologetic, bespectacled fitter was constantly repeating phrases like "Sir may need a small tuck by the Camp tailor at your next Unit" or "We have allowed a little room for growth, sir." When I pointed out that the buckle prongs on the No 1 belt did not align with the sewn eyelets (they had been made much too close together), he reassured me by saying that it was a common occurrence, and bending the prongs inward would easily put it right; before I could stop him, he did exactly that! We were in no position to protest or question; in those days, protesting or questioning wasn't a good idea, so we just said "Thank you" and walked away, each with a large cardboard box.

Our journey out to Rhodesia was by RAF Transport Command in an Avro York; much shorter range than a Hercules, but more noise. The journey took five days, with night stops at Luqa, El Adem, Wadi Halfa, Khartoum, Nairobi,

Entebbe (beside Lake Victoria) and then to Livingstone, where the Captain flew a circuit round the Victoria Falls before landing. The final leg from Livingstone to Gwelo, near Thornhill, was by train - steam of course, and seemingly without springs. At age 19, these five days complemented my education in ways that I couldn't possibly describe. Certainly, little we encountered had been covered in my school geography lessons.

Now, you may be thinking, "What's all this to do with the Earl of Portsmouth?" Well, I'll tell you. After arriving at RAF Eastleigh, in the dark, we were offered service transport into Nairobi, a few miles away, which we readily accepted. Before departing the UK from RAF Lyneham, we had been instructed to travel at all times in No 1 uniform, including any runs ashore. However, after 4 days in the York, and nights out in Malta and Khartoum, our ill-fitting uniforms were even more crumpled. Five of us decided to have our evening meal at the Stanley Hotel, named after Sir Henry Morton Stanley, the explorer who found Dr Livingstone; this was 'the' central establishment, and not to be missed. It has since been renamed 'The New Stanley', after the original was destroyed by fire some years later. The colonial way of life was normal at that time. The laws of segregation were accepted by white settlers and black African tribesmen alike; they showed no outward signs of resentment. These tribesmen were tall and very proud people, who were respected by the majority of the white population.

No sooner had we walked in the door than we were approached by a tall, well-dressed, and distinguished looking gentleman. In a booming voice, he said, "How wonderful to see the Royal Air Force in Kenya, I am absolutely delighted to welcome you here." By now, we were quite seasoned travellers, and this man was an embarrassment - not at all what we had expected. We were proud of our uniforms but, conscious of our visitor status and, with no suntans, we were keen to keep a low profile. After a few minutes of polite but awkward conversation, we asked him to excuse us, as we were going to order a meal. At the time, we had variously assessed him as either the worse for drink, mentally ill, or just a bore. As we walked towards a table, he said, "How splendid, I shall join you and insist on buying you all dinner." After some more failed attempts to detach ourselves, we sat down to eat.

Somehow, we conversed our way through the three-course meal, but the entire evening was dominated by this extrovert who, for all we knew, may have turned out to be a con man, who would leave us to pay for his exotic choice of food and wine. He told us of his three-thousand-acre farm in the north of Kenya, about a thousand miles north of Nairobi. That sort of distance to me seemed to locate him somewhere near Potters Bar. We thought that he might have been the original 'Walter Mitty' but, after all the wine, were past caring. When we finally tried to settle our own bill, he insisted on paying for everything but, before doing so, he introduced us to his favourite liquor, "Kummel" which we drank, having given up the fight. The bill would have been fearsome. Just as we were leaving and thanking him, he said, "I don't suppose you know who I am, do you?" When we politely conceded, he said, "Well, I'm the Earl of Portsmouth." In the coach back to the airfield, we pondered over the evening's experience, and all agreed that he was a fake, albeit a harmless and generous one; we had behaved properly throughout the evening, and were never impolite.

During the months ahead, while on the course, we often talked about this incident, wondered whether his story could have been genuine, and regularly rejected that possibility. However, about thirty-three years later, in 1984, while I was serving with the Elementary Flying Training School at RAF Swinderby, a fellow officer showed me an obituary in The Times. A very brief entry, in small print, said that the Earl of Portsmouth had died on his farm in the north of Kenya, aged 86. Since reading something about his life, I have no doubt now that he was indeed the man who had bought us dinner!

Speechless One

All post-war RAF jet-fighter pilots will recognise this one! Early radios were not too reliable, but these days a stricken Typhoon pilot will no doubt simply take out his/her mobile phone, and ask base for a homing. However, in those days, if our speech transmissions had failed, we could still 'speak' by blipping the transmit button and sending a 'click.' All you had to do, when stuck above the dreaded solid cloud sheet with a bum radio, was to 'click' four times on the base's approach frequency, to announce that you could receive but not speak. The reply would be almost instantaneous.

"Aircraft transmitting for speechless – are you a Chivenor aircraft?" Click (meaning 'yes'). "Aircraft, adopt the call sign Speechless One." Click. "Speechless One, do you require a let-down to land at Chivenor?" Click. "Speechless One, are you short of fuel?" Click. Now this reply usually gingered things up a lot although, when flying fighters, you were almost always "short of fuel."

"Speechless One, one long transmission for bearing." Clic...k. "Roger, Speechless One, steer 160 degrees." Click. "Speechless One, are you above angels 10?" Click. "Above angels 20?" Click. (Good, the boy can fly cheaply above 20,000). "Above 25,000?" Click, click (meaning 'no'). "Roger, are you between 20 and 25 thousand feet?" Click. "Roger, we have you on radar" (because the controller would have checked up on any other blips in that sky segment, in order to identify our hero). "Speechless One, you have fifty miles to the overhead". Click, click, click, click, click! Unfortunately, our brave boy is saying that he cannot accept that distance, because of his parlous fuel state and - by the way – HELP!

"Roger, Speechless One, I will descend you at 20 miles and bring you to cloud-break just off the coast. The cloud base is 800 feet and QFE (pressure setting) is 998 millibars." Click! "Speechless One, begin descent now, range is 18 miles steering 165 degrees." Click. Get it right now, as the boy selects idle throttle, air-brake out with 20 degrees of flap and nose below the horizon, and plunges into the cloud, hoping that the 800 feet cloud-base is an honest one. "Speechless One, you are on track to break cloud about 5 miles to the west of runway 09 but, be advised, runway 27 is in use with surface (wind) of 250 degrees 15 knots."

Click. Then , click, click... click, click! Meaning "I am complete and am below cloud and in visual contact with the airfield." A simple matter, then, to clean-up and reach the downwind leg of runway 27 with minimum fuel use, calling on local control with the same clicking procedure to receive the landing clearance.

I eventually shutdown in dispersal, with just 200/200 pounds (the landing minimum was 310/310) of fuel, and received a right royal 'ollocking for running myself so low. But, at least I had managed to bring Her Majesty's aeroplane back safely, and so I telephoned the Air Traffic Control Tower, and thanked my controller for being on-the-ball. "I'll buy you a couple of beers after work," says I. 'Click' says he!

Credit: Mike Freer

The Fortress Of Youth

The mid-'70s found me on an F4 Phantom strike/attack squadron, at RAF Bruggen in Germany, just across the border from Holland. We were assigned to the Second Allied Tactical Air Force, which gave support to the Northern Army Group. This was all part of NATO's forward defence of the Federal Republic against incursions from the east. Nuclear strike was our primary role, for which we held Quick Reaction Alert (QRA), but we also had conventional attack roles in counter-air, interdiction and close air support.

One of the conventional attacks was to fly in battle formation, with two pairs of aircraft about 2-3000 yards line abreast and the wingman of each pair swept on the outside of his leader by about 250 yards. This gave suitable cross-cover, and was an easy formation to manoeuvre. Approaching the target area, the lead pair would turn to put the other pair into long trail, and each wingman would close up to formate on his leader. With all switches suitably made, each lead aircraft would track the target through the head-up bomb sight and, at the appropriate range, call "Drift – Ready – Pickle", at which point both aircraft would release their ordnance. The "Drift" call was all to do with uncaging the sight. Well, one fine North German day, we were on some major NATO exercise – so many exercises I've forgotten the name. We briefed as a 4-ship, and the very experienced lead pilot was, interestingly, also responsible for target deconfliction profiles. He went, I believe, down to the USAF headquarters at Ramstein, to talk to the other nations' air forces on a regular basis. Perhaps you can now see where this story is going. We were number 4 in the formation, so had little to do other than to check for 'bogies' sneaking up on us. Anyhow our target for today was, I recollect, a radar head on which we were to do a simulated retard bomb attack. Down the dive went our gallant leader, with our pair a suitable distance behind (to simulate bomb fragmentation avoidance). As the lead pair pulled off the target, and my leader started his "D-R-P" spiel, a pair of Mirages suddenly appeared in the bombsight, crossing right to left, and pulled off the dive over our radar head. They had neatly threaded through our pairs targeting, but for real they would have collected our lead's fragmentation and us theirs. There was no sign that they had seen any of us – target fixation? The stunned silence from our four aircraft could be heard. So much for deconflicted routes! Indeed, the nuclear strike missions were also meant to be co-ordinated, and our maps would have "Look left/right" at appropriate points, for which Her Majesty had issued us with eye patches to protect our vision; I still have mine to this day, for whenever I'm invited to a fancy dress party.

On another occasion, as I was taking off into the murk, I was interested to see a Mirage at about 500 feet flash past (what is it about Mirages?) with its gear down, on a GCA[1] to land on the reciprocal runway. It could only have been the mild crosswind that avoided disaster. We carried on unperturbed by this near collision. I believe the Air Traffic Controller was sacked..... ah well.

Strike missions, however, were for singleton aircraft, and each crew had a single dedicated target, which was approached at the lowest level feasible to avoid radar detection. The route was practised endlessly in the simulator, and we were provided with a radar-mapping profile, which fed us through the missile belts and - we were told - would emulate the mapping radar returns of the terrain we were to fly over. We carried a single American (since the F4 was an American aircraft) tactical nuclear retarded bomb, which had two modes of delivery. Ours was LADD (Low Altitude Drogue Delivery), which involved flying in at 500 knots and 300 feet agl[2], if visual, or 600 feet agl if on radar (IMC[3]). At the appropriate moment on the navigator's timer, the pilot would commence a rapid 4G pull-up. When 45 degrees pitch-up was reached, flashing chevrons would announce bomb release. The weapon would float gently down on a parachute, before exploding; meanwhile, we would be rolling inverted and going like a bat out of hell to escape. This ludicrously exposed attack was actually less vulnerable than the "Over the Shoulder" method advocated by the Yanks. This involved doing a partial aerobatic display over the target and, not surprisingly, was known as the "Idiot's Loop." Amazingly, or maybe my memory had gone into protective mode, it never struck me at the time that, whilst all this effort was going on in the cockpit, we would be met with a hail of ZSU 23-4 triple-A gunnery, and all manner of short-range missiles defending the target. We had no Radar Warning Receiver in those days, and our one and only ECM[4] counter-

---

[1] GCA: Ground Controlled Approach using radar.
[2] AGL; above ground level.
[3] IMC: Instrument Meteorological Conditions.
[4] ECM: Electronic Counter Measure.

measure was a Mickey Mouse arrangement of chaff in brown envelopes taped into the airbrakes.

The other mode of bomb delivery was Laydown, which was a level fly-over of the target; the bomb would release and would then, we were told... lie passively on the ground until a timer operated, thus allowing the dropping aircraft to escape. We practised both modes of delivery on the strike target on Nordhorn range. I found that what should have been the more accurate laydown method did not result in my getting very good scores, about which the Boss was getting more than a little peeved. However, while imbibing a "frosty" in the bar with the squadron QWI[5] (sadly no longer with us), he resolved the problem by suggesting I look at the horizon instead of chasing the instruments. Amazingly, this worked, my scores improved, the Boss retired to his office, hopefully forgetting about me, and I got on with squadron life much relieved and happier. Bar folklore regarding flying often produced useful gen. For instance, it was some years before anyone told me that, with a total electrical and instrument failure, one could let down through cloud by descending on south using the standby compass - the E2B, located on the front windscreen. As long as one kept the bank adjustments to maintain 180 degrees, the aircraft could be descended wings level until cloud-break. For a true account of this technique, I recommend Wg Cdr "Bugs" Bendell's autobiography "Never in Anger", relating how he recovered a Lightning F1A with total electrical failure through 30,000 ft of cloud. Why no instrument instruction ever taught this technique has since baffled me – or maybe I just forgot?

Back to our "tactical" nuclear weapon - or "special weapon", as the F4 switchery was annotated. Some wags had decided it was much more economical if, instead of a large amount of uranium (or plutonium) to make a big bang, a smaller amount could be used to compress a mass of heavy hydrogen into helium, thus releasing a vaster amount of energy – just as in the sun. Of course, ordinary explosives were needed to compress the uranium, so really the bomb comprised conventional explosive, which exploded the fission bomb, which then triggered the fusion bomb. All very complicated, but the wags got their way. Apparently, the yield of the weapon was crew-selectable, by allowing more

---

[5] QWI: Qualified Weapons Instructor.

uranium or whatever to be added to the mix. This "tactical" weapon did not strike me in the least bit "tactical." After all, it had a potential yield of 20 kilotons, which was the same as that of the bomb (Fat Man) which ended the 2nd World War in the Far East.

Anyhow, one dank, dark North German winter's day, when nothing much was going on, I and my trusty nav (let's call him "Mac"), were tasked with flying an FRA (First Run Attack) laydown on the strike target at Vliehors Range, situated on Vlieland - one of the string of islands to the north-west of the Netherlands. For this mission, we carried a small practice bomb, which simulated the real thing in terms of ballistics. After take-off, we went straight into the murk, and were not to see the surface again until landing an hour or so later. Crossing Holland at high level, we picked out the Ijsselmeer on radar as we let down towards the range, and then the strike target; checked in with range control; crossed the easily recognisable causeway returns; and wound up the speed to 500 knots, whilst letting down to 600 feet on the radio altimeter. No sight of the ground at all. In the back, Mac was sorting out the required drift and timing. All I had to do was follow his instructions and press the bomb release when told. Everything went well and, after the bomb "pickled" off, we pulled up to return to base. Vliehors came back with the score - 6 o'clock at 60 feet. We thought that was just excellent - all done on misty radar returns – and, with a weapon like that, who gives a monkey's about 60 feet?

Many years later, on a fine clear day and after the Wall had come down, I was flying my Airbus and admiring the scenery far below. I suddenly realised it was the area I had become so familiar with all those years ago. I then vowed to go on holiday in the area and visit it for real. So, just a few years ago, we did just that. It was now a very much-disused military airfield, and had been converted into industrial buildings and a large entertainment complex. Families were happily camping, barbecuing, swimming and playing sports. I walked onto the still existing runway, the centre-point of which had been our 'ground zero', and wandered through the empty hardened aircraft shelters; some still had the aircraft pullback winches in place, and one of the shelters had even been converted into a large supermarket. Later, I visited the small white church whose spire had been the final IP (Initial Point), of which we'd been shown black-and-white photos all those years back. I remembered that the run-in heading from the IP back then was the same as timing to the pull-up point. It was a very poignant and thankful feeling that we had never had to use our MAD 'bucket of sunshine 'in anger - and we were still around to think so.

In 2012, there was an excellent Cold War Fast-Jet Pilots' reunion at the Shuttleworth Collection. The former opposition were there and, as with pilots everywhere, a general camaraderie existed between us all. They were impressed with the importance of my target, but then they had had targets in the other direction even more important. A number of the pilots were MiG 21 drivers, based just down the road on our egress route. Even if we'd escaped the target overflight, as a singleton I don't think we'd have stood a chance against them. But, at the time, even that did not seem to be a worry. And then there were all the mates who had been killed in flying accidents, and this was just when practising for war. But it was never going to be you – was it? Ah the fortress of youth…

Credit: US DoD

The Second Bomb I Ever Dropped

It was early 1957 and I had just arrived on 60 Squadron, flying Venom 1s at RAF Tengah in Singapore. The Malayan Emergency was in its dying phase, and the Squadron was occasionally called upon to take part in operations against the Communist terrorists still holed up in the jungles of Malaya (this was in the days just before Malaya got its independence, and later became part of Malaysia). These operations could involve strikes using WW2 6in drainpipe rockets with 60lb high explosive warheads, and strafing with the Venom's 20mm Hispano-Suiza cannons, but they were mostly bombing attacks, using up the remaining stocks of WW2 1000lb HE. These were done in level flight at 2000 feet and 260 knots, aiming at flares dropped by Army Air Corps Austers from very low level over the jungle canopy. We practised these attacks on Raffles Range, a sea range some miles to the south of Tengah, using 25lb practice bombs, and aiming at a white triangular raft of appropriate size, moored in the middle of the range. The sighting system was, to put it mildly, somewhat crude, involving the gunsight's fixed cross and sunscreen, but we were not exactly involved in precision bombing over the jungle.

Anyway, I was duly briefed for my first attempt at all this by the Squadron PAI[1], (no dual was possible, since the Squadron's only dual aircraft was the Vampire T11 which didn't carry bombs), and was sent off with a cheery, "If you come back with an average of 50 yards you'll have done well." I duly arrived on the range, checked in with the Range Safety Officer (RSO), did a couple of dry runs to assess the necessary wind allowance, and started my first run. It all looked good, 2000 feet, VSI[2] locked steady on level flight, dead on 260 knots and the target's little white triangle tracking nicely down the sight picture. I pressed the bomb release button as the target reached the fixed cross, checked that I'd dropped one, called "bomb gone" to the RSO, and awaited results with bated breath. A few seconds later the RSO calls – "Your first bomb, a direct hit." I think it is fair to say that a degree of over-confidence now began to play a part in the proceedings – "What's all this about 50 yards", for example. Anyway, I

---

[1] PAI: Pilot Attack Instructor.
[2] VSI: Vertical Speed Indicator.

duly lined up for my second attempt and, once again, everything seemed fine, with all the needles in the right places. I dropped my second bomb, checked it had gone, and called "Bomb gone" to the RSO. There followed a pregnant pause, which became more so by the second. Eventually the RSO called "No bomb plotted", and alarm bells started ringing.

I rechecked that I had, in fact, dropped a second bomb, and confirmed my increasing fears. Dropping a wing to see if I could clear up the mystery, I saw to my horror a sampan with a white triangular sail some distance short of the range area, with the tell-tale marks of a bomb-burst in the sea some 50 yards away from it. I cannot remember if I dropped the remaining two bombs, but I rather think the RSO sent me back to base to await the ordure that was inevitably about to fall, deservedly, on my head. Had the second bomb been as "good" as the first, I would undoubtedly have killed whoever was on board the sampan, and, direct hit or not, surely I should have been subject to a civil charge of some sort. That is to say nothing of what the Service's reaction would be. In the event, I have no memory of any action the Squadron took, so it can hardly have been very serious, but I do recall that I was eventually interviewed by the Station Commander, marched "'at on in 'ere" by the Station Adj, with a silly grin on his face. After the inevitable, quite justifiable and, I have to say, memorable "bollocking", I was invited to take my hat off and sit down! It was the first time I had met the Station Commander, and I was welcomed to Tengah, etc, etc. I learned about Station Commanders, and about weaponry, from that.

Credit: Tony Hisgett

Sorry?... I Thought You Said Warsaw!

It was the late 1990s, and I had just finished my last operational posting – I had had a very good run, but the next posting, my last in the Service, was not going to afford me flying, although getting airborne with the AEF[1] would help. More importantly, I was still privileged to be flying 'warbirds' out of Duxford, so really no complaints... except from a long- suffering wife who, a few years earlier, innocently believed me when I said flying vintage aircraft (at that time with the BBMF[2]) would 'only be for a couple of years'. 25years later, and still flying historic aircraft, that lame comment is remembered..!

My phone rang, and it was a good friend who ran one of the outfits at Duxford – welcome respite from the hundred-and-one jobs that come with handing over a fairly large command, moving house, guest nights and goodbye visits. "You've flown the 109 haven't you?" said Chum. "I've flown the Gustav[3]" I replied. He continued "Would you like to fly ours?" I knew he was talking about the Buchon, which is a RR Merlin-powered variant of the 109, given the designation 109J. A vision of a gentle conversion to this tricky aircraft at Duxford... on a sunny day, with 10 knots of wind straight down the strip, came to mind. "Of course" I enthused. "Great" he said "If you're free next week, can you take it to Warsaw?" "Sorry?!....I thought you said Warsaw" came my rather incredulous reply. "That's right, and you'll need to pick it up from Sion[4]" he said, in a voice that suggested going to the local shop for a bottle of milk was no more difficult. "So let me get this straight, you want me to go to Switzerland, pick up the Buchon, fly it over the Alps, and hop from country to country until I get it to Warsaw." He came back "Yes, should be a great trip." My mind went through how many ways there were of saying you must be ******* joking, and therefore said: "OK, what are the details." Oh ye of no moral fibre!

I did have the time between posts, and my CinC[5] (aka - the wife) said alright, which was a bit of a surprise, and therefore the following Monday I was

---

[1] AEF: Air Experience Flight.
[2] BBMF: Battle of Britain Memorial Flight.
[3] Gustav: Messerschmitt Bf109G.
[4] Sion: An airport in Switzerland's Rhone Valley.
[5] CinC: Commander in Chief.

Easy-Jetting to Geneva, and onwards by train to Sion. The plan was to meet up with an old friend of mine, ex RNZAF[6], who would also be picking up a Mk IX Spitfire from Sion, and together we would head out for Warsaw. We had agreed to try and get one leg completed on the Monday but, when I arrived, our engineer was addressing a red-faced Swiss helicopter pilot in colourful Anglo-Saxon, for landing too close to our aircraft and damaging a panel. Not a good start but, looking on the positive side, it gave us time to go over our route, and anyway we had until Friday to get to Warsaw... Tuesday dawned bright, with a great route forecast, our engineer had fixed the panel and, having not been arrested for assault on the helicopter pilot, declared our aircraft fully-fuelled and ready to go. Fully-fuelled is not much in the 109, as 84 gallons does not go far with a thirsty 27-litre Merlin – the Spitfire has the same engine, and normally the same amount of fuel, but the MK IX John was flying had extra tanks in the wings where the guns used to be. I was also conscious that the fuel in my aircraft sat in an 'L'-shaped tank behind and underneath the pilot's seat (really great!), and useable fuel in the bottom part of the tank is, well, questionable when the gauge is low. So, 1½ hours max was the plan, with Augsburg in Southern Germany our first destination. The night before, I had suggested to John that he might like to lead, as he could see a lot more out of the Spitfire than I could from the 109; in that gentle way of all New Zealanders, he said "Bugger off, the sun's in the wrong place!"

Sion has a lovely long runway, at least for a 109, and the wind was kind and blowing straight down 07 at a gentle 10 knots – thank you, God. Much is talked about the 109, in all of its variants, and most have read about the landing characteristics which can be 'interesting',... but the take-off - the take-off can be a trap for players. Willy Messerschmitt designed the 109 with the biggest available engine in the smallest possible airframe – it is smaller than the Spitfire, with a shorter wingspan and automatic slats[7], to improve slow speed handling. The oleos[8] are fixed to the fuselage (the wings can be removed in a heartbeat and, with them stacked

---

[6] RNZAF: Royal New Zealand Air Force.
[7] Slats: Aerodynamic section of the wings' leading edge that, when deployed, allow flight at slower speeds than otherwise would be possible.
[8] Oleos: Oleo struts are shock absorbers used on the landing gear of most aircraft to cushion the impact of landing.

alongside the fuselage, it could be rolled onto a railway wagon, and you are off to invade Russia, I suppose). The unfortunate consequence is that the oleos have to be splayed out to give anything like a reasonable track for the wheels – which also have a degree of toe-in. With a small fin and rudder, which are little better than decoration at slower speeds, no rudder trim, and poor brakes ... result... excitement! (Today our Buchons have modified modern brakes, which have transformed the aircraft). With the control column parked firmly forward and right, gently up with the power old son, catch the swing as the tail-wheel breaks ground and, in a crescendo of noise, we get airborne. John tucks in quickly, and I am not sure if his cheesy grin is because he is enjoying himself, or reflecting his recent close proximity to the blur of the control surfaces on my aircraft during take-off. Sion is about 1600 feet above sea level, and we then start a steady climb ENE up the Sion valley. Surreal does not really catch the moment, as I look along my wing, emblazoned with great black crosses, at a Spitfire bobbing gently in formation, with massive snow-capped mountains seemingly a few yards away.

The Gotthard Pass is around 7000 feet above sea level, so we cross about 2000 feet above the pass, turn north, and then enjoy a 'yee haaa' run (technical term!) down the narrow and very scenic valley towards Altdorf. Still in very high ground, but not the main Alp massif, we strike off NE, and ease out of the mountains, to cross Lake Constance and into Germany. I then check in with Munich Radar, to ease our passage through this busy area towards Augsburg – fuel OK, but not enough to hang around too much. "Golf Oscar Lima formation, you are identified, and you are clear direct track to Augsburg, maintaining 4000 feet QNH[9] 1021" came the clipped and professional instructions from Munich ATC. I read back, and then get the reply "Oscar Lima formation, that is correct, what are your aircraft types?" I reply "Lead is a Messerschmitt 109, and my No 2 is a Spitfire." There is a definite pause..." Ah so... are you armed?!" Everyone is a comedian. "Not today sir", I reply politely, more interested in my fuel gauge. Almost immediately, there is another unidentified transmission on the frequency "Ant who is vinning today!" German sense of humour, you can't beat it! The run towards Augsburg goes well, and I am beginning to relax about fuel... error! An enthusiastic Augsburg ATC greets my joining call "Welcome to Augsburg old timers" (had my

---

[9] QNH: A pressure setting that causes the altimeter to read altitude above mean sea level.

birth certificate been sent with the flight plan?!) "We have 5 aircraft in the pattern, expect a delay." I look across at John, sitting tucked in on my starboard wing. "I've got plenty" – New Zealand sense of humour is almost as good as German. "Oscar Lima formation, what time delay?" hoping that talking through clenched teeth has not muffled my transmission too much. Recognising a measure of tension in my voice, ATC is really on the ball and, without further exchange, "Lufthansa you are now No3 behind a Messerschmitt 109 and a Spitfire, delay your turn for the localiser[10]."

Landing a 109 is not as bad as history sometimes relates... well, not quite as bad. The wheels come down asymmetrically – the hydraulic pump can only manage one at a time – and then there is the considerable manual effort, and time, of winding down the flap. Luckily, she is very speed- stable, and my cockpit gyrations do not displace her from a reasonable approach path. The finals turn must be curved, as the tail-down view out of the front is quite simply appalling. Rolling out of the turn over the runway, gently cutting the power, and then flaring into the 3 point attitude has to be seamless. But she sits down really quite well, and your head is constantly moving left and right looking out of the sides – because there is no view forward. Indeed, it is not so much the touchdown that is fun but a short second or so later... The previously mentioned small decorative fin and rudder, put on by our friend Willy to make it at least look like an aeroplane, start to lose aerodynamic effect quite quickly, as the wings blank the airflow over the tailplane. Brakes (on this early Buchon) are not a good option at high speed either, as they fade dramatically, potentially leaving you with very modest aerodynamic directional control, and no means of stopping. But she behaves impeccably, and rolls out without a wiggle – thank you again, God. As I turn off the runway, I watch John execute an impeccable landing in the Spitfire – showy Kiwi!

Augsburg is the home of the Messerschmitt, and literally thousands were built here during the Second World War. Given the numbers that were produced, it is not surprising that the 109 shot down more aircraft than any other fighter aircraft ever built – a record that will not be broken. Therefore, it was also not surprising that, as we got to the fuel pumps, we were quickly surrounded by a sizeable crowd.

---

[10] Localiser: Component of an instrument landing system (ILS) that guides an aircraft onto the runway centreline.

As we refuelled, there was some amusement and pointing at the fin of my aircraft, and I realised that the speed tape, hastily applied to disguise the swastika, was fooling no one (displaying the swastika is illegal in Germany). Before I was able to get myself an overdue cup of coffee, a young member of the flying club asked very politely if he could introduce one of his club's seniors, a Luftwaffe pilot who had flown the 109. Meeting pilots who have flown these aircraft operationally is almost as big a buzz as actually flying them, and of course I agreed. A short, very dapper, man was duly introduced – the formal nod, handshake and visible stiffening of the shoulders were text-book Bavarian. Introductions over, he then went on what I can only describe as a tour of inspection of my aircraft. I dutifully fell in one pace behind, and we completed a walk-round – with me half expecting to be picked up for an unpolished rivet at any moment. We got back to the cockpit and, with his hand on the aircraft he said, in heavily accented English, "The 109 is a very dangerous aeroplane." Taken slightly aback, I could only mumble "It does have its moments sir." "Ja," he continued, "I crashed three!" I refrained from congratulating him on helping our war effort, and inadequately replied with something like "Oh my goodness." He continued: "So I decided to go onto something much less dangerous." I was anticipating something like Junkers transports or the like but, with a twinkle in his eye, he said "Ja, I went on to midget submarines!" And it was true.

A slightly humbler pilot got airborne from Augsburg, and we set course for our second port of call, Bautzen. Bautzen Airfield lies about 30 miles east of the city of Dresden, and just 18 miles from the Polish border. In truth, this leg of the journey was as unremarkable as it was pleasant. The weather was stunning, as we headed NNE, first over Bavaria and into Saxony, and then around the corner of the Czech Republic that juts out into that part of Germany. Our aircraft required an overflight clearance for the countries we transited, and we did not have one for Czech, so we could not straight-line to Bautzen. Squeezing between the Dresden zone and the German/Czech border, we arrived at a deserted Bautzen airfield, landed – two successes in one day, it can't last – and were quickly refuelled, and tucked away in a very Soviet-looking, but serviceable, hardened shelter. We then wandered to the Air Traffic Control Tower to book in, pay our dues and get a taxi into town – for what we regarded as a well-earned beer. The delightful young chap in the Tower seemed to be a one-man band and, it transpired, had previously been a flying instructor at Bautzen, flying L39 jet trainers – it was then the East German Air Force Advanced Flying Training School. We passed a very pleasant few minutes shooting the breeze, until a very prominent telephone on his control desk started ringing loudly. His demeanour changed instantly - this was a phone that did not ring very often, and he picked it up as if it was hot to the touch. As he talked, his serious face turned to look straight at me, and there was no doubting that I was the subject of his conversation. "It is German Air Defence for you," he said, passing the phone quickly to me. My "Hello" was greeted with a very angry voice which introduced itself as Major Schmidt (I cannot actually remember his name, but Schmidt works for me), the duty controller at the local Air Defence HQ. "Are you the pilot of Golf Bravo Oscar Mike Lima?" he demanded. "I am," I confessed. "You infringed Czech airspace earlier," he shot at me. I countered very firmly, my hackles already rising. "I did not, I could see the actual border crossing point well to my starboard as we turned the Czech corner." One to me! Not beaten, he responded, "You were flying inside the German ADIZ.[11]" I was on firmer ground now, having once been a staff officer in HQ RAF Germany, so came back: " I can fly in the ADIZ, as long as I fly parallel to the border, which we did." Two to me! There was a discernible thinking pause at the other end of the line, and then he came back at me: "You were flying at more than 150 knots in the ADIZ." Damn, that was one I couldn't counter, and admitted that I was flying at 180 knots. I was then subjected to a long triumphal lecture on how I must not fly at more than 150 knots in the German ADIZ. He paused for breath, and then asked what types of aircraft were in my formation... déjà vu. Rather fed up, I replied, "My aircraft is a Messerschmitt 109, and my wingman is flying a Spitfire." A long pause followed and, in a much less confrontational tone, he enquired, "And these are military aircraft?" I replied that, no, they were on the civil register but, as an afterthought, said, "But I am a Royal Air Force pilot." Another pause, followed by, "You are a military RAF pilot... what is your rank?" RAF ranks are not generally understood by most air forces, so I gave him my army equivalent rank, "I'm a Major General." Long, long pause..." You have good day Sir!" CLICK.

The beer tasted good, as we debriefed the day later in the hotel. Still Tuesday, and only one more leg to Warsaw... but that is another story!

---

[11] ADIZ: Air Defence Identification Zone.

Out Of Breath

If you mention North Luffenham, in Rutland, to any RAF aircrew over a certain age, they will immediately know what you're talking about. For many years, this former WWII airfield was home to the RAF Aviation Medical Training Centre (AMTC), which specialised in protective flying clothing and equipment. It was staffed by a team of aviation doctors and assistants, whose primary responsibility was to train aircrew in the use of aircraft oxygen systems and clothing, designed to combat the effects of high-performance or high-altitude flight. The majority of courses were type-specific, because very few aircraft performed the same role or had exactly the same oxygen regulator or system connectors, and this determined the training that was undertaken. Most aircrew could expect to visit AMTC at least every couple of years, either for refresher courses or coincident with moving onto a different aircraft type.

However, regardless of what you flew or were about to fly, every course included some form of torture that involved at least one session in a decompression chamber. For example, those of us who habitually visited the extremes of the earth's atmosphere were introduced to the pleasures of wearing partial-pressure suits, and practising pressure breathing, following a simulated explosive cabin decompression at very high altitude. This was an extremely uncomfortable experience, because the rapid decrease in external pressure caused every gas pocket in your body to expand (if you catch my drift) while 100% oxygen was being forcibly rammed into your lungs. This was required to keep you conscious long enough to descend the aircraft to lower level; meanwhile, the partial-pressure suit was squeezing your chest, to stop your lungs rupturing, and your legs, to stop the blood being forced from your abdomen. Delightful!

A less violent experience in the decompression chamber involved recognising the symptoms of hypoxia, another name for oxygen starvation. We would sit inside the chamber with an instructor, be taken up to a simulated 20,000 feet and, one by one, invited to remove our oxygen masks and perform a simple mathematical task. After a while, the victim would cease to function normally, slump forward, the instructor would replace his mask and he would quickly recover. Common symptoms included a bluing of the lips (not visible if you were wearing an oxygen mask) and bluing of the finger tips (again, not visible if you were wearing aircrew gloves), so the idea was that we would recognise the deterioration in our mental faculties. Unfortunately, I never did, probably because I had very few in the first place. Invariably, the last thing I could recall would be doing something like repeatedly taking away 7 from 501, before coming round after my mask had been replaced. An additional problem was that hypoxia and hyperventilation (over-breathing) produce similar symptoms, and I remember one refresher class being asked how you could tell the difference. My friend brightly suggested turning off the subject's oxygen supply, on the basis that if he improved it was hyperventilation and, if he deteriorated, it was hypoxia. Unsurprisingly, this was not well received by the instructor.

A common danger with being decompressed (and this is the crux of my story) is suffering "the bends." It's exactly the same problem as divers have, in that a rapid reduction in external pressure can cause dissolved nitrogen in the bloodstream to form bubbles. It can have catastrophic effects on your body, and is therefore to be avoided at all costs. In our case, this was achieved by breathing 100% oxygen for at least 20 minutes before undergoing decompression. This process purges the blood of nitrogen and, therefore, removes the risk. Our 20 minutes or so was spent in the cinema (although I use the term loosely), where we sat, plugged into the oxygen rig, and endured old black and white films on first aid. These included such epics as Don't Let Him Die and Stemming An Arterial Bleed. The latter, in particular, plumbed the depths of our intelligence, by forcibly pointing out the dangers of applying a tourniquet around the neck. Eventually, an airman would tap you on the shoulder, ask you to breathe in and hold your breath, transfer you to a small oxygen bottle, and take you down to the decompression chamber.

On one occasion, I was en route to the chamber, when I realised that I could no longer breathe. I stopped walking, pointed to the oxygen bottle, and gave a forcible thumbs down sign to the airman, who asked, "Can't you breathe, sir?" I shook my head violently, whereupon he said, "Stay there sir, and I'll fetch a replacement." Unfortunately, it was some minutes before he returned, by which time I had removed my mask, in preference to asphyxiating myself, and undone all the preparation. The head doctor, who was a few rungs up the promotion ladder from me, was not best pleased, and asked me why I hadn't checked the gauge on the oxygen bottle before disconnecting from the main system. I pointed out

that, firstly, I didn't think that was my responsibility and, secondly, it was dark
in the cinema, so I couldn't have seen the gauge anyway. Unfortunately, I was
in the last batch on the last day to use the chamber, so I was only given a partial
pass and rebooked for the following course.

When I returned to AMTC, the next month, I was careful to check the
gauge on the oxygen bottle. It read full, so I confidently disconnected from the
cinema's system, plugged in and set off for the chamber. Unbelievably, halfway
there I found that I couldn't breathe again so, a short time later, I found myself
in front of the same senior doctor. He was building himself up to self-combust,
when a sheepish airman appeared with the gauge that he had disconnected from
my oxygen bottle.

It still read full!

Fuel Awareness

Once upon a time, a brave young fighter pilot was warding off the Queen's enemies single-handed! We were flying an operation called the "Beihan Patrol," where pairs of armed Hunters would fly a thirty-mile-long patrol line, one low to the ground, and the other five thousand feet above him; this way, each could cover the other's tail for the expected MiGs from just across the border. The army medical site in the wadi[1] below us had been strafed only a few days before and, with no radio contact between aircraft and ground, we were not to know that, as the Hunters went to the north end of the line, the enemy aircraft (a 'Moose' – a sort of Harvard size and shape ground-attack aircraft) had dashed across the border and machine-gunned the distinctly red-cross-marked medical station. As the Hunters turned south they saw smoke in the distance and rushed towards it. By then the Moose had fled, and the army were furious – to use a polite word!

We had to be on patrol on time, to relieve the previous pair so that solid fighter-cover was there from before dawn to after dusk, week after week. So, when my No 2's engine went sick on take-off, I pressed on as a singleton, shouting to Air Traffic Control to fix for either a new No 2 to catch me up, or for the next pair to come up early, because I would be burning fuel a lot quicker than planned for; I could not afford to fly at slow patrol speed, for fear of getting jumped... and faster, much faster, meant much more fuel burned.

Needless to say, there was no spare aircraft for my wingman, and the next pair were late on station. So, I was actually climbing up away from the wadi before the next boys were on patrol. But, I was very low on fuel and, with one hundred and sixty miles to go (if I went around enemy territory, which we were forbidden to cross), as my "bingo" (low fuel) lights came on, I knew I was close to being "soon deep in the horse-dung." Having no choice, I turned south, and flew across the mountains where the enemy lived, and climbed to about thirty thousand feet. I dared not go any higher, as my gauges were by now reading less than I was supposed to be safely taxying in with! I throttled to idle, and lowered the nose to keep my speed up to something half-decent, in case Mister MiG might take a look, though this was very unlikely up that high, as they usually stayed low down.

---

[1] Wadi: A valley, ravine, or channel that is dry except in the rainy season (Arabic).

I watched my last few pounds of fuel dwindle, and thought about getting ready to eject, as the mountains were not the place to force-land a jet fighter. But, at last, I could see the sea, and knew from the angle of descent that I could probably make it. At forty miles to run, I still had about ten thousand feet in hand, and then I knew I was OK – as long as the donkey kept braying!

I landed with nought-nought, and my crew-chief had VERY raised eyebrows when he gave me the Form 700 (log-book) to sign ready for my next sortie. "Just the fumes left Sir!" "I know, Chief, and most of them were coming from me!"

Credit: Alan Wilson

25F Squadron In Cyprus - Summer 1958

The summer months of 1958 found the Middle East once again embroiled in widespread conflict in the cause of Arab nationalism. By July, a civil war in the Lebanon saw the government forces under heavy pressure from the rebel Druze tribesmen, who were being actively supported by the Egyptians, Syrians and Palestinians from Gaza. On the 15th, in Baghdad, King Faisal of Iraq was shot in a military coup, and there was a parallel threat to the King of Jordan. Russia and the Eastern Communist Bloc countries added to the destabilization, by supplying arms, military advisers and pro-communist rebel radio propaganda. The US and British Governments were particularly upset by the Eastern Bloc involvement, and jointly decided that the British should be responsible for settling the trouble in Iraq and Jordan, whilst the US would intervene in the Lebanon. To this end, the US landed 5,000 marines in the Lebanon, from ships in the US 6th Fleet, which they further supplied from their base in Crete, via Nicosia. The British intervention on 20th July comprised 2,000 men of the Independent Parachute Brigade, flown to Amman in Jordan and subsequently supplied by No 70 Squadron's Hastings C2s, based at Nicosia, backed up by RAF Beverley C1s from the UK, and USAF C-119 Boxcars from Germany.

For all of this period, 25 Squadron, equipped with Meteor NF12s and NF14s, was on detachment from RAF Waterbeach, Cambridgeshire to RAF Akrotiri, Cyprus, to provide night-fighter coverage of the island, and deal with any incursion into its airspace. This included the interception of aircraft engaged in gun-running from Greece, to supply the EOKA terrorists, who were in armed conflict with the British forces and Turkish Cypriots, with the aim of political union of Cyprus with Greece. The detachment relieved No 39 Squadron, equipped with Meteor NF13s, which returned to its Malta base. It heralded a long running sequence of three-month detachments of UK Fighter Command N/AW[1] squadrons to Cyprus; No 25's turn came around again in 1960 and 1961.

Because of all this strife, even at night, the sky over the Eastern Mediterranean was busy with military aircraft of many nationalities, operating outside any

---

[1] N/AW: Night/All-Weather.

international air traffic control, with the result that the Squadron's 'Battle Flight' was frequently scrambled to intercept unidentified 'bogeys' approaching Cyprus airspace. It was known that Egyptian MiG 17s were flying to Syria to support the Lebanese rebels, and they were being picked up by our radar on Mt Troodos, flying north-east towards Cyprus, keeping well clear of Israel and Lebanese airspace, before turning east to Syria. During this time, I was a pilot and the Squadron Adjutant of 25 Squadron and, for the duration of navigator Wg Cdr Ken Cook's command of the Squadron, he and I flew as a crew - always taking our full share of operational duties.

Typical of the Squadron's nightly Battle Flight activity, on the night of 23rd July, we were scrambled in NF12 WS622, and identified our "bogey" targets, a C-130 Hercules and four USN AD-5 Skyraiders. On the 28th, in our own aircraft, NF14 WS723, we identified two Hastings and two USAF C-119 Boxcars returning from Jordan, then, on a second scramble, another Boxcar, a Valetta C1 and a Skyraider. The reason for so many of our bogeys being returning RAF or US transport aircraft was that they preferred to fly at night, making no radio calls, to avoid the attention of hostile fighters. On the night of 1st August, we were scrambled in NF12 WS665 to the south, to investigate an approaching high-speed bogey but, as we closed the range, it turned round and, when it faded from our GCI² radar coverage, we were recalled to base. Still in the early hours of the 1st, in Meteor NF 14 WS738, we were scrambled to intercept another high-speed bogey, approaching from the south at about 25,000 feet. With no moon or surface lights visible, and very little starlight, due to desert dust trapped below the tropopause, flying was in a 'black hole'. This time, the bogey did not turn away and, as it continued towards us, Ken achieved AI contact. We commenced our interception to get on his tail, by offsetting our flight path for a 180° turn close behind our target, but then the bogey turned towards us, clearly indicating that he was aware of our presence and not a passive target.

Then followed a dogfight which tested every corner of the Meteor's performance envelope, whilst the Boss demonstrated his outstanding Nav/Radar skills, with accurate assessments and anticipation of target behaviour. Through his steady, positive commentary and directions, for the next 15 minutes or so, with the power

---

² GCI: Ground Controlled Interception.

levers firmly against the stops, the interception was a succession of maximum-G turns, wing-overs, climbs and dives, descending at one time to 1,500 feet above the sea before climbing again. Having no outside visual references, I took care not to topple the artificial horizon, by exceeding its limits of 85° in climb or dive for, if I had done so, I should have had to level the aircraft by reference to the Turn/ Slip and Vertical Speed instruments, and re-erected the instrument by pressing its Fast Erection button for some seconds - by which time we would have been out-manoeuvred.

I soon realised that the night-flying skills of our target's pilot were far beyond what I expected of a Middle Eastern aviator, and that he was under, or assisted by, surface radar control. If our target was a MiG 17, its pilot could be a gung-ho Eastern Bloc 'adviser', attached to the Egyptian or Syrian Air Force, and the surface radar could be located in Syria. Once, our target reversed a turn we could not match and left our AI[3] cover, but we soon found him again and slowly closed the range. Quite suddenly, as we held our target at about 200 yards, 5° up at 12 o'clock, he stopped his violent evasion, and flew straight and level at 15,000 feet. Due to the darkness and lack of starlight, I still had not made visual contact, so I took the opportunity to lift the nose slightly and close right in to get a visual sighting and identify the aircraft. When down to about 50 yards - minimum AI range - I found myself looking into a single, large-diameter (compared with the Meteor's Derwent's) jet-pipe, emitting a dull red glow, but it was too dark to see an airframe shape.

I reported our visual contact to our fighter controller, and requested instructions. The reply was to maintain contact and wait - an order repeated at intervals, whilst higher authority was consulted. After some minutes, the target suddenly lit up like a Christmas tree with navigation lights, white strobe lights, and land-ing lights all displayed in dazzling brilliance. Shortly afterwards, we were ordered to break off and return to base, our target was a 'friendly'. I switched on our own navigation lights, dropped back and returned to Akrotiri, 70nm north-west. Later, after completing our operation report, we learned that our target had been a US Navy McDonnell F3H Demon, a single-seat, carrier-based night/all-weather fighter, launched by the 6th Fleet's major aircraft carrier, the USS Saratoga, to

---

3 AI: Airborne Interception.

provide forward cover over the fleet as it steamed towards the Lebanon, to land a further 1,800 troops. Typical of our NATO ally at the time, the US authorities had not advised the British of their fleet's movements, and it was only when they could see on the Saratoga's radar that their aircraft was in danger of being shot down, that their pilot was instructed to cease his belligerent behaviour and switch on his lights - after RAF Cyprus had been contacted via Naples, to find out if we were an RAF aircraft, and asked to call us off!

Though the early version of the Demon did not have the afterburner4 of later versions, it was, in 1958, the US Navy's latest fighter, supersonic in a shallow dive, yet we in our two-crew Meteor out-flew it throughout the interception. As an experience, it was the most active interception in pitch darkness I ever made, and the most competent intercept commentary by a Navigator/Radar I ever experienced. If ever I needed to be convinced of the superiority of two-crewed night/all-weather fighters over single-seat machines, this event did so, and I remain so convinced to this day. I believe that the Americans adopted the same point of view. One can imagine the consternation of the US Navy 'brass', who had launched their newest fighter type to sweep ahead of the Carrier Group, then had to watch on their radar its interception, being unable to influence the outcome, and having eventually to instruct the pilot to fly straight and level, and later to display every light on the aircraft. It is worthy of note that the USN's next two night/all weather fighters, the very successful F4 Phantom II and the F14A Tomcat were two-crew machines.

By the middle of August, the new regime in Iraq was recognised by the Western Powers. The warfare in the Lebanon eased to a long-term guerrilla campaign, and the American troops were withdrawn. In Jordan, dissidents were arrested and put away. In Cyprus, the EOKA terrorist campaign continued, with attacks on British servicemen, their wives and children (always shots in the back), plus random gunfire through, and grenades over, airfield and barrack defences. On 13th August, the Squadron was relieved by another N/AW squadron, and flew back to Waterbeach. After 63 consecutive days of operations, Squadron personnel were disappointed to learn that, unlike other servicemen in Cyprus, they were not eligible for the award of the General Service Medal, because the Squadron was only on detachment and not stationed in Cyprus!!

A Bit Of A Trial

In early 1965, I was stand-in co-pilot with an experienced Victor B1A crew. We were tasked with taking part in a trial – Trial 494 – to drop 1000lb bombs, which were fitted with experimental radar fuses, on West Freugh range in the Solway Firth. Six of these weapons were loaded on to the Victor, and were to be dropped singly from medium level, so that observers on the range could assess the performance of the fuses, which were set to explode the bombs at 50ft above the surface. We made radio contact with the range and were cleared, having made one dummy run over the range, to make our first "live" drop. With the aircraft lined up on the run, the bomb doors were opened, and the navigator radar/bomb-aimer was issuing instructions to the captain, with an increasingly anticipatory tone, up to the point when it was expected he would announce a triumphant "bomb gone!", like they always do in the war films - but no such announcement came.

Now, the bombs were mounted on a rack in the Victor's capacious bomb-bay, by means of the notoriously unreliable electro-mechanical release units (EMRU's). At the operation of the bomb release switch in the crew cabin, an electrical signal was designed to open the large claws of the EMRU, allowing the weapon to drop. A lanyard, fixed to the aircraft and attached to the bomb, would arm the fuse as the weapon fell about nine inches off the EMRU. In this case, the EMRU did not open. The captain said "(expletive deleted – roughly translated as "Oh dear")", then selected bomb-doors to "close", before informing the range controller of the problem, and turning the aircraft left to position for another attempt at dropping the bomb; but, during the turn, the crew heard a muffled thump from behind the cockpit, accompanied by a slight shudder of the aircraft. Someone asked "What (expletive deleted – roughly translated as "on earth") was that?" It was agreed that the EMRU of the selected bomb had operated at last, and allowed the bomb to drop on to the bomb-doors. There followed a detailed discussion between the crew and the range controller. It was agreed that we would fly over the range again, open the bomb-doors and allow the bomb to drop safely into the sea. So, once again, the aircraft was lined up for this, now unconventional, bomb-run and, when we were safely over the range, the captain selected bomb-doors to "open". Immediately, the "bomb-doors emergency" light illuminated.

Now, the bomb-doors on the Victor were operated by hydraulic power.

Because the aircraft's raison d'etre in event of nuclear war was to drop the atomic weapon on its target at any cost, a device was incorporated in the bomb-door operating system, to allow opening of the doors should the normal hydraulic system fail to do so. This was indicated to the crew by the illumination of a red warning light on the instrument panel in front of the captain (and, if I recall correctly, replicated on the Navigator/radar's panel at the rear of the cabin), and this was precisely what had now happened. I cannot remember (yes, yes, I know, but it was nearly 50 years ago!) what the further consequences were of using the emergency system to open the bomb-doors, but I think it might have been that the whole hydraulic system would be switched to "emergency", thereby limiting some hydraulic operations – undercarriage, flaps, airbrakes, brakes and nosewheel steering were all hydraulically operated. In any case, at this stage it was decided that the trial would be postponed and we would return to base.

At this time, I was still a young and very inexperienced co-pilot. It wasn't quite the situation where the lowly co-pilot was told to "sit there, say nothing and don't touch anything", but I was certainly in awe of these generally older, and undoubtedly very experienced, crew members. Nevertheless, on the way back to base, I was giving some thought to our situation. It struck me, inter alia, that if this bomb had been selected to be dropped, and fused to explode at 50ft above ground by extending the lanyard when dropping off the bomb carrier, it could be "live" to explode as we passed 50ft on the approach to landing. I agonised over this for much of our flight south. Surely these experienced chaps would know all about these things, and would dismiss my thoughts as being ridiculous. But maybe they had NOT thought about it. I really didn't want to die, however gallantly, at this time of life, but equally I didn't want to be made to look like a fool.

At about the time we arrived at the radar entry point, to start our descent to base, I decided that the desire to stay alive, even if I was looked upon as a fool for the rest of my precious life, was the preferable outcome, so I hesitantly and very nervously broached the subject over the intercom. This prompted a short silence (while I cringed in fear of ridicule), followed by assorted expletives from some or all of the crew, and a discussion on the feasibility of my observations and the action to be taken. Much to my relief, the captain decided that, despite the fact that the possibility of the bomb exploding at 50ft height was remote, the Air Electronics Officer was to contact base and get an expert opinion on the subject.

While this was being progressed, a discussion was held on the subject of the rear crew bailing out – they, of course, did not have the luxury of ejection seats. In the event, and after some time, the message arrived from the Armaments Officer at base, who confirmed that the bomb was "safe", and that we should continue to landing. I continued, and I suspect some of the other crew members did too, to feel rather nervous as we flew down the final approach.

The landing, in the expert hands of the captain, was smooth and uneventful. We taxied slowly round the taxiway until we had sight of the marshaller, and turned into the parking bay. I noticed that our marshaller looked distinctly distracted as he waved us in for the final few feet, and his arm actions seemed to slow to an unusual pace. As we went through the closing-down drills, there seemed to be a dearth of groundcrew in front of the aircraft, but the crew chief reported on the external intercom as usual. He did, however, report that "something appeared to be hanging down from the bomb-doors". The crew disembarked rather more quickly than my limited experience would have considered normal – I think I was last out of the aircraft. Once on the apron, we could see what had been causing the consternation. Our selected bomb had dropped on to the bomb-doors as diagnosed earlier, but the bomb-doors had failed to open because the nose of the bomb had penetrated one door (and was now hanging perilously close to the ground), while the tail of the bomb had penetrated the other door, thus locking the doors together.

I never did find out why the weapon was not primed to explode at 50ft, but the event did nothing to endear me to bombs, and I was happy, eventually, to continue to fly the Victor when it was converted to the air-to-air refuelling role.

Credit: Flypast-Key Collection

A Discretionary Commendation

Air Chief Marshal Sir Augustus Walker, GCB, CBE, DSO, DFC, AFC (known as 'Gus'), was born in Yorkshire, and awarded a university commission with the RAF in 1934, when he was at St Catharine's College, Cambridge. He was an extremely good rugby player, playing for the RAF, Blackheath, Yorkshire and England, and captaining the RAF team from 1936 to 1939. He became famous when he lost an arm in 1942, while he was Station Commander of RAF Syerston. A Lancaster belonging to one of his squadrons lost some incendiaries, just as it was about to take off. Racing to the rescue of the crew, he was seriously injured when he was blown along the runway by the force of an exploding 4,000 lb bomb, ignited by the incendiaries. In the early 1950s, when he was Commandant of the RAF Flying College, Manby, one of the students (a wing commander) recalled this experience:

I had been given permission to fly a Meteor Mk7 to Germany for the weekend, with an exchange American student as passenger. It was winter, and the 'met' forecast for Lincolnshire was snow showers, with a gradual deterioration in both the visibility and cloud base; but, the weather in Germany was reported to be good, and staying that way, so I didn't see any problem. We got airborne, and set course for Germany across the North Sea. After climbing to 30,000 feet, with a carpet of thick cloud below us, I called Manby to tell them I was changing channels to a continental frequency. It was then that I discovered I had no radio communication. Furthermore, the intercom had failed as well, so I couldn't speak to my American passenger in the back seat. After a moment's panic, I concluded that, in spite of having no R/T, I shouldn't have any problem map-reading my way to the base in Germany. So, I unfolded my map – only to discover that it finished half way across the North Sea! I had omitted to bring the section which included Germany.

I now had two options: either to press on to Germany without a map and without R/T, hoping I might find an airfield on which I could land; or to try and return to Manby, knowing that bad weather was setting in. I decided to return to Manby – better the devil you know. I wrote a short note to that effect, and passed it over my shoulder to my passenger. I then turned on a reciprocal course and started to let down, so that we would be below cloud before we crossed the Lincolnshire coast. As I approached 500 feet, without breaking cloud, I was beginning to feel a bit apprehensive. So, when I saw the sea at 300 feet below me, you can imagine that I was pretty relieved. I was also confident I could navigate my own way back to Manby once we had crossed the coast, in spite of the low cloud base. The only trouble was that the snow showers had set in, and the visibility was poor.

When I crossed the coast, I looked in vain for a familiar feature – one part of the Lincolnshire coast is very much like any other, especially from 300 feet and when the visibility is less than half a mile. If that wasn't bad enough, a covering of snow made most of the ground unrecognisable! All I could do was to make a square search, to see if anything came up. It didn't. Eventually, with fuel running low, I decided we would have to bale out (there being no ejection seats in the Meteor 7). I scribbled a note and passed it back to my passenger. Within a few seconds, it was passed back with his answer, "I can't! You didn't tell me the drill!"

I then realised, with a sinking heart, that I had no choice but to make a forced landing in a field, knowing that the snow would make it difficult to spot any furrows or surface obstacles. With little time to spare, I selected a field, made one practice approach, and overshot to do a circuit for the real thing. Somehow, I managed to get it down in one piece, just as a farmer was driving across in a Land Rover to intercept us. In the event, he told us we were only about 20 miles from Manby, so I asked him to telephone the Duty Officer, to explain what had happened and to send some transport. While we were waiting for the transport to arrive, I opened the fuselage panel door to retrieve our overnight bags and noted, with some mortification, that my passenger's bag was all-metal and pressed hard against the radio equipment. I said nothing, but I wasn't too surprised when the radio technician told me the following morning that he couldn't find anything wrong!

It was also the following morning that I was summoned to the Commandant's office. I went in fear and trepidation, expecting to be informed that I was likely to face a court martial. I found him walking up and down his office in a state of great agitation, his armless sleeve flapping across his chest. He peered up at me and said, "I have read the reports and have decided to award you an immediate Green Endorsement (a discretionary commendation), for one of the finest feats of airmanship I have ever come across."

I was flabbergasted!

Memories Of A Flight Engineer

As I write this, I am fully aware that my contribution to the Bomber Command war effort was, indeed, infinitesimal. At Branch meetings and squadron reunions, when I hear some of the experiences of my contemporaries, I feel honoured to be in the company of such men. I was glad to have been a part of it, and would not have missed it for anything.

I joined the Air Training Corps, and enjoyed all the training, drill, Morse code, aircraft recce etc. During this time, I made my first flight; it was in a Handley Page Harrow at RAF Montrose. It was just a short flight, but enough to give me the flying bug so, after my 17th birthday, I volunteered for RAF aircrew, but failed the medical. I was told I had some obscure kidney disease, and to forget about any of the Services. The disappointment was intense, and a real low point in my life. On my 18th birthday, I went for a medical for my then employer. They passed me A1, so I went down to the recruitment board again. This time all went well and, after medicals and tests in Edinburgh, I was accepted for aircrew training and a Flight Engineers' course. Great was the joy thereof!

I reported to Lords Cricket Ground in January 1944 and, after three weeks' kitting out, jabs, dentist etc, we were on our way to Initial Training Wing at Newquay in Cornwall. This I enjoyed immensely, and made some good friends. When I went home to Dundee, on my first leave, I had put on over a stone in weight and never felt fitter. The F/E prelim course was next, at RAF Locking near Weston-Super-Mare, during which we were taught the basic principles of engines and airframes. I had a bad experience there! We were doing guard duties, which involved patrolling the camp, armed with pick handles. It was about 2am, and pouring with rain. My companion, who was older than me and already had a few years service, suggested that we take shelter, while he had a smoke. I reluctantly went with him, and almost immediately the Orderly Sergeant appeared. He accused us of sleeping on guard duty, and placed us under open arrest. I was very worried that I would be put off the course, and gladly accepted the CO's punishment of 10 days Confined to Barracks. The 10 days seemed never-ending, as it meant reporting to the guardroom four times a day. At 6am and 11pm, it was in full marching order, with boots and buttons shining, and, at 5.30pm, we had to go to the cookhouse or hospital, to scrub pans and floors. I resolved never to step out of line again!

At a local dance in Locking, I had my first taste of the demon drink. I thought I was Fred Astaire and Frank Sinatra rolled into one, and all this on two pints of the local 'scrumpy.' I'm afraid this experience did not put me off drink for good! The next move was to RAF St. Athan in Wales, where we got down to the serious business of learning about four-engined aircraft. They taught us all about: airframes; engines; fuel systems and management; electric, hydraulic and air pressure systems; and flight controls etc. It was a really intensive course, with much studying to do at night. As final exams drew near, we would fire questions at each other, all desperately keen to get the coveted Brevet. I managed to pass, despite getting "C T Charlie" for my oral test - an instructor who was rumoured to have failed more cadets than anyone else.

With flying on the agenda for the first time, I reported to RAF Stradishall in Suffolk. This was a Heavy Conversion Unit, where I was to meet my crew and learn to fly Stirling bombers. The first person I met there was a New Zealand pilot. We had a drink together in the Mess, and he mentioned that we might crew up together, but for some reason I did not take him up on this. The course went well, with engineers and pilots attending lectures together. At the end, I was approached by a Flight Sergeant pilot to join his crew. He was a Scot like myself, and I liked him immediately; I got my kit and moved in with them. They were all NCOs (Non-Commissioned Officers), and had been together for some time, training on Wellingtons. They made me most welcome, and I realised that I would have to depend on them, and they on me, in the days ahead.

We started flying training, and everything went well until we were on our final night cross-country exercise. This was a six-hour flight on a very cold night. We had icing on the wings, and 'coring' on three engines, a condition in which the oil got too thick in the cooler, the oil pressure dropped, and the engine temperature rose. This was very worrying to an inexperienced crew, but training came to the rescue, and we did all the right things to complete the exercise and land safely. Next morning, at breakfast, we heard that a crew on our course had crashed. The pilot was the New Zealander I had met, and the F/E was a good friend of mine. Lancaster Finishing School at RAF Feltwell was our next station, where we were held up by bad weather for a few weeks. When we started flying, we found the Lancaster much more to our liking, and finished the course with no problems.

At last we were posted to a squadron, No 218 (Gold Coast), based at RAF

Chedburgh near Bury St Edmunds. After the skipper had done two ops with an experienced crew, we were briefed for our first op, as spare crew. We were left behind as the squadron flew off to Dresden. Next night, the target was Chemnitz, and again we were left behind - the frustration was dreadful. At last we went on our first op, which was a daylight raid to Wesel. No fighters were encountered, and the flak was very light. We could not wait for our next trip, but instead we were sent back to Feltwell on a Gee-H course, to master this blind bombing device. The course went well, and we returned to Chedburgh, to find that our aircraft (PD 440 HA C) had three yellow stripes on the tailplane, to denote that we carried the Gee-H equipment.

We started on ops again, and did a few daylight raids to the oil targets, using the Gee-H. No fighters were seen, but the flak was more intense, as the Gee-H took a longer straight-and-level run to the target. Our fifth op was to Gelsen-kirchen, where the flak was very accurate. We were hit by some shrapnel, and the starboard outer engine had to be feathered, as it was trailing smoke and the temperature had shot up. We transferred some fuel to the port side, and the skipper flew us home and landed safely. Our next trip was a night op to Dessau, which is between Magdeburg and Leipzig. We encountered some flak and searchlights on the way to the target, but nothing came too near. We approached the target area on time, but there was no sign of the TIs (Target Illuminators) until the rear gunner saw them dropping astern, so we had to go round again and rejoin the stream. When we made our bombing run, the master bomber was still broadcast-ing, so we dropped our bombs in the right place and headed home. An aircraft passed over the top of us, and flew on a parallel course on our starboard side. We identified him as a JU88. Great consternation! However, he failed to see us, and gradually pulled away. Some time later, the rear gunner reported a plane coming in fast from astern, and we prepared to take evasive action. He must have been using radar, and had not yet seen us visually. When he came within range, both gunners opened fire. The plane reared up to the vertical, rolled over and disap-peared; both gunners claimed hits and identified it as an Me410. About this time we managed to get ourselves lost. Gee was not working, and we could not get a course check, as we could see neither the ground nor the stars. We kept going in a westerly direction, conserving fuel by flying below 10,000ft, keeping the rpm down and the airspeed at 150 knots. After calling MAYDAY for some time, we received a course to take us to RAF Manston. They switched on the flare path, and we went right in. The skipper made his usual soft landing, which says much for his skill and concentration after 11 hours in the air. When the tanks were checked next morning, there were only 30 gallons left - not much between 4 engines. Good fortune had smiled on me again.

We did a few more ops and, after VJ day, the crew was split up, and we went our separate ways. As all ex-aircrew will know, we had a great respect for, and understanding of, each other, and parting was a really sad time. Although there are now only four of us left, we still keep in touch and meet up occasionally.

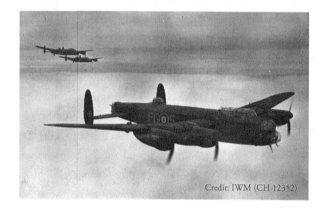

Credit: IWM (CH 12352)

A Turbulent Affair

In 1967, the British presence in Aden ceased after around 128 years. A part of the withdrawal included 84 Squadron's return to the UK, but the Six Day War, in June 1967, caused the Egyptian government to deny overflight for RAF aircraft on the normal route home. So, on 1st September 1967, the first three Beverleys of 84 Squadron departed RAF Khormaksar to fly on the Cento route, on which the staging airfields were Salalah, Sharjah, Tehran, Diyarbakir, Nicosia, El Adem, Luqa, Istres, Brize Norton, and finally to No 27 MU at RAF Shawbury. Then, in November 1967, the last three squadron aircraft departed for England. Unexpectedly, because the British were withdrawing from Aden, Egypt gave clearance for the last three Beverleys to overfly Egypt. On 6th November 1967, the Beverleys took off at 30-minute intervals from RAF Khormaksar for Malta. The lead aircraft (XM111) was captained by Flt Lt John Coutts, the second (XM103) by Flt Lt Dick Barton, and the last by the Squadron Commander Sqn Ldr Stan Hitchen.

This story primarily relates to XM103. The common route for all three aircraft was west to Perim Island, at the southern tip of The Red Sea, then north to a point over the Red Sea, prior to turning northwest to cross the Egyptian coast towards Luxor. After Luxor, the route followed the Nile to the west of Cairo, thence to El Adem, and on to Malta. The weather forecaster highlighted "a weak cold front" north of Jeddah, and on a line southwest to northeast across the Red Sea. On departure, a final farewell to XM103 involved unwelcome small arms fire from a local town called Sheik Othman. Happily no damage was done, but this incident seemed to mark the start of an eventful trip for all three aircraft.

When XM111 met the cold front, the crew experienced heavy rain, hail and turbulence. Messages received from the aircraft suggested that they had experienced some damage, as a result of flying through the storm. However, they did manage to proceed westwards towards Luxor and on to El Adem, and reached the UK on schedule. Onboard XM103, all was well until tracking towards Luxor. A line of ominous clouds extended either side of the flight path, and seemed to reach heights of well over twenty-five thousand feet (well above the unpressurised Beverley's ceiling). After entering the black and threatening clouds at 8000 feet, all appeared well for several minutes; then All Hell Broke Loose! Massive hailstones battered the aircraft, damaged the flight deck windows and the astrodome, and caused a cacophony of sound that most certainly got the crew's attention. There followed a period of turbulence, which not only badly shook the aircraft but really alarmed the crew. The flight instruments were unreadable, and bits of equipment were flying around the front and rear flight deck. Best guess from the information the crew could read off the instruments suggested that the aircraft had climbed several thousand feet, prior to descending rapidly in a violent downdraft. All on board thought that they were unlikely to survive the abuse being meted out to them in the storm. Those who have experienced this level of turbulence will fully understand the definition and effects of severe turbulence.

At some point during this period of severe turbulence, an engine was damaged and shut down; a visual inspection showed it was in a sad state. Then the aircraft settled in much calmer air, and the crew could see that they were quite low over the sea. Instruments fed by the pitot-static system were unreliable. For a while, the aircraft flew in torrential rain, hail and (thankfully) just moderate turbulence; however, the next shock came when it suddenly flew out of the blackness, noise, and turbulence of the storm into bright sunshine. It took a few minutes to realize that the G4B compass was inaccurate, as witnessed by the position of the sun, which did not correspond with the compass reading (the standby compass was a casualty of the turbulence). It also became clear that the aircraft was heading approximately east, almost 180 degrees out from its earlier course towards Egypt.

A distress call was transmitted, and diversion to Jeddah in Saudi Arabia was a simple decision, given that the other options were unacceptable. By intentionally heading to the north of Jeddah, until reaching the Saudi coast, the crew knew that they had to turn south to find Jeddah airport. Several miles north of Jeddah, a second rough-running engine caused the crew some anxiety; a Beverley does not fly well on two engines in high temperature regions. In effect, the arrival at Jeddah was a two- engine approach. After shutdown, it became clear that the crew and their aircraft were not welcome at Jeddah, and were quickly surrounded by heavily-armed Saudi soldiers. The reception was 'frosty' at best, and quite threatening at worst. Communication with the soldiers was tense because of language issues. Even when an English-speaker arrived, the atmosphere remained very tense. The Saudi soldiers demanded that the aircraft and crew depart immediately, but even the soldiers realized that, with an engine failed and obvious damage to the aircraft, it was going nowhere. Meanwhile, Sqn Ldr Hitchen, in the third Beverley, had overheard the distress call, and landed to offer support. His arrival was also not welcomed by the Saudis, and actually raised the temperature of proceedings. However, he was able to leave squadron engineers, who would eventually change the failed engine and rectify several other technical issues. To paraphrase Sqn Ldr Hitchen, "I was ordered to leave Jeddah by several armed soldiers. I attempted to persuade them that I was 'outside crew duty time', but the Kalashnikovs were cocked – so I left!"

During the protracted exchanges between the crew of XM103 and the locals, bad weather approached from the west. Suddenly, all of the conditions that we had experienced in flight fell upon Jeddah. Torrential rain, hail, and strong gusting winds hit the area, with 'biblical' violence. The navigator has a lasting impression of the air engineer who, while sitting on an engine cowling, trying to stop it from being washed away, was swept along on a flood of surface water, to be stopped only by an obstacle at the edge of the dispersal. Eventually, we were taken to a hotel, and remained under armed guard, until British officials arrived on the scene several hours later. The following day, an Argosy arrived with an engine and spares from RAF Muharraq, Bahrain. The Argosy crew reported that one of our aircraft had been fired upon over Egypt; we thought this to be unlikely, but believed that the effects of the storm might have some bearing on the matter. Uncertainty thrived for at least a couple of days, because it was unclear if the Egyptians would permit the Beverley to complete the route over their territory. Furthermore, the crew received more confused messages about the progress of the other two aircraft, both of which had apparently run into serious problems that could make overflight of Egypt problematic.

Radio and signal communications kept the crew alert and busy during their four days in Jeddah. It appeared that the first aircraft had indeed suffered significant damage in the storm, but had been able to continue to El Adem. There was damage to flight deck windows, the astrodome, and to the airframe; any aircraft other than a Beverley might well have been unable to continue. The last aircraft had indeed been intercepted by Egyptian fighters and fired upon. This news generated unease amongst the crew of XM103, with future imagined problems occupying their minds. After the uneasy crossing of Egyptian airspace, RAF Transport Command ordered Sqn Ldr Hitchens to land at El Adem. He was later to write in his log book, 'Beverley attacked by two Egyptian MiGs – one air-to-ground rocket salvo, and two cannon/tracer attacks.' His story is worth the telling, but that is for another occasion, and better told by Sqn Ldr Hitchens himself; I hope he will not mind me quoting him.

On 10th November, XM103 was able to depart for Malta. Cleared to overfly Egypt en route, the tension was palpable on the flight deck until they cleared the Egyptian border with Libya. A clearer understanding of the Egyptian aggression was gained when the crew could see the bomb craters and damage on Luxor airfield, caused by Israeli attacks in June earlier that year. An hour or so after flying overhead El Adem, the crew were instructed to return to El Adem for debrief. The navigator told Flt Lt Barton that they had passed the El Adem/Benghazi critical point, and the captain informed El Adem that he was continuing to Malta. Amazingly, the flight progressed without further query from El Adem. As if they had not already experienced enough excitement for one trip, XM103 lost an engine 100 miles to the southeast of Malta. Fortunately, a quick fix overnight, performed by the crew's new complement of squadron engineers, enabled the aircraft to depart for Istres, and then RAF Abingdon, the following day (11th November1967).

The final chapter is a confirmation of 'anecdotal stories' told about Beverleys flying up the Rhone valley into the Mistral, the effect of which is a strong headwind (in the order of 100 knots) which, for northbound aircraft, can seriously reduce their groundspeed. On departure from Istres-le-Tube military airfield, northwest of Marseilles, the surface wind was northerly at 40 knots, and the velocity increased rapidly with height. The navigator took up his alternative station in the nose of the aircraft to map read; the view was panoramic. After taking a couple of routine fixes, he calculated that the groundspeed of the aircraft was 30 knots! Obviously this had to be wrong, so he repeated the process to find that the groundspeed was 28 knots, representing a headwind in excess of 100 knots. Looking at the valley below, he spotted a train which was rapidly overtaking them! Then he spotted a car on the main road, and it too was leaving them behind! Somewhat agitated, he informed the captain, who dryly replied, "What would you like me to do, Nav, land and taxy? I could make another 40 knots on the road." The Mistral had struck again, but Flt Lt Barton had seen it all before. Once over the Massif Central, and out of the effects of the Mistral, the groundspeed increased to 120 knots. The flight from Istres to Abingdon took four hours, fifty minutes. Overall the planned two-day trip from Aden to England took a challenging six days.

Postscript:

84 Squadron's Beverleys were flown back from Aden to the UK, only to be assigned to the scrapyard. They were delivered to 27 MU, RAF Shawbury, where they were all chopped into scrap metal. One has to wonder why they were not scrapped in Aden!?

Credit: Arpingstone/Wikipedia

Credit: Roy Harper

Contamination

You may wish to sidestep this yarn if you don't have a robust (military) sense of humour – not to say a strong stomach - for the sting in the tale!

If you are familiar with the story of "Operation Attune", which featured in Out of the Blue Too, you will know that the RAF operated the Victor SR2 in the "sniffing" role, which entailed deliberately seeking out, and flying through, the clouds left by atmospheric testing of atomic/hydrogen bombs. We would then take samples of the residue, with devices attached to the outside of the aircraft, and return triumphant to base.

As with that earlier tale, on this occasion we were tasked to operate out of Lima airport, Peru and, because we often had to get to the notional limiting altitude (it wasn't in fact the absolute limit) of 56,000 feet, we were kitted up in both "g" pants and the Partial Pressure Suit, which was an inelegant garment like a bulky flying suit, with the legs cut off well above the knees. The logic was that the combination of the two pieces of kit would keep us more or less intact in the event of a loss of cabin pressure at those altitudes, when we would also have high-pressure oxygen squirted into us, to provide adequate breathing. By the time you add some long-legged underwear and vest, and then a flying suit, you can see that we had become fairly bulky individuals.

We took off in high expectation of finding a good sample when, during the climb, our stalwart Air Electronics Officer (AEO), who was already quite a large chap, shamefacedly admitted that he was suffering from the local "Delhi Belly", which rejoiced in the name of "Inca's Revenge." The aircraft, whilst a triumph of late 1940s design, had not been built around toilet facilities, but the need was desperate. Fortunately, if that's the word, we had several very large and strong polythene bags, which were there in case the inside of the aircraft became contaminated, and we had to put portable stuff into them, so that they could be carried away for decontamination. So, very reluctantly, our AEO climbed into one of the bags and sorted the problem. We now had a contaminated cockpit, and the rest of the flight had to be on 100% oxygen! So, naturally, what happened next was that we hit the strongest source of radiation that our crew had ever come across. As the AEO, who controlled the scoops, very rapidly kept ratcheting up the scale to measure the radiation, he eventually ran out of high-level scales to select! The drill was to select 100% oxygen (so that we would not breathe in any particles) and Return to Base soonest. Well, the first action was already completed, thanks to our crew-member, so the flight home was uneventful.

The thing is - you soon become aware of who loves you when you pitch up with a "hot" aircraft. Our welcoming crew chief, who met us on the ramp with his Geiger-counter, was not impressed - he just turned around and went back to our crew facilities. We were then instructed to place everything we could into the (remaining) polythene bags, climb out of the aircraft, and go straight to our own personal decontam tents and procedures. Not exactly routine, but not unknown on these flights.

The sting in the tale? ALL the bags had to be sealed in lead-lined containers, and shipped back to an atomic facility in Southern England where, some weeks later, they would be opened and disposed of. Not a job for the faint hearted!

Credit: Author

Diplomatic Dealings In Angola

Africa was never my favourite destination on the Hercules although, at times, there were some positive moments. Battling with poor Air Traffic Control, the corruption, the sometimes violent weather, and the dreaded mosquitos did not make for the most pleasant experience. On one of these flights, my crew and I were sent to Angola, to make a delivery of diplomatic bags and supplies to the British Embassy. This was my first, but not my last, visit to the country.

Angola had originally been ruled by the Portuguese; the country gained independence in 1975, but only after 14 years of the Angolan Independence War. This was fought by the Portuguese Forces against the People's Movement for the Liberation of Angola (MPLA) and the National Union for the Total Independence of Angola (UNITA), who were backed by the National Front for the Independence of Angola (FNLA). A change in Government in Portugal halted war operations, and a peace agreement was signed between all parties in Jan 1975. However, later in 1975, the war started again, with the MPLA fighting against UNITA for control of the country. Many other factions and countries became involved, either in direct fighting or in providing weapons and other supplies. The Soviet Union and Cuba supplied and supported the MPLA, and the US supported UNITA. The war continued, apart from some fragile periods of peace, for almost 27 years, finishing in 2002.

It was during a short ceasefire that the crew and I were sent to Luanda and, as you can imagine, an overnight stop was not in the plan! We approached Angola from the east, from our previous destination, so had quite some time overflying Angolan territory. There was not a lot to see, apart from a country covered predominantly by trees. On arrival in Luanda, we could spot several missile and gun sites surrounding the airfield, some military aircraft, obviously Russian, and a few civilian aircraft. As we cleared the runway and taxied to our parking spot, I called the crew to the cockpit window, as I was witnessing a sight I had never seen before. At an intersection of taxiways, a Boeing 707 – a rather aged airliner - was waiting for us to pass by. It certainly showed its age, looking extremely dreary and, on closer inspection, I could clearly see green mould around the rivet lines of the fuselage. I waved to the two local pilots, who were visible through their windscreen. As we passed by the nose, we could not help but notice that the outer port engine had been stripped of its cowlings, and on display was a bare engine, showing the inlet guide vanes, the pipework and ancillary equipment. I have no idea if the engine was working or not; maybe the pilots didn't either, but they managed to take off without any problem! At least it lightened up what, up to now, had been a slightly serious cockpit.

We were met by a number of local military personnel, some armed with the infamous AK47. First up the steps was an officer in dark green uniform, who, we determined, was a member of the MPLA. He was followed by another officer in a lighter-camouflaged uniform, obviously a member of UNITA. There began a lengthy period of formalities. We had hoped that the British Embassy staff would be in attendance to smooth the procedures, but regrettably they were nowhere to be seen. It didn't take long for the inquisitive officers to enquire as to why we were landing in Luanda, and what we were delivering to the Embassy. They wanted us to unload the packages and diplomatic bags, and for them to be opened and inspected. Explaining that protocol (The Vienna Convention) did not permit the opening of diplomatic bags did not seem to change their minds. However, after some minutes of diplomatic conversation, I persuaded the UNITA officer, who was of a senior rank to the MPLA officer, that maybe they should request more advice. He agreed, and made a radio call to request a more senior officer to attend.

We could not understand why the British Embassy staff had not made an appearance and, in the days of no mobile phones, there was no quick way of contacting anyone. As fortune would have it, before the more senior officer arrived, two members of the Embassy finally appeared, apologising for their late arrival, but explaining that they had also succumbed to the rigours of the regimes. I quickly summarised our predicament, and was informed that the staff would attempt to sort the issues out. We also needed to file a flight plan to escape, so one of the embassy staff went with my co-pilot, as he was understandably not keen to leave the relative safety of the aircraft on his own. We waited and waited, and finally the couple arrived back. The co-pilot had collected several stamps on the flight plan, and had been relieved of quite a number of US dollars in fees, not unusual for most countries in Africa.

The Embassy staff bid us farewell, and were escorted away to complete whatever paperwork the locals needed for them to escape back to their hideaway. We had declined their very kind offer of staying the night, and seeing the sights of

Luanda, in favour of beating a hasty retreat. We closed up the aircraft as quickly as possible, as it was time to get the hell out. The co-pilot called for start clearance and - yes, you guessed it - there was no answer. We tried several times, with no success. We tried the other radio set, and again there was no answer. Then we heard a Russian aircraft call for start clearance, and receive an immediate acknowledgement. I called the Russians and asked them to relay for us and I will never forget the reply. "For You, Ascot, It Is Too Late." Note: we were using an Ascot (civilian) callsign. I looked at the others, bemusedly, and asked what the hell they thought he meant by that? We tried again to contact ATC, without success, so we had two choices: start up and go without clearance; or play it correctly, and walk to the tower, which was not too far away, to find out what the problem was. We opted for the latter at this stage. The co-pilot was volunteered, on the premise that he knew where to go. However, as a very unhappy co-pilot was about to leave, we finally made contact with the tower, and were given start clearance for our destination, Ascension Island.

On departure from Luanda Airport, I decided that we would make a rapid turn out to sea, away from the gun emplacements and missile sites, which we hoped were not in a serviceable condition. I held the Herc down quite low until a reasonable distance from the field, before starting a slow climb. Finally we were clear, and heading for some normality. A night in Ascension Island was indeed very welcome, as we were now heading back to the UK with one final stopover in Dakar, Senegal. The crew had a pleasant evening, and were able to relax and enjoy a few beers.

However, the following morning, I assembled the crew and informed them that I had been contacted by the duty operations officer, and that we had to return to Luanda. I explained that the British Embassy staff, and the diplomatic bags and freight, had been impounded at the airport, and no further action would be forthcoming without us returning to Luanda. The MPLA and UNITA had not opened the diplomatic bags, in accordance with the Vienna Convention Agreement, but they would not permit the freight and bags to be taken by the Embassy staff. We had to return to Luanda to collect the items, and only then would the Embassy staff be permitted to return to the Embassy in Luanda. I watched the crew instantly change from upbeat mode to downbeat mode and, to a man, they said "You are joking, aren't you"? "No", I said, "we are heading south again."

There followed quite a prolonged silence. Knowing that we were heading north, I couldn't keep the jape going for too long, but it was fun while it lasted, watching grown men uttering so many expletives. I did have to buy beers at our stop in Dakar, but it was unquestionably worth it.

To this day I still wonder what was meant by "For You, Ascot, It Is Too Late."

Credit: Les Rickman

You Did Say Warsaw!

(A Saga Continued)

With that first shake of the head on rising from my pit, where...? Ah, Bautzen, east of Dresden in Germany, and still one leg to go to get my steed, a Buchon 109 (RR Merlin-powered Messerschmitt 109) to Warsaw. I was in company with a Kiwi chum (mate!), who was flying a Mk IX Spitfire, and we had started this trek yesterday in Sion, Switzerland. Over breakfast, John and I looked at a rather grey overcast sky but, ever optimistic, we decided to get to the airfield and prep our aircraft. Our friend in the Air Traffic Control (ATC) Tower was again most helpful, and got as much met information as he could for our flight across Poland to Okecie International Airport at Warsaw. Still very overcast, and with poor visibility, we rolled our aircraft out of their old, soviet-style shelter, more in hope than expectation – the 10 o'clock clearance was going to be a push (in decades of flying had I not learnt!). The yellow stripe down my back, which was getting wider with advancing years, won the day, and it was back to our friend in the Tower for another cup of coffee. But, within the hour, the sky was much brighter, if still overcast, that lemming-like desire to 'get on' overpowered the yellow stripe and, by 1115, our two Merlins crackled into life.

Anyone who thinks aeroplanes don't have moods has never flown a 109, and today my aircraft would obviously rather have stayed warm and snug in its shelter. The wind was not bad, but a little off the centreline compared to both sorties of the previous day. The aircraft did a vicious swing as the tailwheel broke ground, which gave me an unrequested view of one side of Bautzen airfield, followed immediately by the scenic vista on the other side of the airfield, as it went the other way. With a mental note to stick pins in an effigy of Willy Messerschmitt later, for not providing an adequate rudder, I wrestled the aircraft airborne. Pretty it was not. John quickly slid up in the Spitfire, and I could see him positively laughing – you can go off Kiwis. However, there was not enough time to mentally debrief the take-off, as we were already running into a lowering cloud base, with visibility that was not brilliant. John quickly slipped back into long line astern – sensible move, as it gave me manoeuvre room, and he could look through me and perhaps have a split second to avoid the tree that I was going to hit! It was only 18 nautical miles to the Polish border, and already I was seriously considering doing a 180 and returning to Bautzen. But it was lifting, or at least not getting worse and, just about coincident with the border, the cloud disappeared and we spat out above the flat Lower Silesian expanse of Poland.

While the cloud had disappeared, the visibility was still not brilliant, and we eventually settled at about 3000 feet; this gave me the best combination of available visibility, combined with the chance of seeing the main ground features. The previously- mentioned appalling forward view from the 109 in a tail-down attitude is not much better in the cruise, with the long nose and a front windscreen that is reminiscent of a letter-box. And, oh for the lovely 'P' Type compass that was in the Spitfire (remember this also in the Chipmunk?), but I had to make do with an E2b (little domed standby compass), and a gyro direction indicator – which, to be fair, did not drift that much. And… confession… I did have a very small, first-generation GPS, which had a screen about the size of a business card, and which dropped off line with monotonous regularity. Mind you, I was amazed that it worked at all in the Faraday Cage metalwork structure of the 109 cockpit – so, very much map-and-stopwatch, with the GPS an occasional confidence booster, to reassure me I was still somewhere in the northern hemisphere. It also occurred to me that, if the engine quit, I would have to force-land the first 109 variant in Poland since… Big black crosses on the wings?... Pitchforks? Nah! Now, concentrate on the navigation. Poland is really pretty flat in the north, and more heavily wooded than I had expected, and navigation that day was challenging, but my first major check feature came up on time, although we were a couple of miles south of track. At my next major check, I was still south of track, just to the north of an industrial town called Lodz - 20 minutes flying time to Warsaw. About this time, I checked in with Warsaw, and they said, in not very understandable English – at least with my radios – to hold at 'Woods?' or was it 'Wudz?' I asked several times to 'Say again', while doggedly doing what any aviator does, flying a short range aircraft – keep heading towards my destination. Eventually, I clued up that the aforementioned 'Lodz' was in fact this mystical place 'Wudz' but, by this time, I was well down-track and, in the now further-reducing visibility, and I was locked on to a railway line that I knew went absolutely straight into Warsaw – I was not going back to Lodz!

Suitable bleating about fuel again did the trick; we were allowed to edge our way towards the airport, and held on a very wide base leg for runway 33. I could see a Boeing on finals to land, and was surprised when, almost immediately, we were given clearance to make our approach. I was actually concerned about wake turbulence, but this worry was quickly overtaken when the controller made it clear that this was not an approach to land but to "please make a flypast of the ATC Tower" – a beat up in other words! I pushed the throttle up, noted that the Spitfire had slid up into wide echelon starboard and, having located the tower to the west of the main runway, flew past pretty quickly but at a height and distance that I felt was not unreasonable for doing something that would normally get me locked up. I called 'Downwind to land', but was met with a further call from ATC, asking for a further fly-by, but this time "closer and lower!" I said this would be the last pass, as fuel was now beginning to get a bit low, and I was also mindful of the increasing number of airliners holding above. Closer and lower it was, and the balcony of the tower had a large crowd of people waving enthusiastically... Lord only knows who was controlling the aluminium cloud above Warsaw. There was a tightening crosswind; however, while the touchdown was a knot or two fast, it was a 'greaser'... but, ever-ready to prove the superiority of machine over man, the Buchon swung really hard to starboard and, despite full left rudder, was still heading some 20 degrees off the centreline. Large civilian airports have one very important feature which military airfields do not – high speed exits from the runway. An exit was conveniently lined up with my independent-minded aircraft and, to the casual observer, my departure from the runway was no more memorable than for being a bit fast!

My 'chum', who had set me the original task, was on the apron to welcome us, and he seemed well-pleased that we had arrived – so was I...! It was Wednesday, and the display at Deblin military airfield (20 minutes flying time to the south of Warsaw) was not until the weekend, so the prospect of a relaxing couple of days in the Polish capital was at the front of my mind. I should have seen it coming... I really should have seen it coming. With his most engaging smile, my chum – who was organising this mass push to the air show at Deblin – asked, almost casually, if I would mind heading back to UK and picking up the Hawker Sea Fury. I actually laughed, because he was obviously pulling my leg; but, he had made this request as if he was serious... and he was! An hour later, I was in the international departure lounge and, two hours later, I was winging my way back to Heathrow. A night in my own bed was welcome, but my long-suffering wife was not best pleased when her initial thought that I was back early (shopping, see kids, spend money etc etc) was dashed as I said I was going back to Poland the following day – or so I thought; silly boy!

An early rise, and a 45-minute trip to Cranfield, where I had positioned the Sea Fury just a week or so earlier. The promise that I would be met by one of the engineers, with the aircraft fuelled and ready to go, did not happen and, when he did turn up, it was clear that he had only just heard of the change of plan. A good chap nonetheless, and he quickly set about preparing the aircraft, while I did some further route planning – my initial thought of straight-lining from the other side of the English Channel was really a non-starter. Some of the most congested airspace in Europe, and the pleasures of marginal weather in the German Ruhr, persuaded me that looping north through Holland, for my first stop at the Friesland Airport of Groningen/Eelde, was my best bet. The total journey was over 800 nautical miles and, even with the speed of the Sea Fury, the late start was probably going to mean a night-stop somewhere en route. Many pilots will tell you that the most difficult part of aviation is the messing around on the ground and, true to form, when the magnificent Centaurus radial engine growled into life, I was back in my comfort zone. Not too comfortable though, as the 2400 hp in the engine has to be managed carefully but, in truth, the Sea Fury is a gentleman's aeroplane and, notwithstanding normal prudence on the ground, it is beautiful to fly. After take-off, reducing the engine boost back to cruising power and setting the propeller into automatic, the Centaurus settled to a reassuring purr.

She really is quick for a prop aircraft, and I am soon negotiating the gap between Luton and Stansted and setting track direct for Calais. And joy, unlike the 109, I can actually see where I am going, as the nose slopes away from the cockpit to the massive five-bladed prop. The Fury quickly eats up the miles to Calais, and then it is a left turn up the coast of France, through a bit of Belgium, and then I am weaving my way through the various airfields and restricted areas to the south east of Amsterdam. The weather stays fine and, for a while, a Dutch F16 fighter saddles up on my starboard side before, with a cheery wave, the pilot breaks away in hard turn, with reheat glowing and massive streamers coming off the wings – fond memories! An hour and a half out from Cranfield, I am calling Groningen/Eelde approach frequency and, a few minutes later, I am cleared for a run-and-break to land on Runway 05. I say to Air Traffic that I would prefer 01, which is right into the fresh wind, but am advised that there is temporary work in progress. No problem, and with judicious aileron into wind and a 'wheel' landing rather than a 'three pointer', the Sea Fury runs out down the runway pretty straight, despite the crosswind. I am greeted by the Airport Manager, Fokker (yes, like the aircraft company), an old friend who quickly gets the message that I am pushed for time, and he sets about getting fuel bowsers and the like. Despite the efficiency of my turn-round, I am now going to be pushed to get to Warsaw, and I flight-plan to Poznan in East Poland – with an alternate of one of the many airfields to the north of Berlin. Once again, the Centaurus growls into life and, with a wave to my old friend, I am off. The wind is now starting to blow a hooligan from the north, so I once again ask if runway 01 is available. 'No sir!' comes the cheerful reply, from the man warm and snug in his centrally-heated ATC Tower, "The work party are still painting white lines." Ah well, a careful take-off with not-excessive power on this long runway should not be a major problem... should it? And it wasn't. Airborne, gear up and ease the power... why hasn't the gear moved?! Ah, hydraulic failure... that will do it.

How things can change in a scant few seconds, as now I am confronted with a crosswind landing in a heavy aircraft with hydraulic failure – but at least the gear is down! I declare an emergency and, while my plea for the into-wind runway gets a more helpful response from warm-and-comfy man in ATC, he still can't get the kit off the runway for 10 minutes. Too long, with the potential for hydraulic oil sloshing around a hot engine bay, so I turn downwind to land on Runway 05 – wind now 40-50 degrees from the left, at 22 gusting 25 knots, and a thin film of hydraulic oil beginning to make the windscreen like a frosted bathroom window. Thank you, God, and thank you Mr Hawker, for designing such a great aeroplane – the Sea Fury runs straight as a die, not helped, I am sure, by my enthusiastic flurry of control inputs; I turn off the runway at the end, using the last of my brake pressure, and gratefully close down.

Fokker is quickly alongside my aircraft, in his airfield vehicle with more flashing lights than an American police car and, almost as quickly, the aircraft is under tow back to the main apron. My main problem is not breaking my neck climbing down from the high cockpit on an airframe covered in very slippery oil. The Sea Fury is going nowhere without some serious engineering work so, after it is safely parked, I am back to considering 'Plan B'... or possibly 'Plan C'... even 'D.' Since Monday, I have been from the UK to Sion in Switzerland to Augsburg in Germany to Bautzen to Warsaw, back to UK, and now Groningen in Holland. It is now Thursday and, if it wasn't for the fact that my original aircraft, the 109, is now in Warsaw without a pilot, I would hop a flight back to UK, to be in the Pub for Friday night! A flurry of phone calls to my chum in Warsaw confirms that the Sea Fury is dead, and I now have to get to Warsaw by other means from the wilds of Friesland. Fokker to the rescue... seemingly in a trice, I am booked on the local commuter airline out of Eelde the following morning to Amsterdam, to connect with a KLM flight to Warsaw... simples! Of course, Fokker puts me up for the night, and I enjoy the most relaxed and pleasant evening with him and his delightful wife – and an outstanding wine cellar.

Bidding a fond farewell to Fokker the following morning – aviation needs people like him – I was tossed around in a Shorts commuter aircraft, doubling up as a furniture van, for the brief journey to Amsterdam. The following flight was much more comfortable and, for a while, I was quite relaxed – but it couldn't last, and it didn't. Arriving in the early afternoon, I was met by my chum, the organiser, who nearly had steam coming out of his ears. Apparently the 109 and Spitfire should have been at Deblin – the display airfield, about 20 minutes flying time south of Warsaw – that morning. John, my Kiwi pal, who was flying the Spitfire, looked his normal, calm and relaxed self – he could afford to be, he had been swanning in Warsaw for the last two days, while I rushed around Europe with my hair on fire. Anyway, with reassurances that we would get the aircraft to Deblin soonest, we were strapping in about an hour later. Even the short flight to Deblin was not without a bit of fun – follow the Wisla River for 20 minutes and, at the town, Deblin, with the large railway junctions, the airfield is just to the east. Despite calling on every frequency we had been given, we could elicit no response from ATC so, double-checking we were in the right place and that we were not arriving in the middle of a practice display, we landed. Nobody seemed in the least bit interested in getting us to parking, although there was huge interest from people in general. So, we just parked near some other aircraft which looked like they were visitors, and shut down. For once, we were in the right place and, after a few moments, we were enthusiastically greeted by some Polish Air Force officers, who were much more interested in looking at our aircraft than giving us any idea what, where and when we should be doing. An interesting weekend ahead!

We did, eventually, ascertain a sort of programme and timings of briefings and, importantly, where we would accommodated. In this we were ably helped by a very old friend of mine, an RAF Group Captain (the co-Editor of this book no less), who was at Deblin with a joint RAF/industry sales team. We found our beds, met up with some of the other pilots from our group – we had an assorted collection of aircraft from my 109 up to and including a Hunter – all having arrived from various locations. There was an arrival party if I recall correctly, and we finished up in a hostelry in Deblin town; but, while our hosts seemed to have prodigious appetites for vodka, we were actually (out of character) quite sensible, and were all in our pits at a good hour. Saturday dawned, pretty grey and overcast but flyable, and we eventually found the obscure block where we were to be briefed for the day. This was new territory for the Polish Air Force, as the airshow was the first in Poland since the demise of the Warsaw Pact, and they were keen to get it right. I thought they really did quite well, although application of the rules owed quite a lot to, shall we say, 'pilot interpretation.' John and I were down to open the show in the Spitfire and 109, and it is worth explaining that John's Spitfire was in the wartime colours of a Polish Squadron in the Royal Air Force, and my 109 was in a standard wartime Luftwaffe scheme.

I taxied out past the Polish President's enclosure, where there were a mass of dignitaries, plus a host of visiting NATO senior officers – many of whom I recognised. The general public crowd was truly massive. I got airborne at show start-time and, for the next few minutes, below the overcast, I 'attacked' the airfield with the occasional rolling manoeuvre to show off the aircraft. The Spitfire then scrambled and intercepted me and in the 'combat' – which was me leading John in a tail chase – I eventually switched on my smoke generator, and disappeared over the perimeter, having been 'shot down', leaving the

Spitfire to complete a couple of victory rolls. I then discreetly landed, while the Spitfire completed his show. Almost as soon as we landed, we were invited by a very smart officer to accompany him down to the VIP enclosure, where the Polish President wished to thank us for our display. The President was well fuelled by hospitality drink, and proceeded to give John and myself big hugs and an effusive address in Polish, which I can only assume was thanks for our efforts; separation only became possible when the next noisy aircraft got airborne. I was then tapped on the shoulder and, turning around, there was a Luftwaffe General who I knew well from my very recent NATO appointment. After pleasantries he said "Why does the 109 always lose?!" I replied "Kurt, I was fighting a Spitfire in Polish colours in front of the Polish President and two hundred thousand Poles, what would you do?" After a moment's thought he smiled and said "I would lose!"

The party that night exceeded the one the preceding evening by any scale you wish to use, and the Poles celebrated a very successful day in their own inimitable style. I didn't last much past 9 o'clock, which was just as well, as it gave me a solid eight hours kip, and I awoke surprisingly fresh and with no vodka headache. The programme for Sunday followed the same line as the day before, and John and I completed it successfully, but already our managing pilot was looking to get the aircraft back to UK. Kiwi chum John was planned to go out from Warsaw by scheduled airline later that evening, and the Spitfire was to be flown back to UK by another friend of mine from Norway – with me again in the 109. The weather to the west was not looking good, but the best line (or, more accurately, least bad) was back through central Germany, despite the challenge of the Ruhr. So, after our display, the aircraft were refuelled and, as soon as we could, we set off with, this time, – relief – Rolf leading in the Spitfire. We were heading once again for Bautzen, where John and I had night-stopped the previous Tuesday. Rolf was right on the metal with his navigation and, in reducing cloud base and a darkening sky, we dropped into Bautzen, with our Merlin exhausts beginning to show flames in the dim light. As soon as we had refuelled and put our aircraft to bed in their warm shelters, the heavens opened and we were mighty glad to get to our hotel for another well-earned beer. The weather on the Monday morning was truly awful, and the forecast was dreadful for another two days. Neither Rolf nor I now had time to spare and, by 10 o'clock, we were heading for Dresden Airport to catch flights home – him to Oslo and me to Heathrow.

And so ended a rather eventful week's flying...! I wonder who took the next phone call to pick the 109 up..." It's where? Bautzen? Where the hell is Bautzen?" It wasn't me!

Credit: Tim Felce

Anyone For Cricket...?

My last posting in the RAF saw me spending a lot of my time at JFACTSU (Joint Forward Air Control Training and Standardisation Unit) at RAF Leeming. Now, very few of those who were introduced to the dark art of Forward Air Controlling (FAC) actually arrived with an Air-to-Mud[1] background, so many had little idea what most of the squibs, and such like, that aircraft dropped on ranges actually looked like, let alone what they did when they really went "Bang." To remedy this, the school took it upon themselves to collect examples of much of the hardware that the pilots threw towards the ground (in the hope that they would get reasonably close to the target), in order to educate the tyro FACs.

Over the years, quite a nice collection of inert/training bombs, rockets and other projectiles had been collected, painted blue, and left around for students to look at, examine, generally admire, and ponder on what it would be like to be on the receiving end of them. In due course, they would have the opportunity to see what many of these examples could do in real life but, for now, they just toyed with these blue dummies. Note that little word: Blue. Generally, the colour of a projectile indicates the sort of weapon it is (well, NATO ones do) and blue was the colour of training or drill items (I assume that colour is still applicable).

One of the items on display was a round ball, about the size of a cricket ball and weighing 300gms-ish, with small lugs attached around its circumference. It was frequently to be seen being tossed from hand to hand between the students, or being spun as a spin-bowler might deliver a leg- or off-break in a cricket match. This item was actually a representation of the bomblet contained in a certain type of cluster bomb. When these bombs were dropped, the balls would be released from a selected height, and would spread along the flight path of the weapon, hopefully causing alarm and consternation to those in the target area. The lugs on these balls caught the air and spun the ball as it left the bomb, and this spinning motion armed the bomblet, which exploded when it hit something hard, scattering a lot of nasty shrapnel far and wide. Of course, not all bomblets exploded on contact; perhaps it wasn't a hard enough shock, or perhaps it had not reached a fast enough rotation to 'arm' before it reached the ground. This

---

[1] Air-to-Mud: Reference to close air support and similar roles that involve dropping bombs.

was a very good reason to treat any objects found near a bombing range as both real and live, and not to touch them until proven otherwise. However, all of ours were inert, so they could be handled safely - after all, they were painted blue.

In the late 1980s, there were considerable changes at JFACTSU; the unit was enlarged, new classrooms went up, and somehow we managed to get a number of additional bombs etc for the display. When they were delivered, one of the armourers who arrived with them took a good deal of interest in the collection of weaponry which we had acquired over the years. I was told he took a particular interest in our blue cricket ball, and that he went quite quiet. The cricket ball, and a couple of other items, were subsequently taken away, and replaced by similar looking items a little while later. I remember that the replacement ball was considerably lighter than the old one, and the dots that represented the ball bearing shrapnel were painted on rather than moulded into the surface. One wonders...

Chipmunks Can Be Very Useful…

I wish to set the record straight about a story which appeared in a recent book written by a Canberra QFI. The suggestion was that a very particular phenomenon was "discovered" by one of his contemporary QFIs on Glasgow University Air Squadron (UAS) in 1967 – a man who is, in fact, a long-lost friend of mine, whom I am still trying to trace. No offence to the writer of the previous claim, who could not have known – but the phenomenon was actually discovered two years before that - in Aberdeen UAS, operating at Dyce. I know! I was there! And it happened on the ground – not in the air!

I well remember sitting in the crewroom, indulging in the umpteenth NATO-standard coffee, and waiting for my turn to get airborne, when in came one of the QFIs well known to be a ratbag (albeit held in high esteem by the students) – who had just returned from a sortie with a student. He announced to the assembled students and staff (excluding the Boss, who was busy in his office) that, while his student was taxying into the dispersal from the runway, he had taken the opportunity to fully open the hood and stick his gloved hands out into the slipstream for an experiment.

"If you close your eyes, and hold your cupped (soft cape leather) gloved hands into the slipstream" he claimed, "it feels just like cupping ladies' soft upper superstructure." (well, ok, not his exact words….) Within seconds, the crewroom emptied, as the other staff and students commandeered all the available aircraft sitting on dispersal. A few short minutes after that, all the aircraft on the dispersal had disappeared – in the rush of staff and the more worldly of the students to check the veracity of this claim, while the less experienced students hoped to learn something of the highly desirable experience – even if only a simulation!

It didn't take more than another 15 minutes before the SATCO[1] was on the blower to the Boss in his office – demanding to know what the hell was going on, and why were all our Chipmunks taxying up and down the taxiways with two, and even sometimes four, hands waving out of the cockpits…

I learned a little more about life from that!

---

[1] SATCO: Senior Air Traffic Control Officer.

Incomers!

The strike squadron crewroom was about the size of a front room - very small. But this strike squadron was No 1 Squadron of the Sultan of Oman's Air Force (SOAF), operating Strikemasters at Salalah, in the southern Oman province of Dhofar. It was 1973, and insurgents had scored several successes in Dhofar, as they attempted to take over the country. The adoo (enemy) were hardly irregular forces. Tough, disciplined, well-armed and -trained, well-organised, they were highly effective combatants. They came in from across the border of southern Yemen, which I, and many others in previous days, had known as the Aden Protectorate. The Sultan's air force at Salalah, alongside the land forces, was playing a major part in operations to turn the tide. Aircraft on operations would be fired on, and sometimes hit - one was shot down later - but we didn't expect to receive such nastiness whilst on the ground at Salalah, in the strike squadron crewroom.

Next door to the Strikeys of 1 Squadron were two equally small crewrooms – No 2 Squadron for the Truckies, with their tactical transport Skyvans, and No 3 squadron for the helis, with their Agusta Bell helicopters. The stone-built ops block housing these small crewrooms was, itself, small and basic, but there was a war on and everybody got on with making the place, with its limited facilities, work well. In any case, pilots spent more time on airborne missions than they did in the crewrooms. An exception to this might be Strikey or Heli pilots on operational standby.

Whatever the high-performance aircraft we had flown before, we liked our BAC Strikemasters, an aircraft significantly different from the Jet Provost stable, where the design had started. The Strikemaster had become a small and agile ground attack aircraft with a big punch. It could carry and deliver an air-burst bomb, a ground-burst bomb, 16 rockets and 1,000 rounds of ammunition. There were eight aircraft at Salalah and, for me, although in a job with an office in the north at Seeb/Muscat, I could spend regular time at Salalah, where my previous trade in ground attack allowed me to take turn on operational standby in the small strike crewroom.

On most occasions, the action was up-country, amidst barren rocky hills and wadis[1]. But there was a day when the SOAF Salalah airbase saw the excitement. The coastal plain from Salalah rises gradually northwards for about 10km, before ending in an escarpment, from the top of which one could survey the whole of the territory running southwards towards the airfield. The base had been attacked from the plain in 1972 but, by March 1973, the adoo had obtained weapons with sufficient range to hit Salalah from the escarpment itself. I happened to be there when this occurred, and found myself at the receiving end.

Sitting in the crewroom on standby, there were shouts of "INCOMERS" and the unmistakeable thump-thump of mortar rounds all around us. The ops block had very thick walls, and we dived to the floor, keeping away from the windows. A door then opened, and the Pakistani barber rushed in. He was a friend to many of us who had sat in his chair, but was now very frightened, and joined the assembled company on the floor, loudly lamenting that his barber shop was being targeted. Through the same door then came a dishevelled 3 Squadron Heli pilot, with blood on his arms. This seemed bad, but we quickly learned that, on hearing the alert and keen to join in any action, he had rushed to the ops block on his motor scooter. On the way, and outside the barber's shop, he had driven over a mortar shell hole and fallen off. He, too, joined the rest of the growing company on the floor.

Eventually the shelling stopped. The ops room was picking up information that the attack had been mounted from locations atop that escarpment some 10km north, and exact positons were becoming known, thanks to observations from airfield ground defences. There was every chance that the adoo would have moved on, but the command decision was to respond with an appropriate show of force, and hit where they were known to have been. As four of us rushed out to the flight line, we could see that some aircraft, Strikemasters and helicopters, had been damaged by the shelling. But there were four intact Strikeys, and we 'scrambled.' It was a short sortie north, to mount rocket and gun attacks on the escarpment positions from which we knew the adoo had been so successful in rearranging the day at our airbase.

---

[1] Wadis: Valleys, ravines, or channels that are dry except in the rainy season (Arabic).

Following this event, minds at all levels became rapidly concentrated. Aircraft were more widely dispersed, and each was surrounded by a protective wall of sand-filled oil drums. Most significantly, to safeguard a target with such strategic importance, three key positions were established by troops on top of the escarpment. Salalah saw no more successful mortar attacks, but the adoo were still around on the escarpment, and Strikemasters continued to operate there, supporting the troops during frequent fire-fights. Superficial damage to the barber shop wall was repaired, and the heli pilot was fine, flying the same day, as the incomers had earlier interrupted his off-duty time.

Credit: Les Phipps

Heavens Above

I am reminded of a day, a long time ago, on a gunnery trip out of RAF Akrotiri, in Cyprus. My nose- gunner (pilot) and I had done a few quick passes on the gunnery target, and had a fair amount of gas left to play with. The jet had the gun pod on the centreline, but was otherwise clean.

'Let's see how high we can get this thing' said my airframe driver (pilot – again). Being, at that time, immortal, I said "Sure, why not", and off we set for the tropopause. The plan, such as it was, involved lighting the burners, a level acceleration to about Mach1.5[1], then a 3g pull to about 600 nose- up, then wait. Behind this plan was a complete dearth of research. All, however, went surprisingly well at first. The altimeter spun merrily upwards, the IAS[2] drifted backwards, and the sky took on a very dark blue hue.

After a while, we were pressure breathing[3], the Earth appeared curved, and a very long way down…..and the engines quit. My nose-gunner did the only sensible thing possible and gently, very gently, eased the stick forward, and the nose obediently but slowly headed back towards the horizon. The altimeter topped out at 67,000 feet before it started to wind back. The chances of relighting a RR Spey above 30,000 are pretty slim, so we waited for what seemed a very long time, watching the Mach-meter closely because the RAT[4] had a M1.1 limit, until the airspeed built up to something reasonable, and the Rolls Royce motors lit up with no problem. All that remained was to get back to Akrotiri on the gas available which, from that height with gravity on our side, was no problem.

That's the highest I've ever been and, since I'm now (just) outside the astronaut recruiting age bracket, that's the highest I'll probably ever go. There was no ADR[5] on the F4, so nobody was ever the wiser.

---

[1] Mach 1.5: One and a half times the speed of sound (which is Mach 1).
[2] IAS: Indicated Air Speed.
[3] Pressure breathing: Breathing high pressure oxygen to compensate for the thin atmosphere at high altitude.
[4] RAT: Ram Air Turbine – an auxiliary power plant that is operated by airflow.
[5] ADR: Air Data Recorder - records various operating parameters throughout a flight.

Kai Tak Circuit

The challenge of flying an approach to the old airport, Kai Tak, at Hong Kong was relished by those lucky enough to have the chance. There are plenty of videos (YouTube is your friend for this) of big airliners, threading their way between high-rise buildings on short finals, after flying the Instrument Guided System (IGS), a modified Instrument Landing System approach, which started at Cutters Island. Not many were specifically requested to fly a circuit inside the harbour, and instructed to "make as much noise as you can!"

My story starts well before the event itself. We were a Victor SR2 crew on a "Westabout" training exercise, which had us leaving from RAF Wyton and making our way around the world via Goose Bay, Offutt, Sacramento, Hawaii, Guam and Hong Kong. The plan was then to continue all the way round, and get back to Base after a couple of weeks or so. The purpose was to train crews in operating into unfamiliar airfields, which were usually unsupported by RAF ground crew. This meant that we, led by our Crew Chief, undertook the routine turnarounds of the Victor between flights. The secondary goal was to "Show the Flag."

Having got to Hong Kong, we had a couple of days off before we were due for the next leg to Singapore. However, the then Governor, having got wind of the presence of an RAF 4-Jet, passed the word that, before we set off for Singapore, we were to "Show the Flag" by completing a circuit inside the harbour and, as already stated, "make as much noise as possible", to show the continuing presence of the RAF at/passing through, RAF Kai Tak - simples! The harbour was wider then, and the skyscrapers not as high as the present day.

One slight additional factor was that I, the Squadron Boss's co-pilot and recently qualified in the Left Hand Seat, was now tasked to take the aircraft back to the UK. No worries - and it would be great fun to take off into the visual circuit within the harbour - quite a tight manoeuvre, but not too difficult - and then carry out a go-around and continue on plan. All went well and, at a sensible height, I carried out the go-around and had started to climb away when Air Traffic Control (ATC) called to say that "a panel" had fallen off the aircraft. Cue for immediate Mickey-taking of the Crew Chief, whose last act before climbing into the aircraft was to close the small panel through which the ground power was connected. We were less impressed at being instructed to go the American Clark Air Base in

Manila, the Philippines, which was over 2 hours away. The Boss kindly declined this offer, and said that we would burn off fuel to the Max Landing Weight, before landing back at Hong Kong.

Off we went to hold south of Hong Kong Island, out of everybody's way, and got on with fuel jettison/burn. Whilst there, ATC came back to us to announce that the panel was "about 10 feet by 5 feet" and that the RAF Engineer officer thought that "it was a bit of a wing flap." That changed things more than a little. If, for whatever reason, the flap had been torn off, we could no longer have too much faith in the other functions of the hydraulic system. Patently, we could not rely on the remaining flap, if that was what it was, nor the airbrakes or even the wheel brakes and nose-wheel steering. Complicating the issue was the fact that the runway was not overly long, and stuck out into the harbor, with little runoff on either side. So - the cunning plan was to reserve whatever hydraulic fluid we had left, for critical services of the wheelbrakes and the nose-wheel steering. This would make the approach more than usually demanding, and the nose-wheel steering was only operable from the left hand seat. Unsurprisingly, the Boss decided that he would now like to do the driving, so we had a convoluted dance of putting the ejection seat pins into both seats, (this rendered the seats inoperative) swapping places, and then taking the pins out again.

Then we tried a couple of approaches, without using the flaps or airbrakes. Not in itself a big deal, perhaps but, with a higher approach speed and uncertain braking, it was essential to get the speed accurate and to put the aircraft down right at the beginning of the runway. Trying to get in off a straight approach, over the high ground on the extended runway approach line, meant that we could only achieve the critical parameters if we flew with the throttles completely closed on finals. Glide-landing a largish 4-jet did not seem to be particularly attractive! The choice, then, was to use the IGS, which demanded a very accurate turn at relatively low altitude, so that we could line up and touch down in the right place. The brief was that, if we did, indeed, experience control difficulties once on the runway, I was to blow the canopy off, so that we could all get out before we went into the sea (our ejection seats would not work below 90 knots, and the rear crew had no ejection seats anyway). Naturally, there was, by now, considerable support from the crash team - this included two fire floats on either side and at the end of the runway and, as we touched down, two helicopters from the Search and Rescue squadron took station just off our wingtips, with the winchmen in the doors. It all went terribly well and, when we finally shut down, there was a very bedraggled-looking set of the remaining flaps on the port side hanging down. Off to the bar!

The sequel to the story is that the immediate assumption of the UK-based hierarchy was that we must have overstressed the aircraft with a rather-too-enthusiastic flypast. A unit enquiry was ordered and, because the Boss was very experienced, it took two weeks to find a more senior Wing Commander and get him out to Hong Kong. We therefore had to stay in Hong Kong for longer than originally planned - tough! As luck would have it, prior to the flight, I had just bought a Super-8mm movie camera, (this was a long time ago), and the Crew Chief had filmed the entire initial circuit and go-around. This showed conclusively that we had stuck to the rules!

Credit: Barbara Ann Spengler

Confidence Building

At the time, I was the pilot flight commander on a Nimrod squadron. One afternoon, the Squadron Commander called me to his office, and asked if I would have a full session in the flight simulator with one of the co-pilots, as his captain had assessed him as having a lack of confidence in flying the 'mighty hunter.' Naturally I agreed, and a date was set for the morning session in a couple of days' time. I should explain that the Nimrod MR1 simulator differed from some of the more modern ones, in that the control of 'the box' and training injections were from a separate, external control panel, run by permanent simulator staff members. The aircraft, as many will know, was based around the Comet Mk4C. There had been many changes to that aircraft: Spey engines, in place of the Avons; AC electrics, instead of the original DC; and the addition of an unpressurised weapons bay.

However, the main hydraulic systems were very much of the Comet era, consisting of 4 separate systems, known as Blue, Green, Red and Yellow. There was no manual reversion available for the flying controls, which were powered by the Blue system. The Green system powered the undercarriage, nose- wheel steering, bomb doors and wheel-brakes; it was also the back-up system for the flying controls. The Red system powered the undercarriage (lowering only), the wheel-brakes (no anti-skid), and the bomb doors for emergency ordnance jettison. The Yellow system provided 30-minute back-up for the primary flying controls, in the event of both a Blue and Green system failure. The Blue and Green systems were powered by 3 engine-driven pumps, the Red system was electric, and the Yellow system received its pressure from a large hydraulic reservoir. Got it?

So, on the sim sortie in question, I asked the co-pilot if he would like to fly the first or the second half of the session, and he elected to fly the second. Although our Squadron was St Mawgan-based, the sim sortie was based on Kinloss, so I climbed to the north-east, out over the Moray Firth, up to Flight Level 200 before a spot of general handling, and then elected to carry out a high-level TACAN[1] arc, positioning for the Kinloss 26 ILS. I wanted to keep it simple. The air traffic penetration configuration for the Nimrod was air brakes 'up', undercarriage down

---

[1] TACAN: Tactical Air Navigation aid.

and, as I recall, an IAS^2 of 250 knots. The co-pilot dropped the gear, I extended the air brakes, and we started down the dive arc. No sooner had we left FL200 than the engineer reported a total green system failure, followed rapidly by a double engine failure - leaving us on just 2 of the Speys, with the gear irretrievably locked down, and the air brakes similarly locked up. High drag, 50% power! Plenty of FRC^3 emergency drills for the co-pilot, but not much confidence building going!

We requested a diversion to the nearer RAF Lossiemouth, to be greeted by ATC's "Sorry, the runway's blocked at the intersection with the short runway - collision between a Buccaneer and a fuel bowser - suggest you continue to Kinloss." We intercepted the Kinloss localiser^4 and, just as the glide-slope^5 became 'live', we lost a further engine - so there we were, on a single engine, flapless and 'dirty.' I was still feeling quite confident of making it to Kinloss - but really p****d-off with the sortie profile, for it just wasn't what I had requested, and certainly didn't seem to be doing my fellow pilot's confidence any good. Nevertheless, he was coping well with the emergency drills. Then, to top it all, at about 300 feet, the final engine failed, and we came to a grinding halt amongst the approach lights.

I left my seat to storm out to the directing staff, ready to air my significant grievances - to find the Squadron Commander, the other Flight Commander, and the Navigator and AE Leaders, laughing like a quartet of drains. They had all been in the bar, saying goodbye in style to a departing colleague, and had decided to look in on my simulator session and 'have some fun' at my expense. As it happened, they had been amazed that I had managed to keep the beast in the air so long which, in turn, showed the co-pilot that there was nothing to fear. Maybe it wasn't such a pointless exercise after all... and I am glad to say that the co-pilot overcame his confidence deficit, and went on to become a very good maritime pilot and captain.

---

^{2} IAS: Indicated Air Speed.
^{3} FRC: Flight Reference Cards - contain routine and emergency actions.
^{4} Localizer: The lateral guidance element of an Instrument Landing System.
^{5} Glide-slope: The vertical guidance element of an Instrument Landing.

Junior Pilots Aren't Always Wrong

I recall that, in March 1970, XL 565, a recently refurbished Hunter T7, was allocated to No 8 Squadron in Bahrain. One morning, I was programmed, and duly authorised, for a ground-crew familiarization flight in this T7. After the normal formalities and briefings, we took off on what should have been a straightforward trip.

We flew round the north of Bahrain Island at about 500 feet, before turning south past Umm Al Naasan Island, where there was a notorious prison. The white-washed walls and battlements were clearly visible, as we sped by, with barely a thought for the inmates. This was by way of a bit of tourism for my passenger, who had brought along his camera, which was slung round his neck. We checked out the few bathers at the Sheikh's private beach on the south-west side of the island, and flew on south over the sea, past the Hawar Islands. After a spot of low-level manoeuvring, I opened up the throttle, and bumped the speed up to over 500 knots, just to give the Bernoullis[1] a good roasting to prepare them for the next bit.

The idea was to pull up gently to the vertical, and zoom to medium level for some general handling. As usual, there was a poorly defined horizon, with sea, sand and sky merging into a typical "goldfish bowl". We were soon through 10,000 feet. As we came "over the top", and the nose came down towards the horizon, there was a violent series of oscillations and bangs, as the aircraft departed from controlled flight. We were at about 12,000 feet, and several thoughts flashed through my mind, not least that intentional spinning (which this wasn't) was not permitted but that, if you were still spinning at 10,000 feet, you were supposed to abandon the aircraft, using the Martin Baker apparatus. I throttled back and centralised the controls, as per the drill, but this had no effect. The turn needle was jammed against its left stop, so I applied full right rudder, and the jet immediately stabilised into a dive at around 8,000 feet. Easing out of the dive, my passenger and I exchanged a few oaths, probably aimed at the marital status of this particular jet's parents. I had noticed that his camera was flailing around in the canopy during the event, so I deduced that this had been a fully-developed inverted spin. The rest of the trip proceeded normally, albeit in more conservative regions of the flight envelope.

---

[1] Bernoullis: A reference to Bernoullis' Principle that relates speed with pressure in a gas.

Signing in at the operations desk, I had a conversation with the authorizing officer along the lines that I thought the aircraft may be bent. What knew I, barely 6 months into my first tour, and how dare I blame the aircraft?! Get some time in! For my next trip, I was consigned to be the safety pilot for another chap's Instrument Flying, in the very same aircraft. A few weeks later, we underwent our periodic standardisation checks with the "Trappers". They were a great couple of chaps, who flew with most of us, and reported under their full title, The Central Flying School Standardisation Agents. Once we'd done our bit, the T7s were signed over for 208 Squadron to have their turn with the Trappers. Our Flight Commander seemed reasonably chuffed at his mass de-brief with us. At the end, he commented that it may not have gone quite so well for 208 Squadron. One of the trappers had been particularly unimpressed when one of their chaps had managed to inadvertently spin a T7 – the same aircraft.

Credit: Ronnie Macdonald

Job Done!

In July 2006, with the final flight of a Canberra PR9, the RAF ended 57 years of Canberra operations, the bomber originally intended to replace the Mosquito. The PR9 was undoubtedly the best version the RAF flew, and I know, because I was lucky enough to be posted onto these after doing my time with the Bucket of Sunshine (nuclear weapon) boys in RAF Germany. The PR9, you may recall, was listed as having a service ceiling of "over 60,000 feet." Yup, and the rest – 75,000 feet was the true figure, and I got up to 73,000, where you can see the dark blue of outer space all around you - at least, you can if you're the pilot in his bubble cockpit. We navigators, hidden in the nose cone, had only two extremely small side windows; our best view was downwards. So, some of my best shots were of things I did not get to see until the photos were developed.

At those altitudes, with the specialist camera we had, you could photograph the whole of the UK in very few runs; at least, you could if there was no cloud down there! Our biggest standard camera could mount a 48-inch lens which, producing 9-inch square negatives, could make for amazing detail. However, I was to discover that the RAF, as always, came up with highly creative alternative uses for our skills, "Special Flying Tasks" they called them! Here are four of those oddball jobs.

The first was in April 1974, and concerned the Danish Royal Yacht. They wanted us to film the puffs of smoke from a RN ship, giving a full royal gun salute to the Danish Royal Yacht, as she sailed out of the Thames. Think about this: ships move at maybe 20 knots at sea level, some one-tenth of our flying speed, and they wanted to capture the crew all standing to attention along the sides of the ships! We were given the approximate position and timings of the event; the rest was left to us. We chose a medium-range oblique camera, which would provide the equivalent of close-up photos; pass height around 1500 to 2000 feet, with the best flying speed for the 'task in hand' around 160 knots! We were in radio contact with the London Control air traffic control centre to enter the area, and then direct with the RN vessel; the ship passed us the low-level wind speed, their speed in the water, and the approximate time for the salute. We made a couple of test passes, as the RN ship was finalising its position for the actual gun salute; then, as they advised us of the actual gun-firing, we made our own final pass - my pilot adjusting our speed, in anticipation of the firing of the guns, and me setting the final controls of the camera. Given that I could not see the ships, I had to rely on the information from the pilot as to when to roll the camera. After landing, the film was processed, the Photographic Interpreters (PIs) inspected the individual photographs, and the best three were chosen. Some days later, we received a Telex from MoD, thanking us for our work, and informing us that the Danish Royal Family (and the crew of the RDY) were delighted with the framed photographs, sent as a memento of their visit to the UK. "Job Done!"

Job No 2 was in Northern Ireland. A telex arrived from the PR tasking cell at MoD, ordering a mission to carry out Infra-Red photography along the Northern Ireland/Eire border, trying to locate possible burial locations of murdered British soldiers. We were the duty crew; given the nature of the task, and the parameters of the infra-red camera, it was agreed that we should fly no higher than around 10,000 feet. Due to the sensitivity of the mission, only the military air traffic controllers (M-ATC) in NI, and our own PIs, were informed (it would be up to them to advise the local Civil Authorities, dependent on our proximity to the actual borders!). Very early in the day, we received the weather forecast, followed by a detailed briefing from the Intelligence Officer (IO). I was concerned that the prevailing winds would affect our endurance; given that we were flying at approximately 10,000 feet, our fuel consumption would be higher than normal and, as such, we might have to divert.

Just as we finished our flight planning, the IO came rushing in with new intelligence. The IRA had just received its very first shipment of Russian shoulder-launched SAM 7 missiles; these were capable of reaching aircraft up to approximately 20,000 feet! We could be very vulnerable. The Station Commander said that, in view of this, he would not expect us to fly the mission! After some debate, we decided that the IRA had not had sufficient time to get the SAM 7s 'on site,' nor sufficient training to fire them; we said that we wished to carry out the mission as planned.

We were in constant radio contact with the NI M-ATC. I map-read our routeing just inside the NI border and, as I had predicted, in order to fly the whole route, we did run short of fuel, so a diversion was inevitable. We completed the mission routeing, and declared a fuel emergency direct with the ATC at RAF Aldergrove. After landing, we reported to the Duty Operations Officer (DOO) at RAF Aldergrove, to request fuel. The DOO was very annoyed and indignant with us, saying that the airfield was a PPO (Prior Permission Only) unit and, as such, he was refusing to fulfil our request for fuel. My pilot and I agreed that I would deal with the DOO(!), while he went to instruct the local photo-technicians to download the exposed film and have it processed ASAP. I tried explaining the parameters of our mission to the DOO, and how it was extremely important that the film was downloaded ASAP, and passed to the PIs based at RAF Aldergrove, so that they could process it and send the final photos to the appropriate people based in NI; and, of course, the need for some fuel. He became obstinate, and said his authorities had not informed him of any such impending missions, and he would not co-operate. I said that I needed to talk with our authorising officer; after explaining the matter to my Station Commander, I handed the phone to the DOO, who went red in the face, and merely said "Yes Sir, we will provide all services as required."

However, whilst the duty officer provided what we needed, he still insisted that he would report the matter to his authorities, and complain about our attitude. I asked him if he had ever served in an operational role, and he grudgingly admitted that he had only ever flown in Transport Command aircraft, and never in difficult circumstances! My pilot oversaw the refuelling of our aircraft, while I met with the local PIs, to discuss what to do with the developed photos. Some days later, we received a telex from MoD, thanking us for our work, and informing us the photographs had helped them locate the graves, and also other 'Crime Scene Data.' Job Done!

The third job was in Belize in 1979, and involved the CIA. Recently, I was on a cruise from Miami to Mexico. As we neared some islands off Eastern Mexico, while sitting on the balcony of my cabin, sipping a drink and watching the sea and stars go by, I was reminded of a detachment to Belize in February and March 1979. We were carrying out Operation Bandicoot, the remapping of the Army training ranges in Belize. We had one Canberra PR9, and two aircrews. During such detachments, we always carried our full array of photo-cameras, ranging from the 4" (Low-Level Oblique), 9" and 12" Plate Mapping (Vertical photography), to the 24", 36" and 48" Medium- to High-Level Oblique cameras. All these cameras had specific 'bays' in which they could be fitted. Working with the detachment commander, local Army representatives, IO (Army) and detachment groundcrew, daily tasks were issued to maximise our progress, with the aim of finishing the operation early.

One day, I was asked to see the IO. He looked worried, and explained that the CIA had asked him if we could help to track down a shipment of drugs being transported from Guatemala, along the western Belize border, and into the Bay of Mexico for onward shipment by fast boats. The area in question is covered by jungle, with trees reaching nearly 200 feet in height, so the IO felt that this would prevent us from seeing anything. I explained the performance of our old-fashioned cameras, and how they ought to see through the upper canopy. So, we agreed to try and fit the largest (high-level) oblique camera we could into a low-level oblique bay, and use the 12" vertical camera to help identify our actual physical location on the ground; my idea was to fly along the route the CIA suggested, at around 10,000 feet, and take photos as follows: at the start of the route, the south-western border between Belize and North Guatemala, take a vertical shot; the pilot then to bank as far to the left as possible, thereby pointing the oblique camera downwards, toward the tree canopy; take at least 3 photo shots, level the aircraft and then take another normal vertical shot; check to ensure we stayed in Belize airspace(!); and perform the sequence again and again, until we reached the most north-eastern point heading towards the Bay of Mexico.

The task team were stunned by this suggestion, especially as it had never been tried before. I kept pointing out that this was a one-off situation, and we should show the CIA that we could do it. "Nothing ventured nothing gained," I said. "After all, we are the RAF photoreconnaissance specialists (experts?) and, if we can't do this, then who else can?" (Modesty was always one of my weaknesses). It was agreed that the photo-groundcrew would attempt to install the cameras, and that the IO would contact the CIA, to ascertain the window of opportunity for the task. We carried out the mission. The distance was not great but, given our strange flying attitudes, manoeuvres, and slow speeds, the sortie took 2hrs and 30 minutes. After landing, the photo-groundcrew worked as fast as they could to download the films and have them processed. Then the IO, the PIs and ourselves scoured the photos, and eventually found the trail of drug carriers down in the jungle. This was immediately reported to the CIA. It turned out we had also accurately photographed an awful lot of insects on the jungle floor - David Attenborough eat your heart out! Several weeks later, we received a telex from Belize, saying that the CIA were very grateful for our efforts, and that the mission had been successful. Job Done!

Finally, in June 1980, a telex arrived from the PR tasking cell at MoD: the special mission was to photo the Queen Mum's royal residence, the Castle of Mey, in very northern Scotland. It turned out that the Chief of Air Staff wanted the RAF to present the Queen Mum with a colour picture of the castle for her 80th Birthday, on 4th August 1980. They wanted the photo of the castle on a bright sunny day, with a few fluffy clouds in the background. Sounds easy, sitting behind a desk! I don't think anyone had explained to him just how temperamental the colour film we had was, though he probably had an idea that sunshine in the Highlands could be a tall order too! We chose a medium-range oblique-looking camera, which would provide the close-up photos from a height of around 1500 to 2000 feet. So, in between carrying out regular tasks and training, we watched the weather forecast for northern Scotland. On Thursday 19th June, the forecast looked excellent. We flew there at high level, conserving fuel, then let down to 2000 feet and circled around for some time, choosing the best cloud positioning and formation. In view of my lack of sideways-looking windows, I just had to rely on the information from my pilot as to when to roll the camera; precision was the essence of the day! After landing, the film was processed, the PIs inspected the individual photographs, and we all chose the best three; these were despatched to MoD post-haste. Sometime during September 1980, we received a telex from MoD, informing us that the Queen Mother had been presented with a framed photograph of her Castle of Mey. Perhaps, nowadays, they might figure it would be cheaper to commission Knight Frank, or Savill's Estate Agents to put a drone up. Job Done!

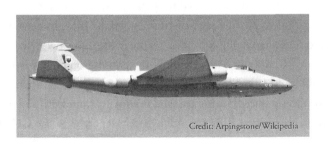

Credit: Arpingstone/Wikipedia

Close Shaves

Before I was selected for pilot training, I flew one tour as an air signaller on Shackletons, and it was whilst flying - or should I say 'being flown' - out of Kinloss that I had the first of two close shaves, neither of which was in any way within my control.

Pilots training to join the Shackleton force did their operational conversion at the MOTU (Maritime Operational Training Unit) at RAF St Mawgan, either on the T4 variant of the aircraft or, later, the Mk 2, both of which were tail-draggers[1]. On 20th April 1964, I was flying as rear crew on a conversion sortie for a pilot newly arrived on the squadron; he had graduated from the MOTU, and was converting to the Mk 3 aircraft, which had a tricycle undercarriage. He, with the Flight Commander in the right-hand seat, was carrying out stalling practice. We did a clean stall, with the stick-shakers operating, followed by another clean stall, but this time without the stick-shakers. Both were carried out without incident. The drama came when, during an approach-configuration stall (no stick-shakers), the port wing dropped; the pilot attempted to rectify this with aileron, the stall deepened and we went into a spin. Although we had carried out the HASELL[2] checks, I was actually standing in the galley, making a pot of tea! I can clearly remember looking directly down through the fuselage at the tops of the pine trees in the Loch Ness area, through the bomb-aimer's window, when as cool as a cucumber, the flight commander stated "I have control", and brought us back to safe flight - after which the new pilot safely carried out another gear-and-flaps-down stall. I really thought that my short flying career was coming to a rapid end!

The second incident occurred some six months later, on a flight back to Kinloss from RAF Ballykelly in County Londonderry, Northern Ireland. We had delivered a spares package to Ballykelly, and the navigator, our new flight commander, decided it would be good to return home via the Scottish Highlands, rather than by the usual Kipper Fleet[3] 'over the seas' route; so, we departed out of Loch Foyle and Magilligan Point, towards the Mull of Kintyre, in cloud at 1,000 feet. Quickly, the radar operator reported "Land on the nose at 30 miles" (a standard

---

[1] Tail-draggers: Slang for aircraft with main and tailwheel undercarriage configuration.
[2] HASELL: Height – Airframe – Speed – Engine(s) – Location – Lookout.
[3] Kipper Fleet: Affectionate (?) term for the maritime patrol fleet.

call), but was advised by the navigator that this was all right, as we were going to coast in at the Mull, and then fly up The Great Glen towards the Moray Firth. I was sitting in the starboard beam seat, mind in neutral, when there was a mighty roar of engines being taken up to full power - and we paralleled the bracken covered hill side, on which I looked down from no great distance at all, as we climbed to height. The navigator had flight-planned to climb from the Mull, forgetting that it extended well above the 1,000 feet at which we were in transit! Many years later, in June 1994, when the Special Forces Chinook ZD576 flew into the Mull while in cloud, with 29 fatalities, this incident came clearly back to mind.

À propos of nothing in particular, after I left the RAF, I flew Boeing 737s for Orion Airways. Most of our flying was holiday-associated, but one out-and-back trip was different from all the others: it was a trooper from London/Gatwick to RAF Gutersloh and return, participating in the major NATO reinforcement exercise, Exercise Lionheart. Our outbound passenger load consisted of 131 Gurkha soldiers, all wearing combat webbing and carrying their rifles. As part of the pre-take off passenger brief, the Senior Stewardess instructed the soldiers to "remain seated, with your weapon erect between your legs." Now, I wonder who thought that wording up?

Credit: Mike Freer

Missing In The South Atlantic

At midnight on Saturday 15th August 1987, an RAF Nimrod of No 120 Squadron, RAF Kinloss, took off from its Morayshire base, beginning one of the most remarkable, marathon, search-and-rescue missions on record. Over the next seven days, it was to search in excess of 200,000 square nautical miles, and burn more than 100,000 gallons of aviation fuel.

The story began a week earlier, at 0810Z on 8th August, when two Cessna 210 aircraft took off from Dakar in Senegal, on a ferry flight to Libreville in Gabon, West Africa, a journey of nearly 2000 nautical miles(nm). Both aircraft had been fitted with ferry tanks and, although their endurance was 18 hours, the pilots had flight planned for a 12 hour flight. Only one aircraft had a serviceable radio, and there was, therefore, a requirement for them to fly in loose formation, thus relying on only one pilot's navigation skill. The forecast weather conditions included a 20 kt tailwind, but the actual wind component was 20 kts headwind, with unusually strong northerly winds, associated with a very active Inter-Tropical Convergence Zone (ITCZ).

At 1430Z, the Cessnas reported at position Devli (0400N 0730W). This was the last routine message recorded. At 2240Z, 2½ hours after they were supposed to land at Libreville, a Mayday message was picked up on HF, by an AFFRETAIR DC-8 approaching Libreville. The DC-8 levelled at Flight Level 125, and attempted to gain radio contact on 121.5MHz, the VHF emergency frequency, but without success. It then flew to a position 100 nm West of Sao Tome (260 nm West of Libreville), but still could not get VHF contact; the DC-8 passed a number of VOR[1] and NDB[2] frequencies on HF, including the Sao Tome VOR, which has a published range of 200 nm, but the Cessna was unable to receive any of them. The DC-8 then, compelled by lack of fuel, landed at Libreville at 0110Z on 9th August, but remained in continual HF contact until shut-down. At 0410Z, three hours after the DC-8 landed, a further Mayday message was received, by a South African Airways (SAA) Boeing 747, en route Frankfurt to Windhoek, this

---

[1] VOR: VHF Omni-directional Radio Range. A type of short-range radio navigation system for aircraft.
[2] NDB: Non-Directional Beacon.

time on 121.5MHz. However, reception was very weak and, although the Boeing 747 answered the call, it received no reply.

At 0425Z, a further distress message was received, and this time the Boeing 747 achieved two- way communications, although assessed to be at very long range. The Cessna pilot stated that he had run out of fuel and was ditching. His position was uncertain, but he thought he was close to Brazzaville. There were no more two way communications but, shortly afterwards, a Personal Locator Beacon (PLB) was heard transmitting on 121.5MHz. The Boeing 747 had insufficient fuel to deviate from track, and contact with the PLB was very soon lost, but the 747 crew relayed the Mayday information to Luanda and Brazzaville ATCCs. A second SAA Boeing 747, en route from London to Cape Town, and approximately 200 nm West of the first Boeing 747 at 0427Z, the assessed ditching time, did not pick up any of the Cessna's transmissions, but did hear the other 747. No SAR[3] or overdue action was taken by any of the local RCCs[4] or ATCCs[5] responsible for the possible search areas, and it appeared that Libreville ATC had not initiated overdue action, despite the non-arrival of the Cessnas, which had been due at Libreville at 2010Z on 8th August. The British Embassy at Libreville had alerted the Foreign and Commonwealth Office (FCO) and, at 1200Z on 12th August, four days later, RCC Plymouth was informed by the FCO that the two Cessnas were missing.

The problem facing the Plymouth RCC staff was simply where to start the search. The theoretical area of possibility encompassed 1.3 million square nautical miles, and their task was made all the more difficult by the fact that the aircraft had ditched some 79½ hours previously, in an area which is not within the coverage of the COSPAS/SARSAT satellite system. However, the RCC set to work, and seven staff were continuously occupied for the next 18 hours, trying to contact various agencies to collate as much information as possible. Indeed, the bulk of the background matter contained in this story stemmed from the detective work carried out in this period. Those agencies contacted by the RCC included: Lockheed Aircraft Corporation (California), who provided final preparation of the aircraft, plus

---

[3] SAR: Search And Rescue.
[4] RCCs: Rescue Co-ordination Centres.
[5] ATCCs: Air Traffic Control Centres.

all route planning; the Captains of both the SAA Boeing 747s, the Flight Engineer from the Affretair DC-8, which had intercepted the first Mayday message on 8th August, the British Embassies at Lagos, Libreville, Luanda and Harare; ATC at Libreville and Dakar; and the RCC at Waterkloof, near Pretoria.

It was established that both Cessnas were fitted with light yellow dinghies, PLB and EPIRBs[6] operating on 121.5 and 243.0MHz, flares, rations for five to ten days, and sufficient batteries to operate the PLBs for up to five days. In addition, the Cessna aircraft company stated that the aircraft could float for up to 14 days with empty ferry tanks, assuming a successful ditching. While the building of the big picture continued, on the afternoon of 12th August, an RAF Hercules of No 70 Sqn, en route from Ascension Island to Banjul in The Gambia, was diverted to carry out a PLB search, from a position just South of Devli, on a North-West track which would cover the initial stages of the Cessnas' route from Dakar. At the same time, a United States Air Force C-141, en route from Ascension to Frankfurt, carried out a PLB search from the same position on an East-North-East track. Although neither aircraft received any PLB transmissions, this negative information assisted RCC Plymouth to determine a primary search area.

In order to determine an area of probability, RCC Plymouth drew 'in VHF contact' and 'no VHF contact' circles, radius 250 nm and 300 nm respectively, around the plotted positions of both SAA Boeing 747s and the Affretair DC-8. The overlap of these circles gave a crescent shaped 'most probable' area. This area, which was then corrected for sea current drift, was too large for a visual search and, because of the information received about the PLB/EPIRBs, the anticipated long battery life, and the fact that a PLB was heard after the final ditching call, it was decided to carry out PLB searches. An RAF Hercules tanker aircraft of No 30 Squadron, captained by Flight Lieutenant John Lines, was used to fly two exceptionally long PLB search sorties on 13th August (15 hrs 10 mins), and 14th August (16 hrs 15 mins). In addition, a Nigerian Air Force Hercules flew two eight-hour sorties on 13th and 14th August. Both aircraft monitored 121.5 and 243MHz throughout, but with no results. It was therefore concluded that the Cessnas' PLBs had failed, had not been activated, or the batteries had expired. The RCC had considered combined PLB and night search techniques, but this was

---

[6] EPIRBs: Emergency Position-Indicating Radio Beacons.

rejected because: a night search would have increased crew fatigue; a night search would have entailed delaying the start of the search by 10 hours; the haze and broken cloud layer at 3000 ft would have reduced visual acquisition range on flares; the survivors probable physical condition made the sighting of flares fired by the aircraft unlikely; and a daylight search presented the opportunity of a visual sighting by the search aircraft. SAA had also agreed to divert flights, on a no-cost basis, over the area of probability, and to maintain a listening watch on 121.5MHz.

As one of the missing Cessna pilots was Australian, there was growing pressure on their government to increase the search effort. As a result, the Australian Defence Staff in London approached MOD with a request for Nimrod participation in the search, and offered to offset some of the cost. The Nimrod's combination of a large SAR specialist crew, Searchwater radar, air-to- air refuelling (AAR) capability, and multiple good look-out positions, provided the best and speediest chance of locating the survivors, should they be either in a dinghy, or attached to, or in, a wrecked aircraft. On Friday 14th August, Flight Lieutenant Peter Rosie, and his crew of 120 Squadron RAF Kinloss, were put on a 24 hours notice to fly, stand-by alert. At 1730Z on Saturday 15th August, he was asked if his crew could make a 2300Z takeoff. By 1900Z, all the crew had been contacted and, by 2100Z, had arrived at RAF Kinloss, to be briefed on the incident so far. On the stroke of midnight, (2300Z), Nimrod XV234 thundered into the rainy skies above Kinloss — destination Ascension Island. However, the Nimrod is unable to reach Ascension without refuelling and, at 0600Z on 16th August, it touched down at Dakar in Senegal: the very airport from which the ill-fated Cessnas had taken off over a week earlier. At 0730Z, the Nimrod was airborne again, for the last leg to Ascension Island, where it landed at 1105Z. By 1230Z, the aircraft Captain, his Navigator and the Air Electronics Officer were plotting out the same areas of probability as RCC Plymouth had done and, by 1600Z, they had finished planning their first sortie for the following day. The AAR rendezvous position and time were confirmed with Flight Lieutenant Adrian Grafham, the Captain of the 24 Squadron Hercules tanker based at Ascension Island and, at 1900Z, the last three members of the Nimrod crew retired to bed, having been up for 36 hours.

The Nimrod crew were awakened at 0315Z the next day and, having breakfasted in the Airmen's Mess and briefed at Operations, were airborne at 0600Z. At 0830Z, the Nimrod RV'd with the 24 Squadron Hercules at position 0900S

OOE/W (approximately 900 nm East of Ascension) and, by 0850Z, having finished refuelling, the Nimrod continued east to its search area, where it started its
radar/visual/PLB search at 0920Z. The presence of ANAPROP[7], or ducting, had
been suspected by the RCC, and was proved on this sortie, when the Nimrod,
which was at 500 ft, managed to talk to Walvis Bay radio station on VHF FM
Channel 16; Walvis Bay was over 1000 nm away on the Namibian coast. The
Nimrod took a detailed temperature profile from 500ft up to 10000ft, and this
information was relayed, via Ascension, to RCC Plymouth. This report prompted
the RCC to request RSRE[8] Malvern to advise on the range at which the Boeing 747 and the Cessna would have achieved two-way communication, taking
into account the power output of the Cessna's radio, the Boeing 747 at FL370
with squelch[9] set to minimum, and the prevailing weather conditions (including
ANAPROP). The Nimrod completed its search at 1445Z, having found nothing of significance, and landed back at Ascension at 1745Z. At the debrief, the
Captain decided that, in future, the Nimrod would carry out some of its search
prior to AAR, as this meant the aircraft would be at a lighter all-up-weight, be able
to take on more fuel and thereby extend its range/endurance. The sortie debrief,
which was carried out between RCC Plymouth and the Nimrod Captain direct,
using the telephone, and the planning for the next day's sortie, were complete by
2115Z, and the crew retired to bed.

On Tuesday 18th August, the Nimrod crew, having had only six hours sleep,
were awakened at 0315Z and airborne by 0600Z, to be on task by first light and,
by 0810Z, were carrying out their search. At 1040Z, they dropped a sonobuoy,
marking its position, prior to breaking off the search to RV with the Hercules
tanker, and at 1100Z started refuelling. At 1125Z, the refuelling complete, the
Nimrod homed to on-top the sonobuoy, prior to recommencing the search, thereby ensuring no part of the area was missed. That same morning, RSRE Malvern
convened a meeting of experts, who came to the conclusion that, taking all factors into account, the presence of ANAPROP would give extended VHF ranges

---

[7] ANAPROP: Anomalous Propagation. Abnormal behaviour of radio or radar waves due to
unusual atmospheric conditions, of which "ducting" is an extreme variation.
[8] RSRE: Royal Signal and Radar Establishment.
[9] Squelch: A radio circuit that supresses unwanted, background noise when not receiving a
transmission.

at altitude, and that the Boeing 747 and the Cessna were probably between 300 and 320 nms apart at the time of the ditching call. RCC Plymouth immediately ordered a change to the Nimrod's search area and, by 1230Z, the Nimrod was on task in its new area. At 1550Z, the Nimrod, with no fuel to spare, finished searching and returned to Ascension, where it landed at 1820Z. Once again, the crew debriefed the day's events and planned the next day's sortie.

Wednesday 19th August dawned, and the Nimrod crew, used to their early morning routine, were once again airborne before 0600Z, and searching the first of two areas by 0900Z. They finished searching the first area by 1030Z and, at 1100Z, once again RV'd with the Hercules to refuel, prior to continuing to their second search area. So far, all the searches, which were based primarily on a radar search looking for aircraft wreckage, backed up with visual searches by the crew, had proved fruitless. But, at 1405Z, the crew located what appeared to be aircraft debris, including a seat and some maps, in position 0642S 00117E, over 500

Credit: US DoD

nm south of the Cessna's flight-planned route. The crew photographed what they found, and carried out a close datum search for any survivors. Although one crew member thought he had had a fleeting glimpse of a body floating just under the surface, this was not seen again and, at 1525Z, the search had to be terminated, due to lack of fuel. At 1800Z, landing back at Ascension, the Captain handed the film from the camera to the Captain of an RAF Tristar, who would take it to the UK for developing. The position of the sighted wreckage was passed to RCC Plymouth who, using leeway and wind history (provided by the Central Met Office at Bracknell) to establish wind driven and sea currents, calculated a most probable ditching position. From this position, a search area for a dinghy was calculated for the Nimrod to search on 20th August.

On 20th August, the Nimrod Captain decided to take off one hour later than on previous days, to enable his crew to get an extra hour's sleep; they had flown 47 hours in four days, and were starting to show signs of fatigue. So, at 0700Z, the Nimrod took off, and commenced its search at 0900Z. At 1030Z, the crew spotted what could have been an uninflated life-raft pack. There was no sign of any survivors and, at 1200Z, the search was broken off, to refuel from the Hercules tanker. At 1430Z, the crew came across a Spanish fishing vessel and, with the assistance of an Ascension-based RAF Corporal, who was learning to speak Spanish and happened to be on board the Nimrod, established that the fishermen had seen nothing untoward. At 1630Z, the Nimrod completed its search and, at 1915Z, the aircraft landed at Ascension. During the subsequent debrief, the crew were told that the photographs taken the previous day had been analysed by experts at the Joint Air Reconnaissance Intelligence Centre (JARIC), and had been confirmed as aircraft wreckage.

As the Hercules tanker had another commitment on 21st August, there was no Nimrod flight planned. This enabled the Nimrod crew to have a well earned rest, and for some of them to see Ascension Island in daylight for the first time! On 22nd August, the Nimrod was airborne once again by 0700Z, and had commenced the search by 0830Z. It refuelled with the Hercules tanker, now being flown by a crew from No 30 Squadron, at 1200Z and, by 1230Z, had recommenced its search. At 1330Z, the crew spotted more wreckage, and the body of a man floating face down, just below the surface. The Nimrod's camera was unserviceable and therefore no photographs were taken. Another close-datum search was carried out, but failed to find anything else of significance, although the body was sighted twice more by two other crew members. At 1625Z, just as the Nimrod was going off task, it picked up a small radar contact, but was unable to investigate due to lack of fuel. The Nimrod landed back at Ascension at 1825Z.

A final sortie was planned for 23rd August, to try to relocate the small radar contact, and then to complete a search for a dinghy in a second area, calculated from the original wreckage sighted on 19th August. Once again, the Nimrod was airborne before 0700Z and at, 0940Z, relocated the small contact, which was identified as a blue vacuum flask or similar object. There was nothing else significant to report, and the aircraft landed at Ascension at 1825Z. The search was called off after the 23rd August sortie had landed with nothing significant to report.

Due to the extraordinary amount of flying the Nimrod crew had carried out over the past week, they spent 24th August resting, prior to starting the 12-hour transit back to Kinloss, stopping only to refuel at Dakar. Over the previous 10 days, Nimrod XV234 and its crew from 120 Squadron had spent 92 hrs and 55 mins in the air, burned 850,000 lbs of fuel (of which over 240,000 lbs was transferred during AAR) and searched an area equal in size to twice the land mass of the United Kingdom. The Nimrod crew had found two areas of wreckage, which were too far apart to have belonged to one aircraft. Although it was impossible to identify the type or details of registration, the crew were confident that both areas contained aircraft wreckage. Photographs taken in the first area on 19th August were confirmed by JARIC to be of aircraft wreckage. The fleeting glimpse of a body in this area by one crew member, and the confirmed sighting of another body on 22nd August in the second area by three crew members, along with the widely dispersed nature of the flotsam in each area, indicated that neither pilot was successful in completing a night ditching. The fact that both pilots, neither of whom was very experienced, had just had a thoroughly traumatic 20-hour flight, coupled with fatigue, a possible lack of engine response due to fuel exhaustion and, in my opinion, a total lack of a visual horizon at night, all mitigated against a successful ditching.

Visibility and general search conditions were excellent and enhanced by good radar backup. Once wreckage had been located, the RCC had planned the search areas, looking for a dinghy with a drogue anchor, a dinghy without a drogue, and an aircraft afloat. These areas were well searched, with a 70% probability of detection of at least one pilot and possibly both. The RCC was confident the search areas were accurate, and the subsequent results appear to justify this confidence.

Although, sadly, the two missing pilots were not found alive, it is a tribute to the professionalism and dedication of all the people involved that such an operation was mounted at short notice, and carried out so efficiently, over 4000 nm away from the Nimrod's home base. This was the result of exceptional teamwork, involving: the Hercules crews of both No's 24 and 30 Squadrons; the operations staff at Ascension Island and, in particular, Squadron Leader John Petts who, in his capacity as OC Ops, was involved in every crew brief and debrief; the staff at RCC Plymouth; and, last but not least, all the members of No 120 Squadron 'Crew 8', the team which I have the privilege to captain, who flew each sortie with minimum rest in between and yet, although visibly fatigued in the latter stages, were ever vigilant, and, as often happens, quietly got on with the job.

'Oly Highland

After some years flying Canberras, instructing on Chipmunks, and then flying Lightnings - the most superb aeroplane on the RAF's then inventory - I was moved onto helicopters, to become the Sqn Ldr CO of one of the two Search and Rescue (SAR) Squadrons, No 202, which looked after the northern half of the country. There were four flights, situated along the east coast from RAF Lossiemouth, via RAF Leuchars and RAF Acklington down to RAF Leconfield. As the CO, I moved frequently between the flights, to keep an eye on them, and to support and encourage them by showing my face; however, they tended to run very well on their own, under some very good Flt Lt flight commanders. I took advantage of visiting the flights when aircraft were changed over, as all the second-line servicing of the Whirlwind helicopters was done at the Squadron Headquarters at Leconfield, under an excellent young engineering officer called Ian Jones. Apart from these fairly frequent visits, I also managed to spend a week alternating between flights each month, so one month it would be Acklington, and the next it might be Leuchars. Alongside the Squadron Headquarters at Leconfield, I had an Adjutant and a wife, both called Liz, which caused the occasional bit of confusion and the odd bit of mirth. "Which Liz are you bringing up to the Flight, Boss? One bed or two?"

On one occasion I had to go up to Leuchars, and this coincided with a visit from Jones The Engineer and the Squadron Qualified Helicopter Instructor (QHI). When it came time to leave, the weather, while delightful at Leuchars, was forecast to worsen as we progressed south, to return via Acklington to Leconfield. We rang the Coastguard stations down the coast, who confirmed that, at St Abbs Head, the weather clamped to low cloud and poor visibility. Jones had hoped to get a bit of time in on the controls, under the wise eye of the QHI, while I relaxed in the cabin but, as there was some need to 'press on', we decided that the QHI and I would fly up front, and Jones would slum it in the cabin; if it got too bad, we could always return to Leuchars. There was a well-practised low-level poor-vis recovery route, from the coast near Coquet Island, by following roads, lines of trees and electricity lines, to get back into Acklington, so we were happy that, if we could make Coquet Island, we would soon be home and dry. Alternatively, if the weather was too bad, we could always take the Leuchars option.

We set off and, as observed by the coastguard stations, the weather did clamp at St Abbs Head. In fact, it came down to about a 100 foot or so cloud-base, with in-flight visibility around half a mile, sometimes less. However, we were fine, as we could simply follow the beach, making good, albeit slow, progress south; the joy of helicopter flying was that one could fly as slowly as was necessary, and even land on if needed. After about 20 minutes flying, there was a call from the back saying, "I am sure I've seen that castle down there before." "Rubbish," we both replied from the front, "this bit of the Northumberland coast is covered in castles." A moment or three went by, before Jones observed, with some concern in his voice, "There it goes again!" The two of us in the front started to wonder, checked our maps again, and looked at the compass a bit more carefully, realising that we had been concentrating so hard on following the beach in the appalling visibility that we had flown right round Holy Island twice, and were starting off on our third circuit!

The weather improved sufficiently for us to make it into Acklington, using our special low-level feature-following route and, in the hotel that evening, we discussed the navigational anomaly. Jones was gloating, as engineers do when scoring off pilots. For years to come, he was heard to re-tell the tale in his best Yorkshire accent, referring as he did in the telling to "Oly Highland."

Credit: Tony Higsett

Bomber County

The skies are empty now that darkness falls,
The bare, deserted runways scarred with weeds.
Across the lonely fen a night bird calls,
The wind sighs softly in the whispering reeds.

A fitful moon rides through the cloudy blue,
A bomber's moon, remembered now no more,
Where once the very air vibrated to
The mighty Merlin engine's roar.

Dispersal huts stand crumbling and forlorn,
Their broken windows open to the rain.
The taxi track is fringed with waving corn,
The echoing hangars used for storing grain.

Upon the cracking tarmac wander sheep,
A derelict crew-room door creaks in the breeze,
The silent world around is lost in sleep
And stars are twinkling far above the trees.

Those very stars which were a friendly aid
To those who flew upon the wings of night,
The crews who never grudged the price they paid
To keep aglow the flame of freedom's right.

There is no flarepath now to show the way
And guide the homing bombers to the ground.
The old control tower stands in gaunt decay,
In silence and in darkness wrapped around.

Remember those who flew, across the years,
Those bright young lives they gave so long ago.
No looking back with bitterness or tears,
But thankfulness - for they would wish it so.

It Was A Dark And Starry Night…

RAF Phantom training took place at RAF Coningsby, and below the "enormous skies" of Lincolnshire that (some) people raved about. I didn't; my memories were of a bleak landscape and perpetually muddy fields, home brew, Lincolnshire snarlers (sausages), and the three-day week. From there, it was a relief to be posted to Northern Germany which, although it still had muddy fields, offered proper beer and wine, currywurst mit frites und Local Overseas Allowance. Much better.

In a later life, I found myself at RAF Leuchars in Scotland, near the charming town of St Andrews and the sea, with low rolling hills and easy access to the Highlands. Checking out new pilots and navigators on the Leuchars squadron (which was in the air defence role) of course necessitated low flying, and what better way to introduce them to this new theatre of operations than to fly the glens which led north through the mountains. Since the clouds were often down on the hills, these gaps provided the only way to counter a potential low-level overland threat from the north. The mountains of Scotland are literally littered with the wrecks of aircraft (mainly from WW2) that have diced – unsuccessfully - with the clouds. Thus it was we flew Glencoe, the Lairig Ghru, and the Drumochter Pass etc, by way of introduction to this theatre of operations.

We had a French squadron exchange one year – and yes they flew Mirages – oh dear – so I led four of them around the Scottish Highlands after some practice interceptions. On recovery, we closed into tight arrow formation to negotiate the steep and narrow sides of Glen Tilt, which led down to Blair Atholl. Looking in the rear view mirror, I could see the four Mirages, and that they were holding a nice tight formation. Then a strangled voice came over the radio, saying something that sounded like "Showsha", which I couldn't make out; the reception on the Phantom radio was not renowned as brilliant. No one else said anything despite my queries. Nevertheless, we progressed back to base, as the Mirages, which had much less endurance than the Phantom, must have been getting tight on fuel. I had briefed that I would overfly the field and waggle my wings, at which sign the Mirages would break off independently and land. We, meanwhile, would go off and do something else exciting before landing. All went well as we approached the field, with the Mirages tight in there. I waggled, but alas, and to my chagrin, nothing happened, as the Mirages hung grimly on to me as chicks to their mother hen.

As a neat and impressive formation, we overshot the field, no doubt with both resident squadrons applauding this astounding demonstration of airmanship. All I could do was advise Air Traffic Control, and repeat the run-in and break. Having led the break and overshot the runway for the second time, the French all landed safely. And the "Showsha"? Well it was apparently "Joker"[1] distorted by the radio. So, what they eventually landed with, we never did find out. The Froggies did seem to thrive on fumes - maybe it's the wine they have with lunch - and they certainly possessed eclat, by opening champagne bottles with a slicing squadron sword at a party they threw for our ladies and us. But I get nervous anywhere near Mirages.

The main peacetime role of the UK Phantom Air Defence Force was Quick Reaction Alert (QRA), in which 2 aircraft held a permanent 10-minute readiness. In those days, there were many incursions into the UK Air Defence Region by Russian military aircraft which, I hasten to add, was just an extended area of UK surveillance; at no time did the Russians ever intrude into our national airspace, which is what the popular press seems to imply nowadays. "RAF fighters see the Russians off." It's all garbage.

The Phantom we had at Leuchars was the ex-RN version – the F4K/FG1. This had various aerodynamic modifications to cope with life on board ship, but what it didn't have was the good inertial navigation and HF communications that the RAF version, the F4M/FGR2, possessed. The nav kit consisted of a Mickey Mouse arrangement of cogs and wheels, which became inaccurate soon after take-off, and conventional radio aids. The F4K/FG1 Phantom was not planned to operate far from the support of the Fleet. In terms of navigation, we were no worse off than the single-seat Lightning, but that aircraft more usually operated close to land as a point-defence fighter, unless it had tanker support. However, the F4 - with three external fuel tanks and some 3 hours endurance, without tanking - could often find itself a long way from any land-based navigation aid. Thank you, Air Staffs – a brilliant piece of work by you all. So, when operating a long way from land, as the Leuchars role often dictated, there was no way of knowing precisely where one was without outside help. Indeed, one crew ran themselves so

---

[1] Joker: A transmission indicating that the caller is down to recovery (return to base) fuel.

short of fuel, due to navigation problems, that they had to jettison their empty fuel tanks and a bunch of expensive missiles, just to make it back to a tanker which had been vectored north for the emergency. That was a close call for the junior pilot and navigator involved.

One cold winter's night, we were scrambled from QRA. Word had come from the Norwegians that a couple of Russian Bears had rounded the North Cape and were heading our way. A Victor tanker had been scrambled from RAF Marham down south, in good time to meet up with us as we headed north. From our Buchan GCI controller, we were handed over to our last fighter controller at Saxa Vord, on the most northerly of the major Shetland Islands – Unst. After a while, we intercepted two Tu-142 Bear Foxtrots, coming down the north Atlantic at high level, to head through the Iceland-Faeroes gap. The intelligence bods were very interested in this maritime variant, as it was specifically designed for anti-submarine warfare. It had been brought into service as a response to the threat from the American Polaris submarines, of which the UK had four. Our people were dead keen to know the airframe number of the aircraft, which was painted on the nose wheel door. This seemed to be a priority although, had I been a Russian general, I might have altered the numbers occasionally with sticky lettering to confuse. Who knows – maybe they did? How to see the number on the nose-wheel door at night, I leave to your imagination, as this was all before the advent of night vision goggles. All I will relate is that the throbbing beat of the four contra-rotating Kuznetsov turboprops though our airframe was really impressive. But we got the details and, after refuelling to full as the tanker headed home, we asked it for an HF 'phone patch' to the controller at Strike Command. "Proceed to your prudent limit of endurance," he said, "and, by the way, there is an American AWACS[2] out of Iceland that will update your position."

So, we were now on our own, trailing the Bears through the Arctic darkness and plotting our position from time to time with American help – fat dumb and happy, and confident all would be well. Monty Python's foot comes to mind now. We droned along, behind the two Bears, with nothing much exciting happening, for a couple of hours and, when we reckoned we were somewhere south of Iceland,

---

[2] AWACS: Airborne Warning And Control System aircraft.

and should be thinking of going home, I requested our new position from the AWACS – "Aw gee shucks we're just refuelling right now, so our radar is turned off. Sorry Bud – have a nice day." (Or words that amounted to the same thing.) Well, thanks a bunch to our great NATO allies! Just the help we needed when alone in the dark Arctic night. Tracking the Bears seemed to suddenly lose our interest, as thoughts turned to where we really were, and how much fuel remained. However, being at high level, we should have been able to see Iceland on the radar from our estimated position, if we turned to the north. To our dismay all we saw were sea returns.

We were not lost of course, just – as the old saying goes – temporarily unsure of our position. "Oh s**t," or words to that effect, "maybe we'd best turn southeast to hopefully pick up the line feature of the British Isles." We both agreed that this was a jolly fine idea, but it felt very cold and lonely droning along in what was presumably the Shanwick Oceanic Control Area, inhabited by airliners plying the route across the pond. But we saw no one else. It was a beautiful starry night, and I even checked the compasses against the Pole Star, to make sure we were going in the right direction. One gets nervous you know. Time dragged slowly by as the fuel continued to decrease. However, after about an hour, the cheering green outline of the Outer Hebrides started to appear at the top of the radar screen, and we made contact with the fighter controller on Benbecula, and thereafter started a cruise descent back into Leuchars. In retrospect, we must have been further to the south and west of our dead reckoning position, or had the availability of the AWACS led us to a false sense of security? We never did find out, but still had enough fuel on landing so really couldn't have been too far wrong. Afterwards I 'phoned the Strike Controller. "Oh yes we wondered where you were," came his laconic reply.

The Bear was an impressive aircraft – a beautiful silvery-grey, 163 feet long, a wingspan of 168 feet, and with a crew of up to 13, including the resident KGB officer, so were told. Having recorded the very important nosewheel door number, we would drop back towards the tailplane where resided the duty rear gunner. Once, when behind a Bear F in broad daylight, I was filming with my cine-camera, when a small door opened and a sonobuoy popped out, passing close under the starboard wing. I steered clear of line astern after that. At the rear end were a pair of 23 mm cannons pointing upwards, so no threat to us, and the rear gunner could be clearly seen, looking out of his side perspex blisters, as we formated beside the enormous tailplane. We would wave cheerily at him – 'cos we are all fellow aircrew after all - and he would invariably wave and smile at us in response. However, there was a then protracted period during which he manoeuvred a large camera on a tripod into position to photograph us. When he was just about ready to capture us for the Kremlin archives, I would move over to the other side of the aircraft to watch the whole process being repeated. And repeated it was, without success. On one occasion, we had been fitted with new Skyflash missiles to replace the old radar-guided Sparrows. These, as before, were partially recessed in the under-fuselage. The Russkies were obviously fully aware of this, and the rear gunner made repeated hand gestures for us to turn our belly up to him, so he could photograph the new fit of missiles. I politely declined. It was all a friendly game, but with potentially disastrous consequences. In my time at Leuchars, I carried out over 40 interceptions of the NATO code-named Russian Bear, Badger, Bison and Coot aircraft. I remember one amazing night, transiting north into the green and red shimmering curtains of the Aurora Borealis, whilst below the many oil rigs flared off enormous plumes of gas. It was like a vision of Hades. I suspect those times saw an interception frequency greater than we hear of the Typhoon nowadays. In none of the interceptions were any counter-measures taken by Warsaw Pact aircraft, to place us in an invidious position; a manoeuvring Bear could easily embarrass a swept-wing fighter at close range. None of this happened to us; maybe others have their own tale to tell. But it was the Cold War back then, and a game of cat-and-mouse. Thankfully we all settled down after the faults and suspicions on both sides. Let's not have another one...

Credit: Mike Freer

Out Of The Jaws Of Defeat

In 1981, I was posted to Belize, to command the Reconnaissance Intelligence Centre (RIC). The RIC's function was to provide intelligence to the garrison commander, whose command included a company of the Gordon Highlanders, and RAF Belize, a force made up of 4 Harriers and two Puma helicopters. We had an important mission to keep an eye out for any potential military action by Guatemala, which had, for many years, maintained a claim on the territory of Belize. Autumn 1981 was a particularly critical period, as Belize was about to gain full independence, and we were concerned that Guatemala would try and disrupt the change of status of Belize. RAF Belize was also busy supporting army training, and keeping a watch for drug smugglers and other malcontents potentially causing disruption to this otherwise quiet corner of the fast-shrinking British Colonial area of responsibility.

During one of our regular airborne patrols, a coastal freighter, the Orca 11, was seen unloading a suspicious cargo on one of the quays in the south of the country. This information was fed into the force operations centre, and immediately elicited interest. We tasked a Harrier to 'have another look' and, when the aircraft returned with some rather hazy imagery, it was my task to puzzle out what the ship was unloading. The army, having heard that something exciting might be in the offing, immediately bombarded me with questions about potential arms smuggling. I produced the images for the force intelligence staff, with a rough measurement of the boxes being unloaded, whereupon the 'intelligence' on the crates took on its own momentum. The crates were continually referred to as possible – then probable - arms cases, and the army, itching for some action, were soon briefing a platoon to carry out a lethal assault against the arms smugglers. Any caution as to the veracity of the limited intelligence was swiftly bypassed and, within an hour, the Gordon Highlanders were 'tooled up', ready to go into combat. I watched the proceedings with growing alarm, that we might be 'going nuclear' on a situation which the local bobby might have been able to deal with!

Soon, a helicopter launched, with a platoon of Scotland's finest, ready for a jolly good punch-up, while I sat nervously in the ops room, awaiting a report on the action. The troops descended en masse on the jetty, captured everybody in sight, and pounced on the arms crates. The report from the troops came through the radio net. "Those are not arms crates – they are lobster pots!" I put my head in my hands, imagining what great stories would be told at Intelligence dining-in nights at my expense!

The Company Commander of the Highlanders went slightly white-faced, and ordered the troops that, as they were there, they might as well search the ship. Salvation! Twenty tons of cannabis was found in the hold. All the ship's company were arrested, the ship was impounded and, later that week, when the reports were made, the Foreign Office congratulated all at British Forces Belize for a great humanitarian operation, saving the local community from the ravages of drug addiction - only slightly spoiled when the Belize Police burned the bales of drugs upwind of Belize City – so everybody was on a high!

Credit: Rob Schleiffert -

How Not To Get Bounced

RAF Murrahaq Air Movements Squadron in 1971, and on the day shift. The scheduled Argosy freighter is inbound from Sharjah, and I suggest to the shift chaps, who do the loading and unloading, that it would be a good idea to wait for their lunch break until the aircraft has landed, and the freight has been taken off. They will then get an extended break, as we are well ahead of the days' tasks in hand. But no, it's their lunch break and they are going to take it.

My No 2 and I thought that, instead of us just sitting in the office to await their return, we would go out and do the unloading; that would show them who really were the bosses. So, the aircraft landed, shut down, and the crew departed for their crew room. We jumped into our yellow-painted Land Rover and drove out to the aircraft. The Land Rovers were used for all sorts of jobs around our movements parish. The canvas hoods and frames had long since been removed, and the back was normally full of a couple of aircraft chocks, chains and strops for securing freight in the aircraft. They were also fairly unreliable and so, when we stopped at an aircraft, we tended to leave the engine running.

At this point, I should mention that our four resident Argosy aircraft were parked in a line in front of the 84 Squadron Andovers. As we arrived at the aircraft, we saw that the rear clamshell freight door was open. Peering inside, we saw that there was only one piece of freight, and it was a tyre. Not just any tyre, but the main wheel assembly off a Shackleton, which was about the same size as that of a Lancaster. It was far too heavy to move by manual effort, so we decided to put one end of a chain into the hub of the tyre, and hook up to the Land Rover. We would then slowly drag it rearwards, until it was neatly balanced over the edge of the clamshell door. We would then unhook the chain, and gently ease the tyre over its' point of balance', so it would drop onto the concrete behind the Argosy. Easy.

All went well initially, but we had not factored in the diameter and weight of the Shackleton wheel. As it slid over the edge of the ramp and dropped, it hit the concrete pan, rubber first… and bounced. The energy in the wheel was such that it bounced again, higher this time, and headed off towards one of the Andovers. Another disaster was about to unfold. My No 2, realising what was about to happen, seemed to leap from the aircraft into the driver's seat of the Land Rover all in one motion. Accelerator hard down, he chased the wheel, and literally rammed it so that it fell over, just a few feet away from the nose of the target Andover. A long, deep silence ensued, followed by hysterical laughter and a change of underwear! We drove across to the Cargo Shed, and returned with our large forklift truck, to scoop up the wheel and deposit it in the "Inbound Freight" pile.

About half an hour later, the chaps came back from lunch, and announced they were going to unload the Argosy. "Don't bother lads" said I, "We did that while you were sitting around at lunch, and by the way, the Land Rover needs to be refuelled." The response – a shrug of the shoulders and feet up in the crew-room until the next aircraft arrival.

Happy (lucky!) days.

Credit: RuthAS/Wikipedia

An Agricultural Adventure

I was instructing on that delightful little aircraft, the Chipmunk. My "Bloggs" in the front seat was a young man who aspired to train as an RAF pilot under the, then new, Graduate Entry Scheme. His progress to date had been less than meteoric, but these were early days, and we had reached the phase where he was flying circuits and bumps, in preparation for his first solo flight. To achieve that standard, it was necessary for Bloggs to demonstrate that he would be able to cope with an engine failure after take-off (EFATO). This would involve selecting a suitable field for the engine-off landing, planning the approach, carrying out safety checks, checking his harness was tight, and so on. In training, of course, we didn't actually carry out these actions, but instead did "touch drills", only chanting out the check-list, and touching the appropriate controls to simulate the action required.

We briefed very carefully for the flight: a few circuits and landings to allow Bloggs to get his hand in, and then, to build on his past - not very successful - attempts on a previous flight, we would simulate engine failure, and go through the drills for an EFATO. The weather was benign – ideal for the flight. The northerly runway was in use, beyond the end of which there were a few hundred yards of rough ground, leading down to a substantial river. North of the river, there was a large stretch of agricultural land which, it being winter, was almost all ploughed land – not suitable for an emergency landing – but there was one solitary, grass field in which it would be possible to land a Chipmunk, if the need arose. It was satisfactory for training purposes because, of course, we wouldn't actually land in the field during this exercise, but apply engine power and climb away once the practice was complete.

Initially, the flight went well, but the EFATO was causing problems for Bloggs. He just could not carry out all the actions in the correct order. He would select the field and plan his approach, but forget to carry out the checks, or he would get the checks right but let the aircraft stray off the approach path, so that a landing could not have been made in a real emergency. It was clear to me that Bloggs was overloaded, so there was nothing to be gained by continuing with the exercise at this point; however, I felt that it would be good to boost his confidence with a little progress before the end of the flight. Therefore, I planned to allow him a very gentle attempt where, with a little prompting from me, he could carry out a satisfactory drill and approach to the field, before we returned to the flight line. Accordingly, I landed the aircraft and taxied round to the holding point, where we stopped for a comprehensive brief on what was to happen. I told him that, when safely airborne after take-off, I would ask him if he was ready. When he had told me he was, I would gently close the throttle to simulate engine failure. "What would you do next?" By question and answer, we went through the entire procedure. "Do you understand?" "Yessah!"

I informed the local controller in Air Traffic Control (ATC) of our intentions. I can imagine the controller, reluctantly raising his eyes from his Sunday newspaper to press his transmit switch, sighing with boredom, and clearing us for take-off. Off we went. At about 500 feet, I asked Bloggs, "Are you ready?" "Yessah!" I slowly reduced power to idle. Bloggs put the aircraft into a descent, selected the (only suitable) field, and turned towards it. So far so good! Then he commenced to carry out the touch drills, still aiming at the field. Splendid! Then, as Bloggs said "Fuel off", out of the corner of my eye, I saw the fuel cock (there are two, connected together, one between each pilot's legs) move to the aft (OFF) position. Instead of doing the touch drill, Bloggs had actually switched the fuel off! I looked up again in time to see, over Bloggs' left shoulder, his left hand pressing the magneto switches down to the off position. We were now without a running engine.

I took control of the aircraft, and quickly realised that there was insufficient time to attempt a restart, so I called air traffic, "Mayday, Mayday, Mayday, One Seven landing in a field," and continued the approach, landing without further incident, to the surprise of a handful of curious cattle and, no doubt, to the consternation of the startled controller who, I imagine, after a moment of disbelief, hurriedly discarded his Sunday paper and initiated crash procedures. Once we had rolled to a halt, I was able to communicate with the Squadron Boss, who was airborne in the area at the time, and who relayed the information that we were safe to interested parties on the airfield. As a precaution, I had the aircraft checked over by our ground-crew, who also herded the cattle away from my take-off path and took Bloggs back to the crewroom. I flew the aircraft back to the airfield, with nothing more than some cow dung on the tyres to show for the adventure.

Pollarding – RAF-Style

In 1961, after flying training on Vampires at RAF Oakington, I was turned down for the 22 Squadron advanced, rocket-propelled Whirlwinds, and ended up on the plywood, elastic, Search-and-Rescue Sycamore helicopters in Aden instead. After all my Vampire training! I was assured it really wasn't a punishment posting!! I suppose my only claim to fame was holding the record for a forced landing at 4000 feet, after hitting the only tree on the Jebel Shamsan (better known as the Barren Rocks of Aden...) – but avoiding the Court Martial...

It was early one May morning in 1962, just as the sun was rising; I took off, (or was I pushed?) in my trusty, overladen Sycamore, XG504, from Khormaksar, heading hopefully for somewhere in the hills near Dhala, near the Yemen border. On board were navigator Bill Hughes, and two army intelligence officers, Colonel James and Major Abel. Not surprisingly, we found the hilltop we were supposed to land on, and tried an approach, which wasn't looking successful, so we went round again. On touching down at the second attempt, a severe dose of ground resonance resulted; Sycamores were prone to this, with often earth-shattering results.

On pulling off, the ground cushion was soon lost and, in spite of an attempt to bend the collective and wind on more power, we continued to advance towards the ground rather than the sky. A small valley beckoned, and a forced landing arranged. I realised that some of the rotor blades had been in contact with what seemed to have been the only tree in the area. As the blades came to a stop, we could see that this had been the case. A delicate new aroma began to percolate the cabin! On noticing Bill (an old Master Navigator), calmly writing in his log, I suggested he would be better employed inspecting the damage. He quietly informed me that the time of landing (0810) would probably be of note at my Court Martial!

As we stood inspecting the damage, and realising a take-off would not be possible, a rather irate Arab appeared, clutching a branch of said tree. After speaking to Major Abel, he thoughtfully retired. It appeared that he wanted compensation for his tree, but changed his mind when he was informed the RAF would counter claim, as the tree shouldn't have been there in the first place. We then had to try and contact Khormaksar, regarding the change of plan. This was done via Morse Code from fort to fort, manned by non-English-speaking operators, so the simple message, by the time it arrived in Aden, had escalated to Third World

War proportions! It wasn't long before the trusty boys in blue, in their 8 Squadron Hunters, were overhead, ready and willing to settle the score for a downed Sycamore! I am sure they were very relieved to be informed, via the helicopter radio, that everything was under control. We then had the honour of selecting a goat for our lunch, at which event I was presented with the eye delicacy. Being a lowly Flying Officer, I indicated to the bearer that it was more appropriate that Bill should receive it, as his badge of office was bigger than mine. New blades were transported from Aden, and it is said that some enterprising Arab was selling clocks in sections of plywood from the old blades within 24 hours.

"How about the Court Martial?" I hear you say. Well, my pal the WingCo (he sometimes tried his hand at flying the Sycamore) informed me that there would be no Court Martial. Was I relieved?! I can only think that this might have been due to the flight having been authorised by the flight commander, and the operation was probably outside aircraft operational limits. It also turned out that some of the rotor blades were time expired...

Credit: RuthAS/Wikipedia

Never Volunteer

If you are going to have an easy life, stay in one piece, and keep out of trouble when you are in the armed services, there is one thing that you must learn and always stick to: never volunteer! It seemed to me almost to be a mantra, repeated many times by all those who were the more sensible types, and had anything to do with our training. So, I learned it early on during my career, and made a firm resolution to stick to it. The problem was that I repeatedly ignored the resolution, and that inevitably resulted in trouble. It certainly did on this occasion.

It was during my time on 1340 Flight in Kenya, flying the armed version of the Harvard, on army support work, during the campaign against the Mau Mau. At the time, we were based at Nanyuki, near the northwest corner of the Mount Kenya massif, where there was a good airstrip and old wartime army accommodation. It did not turn into a boggy morass whenever it rained, but was often very dusty. Someone had the notion that it would be a good idea to keep the Mau Mau awake at night, so it was planned that we would scatter anti-personnel bombs in the small hours, across parts of the forests in the Aberdare mountains, where they were known to be. We would take off at about midnight, but this seemed to me to be a means of keeping us awake as well. We still had to do our normal daytime strikes, and there would not be much night left for sleeping, as the first wave entailed a dawn take-off. One aircraft was to carry a parachute flare in place of a bomb. This would be released over the target area, in order that the target itself could be illuminated, accurately identified and pinpointed. One of us was asked to volunteer to carry the flare. 'Oh yes,' I thought, 'That'll be interesting, something that I've not done before, and a change from just bombing as usual.' 'Yes Sir, I'll have a go at that!' I didn't think; I had dropped myself right in it.

The flare was carried on one of the underwing bomb racks, and released in the same way as the bombs, just by pressing that particular bomb release switch, after which it would simply drop away behind. It remained attached to the aircraft by a long cord, which unravelled to its full length and, in so doing, operated the fuse which lit the flare up, and also deployed the parachute. It was then supposed to become detached from the aircraft, and so could drift down and do its job of illuminating the target, enabling the attack to go ahead. On time, at midnight, six Harvards started their engines and taxied out, with the CO leading. As usual,

I flew as his No 2. Also as usual, our propellers sent up clouds of dust through which we had to taxi, especially at that time during the night, when there was no wind and the dust cloud just hung there. We then took off in stream, and there was more dust. This was not at all unusual, and sooner or later would result in a blocked pitot tube, the result being no airspeed indicator for that flight. We accepted it; it was something that we were used to and, in that event, we just had to fly by power and attitude. I got airborne in my turn, and automatically checked my airspeed. 'Oh!' It read zero. In the fully dark conditions, power and attitude would not be quite so easy but, at least initially, I was formating loosely on the Boss. Also, nobody seemed to understand a word that I said on the radio, which did not surprise me. My aircraft had a long history of transmitter trouble, to such an extent that I had got used to it and did not bother to say anything. The receiver always worked, so I could hear the Boss shouting at me, but now however, the transmitter would really be something that I would regret not having.

As is usual in Africa, it was a beautiful night, black and full of stars; wonderful to fly beneath. Satima, the northern peak of the Aberdares, was a great black shadow, stretching above us as we came over the forests on its eastern slopes, where our target lay. Mount Kenya stood away in the distance to the east, and the white snows on its three peaks were just visible. The Boss had an uncanny knack of knowing just where we were over those forests and, even now, in the dark, could pick the target area. 'Right Mike, drop the flare now.' I selected the required bomb release, and pressed the button. Away went the flare canister, and I saw it blaze out satisfactorily behind me, but I soon realised that it was not drifting away; it was following along behind me, still attached to the cord which was attached to my aircraft. I was pulling a load of fire through the sky, and it was not illuminating the target as it should have. I operated all the release mechanisms and fuses for all the bomb points that I could, in an attempt to get rid of it, but no luck; the fire stayed there, firmly attached to me, being dragged through the sky behind me. The best that I could do was to fly round in a circle, as slowly as possible, just above stalling speed, and so light up the forest below. Whether it lit up the actual target, I have no idea but, as planned, the other aircraft formed up in very loose line abreast, flying lower than I was, I'm glad to say, and dropped their bombs across the area.

That was all very well for them, but I was far from happy. I had visions of the fire working its way up the cord and reaching me. Of course it did not do so, but just went out when the flare was finished. However, until then, I was a very worried pilot, continually twisting my neck round and looking over my shoulder, to make sure that all was as well as could be, and that there was no little flame licking its way towards me. The bombs had been dropped, the task was complete, so we all closed in together and turned for home. All that I had to do now was to work out which of the navigation lights that I could see belonged to the Boss's aircraft, and then join up into close formation with him. Without an airspeed indicator, it would be necessary for me to remain in formation for the landing, and that was something that I had seldom done at night. Close formation flying in the dark was not one of my favourites, especially the landing, but it could not be avoided this time. I found the Boss, and tucked in on his wingtip; so far so good, but I was still towing a long cord out behind, and I hoped that nobody would get their prop wound up in it. They would have a problem!

Then I realised that, when I was low, just before touch down, the cord would be dragging along the ground. There were the usual African bushes and acacia trees close to the airfield boundary, and the Boss would come in low over these. Would the cord catch in them, or perhaps the barbed-wire fence, and then, would it jerk me down before breaking? I imagined all sorts of problems. Common sense told me that my imagination was running wild and that, as long as I kept a bit high, so avoiding the obstacles, all would be well.

It was, and I dragged the cord along the ground as I taxied up to the ramp, but was very pleased to shut my engine down and walk away after that flight. One that I had volunteered for!

Credit: Leo za1/Wikipedia

One Final Act

It was the north of Scotland, forty-four years ago. A clear blue sky, and my first ever trip in a Buccaneer, a two-seat low-level strike jet of the Royal Navy. Jerry Yates, a tall lean flight lieutenant on an exchange tour with the Fleet Air Arm, was my pilot, and he was keen to show me an aircraft over which he was master. Throttles fully open, we accelerated down the runway with a vengeance and, lifting off, wheels in the well, we sped low over the beach of the Moray Firth. A few small boys looked up in awe at the shiny machine. In not very long, we were at 560 knots, the limiting speed of the Buccaneer, and cruising at low level over a smooth sea, low enough to leave a trace on the surface. Jerry caught my eye in the mirror. "There are not many aircraft you can do this with at deck level with any confidence", he said – taking his hands from the controls and placing both on the canopy. Impressive. The Buccaneer was designed for high-speed low-level flight, and it was in its element – so was Jerry.

That first experience of the Buccaneer clearly left its mark on me, for I was to remain with it for a number of tours and three thousand hours. Sadly, one of my last flights was once again with Jerry, over the Moray Firth, but this time I was carrying his ashes. He had been tragically killed in a flying accident in Oman and Linda, his widow, wanted Jerry to return to that part of the world they had both loved so much. Being on 12 Squadron, a unit Jerry had commanded, we wanted to catch the moment. Jerry's ashes had been carefully packed in a very large brown manila envelope with 'On Her Majesty's Service' on the side. Jerry would have liked that. The envelope was then placed between the petals of the massive airbrake at the rear of the aircraft. We decided to commit Jerry at 12 seconds past 12 minutes past midday on the 12th day of the month – it was a bright day in November.

We called Air Traffic for a priority take-off. They wanted to know why this was a priority take-off – we didn't tell them; this was personal. Throttles fully open, we accelerated down the runway with a vengeance and lifting off, wheels in the well, we sped low over the beach of the Moray Firth at 560 knots. I read the words of the committal that had been prepared by the padre and, with a blip of the airbrakes, Jerry was gone.

Whenever I visit there, I often look over the quiet waters and think of Jerry. I am sure the Moray Firth holds many secrets, but I wanted to share this one.

Where's My Medal?

What follows took place on HMS Implacable, while in the Pacific in late May 1945.

A Fleet Signal was received on board as follows:

TO: All Ships Pacific Fleet   Confidential   FROM: Admiralty

The Admiralty is aware that there is a discrepancy in the award of recognition to Fleet Air Arm Aircrew for gallantry and success in air combat. Aircrew who have 5(five) or more destroyed aircraft to their credit, and which have been authenticated, should be put forward for the Distinguished Service Cross.

ACTION: Commanding Officers   XXO545

Roughly that's what it said, so having 6(six) aircraft to my credit, I applied accordingly:

HMS Implacable
At Sea
XX May 1945

The Commanding Officer
880 Squadron

Sir,
I have the honour to request that I may be considered for an award in accordance with the terms of Fleet Signal XX0545.

I enclose my Flying Log Book, annotated at the appropriate pages.

I have the honour to be,
Sir,
Your obedient servant
Sub/Lt(A) RNZVR

The reply was swift and to the point:

TO: Sub/Lt (A) J. RNZVR   FROM: Commanding Officer 880 Squadron

XY May 1945

Your letter of XX May 1945 is not in the spirit of the Fleet Signal, and cannot be actioned. The signalled numbers applied to ENEMY aircraft, not our own.

Lt/Cdr R M Crosley DSC RNVR

Scrubbed

On completion of training on 1663 Heavy Conversion Unit at RAF Rufforth, in December 1943, we, as a crew, were posted to 76 Squadron at RAF Holme-on-Spalding-Moor. However, before beginning operations there, we were asked if, as a crew, we would consider joining a Special Duty Squadron. As most of the crew were in agreement - although not all - the democratic vote won, so we joined 624 Squadron, stationed at Brindisi in Italy, and engaged in supply dropping over the Balkans, I in my capacity as Flight Engineer.

After four sorties from Brindisi, we were posted to Blida in North Africa, and it was there that the incident referred to in the title occurred. The exact date I cannot remember, as it is not recorded in my log book for obvious reasons, but we were briefed for a sortie to a target in South Eastern France. From early morning, the rain had been incessant, and the Met Officer stated that we would experience showers all the way. The rain was bouncing off the ground, and one wag asked, "Like we are having just now?" to which the Met Officer replied, "Exactly!"

I think there were 14 aircraft on 'ops' that night. We were No 1 to take off and, having started up the engines, checking for mag drop, pressures etc, we moved round the perimeter track to position ourselves for take-off. However, we were told to hold, as a Wellington with engine trouble had requested emergency landing. That aircraft tried to abort the landing and overshot, but crashed into a farmhouse, killing the five crew members and three civilians.

By this time, our engines were overheating, so we asked permission to cut them and join the queue further back. This was granted, and No 2 was detailed for take-off. Opening up to full power, the Halifax sped down the runway and began to lift off but, for some unknown reason, nose-dived into the ground at the end of the runway, bursting into flames and killing all seven crew members.

With one fire burning at one end of the runway, and another on the left, No 1 was again told to prepare for take-off. Fortunately, before we actually positioned ourselves, a vehicle with flashing lights travelled the length of the queue, signalling that operations were 'scrubbed.' I personally was never so glad to exit an aircraft at the hard standing although, two nights on, all was forgotten as operations continued.

The victims of the two crashes were buried with full military honours, and representatives of the station attended the funerals of the civilian victims.

Chinook In The North Sea

We say that the hour of death cannot be forecast but, when we say this, we imagine that hour as placed in an obscure and distant future. It never occurs to us that it has any connection with the day already begun, or that death could arrive this same afternoon, this afternoon which is so certain and which has every hour filled in advance. ~ Marcel Proust

The Chinook is a warm wind that blows over the Canadian prairies, raising temperatures and melting snow; it is also a large helicopter, built by Boeing since 1962, and in military use with many nations. Less well known is that the Chinook (or CH-47) is used by many commercial operators, in a variety of roles, principally for its load (and passenger) carrying capacity; and, for all but two of the 47 unsuspecting people who boarded a British Airways Chinook 234 on the beautiful morning of 6th November 1986, the hour of death was not 'in an obscure and distant future', but a scant four hours away. The two people whose survival was nothing short of miraculous were a 20-year old passenger, Eric Morrans, and me.

My name is Pushp Vaid, and I was born in 1941, in what later became Pakistan. My family migrated to Delhi during the partition, and I joined the Indian Air Force in 1963 as a helicopter pilot, served for eleven years and received the Vir Chakra – an Indian gallantry award - in 1971 for bravery during the Bangladesh War. In 1974, I migrated to the United Kingdom, where the civil helicopter industry was set to mushroom. I joined British Airways 9 months later, and flew with them until 1993. In November 1986, I survived the worst helicopter accident in civil aviation history.

At that time, our company – British International Helicopters (Robert Maxwell had recently bought out the rotary-wing division of British Airways) - operated 6 Chinooks for Shell, ferrying company personnel to and from oil rigs in the North Sea. Aberdeen was then, as it is now, the oil city of the UK, with many big oil companies based there. Its airport hosted the biggest heliport in the world, base for between 50 and 60 helicopters. The Chinook 234LR (Long Range) had an empty mass of about 27,500 pounds, with a 21,000-pound payload capacity. It was like an airliner, with headroom, luggage racks, a toilet, and inflight service! Helicopter pilots generally struggle with small payloads and limited fuel capacity; the Chinook was a helicopter pilot's dream – it could always carry the full

47-person contingent, with enough fuel for over 6 hours of flying, and it had very powerful twin engines. At the time of the accident, I already had over 2,500 hours on type and, despite the nightmare that the 1986 flight turned out to be, and after 45 years of flying and over 17,500 flying hours, I maintain that the Chinook will always be the best helicopter I have ever flown.

The Monday before the accident, 3rd November, I had taken one of the Chinooks – G-BWFC - to Sumburgh, in the Shetland Islands. We would operate out of Sumburgh for five days, heading back to Aberdeen on the Friday evening. There were 2 crews, one for the 2 morning flights to East Shetland Basin (a little over 100nm north-east of Sumburgh), and one for the single afternoon flight. As they say, when someone's time is up, the whole universe unwittingly conspires to make it happen. First Officer Neville Nixon, who died in the accident, was not even supposed to be on the ill-fated flight; he had been allotted the afternoon duty, but swapped with First Officer Mike Stanley, since Neville was totting up flying hours after being off flying for 3 years. He was 43, and had left Bristow Helicopters a few years earlier, giving up flying to help his wife, Pauline, to set up a chemist shop in York. After three years, the shop was doing so well that Pauline could manage by herself; this meant he could return to his first love, flying. Neville was at the controls on the return trip, characteristically leaning forward a little in his seat, rather than resting against its back; he was killed by whiplash while I, next to him, survived. Yet another bizarre twist of fate directed events that day. The original flight schedule included two stops – oilfields Brent Bravo and Brent Delta - and then back to Sumburgh; but Brent Alpha was unexpectedly included in the outgoing schedule, adding ten minutes to the flying time. Under the original schedule, the accident, which occurred a couple of minutes short of landing, would have caused no fatalities.

The outbound sortie, for which I was the handling pilot, was uneventful, with not the slightest portent of what lay ahead. When Neville took over for the return trip, the weather was sunny and clear. We got airborne at 1043hrs, with a full complement of 44 passengers and 3 crew, quickly climbed to 2500 feet, and switched to auto-pilot, chatting meanwhile of inconsequential things. All this time, the technical fault, which was to culminate in disaster, was developing above our heads – as I discovered later from listening to the Cockpit Voice Recorder tape, on which the sounds of imminent failure were clearly audible throughout. After about an hour of flying, and 40nm short of Sumburgh, we switched to approach frequency, began a slow descent to 1000 feet, and then continued descending to 500 feet. I contacted the company to give them the 'two minutes from landing' warning, which was routine. Meanwhile, in the Bristow hangar at Sumburgh, Capt Gordon Mitchell and his Coastguard crew were getting ready for a search-and-rescue training sortie. Their Sikorsky S-61 was fuelled and ready; they were just waiting for one of the crew to return from an errand, otherwise they would have been airborne earlier. It was a coincidence that they got airborne just after 1129, when we were on our approach to land. The control tower advised the Coastguard helicopter, "Oscar Charlie," to look out for the Chinook on finals.

When we were 3.5 nautical miles from the runway, a whining noise became audible in the cockpit. It didn't sound dangerous, and didn't worry either of us. We were 2 minutes from touchdown, and would get it checked as soon as we landed. The noise was getting louder though, and we wondered where it was coming from. Just then, our cabin attendant, Mike Walton, entered the cockpit to inform us that the passengers were strapped in and ready for landing. He heard us discussing the noise, and immediately realised that it was coming from the gearbox above his head; he didn't seem alarmed by it either. We were now roughly 300 feet above the water, speed was reducing to below 100 knots, and we were cleared by the control tower to land. Mike went out, closing the door behind him; almost immediately, there was an almighty bang, and, all of a sudden, I was looking straight up at the sky.

The whining noise had actually been the front gear (Spiral Bevel Ring Gear) breaking up. Once the gearbox failed, the front rotor began decelerating and it was only a matter of time before the two rotors, which intermesh as they counter-rotate, collided, with another loud bang. The rear rotor and gearbox broke away and fell into the sea, causing the rear of the helicopter to drop down (the two rotors work together to keep the fuselage level), while the nose pitched up. The airspeed almost instantly went from 100 knots to zero, the rapid deceleration causing severe whiplash. Half the passengers, and Neville, probably died at that moment. When they retrieved Neville's body from the seabed, the only injury on it was a broken neck. I, being the non-handling pilot, had my back against the backrest; the whiplash effect on me was not as great, although thinking about it or talking about it, like right now, I start feeling the pain in my back.

The helicopter was now falling apart, and dropping backwards into the sea like a stone. I grabbed the cyclic control and pushed it all the way forward, to level the helicopter, but only the front rotor responded; the rear rotor was gone. This action, however, flipped the cockpit section of the helicopter over, so that the front and rear sections were only attached at the floor, like a hinge, and we were now diving head first into the sea. The front rotor had broken part of the windscreen, and debris was flying into the cockpit. There were cuts and bruises on my face, but no damage to my eyes or ears. When we hit the water, the rear end of the helicopter took the impact, and all the remaining passengers, save one, died as a result of it. Meanwhile – as I discovered later – the cockpit had broken off from the main cabin on impact and, with me still in it, seemed to keep going down and down and down. It must have gone down at least 30 feet below the surface, before it stopped moving. I could see sunlight, and I knew which way I had to swim. However, when I left my seat and started to move, I discovered that I was going the wrong way; it was getting darker. I turned around and headed towards the sunlight again. I passed through the emergency window, which had blown away on impact, I think, and started to swim up towards the surface.

I surfaced, alive, and coherent. I have no recollection of undoing my straps – they were found intact later, save one which had broken – but I still managed to get free and make my way up. I held on to what appeared to be a piece of the fuel tank cover and floated. It looked like a big bowl, and I managed to climb into it but, two seconds later, a small wave tipped me over, and I was back in the water. I wasn't worried; in the back of my mind I knew the rescue helicopter would be overhead in a few minutes. I was just waiting for them to come and pick me up. My survival suit, which I had had no time to zip up, was full of water; the temperature of the water was about 7-8 degrees centigrade. In my own words at the time, "Not for a moment did I think that anybody was going to die!" But then a body popped up next to me, and then another and another. There must have been at least seven bodies floating close to me, and not moving. That is the first time it occurred to me that perhaps some people were dead. There was a lot of hydraulic fluid and pieces of the helicopter were floating around in the sea near me; I could see broken pieces everywhere.

When Oscar Charlie started his turn towards his training area, he asked the control tower where the Chinook was. The controller looked up and couldn't see the Chinook on finals; this amazed him, because he had seen us just 30 seconds earlier, and had given us clearance to land. Luckily for Eric Morrans and me, the Coastguard crew spotted the debris in the sea, and headed towards us. As soon as I saw them, I waved; the helicopter came overhead, and the winchman came down, put a strap around me and winched me up. My shoes were coming off but, for some reason, I kept hanging on to them; however I never saw them again!

Only one 20-year-old passenger, Eric Morrans, survived the crash. He was sitting in the front row of seats, which faces backwards; thus, he was protected from the whiplash. He was facing the other passengers, and saw the fear of death in their faces, as the helicopter was plunging vertically backwards into the sea; he was not to know that many were already dead. Eric was just plain lucky like me. Instinctively, he had zipped up his survival suit when he heard the big bang. There was a lot of debris flying around the cabin, and he was injured and lost consciousness. When the helicopter plunged into the water, he went with it; however, when he was about thirty feet under water, his survival suit, which was full of air, acted like a football, and threw him out through the hole behind him. When he reached the surface, a wave broke over his face and woke him up. Luckily for him, just as his eyes opened, a dinghy inflated next to him. He quickly got hold of it, wrapped its rope around his wrist, and passed out again. Then he heard the helicopter overhead, saw me being winched up, got worried that he might be left behind, and started waving frantically.

The Coastguard training mission had morphed into a real emergency but, as they searched for more survivors, Eric and I began to suffer from hypothermia, myself not least because my survival suit was still full of cold water. When the crewman saw that we were both closing our eyes, he persuaded the captain to take us to hospital; by this time, other helicopters were on the scene, and a rescue ship was also on the way. On arrival at Lerwick, my body temperature had fallen to about 33oC, and they cut off all my clothes and wrapped me in a space blanket. At this point, and with my eyes still closed, I heard a voice talking to me in Hindi, and wondered if I had reached heaven!… by a strange coincidence, the doctor treating me was a fellow Indian.

Apart from my brush with hypothermia, and a few cuts and bruises, I was apparently uninjured; the whiplash had only caused me a painful jerk. While the rear of the helicopter had taken all the impact, the cockpit had gone into the water as if from a 10 foot high diving board. A month later, when my wife insisted that my nose was crooked, the doctors found I had broken it; I had no recollection of the injury. The mechanical failure which caused the gearbox breakdown was a one-in-a-million chance; that it resulted in so many fatalities was a terrible orchestration of events. The Chinook was subsequently withdrawn from civil operation, though it is still widely used by the military. Friends advised me not to go back to flying. After all, the company would pension me off comfortably, but I knew "money wouldn't fill the hours"; flying was all I had ever wanted to do. By February, I was ready to fly again; however, the company insisted on psychological checks, and I actually resumed flying in April 1987. I was 45 at the time of the accident, flew for another 20 years, and enjoyed every minute of it.

Credit: Pushp Vaid

There But For...

I joined the Royal Navy in January 1961 as an Officer Cadet at The Britannia Royal Naval College in Dartmouth. After six months basic training, I moved on to flying training with the RAF at Linton-on-Ouse in Yorkshire, to aim for pilot's wings. At the end of that stage, there was a split to either more swept-wing jet training, or to the turbo-prop Fairey Gannet at RNAS Culdrose, in Cornwall. I qualified on the Gannet, and gained further experience in order to fly the AEW Mk3 (Airborne Early Warning) with the Headquarters Squadron, and eventually be assigned to a Flight on board ship. There were four Flights, each with four aircraft, and each Flight was attached to a particular aircraft carrier. This incident occurred when I was on board HMS Eagle in 1965.

It was the final day's flying before the ship sailed for Mombasa, and I would be travelling back to the UK for a new appointment. On the flying programme, I was down for the first launch of the day. The night before, I was in the bar. "Better stick to a small beer and turn in early, as first launch was at 0700," I thought. Just then, the Senior Pilot approached me. "Bob, I'm taking you off the flying programme tomorrow – I'm sorry, that's it, you've done your last sortie from the ship." Rather surprised and a little upset, as I was looking forward to my last catapult shot and deck-landing for some time, I enquired why? "I've seen too many people have something happen or do something silly on their last trip, so that's that and the Boss agrees. On the plus side, you can have a few more; I'll buy you a G&T or a beer."

I could see it was pointless to argue, so I took up the offer and got slightly merry before turning in for the night. Next thing I was aware of, through a thick head and bleary eye, lying in my bunk, was that the whole ship was vibrating very heavily; the ship's propellers were going 'Full Astern.' The cabin door was flung open, and Dai R---, one of our Observers, shouted, "The Gannet's in trouble," and disappeared up to the Quarter Deck, which is at the stern of the ship and open to the sea. Instantly awake now, I swiftly threw on my shorts, uniform shirt and sandals, and bolted up the ladder to the weatherdeck. We could see the ship's Wessex helicopter plane-guard hovering, and someone being winched from the water. "We think they've all surfaced." said someone. "Thank God."

What had happened? The aircraft was loaded onto the bow catapult, and was in the process of being tensioned and wound up to full power. The tail holdback failed prematurely, and the aircraft proceeded down the catapult track under its own power, without the launch force of the catapult. The pilot, Roger J--, throttled back to idle, and stood on the brakes, but was unable to stop the aircraft pitching over the front of the flight-deck into the sea. Roger and one of the Observers, Dusty M---, managed to exit the aircraft as it hit the water, but the second Observer, Mel H--- went down about 120 feet with the Gannet. He managed to free himself from the rear cockpit, however, and shot to the surface, rupturing an eardrum in the process.

That would have been my last sortie, had the Senior Pilot not removed me from the flying programme. We never discussed his decision to change it; was it a premonition, was it an impulse? Nearly fifty years on, I still wonder.

Post Script:
Of the 44 AEW Gannets built, 22 were lost to accidents or misfortune.

Credit: greenacre8/Wikipedia

The Met Balloon

As a young pilot, Roger Dimmock survived a spectacular Sea Hawk fire and crash at the 1958 Farnborough Air Show. He eventually rose to be a Rear Admiral, and Flag Officer Naval Air Command. His death at 78, brought back vivid memories for me of the time, in 1970, when he was a Buccaneer pilot, and Senior Naval Officer at RAF Honington. I was a brand-new Buccaneer navigator, and a Flight Commander on No 12 (Bomber) Squadron. The story of our involvement in the infamous Meteorological Balloon Saga is best recounted over several pints of beer. However, I shall try to write as I remember it, 40 years on.

RAF Honington was then home to the RAF's first Buccaneer squadron, 12 Sqn, and the Buccaneer Operational Conversion Unit, 237 OCU. The Royal Navy Buccaneers had always disembarked to RAF Lossiemouth as their shore base, but now 809 NAS Buccaneers and crews came ashore from Ark Royal's latest commission and joined us at Honington. It was very much a gathering of the Buccaneer "Brotherhood". Most of the RAF and RN aircrew had trained with 736 NAS at Lossie, and some of the "Light Blue" had flown to the deck with 809 and other "Dark Blue" units. The welcome ashore was enthusiastic; the first joint Guest Night in the Mess was outstanding/outrageous. Every dining-in wheeze, perfected over the years in wardrooms and messes, was wheeled out and/or exploded: black cotton, tied to opposite-side chairs, cleared the tables of cutlery; flower displays and cabbages exploded etc, etc. It was great fun, but MESSY!

The Station Commander ("The Bear") called together all officers and decreed, in his usual very positive style, that the next Officer's Mess Guest Night was to see "NO HORSEPLAY WHATSOEVER." Meanwhile, in a good political RAF/RN "Jointery" move, The Bear appointed the Senior Naval Officer, Commander Roger Dimmock, as President of the Mess Committee (PMC). The "No Horseplay" decree just had to be challenged! This was a task which really had to be down to 12 Sqn and, accordingly, the two Flight Commanders decided to risk our careers. I had heard that a (radio-sonde) met balloon, inflated under a mess carpet, could be impressive. We persuaded a reluctant Met Man to donate a balloon to research, promising that it would not be released to the upper atmosphere; it came folded in a long box, with a lot of talcum powder. It was, in fact, a lot of balloon for indoors!

A quiet recce as to the potential of the mess carpet revealed that the heavy dining tables for a sold-out Mess Guest Night would prevent a spectacular carpet rise. So, the boxed balloon was placed behind the long, red velvet curtains behind the top table, and connected through a window to a trolley bearing multiple cylinders of compressed air. Timing of the inflation had to be immaculate, so a reliable, fully-qualified Buccaneer pilot agreed to take on the duty. The Guest Night, chaired by the PMC, Roger Dimmock, and full-to-bursting with officers in their best light and dark blue mess kits, was enjoyable and EXTREMELY well-behaved. The Bear, seated beside his new PMC, watched fiercely for any sign of trouble; there was none and, after the Loyal Toast, he rose to speak. There was a faint "flubba-lubba" from behind the curtains in his 6 o'clock - undaunted, he continued and welcomed the guests.

As the valves of more air cylinders were opened, the "FLUBBA-LUBBA" noise rose to prevent further speech, and the Station Commander sat down, looking less than pleased. Much to the delight of their juniors, who were beginning to work out the cause of the disturbance, the ballooning curtains began pushing the senior occupants of the top table over their port glasses. The balloon was not yet fully inflated when the pressure became too much for its jury-rigged, sticky-taped connection to the air trolley. It burst through the curtains, over the senior diners, and took majestic undulating flight the full length of the dining-room. As it did so, a dense cloud of talcum powder filled the room and, despite all of their mess kits now being a talcum-powder-modified uniform bluey-grey, the crowd went wild. The Bear did not look pleased; a lesser man would have been apoplectic. Roger Dimmock saved the day, banged the gavel for good order and, with great aplomb and quick wit, showed his Admiral potential: "Gentlemen! I have often heard of The Immaculate Conception; this is the first time I have witnessed it."

At the end of an impressive, spine-trembling "hats on" interview for we two Flight Commanders, our Station Commander conceded that, notwithstanding conduct unbecoming of Squadron Leaders, the Met Balloon had been a Good Wheeze.

... But Modesty Forbids

I was accepted for aircrew 'PNB' (Pilot/Navigator/Bomber) in May 1943, but was informed that there was a deferment period, often months. I was 17 years and 8 months old at the time, and this seemed like a lifetime; but there was a lifeline, as I had been under 14 on 3rd September 1939, so my education was of elementary standard. I was, therefore, eligible for a PACT (Pre-Aircrew Training) course of 6 months duration, which I gladly accepted, and my improved educational standard laid the keel for what, in later life, amounted to three professional qualifications and a directorship.

After PACT, I was posted back to the Aircrew Receiving Centre at St. John's Wood, where I gained first-hand experience of 'Doodlebugs' and V2s. Next, I was sent to Marshall's Flying School, Cambridge, where I did my twelve hours on Tiger Moths, and was then posted to 17 Initial Training Wing at Scarborough, only to find that it had been closed the week before; cadets were being sent to work on farms, and do menial tasks on RAF stations. By a crafty move, too detailed to explain in this narrative, I wangled a posting to RAF Lossiemouth, as Clerk (Special Duties Intelligence), where I had a minor role in the work leading to the sinking of the Tirpitz, and I have a piece of the Tirpitz with an engraved plate, presented to me and other members of what was to be my first Squadron (617), from the people of Tromso.

My regular RAF career lasted until 1950, during which time I was a flight engineer on Lancasters, Lincolns and B-29s, and which contained its fair share of amusing incidents and narrow squeaks. My first flight in a Lincoln was an air test and, halfway through a 'corkscrew', there was a loud cracking sound from the starboard mainplane. The pilot shouted, "What was that, Flight Engineer?" "I haven't a f****** clue, but get down fast!" I replied. We landed with due haste, and an examination showed that, out of the four high-tensile steel shackles which fixed the mainplane to the centre-section, one had sheared and the adjoining one was cracked halfway through. Our groundcrew Flight Sergeant reckoned that, in a couple more minutes, the starboard mainplane would have fallen off, and we would have ploughed into the deck.

Some time later, a Warrant Officer flight engineer on 100 Squadron at RAF Hemswell obtained a compassionate posting to 617 at RAF Binbrook, as his wife, who lived in Louth, was expecting their first child, and a difficult birth was anticipated. In order to decide who should replace him on 100 Squadron, we drew blades of grass, and I got the short straw. I was furious, as my crew had been detailed to do an exercise 'Sunray' to Shallufa (near Alexandria), and this guy had taken my slot; my pilot tried to intervene on my behalf, but the CO would not budge. On the way home, the Lincoln ran into huge Cumulo-Nimbus clouds. It broke up, ploughed in at Istres (near Marseilles), and all the crew were killed - including nine ground staff, who were returning, after having completed their duties. I still have a copy of a summary of the findings of the Court of Enquiry.

On another occasion, I had been flying with a different captain (Paddy), as his Flight Engineer (Bob) was grounded for health reasons. Bob eventually returned, and the crew were detailed for a cross-country. The usual checks were done, and Bob told Paddy that a split-pin, which locked the pilot's seat at the required height, was missing. Paddy, who was about 5ft 5ins tall, said, "I'm not declaring the aircraft U/S for a bloody split pin!" I watched the take-off from dispersal; the tail had just come up when Paddy's seat collapsed, the Lincoln slewed to port, wiped off the undercart and bent all the props. All the crew, except the Flight Engineer, were out in record time, in case the aircraft caught fire. Bob eventually emerged, in a leisurely manner, through the pilot's canopy; when I asked why he had taken so long, he said he had followed the baling-out procedure, gone into the bomb aimer's compartment, and lifted the escape hatch. He was puzzled to find his means of escape blocked by terra firma, and it took some little while for him to realise he was looking at the grass verge.

I had done 199 trips, and was due to do my last, before deciding whether to stay in the RAF or come out. I was with 7 Squadron at RAF Upwood at the time, and I was detailed to do a seven-hour cross-country with an unfamiliar pilot, a Czech called Flight Sergeant Kijack. During the take-off run, we were in a tail-up attitude, just before lift-off, when he shouted, "Cut power, Engineer!" I quickly slackened the throttle lock, and pulled the throttles back. He then added, "The aircraft just wouldn't unstick." I assured him that he had had full power for take-off, and that all was OK. He said, "We will try again, but do not lock the throttles." We tried again, and the same thing happened. We taxied to dispersal, and I thought, "This lazy b*****d probably has a date, and is skiving out of a long trip." The CO was awaiting us, and demanded an explanation; he was not a happy bunny. He ordered Kijack and myself to wait while he tried himself, with the dire threat that, if he managed to take off, we were in the s*** up to our necks. We watched his attempted take-off with some trepidation, but the same thing happened for a third time. I spoke with the groundcrew Flight Sergeant, and we eventually jacked up the Lincoln into what was similar to a tail-up take-off position. We then looked at the aircraft from some distance behind it, and immediately saw that the twin fin and rudder assembly was not horizontal, but had a pronounced list to starboard. The Lincoln fuselage was built around four 'drainpipes,' one of which had fractured. In the pre-flight check, and in a tail-down position, the fractured ends met and, as the fuselage was dark and dirty, neither the pilot nor I had spotted such an unusual and unexpected structural failure. If the pilot had forced the aircraft into flight, it would probably have broken its back.

During my time with 100 Squadron at RAF Hemswell, we had had a 'twinning' arrangement with the 345th Bombing Squadron of the 9th US Airforce at Sculthorpe, which was operating B29 Superforts. Some of their personnel qualified on Lincolns and I, for one, qualified as a Flight Engineer on B29s (later used by the RAF and renamed Washingtons). In 1952, after I retired, I was still a 'First Call' reservist, and was called up and posted to 15 Squadron at RAF Woodhall Spa, where they were operating Washingtons. I was kept there for a few weeks, mainly on long cross-countries and bombing from 30,000 feet; then I was allowed to return to my civvy job, but I always wondered: "Why did they call me up?" Many years later, my wife and I were having a holiday at Eaves Hall, a country house in Lancashire, only available to Civil Servants (active or retired). As happens on such occasions, the 'hangar doors' got opened, and I happened to get into conversation with a retired senior Air Ministry official. When I told him of my call-up, he chuckled and said "I was one of the officials responsible for that." He told me that, at that time, there were only six qualified Washington Flight Engineers on the Reserve, and we were all called up and posted in accordance with requirements. He added that, at that point, whether or not to 'nuke' North Korea hung in the balance, and the only RAF aircraft capable of carrying the nuclear weapon was the Washington. When it was decided not to carry out this option, the reservists were sent home. My mind still boggles at the possibilities.

Thunderbugs Are Go!

In the very early hours of the morning of Wednesday 8th July 1970, when RAF Kinloss was undergoing TACEVAL[1] and we were sleeping in the Mess, my captain came knocking on my door, with the news that we were to get airborne and fly south to one of the weapons ranges off the south coast of Cornwall. Once there, we were to carry out practice drops of two inert Mk 30 torpedoes against a padded target, in the form of a marine craft out of Falmouth.

After a pleasant flight down the spine of the country in the early morning sunshine, and an excellent breakfast, we let down towards the ranges, and the skipper carried out the first exercise, a dummy run followed by the actual weapon release. Unfortunately, on this lovely summer morning, the air was filled with 'thunder bugs' and, down at 200 feet above the glistening sea, the windscreens quickly became obscured by these tiny flies. Not a problem though, as the aircraft's massive windscreen wipers and high pressure sprayers quickly cleared them away. I then flew my dummy run, cleaned the windscreens and carried out the drop but, as we climbed away this fourth time, there was no water jet to accompany the wipers, and both windscreens were transformed into a dark, impenetrable mess.

"Washer bottle's run out, Eng" I intoned, only to receive the reply: "No. There's plenty of water still in them; the float is still only half way down the sight tube. I've checked the circuit breaker, and reset it, but it hadn't popped."

With not a rain-cloud in the sky to act as a water source, we set off to attempt a landing at close-by St Mawgan, but I wouldn't even have driven my car out of the garage in such a state. St Mawgan Radar picked us up, fed us across to Talk-down, and we positioned ourselves for a landing on Runway 13, with virtually zero forward visibility. Then, just as the final controller reported that he had us on radar and that we were approaching the descent point for an azimuth-only radar approach, the engineer came back on the intercom. "Sorry guys. My mistake. The reservoir is empty - that's a dirty mark on the sight glass!" The AEO[2] came forward with a couple of kettles full of water and some washing up liquid, topped up the reservoir as necessary, and we carried out an uneventful landing - but it could have been so very different!

---

[1] TACEVAL: Tactical evaluation of NATO declared units by NATO staff.
[2] AEO: Air Electronics Operator.

You Go Left, I'll Go Right

Back in the 70s, most front-line flying stations had Open Days, including whatever flying displays they could muster, and the resident squadrons looked forward to this annual opportunity to have a good time and make a lot of noise, without the brickbats normally associated with such exuberance. One year, some bright spark at HQ RAF Germany decided that it would be a good wheeze if each squadron was allocated a different type of display to perform, thus varying the spectacle for the punters, and also allowing each display team to support the other Open Days, thus maximising the breadth of each show.

So it was that, in the summer of '75, RAF Guterslöh and RAF Laarbruch were designated as the host Stations, and 19 and 92 Squadrons were required to work up a display each: 19, a Diamond 9 formation, which then degenerated in to an 'airfield attack' (essentially flying as low, fast and noisily as one thought one could get away with); and 92, a 5-ship formation aerobatic team. The authorised callsign was 'Cobra Formation'; however, since our Lightning F2A's were painted green, it didn't take long for this little combo to be christened 'The Green Marrows' – can't think where the name came from. Obviously, this scheme generated a lot of fun for a limited number of people, so some compensatory plan for the others was in order. 92 were due to undertake a Squadron Exchange with 723 Squadron, Royal Danish Air Force (RDAF), an F-104 outfit based at Ålborg, in the September, and it was decided that the 'Away' team would be selected from those who were not in the formation.

Ah, the best-laid plans of mice and men! It so happened that watching the display at Laarbruch was the Chief of Staff of the RDAF; he was clearly so impressed that he prevailed upon our C-in-C to authorise us to display at the planned RDAF Silver Jubilee celebrations at Ålborg and Karup which, as luck would have it, fell during our planned Squadron Exchange. Thus it was that The Green Marrows (aka Cobra Formation) got the best of both worlds; we muttered some platitudes about the 'fortunes of war' to our less fortunate comrades (from a safe distance), and departed for Denmark. Now, it will not have escaped the notice of the cognoscenti that Squadron Exchanges, by their very nature, were extremely convivial affairs, during which the flying took very much a back seat to the socialising; stupid games involving beer, aqvavit, skittles and pianos were de rigueur and, indeed, the programme was tailored to take account of it. It was not unknown to have a 'flying team' and a 'drinking team', the duties being alternated on a daily basis, to take account of the fact that we were heavily outnumbered by the home side. However, here arose a problem, in that the 'flying team' for the planned practices and displays had, de facto, picked itself. The display routine was not inordinately ambitious by professional formation aerobatics standards, but the Lightning was a big, heavy, powerful beast, not ideally suited to such antics, and it was hard work. Moreover, the Danes are, by nature, a sociable lot, and Ålborg – both the base and the town – was a lively place. I have an abiding memory of a little number called a 'Depth Charge', which consisted of a litre mug of ice-cold beer into which was carefully dropped a shot glass of aqvavit. This had to be 'downed-in-one' and, at first, to those accustomed to such pastimes, it all went quite well. This was until the beer mug was nearly empty, at which point the shot glass fell over, and the last few mouthfuls were pure firewater. I will not perjure myself here by reporting to what extent the 'flying-' and 'drinking-team' plan worked; suffice to say that the hard work was not confined to the flying team; the drinkers needed a day off, too.

The weather for the practice days was ideal – light winds, high cloudbase and mostly sunny – and we were getting quite good at this malarkey. There are a limited number of formations one can present with 5 aircraft, but we were becoming quite slick. At one point, the two outer wingmen – Nige and me – would break out from the formation on a call from our trusty leader, Lloyd, and position for an opposition run down the runway at many knots and not many feet, followed by another couple of 'whifferdills' and then a rejoin; this latter could be the most demanding, since catching up in the Lightning tended not to be a problem; stopping once you got there, however... One of the challenges for this 'Poor-Man's Synchro Pair' was adapting quickly from close formation mode to airfield flypast mode, since we had, until the break-out, been alternating our view between all-white-and-blue and all-green-and-brown, both with four large lumps of metal oscillating in the near foreground. The timing also depended fairly critically on our being ejected from the formation at the correct moment, pointing in the right direction.

The displays at Ålborg and Karup had been cunningly planned on successive days, in order that the great and good could attend both, and also so that the maximum number of flying 'acts' could partake in both. The weather on display day at at Ålborg was pretty grobbly, but the coastline helped the orientation and the display went well. Came the day for the display at Karup, however, and it was a different story. The cloud was low, the sun was nowhere to be seen, and the vis was 'pants' (not a word we used in those days, but suitably expressive none the less). The view from the wings alternated between grey-grey and green-grey, still with the oscillating lumps of metal, but without a discernible horizon. The 'call-to-arms' from our trusty leader (which, I have to say, was smack-dab in the right place, and pointing in the right direction) pitched Mutt and Jeff off into a murky world, which was every bit as bad as we had feared. The problem was that we could not just turn tight enough to keep the airfield in sight (although the Lightning was perfectly capable), because that would screw up the timing. So, we had to stick to the plan and hope for the best; I even remember cross-referencing the TACAN[1] range, for what good that might have done me. Fortunately, some gem of an air-trafficker had left both sets of approach lights on full, and it was with no little relief that I rolled out in about the right place at about the right time, and eventually spotted Nige. I hear much these days about the ability of the fairer sex to multi-task, and this capacity might also, under normal circumstances, have been ascribed to Lightning pilots and one-armed paper-hangers. Sad to say, at this particular point, the tasks had got a bit too multi-, and observing the priorities (not hitting the ground and not hitting each other) had, so to speak, put other things slightly on the back-burner – or, more accurately, both burners. As we approached the cross-over point at mid-runway, it all seemed to go a bit quiet – in the cockpit, at any rate - and I observed the relevant needle to be hovering just the wrong side of the figure 1[2]!

We found the other three, and joined up – no mean feat in itself – for the return to Ålborg. This helped to take my mind off the roasting which undoubtedly lay in store and, sure enough, we hadn't been on the ground long before the rumours of mayhem at Karup began to filter through. Aided and abetted by a very supportive Ålborg Base Commander, Lloyd made the obligatory apologetic phone call to Karup – to be told by the Karup Base Commander that, in the opinion of the RDAF Chief of Staff, broken glass in the spectator car park was an occupational hazard for those attending airshows, the Base had insurance, the sonic boom had been impressive and, under the circumstances, it had been a damn fine show.

There were two drinking teams on duty that night, and copious quantities of Depth-Charge were had by all!

---

[1] TACAN: Tactical Air Navigation equipment.
[2] Figure 1: In this context it refers to Mach 1, the speed of sound.

QRA Is Not All Waiting Around

Life on a Phantom Squadron at RAF Leuchars in the mid to late 1970s involved spending a rewarding number of days of the year on 24-hour Quick Reaction Alert (QRA) - rewarding, because QRA was often launched to intercept Soviet aircraft which had entered the UK Air Defence Region (ADR). Indeed, it was not unusual for aircrew to achieve, annually, double-figure numbers of intercepts, mostly Badger D and G (Maritime Recce and Strike respectively) and Bear D and F (Maritime Recce & Targeting/Electronic Surveillance and Maritime Recce/ Anti-Submarine Warfare respectively), and the occasional Coot A (Electronic Intelligence Gathering) aircraft.

The sorties flown by the Soviets generally originated from bases in the Murmansk Area, and involved transits around the North Cape of Norway to the UK's area of interest. These flights fell largely into 4 main categories: high level transits, close to Iceland, by aircraft en route to Cuba; high/low transits to the west of Scotland and Ireland, by aircraft en route to operations with Soviet naval forces in the Bay of Biscay; operations at all altitudes by aircraft in support of Soviet Naval Forces operating within the UK ADR, usually between Scotland and Iceland; and random reconnaissance and electronic intelligence gathering sorties, sometimes involving Coot and Bison aircraft. Generally, the busiest time of the year for QRA in this Cold War era was late September and early October, when both NATO and the Warsaw Pact engaged in large naval exercises to the north of Scotland. These exercises always coincided with the Station's Annual Battle of Britain Reception Party, which regularly featured a frantic search for sober aircrew to man additional QRA aircraft. Indeed, in this busy autumn period, it was not unusual to have as many as eight armed aircraft on stand-by to intercept the Soviet aircraft. During the rest of the year, there would be just two aircraft on 24-hour alert in the northern half of the UK. The late summer of 1978 was no exception to the norm, and I recall vividly 2 sorties in particular.

On the first, Al Richey and I - who flew as a constituted crew for around 2 years - were scrambled to intercept 2 Badger G aircraft, supporting Soviet Fleet operations in the Iceland/Faroes Gap. Although we acquired radar contact with the pair whilst they were still at high level, we failed to intercept them before they entered cloud in a descent; we therefore followed them through the cloud at a range of about a mile. Finally breaking cloud at around 2,000 feet, we saw the Badgers and some Soviet ships ahead of us; we also had a range of lights and sounds emanating from our Radar Warning Receiver (RWR). Closing in on the Badgers - as we were required to do to photograph them, so that the Intelligence Experts could check for the addition of new aerials and equipment - we noticed that each aircraft had what appeared to be a large stage arc light strapped under the rear fuselage. At about the same time, the Badger aircrew clearly became aware of our close presence, and commenced fairly aggressive manoeuvring, to prevent us getting a clear picture of their fuselage. To put the situation into context, I would add that, unlike the much larger and less manoeuvrable Bear, the Badger was akin to a large Canberra in terms of its agility and manoeuvrability. Although it took some time to get in position, we won - we got our close-up pictures. However, despite completing the usual post-flight reports, we never did find out the function of the devices located under the fuselage!

The second sortie occurred during the week following the Annual Reception. Al and I were tasked to take part in an exercise, in support of NATO naval forces exercising off the Scottish Coast. After an early morning launch, we had completed the first part of the mission, and were just finishing refuelling from a Victor tanker, when we were suddenly allocated a QRA task. This was despite flying an unarmed aircraft, and not carrying the obligatory QRA camera - a situation that would later prove to be extremely unfortunate. It was a beautiful autumn day, with not a cloud in the sky, as we headed north-east to intercept an aircraft which had just come around the North Cape. Al got an early pick-up on our radar, and we set up a stern intercept at a height of just over 30,000 feet. As we approached, we found it to be a Badger G, armed with two Kelt air-to-surface missiles. As mentioned before, the Badger is slightly larger than the Canberra, while the Kelt missiles it was carrying, one under each wing, looked like mini-aircraft. On account of the weapon load, we assumed that it was on some form of simulated attack profile against a land- or sea-based target. What we did not know at this stage was how dynamic this profile would become!

Al and I decided to sit loosely off the Badger's right wing. As it reached about 150 miles from the UK coast, it entered a slow descent; it was not an unusual event for a Badger to simulate the launch of a Kelt missile, and then to simulate the weapon's profile. Some ten minutes later, having done some deductive work,

Al announced that he thought the target was an oil rig, and he was right. By now, the Badger had descended below 5,000 feet, and I had closed to a tight formation position on its right wing; to our surprise the aircraft kept descending, eventually ending up significantly below 500 feet, and well below the height of the main platforms on the rigs. At this point, Al in the back seat became a little agitated, as we both realised, at the same time, that the right-hand turn which the Badger had entered, to fly between two rigs, put us extremely low, and in danger of being flown into the sea. Common sense prevailed, and we dropped back to shadow the Badger, as it flew a most impressive profile between the oil rigs, at a height well below 250 feet, with workers gazing down on it from the main platforms.

On our return to base, we filed the usual Intelligence Report but, as we were not carrying a QRA camera, there was no formal evidence to confirm what we had witnessed. Suffice to say that, some days later, we were accused of exaggerating what we had seen, and were advised that Soviet pilots were extremely professional and well-disciplined, and would never fly profiles so low! Al was incensed that our report had received such off-hand treatment, and he was in favour of writing to the owners of the rigs, to try and acquire any photographic evidence of the event which may have been taken by their workers. Wisely, I think, we decided to let the matter drop.

QRA duties did, however, have a lighter side as exemplified by two other memories. Firstly, the entertainment we used to have with Bear aircrew, as they tried to take pictures of our aircraft. The Bear has two large observation blisters, one on either side of the fuselage, just forward of the aircraft's tail, and it was commonplace for the Soviet aircrew to use these to try to take our picture. The only problem was that they employed tripod-mounted cameras, which took some time to set up; it was thus great fun to move from one side of the Bear to the other just as our picture was about to be taken. After a few cycles of this cat-and-mouse game, we generally got a glare and an abusive gesture from the camera operator! Secondly, my favourite profile: a launch around midnight in mid-summer, supported by a tanker, to intercept the two Bear aircraft doing the routine Cuba run. At that time of year, it is virtually permanent daylight at 60o North and so, after the intercept, we were able to refuel to full and then to transit home at low level along the coast of the Outer Isles and Eastern Scotland, the whole environment being extremely quiet and serene so early in the morning. Generally we arrived back at Leuchars in time for breakfast, and the 8am shift-change.

Night Fright - RAF Jever 1952

After completing my flying training in Southern Rhodesia, I was posted to Moreton-in-the-Marsh for a two-week 'weather acclimatisation' course, on the Harvard IIB. This former RAF airfield is now home to the Fire Service College. After that, it was to the Advanced Flying School at RAF Valley, for conversion on to the Vampire. There were no two-seat Vampires then, so you flew the pre-solo in the Meteor TMk7, before being sent off on your first Vampire sortie. As courses were running late, our night flying phase was cancelled and "would have to be completed on the Squadron later."

Before joining our first squadron we were posted to RAF Chivenor, the fighter Operational Conversion Unit (OCU), to be taught how to aim the four 30 mm cannons; performance was assessed by cine-film taken from a camera attached to the gunsight. One live air-to-air firing sortie and air-to-ground rocketing was also included. Flying close formation, in all weathers, was also quite a test for us. While walking to the mess for breakfast on the first morning, at about 0700, I heard a fast, low flying aircraft approaching the airfield. I had a brief glimpse of a Meteor flying between the hangars very low, at less than 100 feet. It was inverted, and I thought that it might crash; of course it didn't and, seconds later, I saw the aircraft climb steeply, still inverted and then rolling through 180 deg (the Meteor had a maximum of 11 seconds inverted flight at low level). The pilot, Flt Lt Ken Goodwin, had just returned from the morning weather recce. Everyone said that he would kill himself, but he never did. Some years later, he became the RAF Aerobatic Champion, piloting a Lightning, and then won the inter-services competition. He retired as a Group Captain.

The OCU Staff were well known for their "press on" attitude during that period, and student pilots were encouraged accordingly; at least we were a bit prepared for what to expect on our first squadron tour! On the 12th November 1952, I was posted to the 2nd Tactical Air Force in Germany, to join No 112 Squadron in the Day Fighter Ground Attack (DFGA) role. The journey was by train from London to Harwich, then by ferry to the Hook of Holland. After that, more trains, and finally by RAF coach to RAF Jever in the north of Germany, a former operational fighter 'flugplatz' for the Luftwaffe. As I stepped out of the RAF coach at the Mess (in the dark), I was greeted by one of the squadron pilots who said, "Don't bother to unpack, we're off to Sylt in the morning." Not knowing what he was talking about, I was taken to the Mess bar for a briefing about the forthcoming detachment; I don't think I remembered a thing, apart from being told that I would be having a Flight Commander's arrival check with Flt Lt Blair in the two-seat Meteor the next morning, before departing to Sylt. I hadn't a clue where it was, why we were going, or what APC[1] stood for. Sylt, I later discovered, is an island joined to the mainland by a causeway, close to the German/Danish border. The island was, and still is, a long-established holiday resort, well known for its nudist beach.

The next morning, I was met by the Flight Commander, who gave me a short pre-flight brief, prior to my arrival check; the brief was "Follow me and jump in" or something like that. I do remember that it was a bright sunny morning, and I wasn't being treated like a student for the first time since I joined the RAF. The sortie consisted of a sector-recce, and lasted for about 35 minutes at low level, which was about the longest you could stay airborne at lower levels in the Meteor 7, without drop tanks. After I had been shown the local landmarks, we approached the airfield; I was instructed to position for a 'Run in and break' as per Standard Operating Procedures. I made what I thought was a spirited low approach for the run in but, at this stage, the Flight Commander commented that I was rather high, about 300 feet, and took control. RAF Jever had been cut out of a dense pine forest; he approached, just over the treetops at about 270 knots, climbing to about 400 feet on the downwind leg. At that stage, I vaguely remember being handed control to complete the approach to land. The debrief would have been short. Flt Lt Blair had flown Tempests and Typhoons against ground targets in German-occupied France during the latter stages of the war; he now lives in Devon.

Later that day, I joined the ground party for the two-day road journey to Sylt. Only the senior, or more experienced, squadron pilots flew up in the Vampires; the rest went by road, apart from two or three who were 'supervising' the others, because there weren't enough aircraft for all senior pilots to go by air. There was a hierarchy among the squadron pilots; where you fitted in was never said, but you just knew. For the first six months, you were definitely at the bottom, unless you could drink copious amounts of beer, or distinguish yourself in some way without causing offence or being arrested. The journey, via a night-stop in Hamburg,

---

[1]APC: Armament Practice Camp.

could be the subject of another story. Suffice to say that nobody slept, as far as I was aware, Dortmund Brewery made a lot of money, and we all had headaches the following day. The senior pilots had taken us on a guided tour of the once-famous Reeperbahn, where some of our ground-crew were already located in the best night clubs. As we were not allowed to fraternise in those days we had to find alternative venues.

Firing on the flag target (towed by a Tempest MkVI) was exciting and very competitive; this was our 'raison d'être.' The Flights were divided alternately into PM/AM shifts, so every other evening was free, and you had the next morning to recover. You could expect up to five of these detachments during a tour, and you were judged by your ability to hit the flag; the most successful pilots approached the target at very close range before firing. Occasionally, someone would collide with the heavy bar to which the flag was attached, always with considerable damage to the aircraft. On one detachment, a pilot fired a 30mm cannon round into the cockpit of the Tempest, destroying the instrument panel; the Tempest landed safely, but the squadron pilot was subsequently dismissed from the squadron, and sent back to the UK. Similar misdemeanours were not uncommon, and time was not normally wasted on Unit Inquiries or Courts Martial.

After the month's detachment was over, a list of pilots who were due to fly back was read out, and I was surprised to hear my name called. I was not a heavy drinker, nor had I achieved high scores on the flag. As the most junior member, the kudos associated with flying back with some of the hierarchy was considerable. On the final day, the air party was briefed to take off at dusk (about 5:30PM – the month was December), to land back at Jever about 45 minutes later, in the dark; this would make us night current, which was a quarterly requirement. Night flying was always unpopular with the Flight Commanders, and scheduled programmes were usually cancelled 'for weather reasons.' Having never flown a jet aircraft at night, I wondered whether I should declare it or not; my last solo night flight had been in a Harvard, during the FTS in Southern Rhodesia, more than a year before. The real possibility of appearing 'naff' by the other pilots, and even by the Boss, flashed through my mind; students on flying courses were occasionally suspended due to LMF[2], and I couldn't risk that tag. Of course, had I spoken, I

---

[2] LMF: Lack of moral fibre.

would immediately have been transferred to the ground party and the thought of that reinforced my decision.

We took off in 'stream', and I joined the others as No 4, flying in a 'finger-four' battle formation; as we approached the airfield, we were split up, to join individually and fly only one circuit to land (which fulfilled the Group requirement to maintain night currency).

At this point, I was feeling quite confident, having enjoyed the transit flight without any responsibility for navigation. I remember thinking that a long low steady approach would be the sensible thing to do, making sure that I landed off the first approach as briefed. The weather was good, and the airfield lighting spectacular. I wisely extended downwind (so I thought), feeling quite pleased with myself that I had kept my mouth shut.

After turning onto the final approach, having lined up with the runway, I selected the flap etc; all seemed to be going well, when suddenly all the airfield lights were extinguished. I immediately reported this to Air Traffic Control, keeping as calm as possible. Their response was immediate, "The Airfield lighting is fully serviceable!" I suppose it took about 3 or 4 seconds for me to realise that I had descended below the tree line. I applied full power and climbed steeply (the engine could have surged but, thankfully, it didn't). After what seemed like an age, the runway lights re-appeared. Back in the hangar, those that had already landed were heading for the Airmens' Mess for a night- flying supper, or direct to the Mess bar for more drinking. No one ever spoke to me or queried my R/T call on finals; perhaps no one else heard it. The ATC controller never mentioned it, and so I just debriefed myself; in those days, no one wanted to make a fuss.

I learnt many lessons during that tour, but that was one I shall never forget.

Credit: digitaltmuseum.se

We Seem To Have Mislaid An Aeroplane

It was sometime in the 60s, on board a big NATO aircraft carrier. Flying Operations had finished for the day, and the flight-deck teams were re-spotting aircraft on the deck, in readiness for flying next morning. It was dark, the sea state was flat calm, no wind, a beautiful evening somewhere in the Indian Ocean.

A flight-deck crew would consist of a tractor (with driver), towbar attached to the aircraft, and two accompanying crew, carrying chocks, who would walk alongside during the move. When on the designated spot, No 1 in this case, they would secure each aircraft by means of chain lashings to ringbolts in the deck, and place chocks under the main wheels. The rule was to have at least two lashings attached, and two chocks in place, before un-hitching the tractor and moving on to the next aircraft. The end of the watch was very near, and the crews were keen to finish their task, before heading below for a well-earned meal and a rest. One crew had just positioned their aircraft right on the stern (back end or blunt end for the Crabs), and realized that they were short of lashings, but had two chocks, which were hurriedly placed around one mainwheel. "I'll bring more lashings with the next airplane," said the driver, as they unhitched the towbar, and hastened back up the deck for the next aeroplane.

The ship was under way, making about ten knots, with no movement of the deck, as it was a calm sea. Only those on the Bridge seemed aware of a Supertanker heading the other way, passing abeam about half a mile from the ship, and creating a large bow wave. Our deck team had hooked up the next aircraft, and eventually found some more lashings, and moved back sternwards to the next parking spot. They approached the stern, just as a Squadron engineer came up on deck to investigate an unusual "tearing noise" he'd heard, as he described it. Meanwhile, a very puzzled tractor-driver was thinking to himself: "That's funny, I thought we used No 1 spot!" But there was nothing on No 1 spot, or anywhere around it! The flight deck and lifts were thoroughly searched, but not a trace of the missing aircraft was found. It was if it had vanished into thin air – or had never existed.

What they hadn't realised was that, while they were otherwise occupied, the huge tanker passing abeam had made just enough disturbance in the sea to cause the ship to pitch slightly, which caused the aircraft [no brakes] to jump the chocks, roll gently over the side and plunge to the bottom of the Indian Ocean… where it rests to this day!!

Blundell's Night Fright

In April 1964, I had reached the end of my Canberra flying tour. Most Canberra drivers at that time progressed onto the V-force, but I still had a yearning for fast jets – there had been no Hunter postings from my course out of flying training. In order to avoid having to fly around at 60,000ft attached to a bucket of sunshine[1], I applied for Central Flying School (CFS), hoping that I might get sent to RAF Valley to fly the Gnat and thence onto faster things. The posting staff had other ideas, and sent me to fly Chipmunks at a University Air Squadron (UAS); and, being a bachelor, I had to live in a Mess, and the only available slot from my CFS course was on St Andrews UAS, which flew out of RAF Leuchars.

Leuchars, at that time, was home to two Lightning Squadrons, 23 and 74. The Russian Bear crews knew who was intercepting them by the coloured tails, 23 being white with a red eagle on it, while 74 was black with its Tiger's head. The UAS normally flew at weekends, as Leuchars was an MDA[2], but we could also fly during the week, and fitted in well with the Lightnings without any conflictions. They flew circuits to the north of the airfield, while we flew ours to the south. If we were airborne when a pair of Lightnings was returning to base, we simply flew a racetrack pattern to the south of the airfield, using an into-wind track parallel to the runway, half way between the downwind leg and the runway. It worked very well. We had the additional safety precaution that the Lightnings would fly their circuits at 1200ft while we stayed at 800ft – I cannot imagine such common sense being displayed these days.

One element of the training we had to give the UAS students was night flying. This could be done at any time of year; however, we tended to do it during the winter, as the summer nights were very short, and did not start until far too late for the student leadership training required in the Mess bar. The weather in Scotland was not always reliable, and this meant that, in order to achieve the task, we occa-sionally flew on weekday evenings. We needed a gentle cross-wind, so the instruc-tor in the back could see out on the approach, but not strong enough to give the student difficulties. If there were Lightning sorties, we endeavoured to time our

---

[1] Bucket of Sunshine: Aircrew slang for a nuclear weapon.
[2] MDA: Master Diversion Airfield.

flying between them, or while the fighters were away practising interceptions over the North Sea. If the Lightnings returned while we were in the circuit, we adopted the same racetrack pattern south of the airfield until they had landed.

On the night in question, I was detailed to fly with an experienced and very mature student, a medic called David Blundell, who later joined the RAF as a doctor. He was approaching the end of his degree course, and had been on the Squadron some 5 years. We did the initial exercises, which went as expected, and then it came to his solo. I got out of the aircraft near the Air Traffic Control tower, and briefed Blundell to taxy onto the runway by an access taxiway, and take off from there. Two Lightnings had recently landed, and had left their drag-chutes on the runway - as it turned out, close by the access from which Blundell was due to depart. It being dark, none of us saw the 'chutes by the side of the runway and, when Blundell got airborne he complained that "The aircraft was not climbing very well". I soon realised what had happened, and told Blundell to keep on full power and make all his turns gentle ones - I think he was ahead of me on this. He kept a cool head and, having made about 700ft at the bottom of downwind, he turned onto finals and reduced power from full for the first time. He made an excellent, rather steeper than average, approach, landed successfully on the runway, and we all went to have a beer, Blundell being the recipient of several glasses bought for him by the instructors and other members of the Station. Happily the mesh of the canopy of the 'chute' had caught around Blundell's tail wheel. Had it caught in the shroud lines, allowing it to deploy fully, Blundell would not have got very far!

Credit: Tony Hisgett

Six Red Eagles Stuck High Up In Ankara

Apart from my first Burns' Supper, 1969 had started uneventfully but, in March, I was presented with what, even at first sight, seemed a stern test of our capabilities: the largest staging exercise, in terms of number of aircraft and distance flown, that the UK Lightning Force had yet undertaken. Lightnings had previously flown non-stop, with air-to-air refueling, from UK to Bahrain, but none had ever staged through the CENTO (Central Treaty Organisation) route. The main aim of Exercise Chicanery in 1969 was to prove the operational feasibility of staging Lightnings through Turkey and Iran to the Gulf, and thence to Masirah Island, Oman. While in Oman, it was planned that we should participate in a one-day air defence exercise, opposing Bahrain-based Hunters, before returning to UK.

I was to command a detachment of six Lightnings for the task, with three C130 Hercules acting in support, to transport groundcrew, equipment, and spares. The exercise envisaged a non-stop flight from RAF Leuchars to Ankara (Esenboga airport) in pairs, using in-flight refuelling, for a night-stop at Ankara, before flying, unsupported by tankers, to Hamadan (Shahrokhi), in Iran, for a further night-stop. The third and final day of the deployment would involve flying to Masirah Island, via a ground-refuelling stop at Sharjah. A senior pilot spent an exacting two weeks preparing flight plans, showing details of radio frequencies, TACAN (Tactical Air Navigation) beacon positions and frequencies, diversions, restricted areas, air traffic control procedures, airfield layouts, fuel consumption and required reserves, tanker refuelling arrangements, and so on. He was a busy man!

The preparations included selecting tools, spares and equipment to be carried by the Hercules aircraft, and fitting 5,000-metre (just over 16,000 feet) barostats in the ejection seats the night before departure. To put the latter action in perspective, when a pilot ejects, a barostat dictates the height at which he is automatically separated from his seat and his parachute deploys. We would be flying over territory in eastern Turkey and Iran, where much of the terrain was over 10,000 feet, with some mountains, like Ararat, well over 15,000 feet. If a pilot had to eject over such terrain, he would need a barostat which would operate before he hit high ground!

The flight to Ankara was fairly uneventful, and some minor unserviceabilities were quickly rectified that evening, in preparation for the next leg to Hamadan the following morning. We planned to take off from Ankara in pairs, with the C130s following, when all six Lightnings were safely on their way. This is when we hit our first problem. Our Rolls Royce engines were each fitted with an Impulse Turbine Starter, supplied by a common three-gallon tank of starter fuel (AVPIN) located in the spine. When I pressed the starter button, I heard the familiar whine, followed by a burp and then a depressing silence. This sequence was repeated during further attempts to start an engine. Alarmingly, all six Lightnings responded in the same way. An initial inspection revealed nothing amiss, but we had no choice other than to cancel our allotted flight plan slots, while a more thorough investigation was carried out. The first theory to be explored was that the AVPIN was contaminated. So, an aircraft AVPIN tank was emptied and refilled with AVPIN from a sealed container. The result was the same. When the combined expertise of the detachment was exhausted, the USAF detachment in Ankara gave me permission to use their sophisticated Logistics Communications' Center to contact 11 Group HQ in Bentley Priory. We were able to set up a conference line, which allowed the engineering expertise of 11 Group and Strike Command to discuss the problem with me and my technicians. After two days of abortive trial and error, someone recalled that the Lightnings delivered to Khamis Mushayt, Saudi Arabia, in 1966 had experienced similar problems, until it was discovered that the ambient pressure at Khamis Mushayt (at an altitude of 7,000 feet) wasn't great enough to produce the required volume of flow of AVPIN to sustain the starting cycle. We were stuck in Ankara (about 6,000 feet up) so perhaps the same diagnosis applied.

In parallel with these discussions, 11 Group had contacted Cyprus, to arrange for a Hercules to fly from there, with additional engineering expertise from 56 (Lightning) Squadron. When the reinforcements arrived, one brave and resourceful chief technician invited one of our pilots to attempt to start an engine while he blew into the AVPIN tank. Hey presto! The lung pressure he was able to bring to bear on the AVPIN did the trick. Diagnosis confirmed. All that then remained was for the engineers to construct a makeshift rig which applied pressurised nitrogen directly into the AVPIN tank during the starting cycle, and which we employed, with a 100% success rate, at Ankara and again at Hamadan (also high and hot). The rest of our journey to Masirah was without incident. The resident RAF contingent made us feel very welcome, but my most pressing concern was that we had lost three days in getting to Masirah. We had several aircraft unserviceabilities, which had to be sorted out, but we still managed to exploit the subsequent air tests by practising low-level interceptions on each other over the calm, clear seas around Masirah. However, with time running out, I decided that ensuring all the Lightnings were fully serviceable for the return to UK took precedence over the air defence exercise with the Bahrain-based Hunters. The Ops staff at Bahrain were disappointed, but I was obdurate. I sensed that there might be yet more drama to come.

We left Masirah, refreshed and fully serviceable, flying the first leg to Muharraq, Bahrain, where the weather forecast for Hamadan, our next stop the same day, was excellent, with winds forecast to be 'light and variable.' This was important, because of the shortage of suitable diversions in the Hamadan area, and also because we were carrying over-wing tanks, which reduced the crosswind limitation on landing to 20 knots. Half-an-hour before arriving at Hamadan, their Air Traffic Control informed me that the wind was variable at four knots. I was, therefore, surprised and concerned to find that, when I arrived in the circuit, the wind was blowing at 90° across the runway at 30 knots. I told my No2 that we would hold off until it reduced to acceptable limits. After 15 minutes, we were able to land, though I requested the ATC controller to give a continuous transmission of wind velocity for the final part of our approaches to the runway. So much for the forecast of 'light and variable' winds! Fortunately, the wind had reduced to 10 knots for the following two pairs, who landed without incident. The following day, I led the first pair of Lightnings to the runway for take-off to Ankara. The wind was 15 knots, with visibility of six kilometres; quite acceptable. However, as we lined up on the runway, the wind increased to 35 knots (25 knots crosswind component), with thick, swirling dust reducing visibility to 500 metres. I decided we should return to dispersal. It was the onset of the worst dust storm (unforecast) in seven years, with winds in the local mountains reaching 95 knots (110 mph). I delayed our departure for Ankara by 24 hours, in the hope that the weather would improve, and we rearranged our flight plans accordingly.

On the following morning, the wind was still gusting and variable in direction, and the horizon was obscured by sepia-coloured dust, but I judged conditions to be within limits. The Met forecast was for a surface wind of 15 knots. As an insurance, I detailed a spare Lightning pilot to sit in the Air Traffic Control tower, to be ready to advise the nominated pilots of any significant change in wind velocity as they prepared for take-off. Once bitten ... I took off first, followed by my No2, Del Bassett, a US Marine exchange officer. He was to keep his distance until we were airborne, and then close up in formation before the climb. Almost as soon as I was airborne, I entered the dust cloud. A few seconds later, Del reported that I had disappeared in a self-generated dust storm, as soon as I had engaged reheat for take-off! I instructed him to climb on the briefed heading, with the aim of regaining contact when we were in the clear, forecast to be at 20,000 feet. We then discovered that we could not communicate with each other. Worse, we also discovered that we could not communicate with any ground station on any frequency. I broke out of the dust cloud when I was above 30,000 feet, and made several orbits trying to locate Del's aircraft on my radar, but without success. He later reported that he had done likewise, before concentrating on navigating to Ankara, knowing that it would be easy to stray into Iraq or the USSR. In my anxiety to locate him, I landed at Ankara five minutes after him. The total lack of radio contact with any ground station or other airborne aircraft was a strange and disconcerting experience, made even more so by the solid floor of the sepia dust cloud below me. The cockpit was my world, the instrument panel represented the outer limits of that world, and every slanting shadow and beam of sunlight illuminating the instruments was as sharply defined as a laser.

I cannot remember how long it was before I was able to get bearings and distances from Tactical Air Navigation (TACAN) stations, which could be interrogated with our onboard system, but first sight of ground was near Lake Van in Turkey, 400 miles from Hamadan, and less than 100 miles from Mount Ararat. It was a great relief when all six Lightnings arrived safely at Ankara. Every pilot had lost all radio communication for several hundred miles. One had taken off from Hamadan as the wind swung round in a matter of seconds, producing a tail wind of 25 knots, with a crosswind of 15 knots. Our pilot in the control tower had watched with incredulity as this happened, but the Lightning was already committed to take-off before a warning could be transmitted. With full over-wing tanks and a 25 knot downwind component, the lift-off groundspeed would have been over 200 knots. It was just as well that Hamadan had one of the longest runways in the world, at 15,000 feet. And it was hardly surprising that, on his arrival at Ankara, the pilot was refused permission to taxi after clearing the runway because the tyres were seen to be so badly threaded. None of us could understand how they had not burst on landing. The bizarre events at Hamadan, especially the effect of the dust cloud on radio communications, came vividly to mind 11 years later, during the abortive attempt by the Americans to rescue American hostages in Teheran. By all accounts, the failure of that operation was due to the pilots of the rescue mission encountering abnormal dust clouds similar to those that we had.

After a brief licking of wounds, we were airborne from Ankara that same day, to position ourselves at Izmir (Cigli), on the coast of Turkey, for the final leg to UK the following day. Departing Izmir to rendezvous with the tankers over Catania, Sicily, for the accompanied flight to RAF Wattisham, seemed like child's play after what we had been through. Our faithful Hercules aircraft, which had provided such staunch and uncomplaining support, left us at Ankara, but not before the crews sang their variation of the Caribbean song, Yellow Bird:

> Silver bird, stuck high up in Ankaree,
> Silver bird, inconveniencing folk like me;
> Stuff your Avpin in,
> Or fill up with gin,
> If you gotta fly
> Then why don't you fly?
> Twenty four hours' delay
> Ain't the thing to say.
> Hercules wanna go home.
>
> Long time past, we took off from Leuchars 'drome,
> Multi-Mach, we zoom round the Gulf to roam;
> Now so far away
> Static display they say,
> Cannot take off today,
> Twenty four hours' delay.
> Stuff your Avpin in,
> Or fill up with gin.
> Oh, how we'll blush when we're home!

But we did not blush! During the two week saga, I had been tremendously impressed by the stoicism and professionalism of the groundcrew, who had battled against the severe weather conditions while servicing the aircraft, and then had to endure the discomfort of flying in the back of Hercules aircraft from one location to the next. We were met on arrival at RAF Leuchars by the Station Commander, Group Captain John Nicholls, who asked if he could have the film rights. That was fine by me - so long as I was not asked to do it again for the cameras.

Credit: Geoff Parselle

Credit: Geoff Parselle

An Unauthorised Passenger

1960 started, for me, with some unsought excitement, when a senior officer visiting RAF Eastleigh, Nairobi, asked me to check him out in a Twin Pioneer. The familiarisation flight was uneventful, but the only aircraft available for his second flight did not have dual controls. I occupied the navigator's seat, knowing that I would not be able to take control if anything went wrong – which, of course, it did.

This senior officer had a reputation for being stubborn and pugnacious, but we seemed to hit it off, and all he wanted was to fly over the Amboseli Game Reserve, north of Kilimanjaro, and back. The weather was perfect, with unlimited visibility. I would give him headings to steer, remind him of airspeeds, and keep an eye on the engine instruments. Yes, sir, all very straightforward – or it should have been. When we reached Amboseli, we saw some vultures at a similar height, circling lazily ahead of us. "A kill!" he shouted in glee, "There will be lions below them. Let's have a look!" "Please be careful about those vultures, sir," I warned, "they aren't very agile!"

I might as well have been speaking to myself. We hurtled into their midst. Using a boot-full of rudder, he managed to avoid one, which was on a direct collision course. The next moment, however, another one exploded through the nose of the aircraft, passed underneath the instrument panel, and smashed against my legs, in a bedlam of feathers, fleas and rushing wind. Not knowing whether it was dead, I stamped vigorously on its neck, and recoiled at the stench, while checking to make sure that the instruments, flying controls, and engines were unaffected, and that the 'pilot' had got the message! I was greatly relieved to find that the vulture was well and truly dead and that, in spite of torrents of air rushing noisily into the cockpit, the aircraft was flyable.

I radioed base, advising them that we were carrying an unauthorised passenger, now deceased, and asked that emergency services should be standing by in case any further problems developed. I supervised my unrepentant pilot as he checked the low handling characteristics of the aircraft, so I told him to add ten knots to the approach speed for landing, as a safety measure. When the ground-crew removed the Ruppell's Vulture (for that is what it was), they measured its wingspan as seven feet, and its weight as 7 lbs (just over three kilos) . A lucky escape. If the vulture had hit an engine, we would have had to force-land in the game reserve (perhaps near the lions!), with only the remotest chance of the pilot, with his inexperience, bringing us down safely.

I was starkly reminded of Michael Grzimek, who was killed when his aircraft, a zebra-striped Dornier, crashed after colliding with a Ruppell's Vulture, when flying north-east of the Ngorongoro Crater on 10th January 1959. He was buried on the lip of the crater, where the epitaph on his gravestone reads: "Michael Grzimek – 11.4.1934 to 10.1.1959. He gave all he possessed for the wild animals of Africa, including his life." He had worked with his father, Bernhard, recording the movements of herds of wildebeest and zebra in the Serengeti, which resulted in a classic wildlife film, Serengeti Shall Not Die, filmed by Alan Root.

Finally, of ornithological interest, a Ruppell's Vulture was flying at 37,000 feet, when it collided with a commercial aircraft over Abidjan, Ivory Coast, on 29 November 1973. Feather-remains enabled the US Museum of Natural History to make a positive identification.

Credit: Oldsoldier38/Wikipedia

The Jetstream Parking Brake

In 1989, I was serving in an appointment which one of my previous Station Commanders had described as the aviation equivalent of having a license to print money. He was correct; I was current on no fewer than seven quite different types of aircraft, one of which was the Jetstream. This was a small twin-turboprop commuter aircraft, which the RAF used as a multi-engine trainer. In the autumn of 1989, it was clear that the Cold War was coming to an end, with the breaching of the Berlin Wall. I, too, was about to move on to another posting on promotion, so I decided that a good way to finish my money-printing tour would be to take a Jetstream to Berlin for a weekend, on one of our authorized overseas training flights. I could fill the Jetstream with a selection of suitable mates, and our wives and girlfriends (WAGs) could travel to Berlin by British Airways, and join us there. My co-pilot for this venture was a large and amiable man called Fred who was, without doubt, the world's expert on the Jetstream, whereas my knowledge and skill on that aircraft was distinctly limited.

The rules for flying into Berlin required the aircraft to arrive with enough fuel to divert back to Hannover in West Germany; therefore, we planned a refuelling stop at RAF Wildenrath. After despatching the WAGs, we set off for Wildenrath from RAF Finningley late on Friday morning, and arrived early afternoon for our refuelling stop. The Wildenrath Station Flight personnel were keen to get rid of us, as they were looking forward to packing up for the weekend. We taxied out, with me in the left hand seat and Fred in the right, stopping at the runway holding point to copy our airways clearance into Berlin. I applied the parking brake.

Now the Jetstream's parking brake looked identical in shape and function to the type of handbrake fitted to cheap Ford motor cars of the 1950s, like the Popular. It had an L-shaped handle, incorporating a bakelite trigger, which had to be squeezed to allow the handle to be moved forward to release the brakes. As soon as we received our airways clearance and read it back, we were cleared to depart. I attempted to release the parking brake, but it was stuck firm, and would not move. I told Fred, whose response was "Don't be so wet Sir, I'll have a go", and he leaned across to try. It was still stuck firmly on. Visions of us being stuck for the weekend at Wildenrath, whilst the WAGs burnt through the plastic, unsupervised in Berlin, floated before our eyes. In view of the gravity of the situation, and my lack of Jetstream experience, I handed over the role of aircraft captain to Fred. He summoned help from Station Flight, but the man who arrived was no use, so he was dismissed. Fred then produced, from a pocket in his flying suit, the largest Swiss Army penknife I had ever seen, and undid the panel surrounding the parking brake, revealing two cables which were attached to the parking brake handle by a split pin. Deploying the pliers function on the penknife, he removed the split pin, and the cables slithered away into the bowels of the Jetstream like two frightened snakes. "There you are," he said, as he replaced the panel, "the parking brake is off now, so we can proceed."

Throughout the flight to RAF Gatow in Berlin, and all the way back to Finningley, the parking brake handle stuck out from the instrument panel like an accusing finger. On arrival at Gatow, Fred jumped out, and ensured the Jetstream was double-chocked before I shut down. We had a great weekend in Berlin, returning with our bank balances depleted, and chunks of the Berlin Wall in our pockets. On arrival back at Finningley, Fred announced that he would deal with the engineers, and we left quickly. A few weeks later, in my new rank and appointment, I was grappling with my wider responsibilities, when the squadron leader desk officer who looked after Jetstream matters came in. "Have you heard about this incident concerning the unauthorized tampering with a Jetstream parking brake?" he said. "Don't worry," I replied, "I know all the facts, and have the matter well in hand." I never heard another word about it.

Credit: MilborneOne/Wikipedia

Cable

Observatory Buttress is part of that morose and daunting Scottish monolith, Ben Nevis – in Gaelic: Beinn Nibheis. Climbers challenge their physical – and nurture their mental - hold on life, by scaling its vertical slopes, and their daring sometimes results in falls. Plummets from this mountain are often fatal.

It's 1980, and we have been scrambled in our yellow Wessex helicopter to four fallen climbers, who have clung for hours below the menacing Ben, cold, bruised, frightened – but alive. Providentially, their connecting ropes have snagged on an outcrop, swinging them back enough to grasp a welcome but precarious perch. We arrive at Fort William after dawn, having flown through the dark Highlands from our base at RAF Leuchars. Hover-taxying just outside the grasp of turbulent mountain winds, we see small figures pressed close against the sheer face. The summit is invisible, cloaked in cloud of its own making. The Ben lures, challenging us.

To enable the winchman to descend on the winch wire precisely onto the target casualties, the helicopter must sit vertically above them. On an incline which is near-vertical, we must hover very high above the target to find a place where the tips of our whirling main rotor keep just clear of the steep rocky face. That's why we have 300 feet of cable available. Even then, we have to snuggle right in close to the mountain, to deliver Master Air Loadmaster Mick Bush right onto his target. The main rotor tips and tail rotor will still be very, very close to the rocks on our right. 'Nibheis' translates as 'malicious' or 'venomous' - uncomfortably apt, when one can save lives only by edging ever closer to the Ben's intimidating embrace. Observatory Buttress gouges a massive cleft into the mountain, narrowing the further in you fly. Our rescue hoist is on the right hand side, and it must face the mountain as we hover. So we must face the way we entered, and we hover in backwards (we realise later that reversing in was a blessing in disguise). From now on, my winch operator, Master Navigator Joe Nichols, is the absolute boss, for I can see nothing but a small area of rocky slope, to my right. I dare not move the mighty Wessex in any direction, nor yaw the tail, until Joe has cleared the area and authorised the move.

When learning to hover a helicopter, it is essential to see the horizon. Then, any undesired pitch or roll is immediately obvious, and can be corrected (at the learning stage, often embarrassingly over-corrected!). In the mountains, a sloping ridge can give the illusion of a horizon, and orientating the helicopter's attitude on this false friend will surely send you veering sideways to disaster. In Search and Rescue (SAR), one must be able to maintain a steady position, with only a small bit of terra firma in view. Hovering becomes instinctive; consciously thinking about it would be too slow. Any unwanted movement of the aircraft sends information directly from the eyes to the hands and feet, which make tiny control inputs to stay in position. This information and action bypasses the conscious brain - just as well, in my case, my colleagues tell me ...

We're hovering about a hundred feet above the casualties, rotor tips whipping past the rock face as close as we dare. Mick hooks up at the starboard door, and (no doubt apprehensively) leaves the relative security of the cabin for his vertiginous descent. Joe winches him down, giving me a continuous commentary, punctuated comfortingly with a regular "Steady, Steady." This tells me that the heli is not wandering about, which would wrench Mick from his foothold, and swing him giddyingly in space. Joe's voice gives me a word picture of their calm, professional progress in this potentially lethal work environment. Our faith in each other's ability and commitment is absolute. My cockpit is my familiar world; I am at home. With eyes for only my chosen stable datum - a rock on a grassy hump - I hold our friendly Walter Wessex steady in space, despite the buffeting winds.

On arriving below, Mick examines the casualties, renders First Aid, and ensures that the lift will not exacerbate any injuries. Mountainside diagnoses are necessarily fast, and surprisingly accurate (Mick always visits his rescuees in hospital). He must be deliberate and thorough, despite working on a near-vertical cliff, under the helicopter's clattering noise and powerfully-descending winds. If gusting winds, coming down from the summit, suddenly render the helicopter uncontrollable, I must pull away into clean air. If those below are secured both to the winch-hook and their climbing gear, this would seriously injure them. However, on such extreme slopes, whilst being clipped to the winch hook, Mick and his casualty might momentarily have to remain attached to the mountain, to avoid the risk of falling. It's crucial that I keep the helicopter really steady, at all costs.

Joe tells me that they are all on the winch hook, and he is bringing them up. "Steady." Good, obviously no stretcher is required. That would have been very difficult on such an exposed slope. Now they've arrived safely in the cabin! Much relief all round. But, as we hover-taxy towards the other casualties' position, a strong gust catches us, and I must pull away into free air.

Me: "Shall we take these first two down to Fort William, or go straight back now for the others?"

Mick: "Better go straight back – before I have time to think about it!"

So, for Act II, we reposition against the mountain, not far from Scene I. With the extra weight now on board, I have a bit less power available, but we have burned fuel, which compensates. Cloud is thickening, so I note carefully the compass heading to fly, which would take us safely away from obstructions. Fortunately, we are already pointing towards the exit from this hanging valley, for we are too close to rock-faces on three sides to turn around safely in cloud. I keep a careful eye on my faithful rock, for we are now completely enveloped in cloud. Joe confirms that everyone is in the cabin, winching complete. I know this already, for the aircraft rolls left, as weight transfers from the winch to the cabin. I ease the helicopter away from the slope. My precious reference point disappears, but we now have clearance to yaw the nose safely onto the escape heading. I stuff the nose down to gain flying speed, and escape the spectre of the Ben. We wait.

Still in dense cloud, now flying on instruments, we descend rapidly. I noted earlier that there is a ridge ahead. If I don't get below the cloud by altitude two thousand feet, I must climb to avoid hitting it, hoping we won't then find heavy icing at Safety Altitude. Flying blind in cloud around mountains is dangerous, for it might be 'Cumulus Granitus' – clouds with very hard centres! Suddenly – Oh Joy! We pop out of cloud. I can still see that welcome view, thirty-six years on. Relief floods through us, tension evaporates. We land in the car park at Fort William, where ambulance, onlookers and the Press await. The helicopter shuts down, and our exhausted, cold and battered (but happy) mountaineers climb out.

Press reporter: "Stop, stop, I need photos of you in the helicopter."

Mountaineer: "Have a heart mate; we've been out on the Ben all night."

Reporter (indignantly): "I had to get up early too, you know."

The newspaper photo shows us all laughing.

Sailing In The Bay Of Biscay

In October 1977, Exercise OCEAN SAFARI, a major NATO maritime exercise, took place, beginning off Gibraltar and ending at the western end of the English Channel. At that time, 819 Naval Air Squadron, based at Prestwick, provided anti-submarine protection for the SSBNs[1] of the deterrent force as its primary task, but additionally conducted a great deal of Search and Rescue work. For this exercise, I flew to Lisbon, as part of a detachment of 819 Squadron aircrew and maintainers, to join the aircraft carrier HMS HERMES, which was to be our home for the next fortnight or so. We would be flying Sea King Mk1 aircraft, belonging to 814 Squadron.

Early on 25th October, whilst the fleet transited the Bay of Biscay, we launched from HERMES in airframe XV 646, for a long-range anti-submarine patrol - part of a rolling flying programme, which was planned to continue on a 24-hour basis throughout the exercise. The fleet was operating in radio and radar silence, due to the close proximity of Soviet intelligence-gathering vessels. Following standard routine at the time, aircraft departed for their respective missions, and were expected to return to the ship in silence some hours later, at the end of their sorties. The sea state was moderate to rough.

As the aircraft, with full fuel load, began the transition into the initial hover, in order to lower the sonar[2], we heard two loud bangs overhead, and the Sea King began to rotate extremely rapidly. Very shortly afterwards, and following several turns, it struck the water with tremendous force, capsized and sank. It transpired that the flotation bags had been ripped off, and the two sponsons[3] were too damaged to provide any stability. All four of us managed to escape, as the aircraft foundered, manned our individual life rafts and secured them together. As a result of the impact, most of us had suffered compression injuries to the spine, which made embarking in the rafts something of a challenge.

---

[1] SSBNs: SS (submarine) B (ballistic missile equipped) N (nuclear powered).
[2] Sonar: A system for the detection of objects under water by emitting sound pulses and measuring their return after being reflected.
[3] Sponsons are projections which extend from the sides of the helicopter to provide stability and storage.

We activated our SARBE[4] beacons and fired our flares - but with little apparent effect. We could occasionally see the masts of ships in the distance, over the top of the swell, but unfortunately the ditching had gone unnoticed, and it later transpired that no ship or aircraft had heard any of the SARBE calls. The red flares, however, were eventually sighted some hours later, and it was immediately assumed by the Command that a submarine was in distress; however, a check of the operations plot indicated that no submarines were in the area, and it was then surmised that a Buccaneer from ARK ROYAL (in the opposing force some 100 miles distant) had crashed. Subsequently, the radar was switched back on, and XV 646 was found to be missing; an alert young seaman in HERMES, on his first trip to sea, then spotted a flare, prompting a more focused search. In due course, the frigate HMS ARROW arrived impressively at maximum speed and, following recovery by seaboat, our crew was transferred by Wasp helicopter (single engine, no doors!) to HERMES, where we passed the remainder of the exercise in the sick bay.

The aircraft was never recovered from the depths of the Bay of Biscay but, following several months of careful analysis and deliberation, the accident investigation team came to the conclusion that there had been a catastrophic failure of one the gear-boxes leading to the tail rotor. The fundamental problem was with the grease packing the gearbox which, over time, was apparently prone to hardening, thus losing its effectiveness as a lubricant. All Sea King aircraft were then grounded for a period, whilst the issue was addressed by the manufacturer; the aircrew were back in the air within three months.

In 2015, my wife and I enjoyed a cruise which happened to transit the Bay of Biscay in a full gale. We reflected that luck was with our Sea King crew on that day in 1977.

Credit: Mike Freer

---

[4] SARBE: Search And Rescue Beacon Equipment.

The Little Pilot Officer

In 1965, I was one of a number of RAF Photographers based at RAF Wattisham, supporting 56 and 111 Squadrons with their Lightnings and, of course, the Station as a whole. One day, the phone rang in the office, with a request for a photographer to head for 111's flight-line, to photograph a new Pilot Officer who had just arrived - an unusual request, as new pilots were not, generally, photographed. We were informed that the new officer was a very small person, and someone very special.

I was allocated to this task, so off I went with my trusty Rolleiflex "T" camera and, as supplied in those days, black & white film. Arriving on the pan, I found a number of officers gathered around the new temporary member of Treble One who was, indeed, a very small person. He was wearing a white metal helmet, a standard light brown flying suit with pilot's wings, and one or two metal badges, together with black boots on his short, stubby legs. His ears were hidden beneath

Credit: Geoff Parselle

the helmet and he had a sort of fixed smile. He was very short, at about 30". He didn't say very much; in fact, he didn't say anything at all - just grinned. He was also covered in a light brown/reddish fur. He was, in fact, a teddy bear.

Pilot Officer Dudley Peasfold Gruntfuttock was the first Red Arrows mascot. He was already a genuine sky-diver, having landed safely after being thrown out of an aircraft, while wearing a delayed-opening parachute, and had flown at Mach 1 in a Hawker Hunter. He had come to 111 Squadron for his Mach 2 qualification in the Lightning, something he had just achieved, as a passenger in the "boot" behind the cockpit.

Back at the Photo section, my sergeant threw a fit when I told him who the small Pilot Officer was, until he saw the joke; films processed, prints done and thank you all round. Later, I heard through the grapevine that Pilot Officer Dudley Peasfold Gruntfuttock had been "killed" (flattened) by being run over by an aircraft, and had been buried with full military honours alongside the runway.

Wheels-Up 1966

After a PR Canberra tour in Germany, I became a Qualified Flying Instructor at RAF Acklington, No 6 Flying Training School, in Northumberland, on Jet Provosts Mk 3 & 4. My mix of students included Jordanian, Malaysian and English. Doing circuits and bumps with my Malaysian student one day, we got red and black main undercarriage lights, with a green indication only on the nose wheel. I managed to persuade my student to refrain from ejecting! We climbed to 2000 feet, informed Air Traffic Control, and circled, whilst we checked the Quick Reference Handbook (QRH), and recycled the undercarriage. Then I noticed three staff cars with the Wheels (CO, Wg Cdrs Flying and Eng), rushing across the airfield to the tower. Several more fly-bys ensued, and I realised that the Board of Enquiry had already been convened. Great! All I needed to do was to follow their recommendation, and I was home free! Remarkably quickly, I was ordered to burn off fuel to minimum, and land, wheels up, on 02 (not the main runway).

Whilst orbiting to burn off fuel, my student had calmed down, and requested that he do the landing - I promised he could do it next time! Then we saw flashing blue lights converging on the airfield from all points of the compass. I found out later that the Duty Instructor had phoned the local fire brigade to request domestic cover, as our own firemen stood by for a crash in 40 minutes. The word spread like wildfire round all the nearby fire stations. When I landed, there were 10 fire engines lined up on the other runway, determined to see the spectacle - and probably, for the part time firemen, to get a call out fee!

I later found out that, in the Jet Provost, there was only one hydraulic jack for the undercarriage. This worked the nose wheel directly, and the main wheels by a pulley and leather belt. However, in this instance, the buckle on the belt (!) had come undone. The landing was incredibly smooth, with the ground effect from the low wings forming a cushion. First you heard the aerials scraping on the ground, then a louder grinding noise from the fuselage, then silence. The belly was patched up, and the aircraft back on line in a few weeks. The Search and Rescue helicopter arrived as we jumped out, and whisked us to Sick Quarters, which was uninhabited, since the entire staff were in an ambulance - also lined up for the show! Eventually, the Medical Officer showed up, and gave us a brandy laced with coffee. Purely medicinal! My married quarter overlooked the airfield. When my wife noticed all the commotion, she watched for about 20 minutes, and then went away, thinking it was another exercise. "What was all the fuss this morning," she asked, when I got home.

My next posting was to RAF Leeming, No 2 FTS. Walking into the line office to sign the F700 (aircraft authorisation) on my first flight, I was greeted with a large poster, displaying my aircraft, with the text "Don't forget your undercarriage like this stupid pilot!"

Editorial Note:
I also clearly remember this poster being displayed in the line office, when I started flying training in 1967.

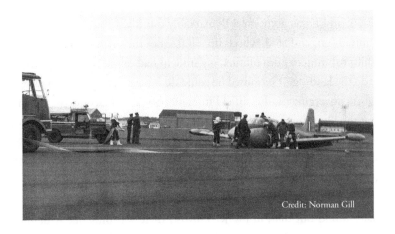

Credit: Norman Gill

How Low Can You Go?

Mid-summer 1967, and it was near the end of the four-and-a-half months of No 238 Course at Central Flying School, Hell-on-the-Hill, aka RAF Little Rissington. Usual make-up of the course in those days, including some 'creamies' - straight out of the end of their own advanced training, diverted away from their hoped-for first tour as demi-gods, and destined to wreak their revenge on yet more embryo demi-gods at the (probably) basic stage of their flying training. Not necessarily a happy bunch. Similarly perplexed were the folk who had just completed a blameless tour, or several tours, in charge of something big or small in the then RAF inventory. Remember, those were the days when there was still fun to be had on Hunters in Singapore or, closer to home, out of RAF Chivenor, trying to sink the 'Torrey Canyon'. There was also some Gulf region action to be had, before the evacuation of Aden; the Defence White Paper included the plan for merging Bomber and Fighter Commands to form Strike Command. Transport Command was to become Air Support Command, and its Belfasts would form part of the huge airlift to empty out the Aden garrison, as would Britannias and Beverleys (one of the latter was damaged when running over a mine on an up-country Aden airstrip in June '67). Lightnings had been in service for seven years, and the Javelin was to retire in about a year. Canberras were still everywhere, as was the remaining V-Force, with Valiants now fatigued and withdrawn from service. The Cold War was still chilly, and Israel had run its 6-Day War plan, and scored almost maximum points.

For extra leavening in the make-up of our 23-strong course, there were two pilots from Ghana, one from Lebanon, two from Kenya, and finally two from the Fleet Air Arm. For the RAF trainees, the course was designed and delivered to generate Qualified Flying Instructors (QFIs), who would bring their newly-acquired skills to bear on either basic students at the Jet Provost Flying Training Schools, advanced students on Gnats or Varsities, or, finally, on cadet pilots at one of the 15 University Air Squadrons (UAS) flying Chipmunks. I was destined for a UAS slot on Chipmunks, along with two other RAF colleagues, and the two Kenyans and one of the Ghanaians were also going to be trained as Chipmunk QFIs. The standard pattern for the course in those days included a fair proportion of the 90 hours of flying spent on 'mutual' instructional practice. Two students took it in turns, from their respective seats in the aircraft, to see if they could get all their instructional 'patter' out, before running out of either authorised time or fuel. The chance was also taken to sit alongside our fellow trainees, as they did their early consolidation sorties after first solos – much fun to be had as two formerly single-seat aviators clattered around the airspace in a Varsity, flipping over endless pages of Flight Reference Cards, wondering where the gill switches were (or, indeed, what they were?), and so on.

With over four months of this routine now past, the last phases were nearing completion, and this led up to the challenges of the last couple of weeks, when there were competitions for aerobatics (excluding the Varsity, of course, but there had been moments in those consolidation sorties when the envelope had been strenuously 'examined'). There had to be a few practices, a dual then some solo, with height limits progressively coming down, but I recall that the final base height was to be a nominal 500 feet. As far as the Chipmunk was concerned, that meant staggering up to about 3500, before starting a furious descent to allow probably a 'square loop', leading to a series of more elegant rolling and looping manoeuvres, stall turns, Cuban and horizontal eights. If energy could be maintained as well as height, an attempt at a 'Porteous loop' was likely, and probably a closing and racy 'Derry turn' towards the judges, lined up with their marking sheets on the balcony of the Little Rissington air traffic control tower. I look back in my logbook and see I had my dual check, with Tony Langmead in the back, on 19 July, and a solo practice that same day: it made a noticeable difference, not having his 14 stone of body and equipment behind me. Another practice was flown on 20 July, another – cleared lower – on 21 July, and the competition proper later that same day. There were six of us Chipmunk pilots having a go, and I was going to be the fifth to perform. First up was one of the Kenyans, who had been a spirited pilot in all course phases, and his aeros sequence was vigorously flown. But – watching, as I sat in my Chipmunk on the pan, waiting for start – it was pretty evident that Larry (for that was his name) was not maintaining height as well as energy. And, although his manoeuvres were eye-catchingly intricate, it was for sure that he would have trouble keeping above the base height. His pièce de résistance was very much 'in your face' (and outside the limits of display flying even in those days): he rolled wings level out of his last manoeuvre, turned hard to aim directly at the tower, and then rolled inverted to pass over the judges and out of their sight. It was reported - perhaps apocryphally, although truth not to be completely ruled out - that at least one marking sheet had some engine oil splatters on it.

By now, the second competitor was running in, and the third aircraft was on its way from pan to holding point, as the fourth one started his Gypsy Major engine. I was still on the pan when Larry landed, and he was quickly back alongside me and shutting down the engine. Just before I started mine, I leaned out and shouted, "Well done!" He grinned, and started to remove a sheet of paper which had been stuck over the left hand side of the instrument panel. As I taxied out, it dawned on me that he had - as we all did in that learning phase - prepared himself a 'crib' for the lesson content or whatever. No doubt he'd written and diagrammed his 'sequence' for the competition. But - unlike the crib for any other phase, slipped into the knee pad and referred to as the need arose, to get that instructional 'patter' correct - he had fixed it over his primary instruments! The airspeed indicator and the altimeter! Gordon Bennett! No wonder his final pass over the tower had been at something less than 100 feet! One more manoeuvre, and it seems certain he would have had contact with unyielding terra firma, probably just in front of the tower.

Maybe he was a risk-taker by inclination. Many years later, I heard that he had been involved in a coup against the then Kenyan President. After a spell in jail, he – and three other co-conspirators – had died separately, but all in similarly unexplained circumstances, in car crashes. Sic transit etc….. Anyway, it wasn't his risk-rich display that won the De Havilland Trophy for Chipmunk aerobatics. It was mine: neat but not gaudy!

Credit: Tony Hisgett

Flying With Robin

Robin Olds, a legend in his own time, a double ace with 12 kills in WWII Europe, assumed command of the 8 Tactical Fighter Wing at Ubon, Thailand in September 1966. By June of 1967, he had been credited with the downing of 4 MiGs, making him a triple ace, and within one kill of being an ace in two different wars. More important, he was a true combat leader. He demanded excellence, and wouldn't ask us to go anywhere he wasn't going or hadn't already been. And we loved to fly with him. We knew he would do his job and, if we did ours, we would have plenty of excitement and fun (a true junior officer perspective).

It brings to mind one specific mission in August '67… hit the Thai Nguyen railroad yard with 32 strikers (half Thuds[1] and half Phantoms) and Iron Hand[2]. Given the target's importance and short distance north of Hanoi, we should expect plenty of AAA and SAMs. In view of the recent lack of aggressiveness of the MiGs, we would have no air-to-air support. The briefing was pretty much standard, covering air-to-air refuelling, join-up with the Thuds, navigation, defences, and bomb release. Then came what we'd been eagerly awaiting, Col Olds' post-strike plan to stir up the MiGs. The ROEs[3] of the day precluded overflight of MiG bases unless under attack, thus we had to stay clear of Phuc Yen AB.

Col Olds briefed that we would come off the target, as elements in 5 nm trail, in the dirt, heading north-west up the backside of Thud Ridge. At the north-west end of the ridge, we would do a left 180, to head south-east down the south side toward Phuc Yen Airfield, just north-west of Hanoi. The intention was to get a full system radar lock, in range, with a target aspect which would facilitate a reasonable AIM-7[4] shot at a MiG in the traffic pattern. Col Olds, leading the first element toward the airfield, would ensure the area clear of friendlies, and work to get a shot. Regardless of his success or lack thereof, he would exit left abeam Uncle Ho's palace swimming pool, and call "off", giving the following element missiles free. As each element exited over the pool, they would rejoin on the north side of the ridge for a normal egress. There would be no second tries.

---

[1] Thud: Republic F-105 Thunderchief.
[2] Iron Hand: A Suppression of Enemy Air Defence (SEAD) Mission, also known as Wild Weasel.
[3] ROEs: Rules Of Engagement.
[4] AIM7: Raytheon Sparrow semi-active air-to-air missile.

The mission went as briefed, bombs on target. The post-strike plan was executed flawlessly, with one basic hitch… MiGs in the pattern, no valid locks, no shots fired, no kills. I think you haven't lived until you've tried to gain a good lock, while flying in the dirt at 500+ knots, in a high-threat area, with that old radar continually transferring lock to the ground. On the positive side, we suffered no losses. In fact, I don't believe that we were even fired upon from ground or air during the post-strike phase. Not unusual, and a tribute to Col Olds' mission-planning style. That would probably be worth an article in itself.

Credit: USAF

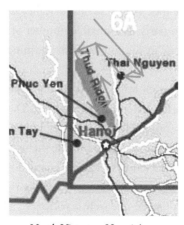

North Vietnam, Hanoi Area

With Friends Like That...

It was sometime in the middle of last century – in the days of yore granny. A bunch of us young RAF officers had arrived a few days earlier at RAF Colerne, a piece of desirable real estate near the posh city of Bath, and once owned by the Queen. It was also known to be inhabited by aviators apparently engaged in the express purpose of annoying the locals. I was fortunate enough to have been there for a short time a couple of years earlier, and had made some acquaintances – including a rather pleasant young lady, with whom I had spent happy hours of dalliance – so I lost no time in looking her up again, hoping for a little light entertainment, to pass the hours not otherwise engaged in committing aviation on behalf of Her Majesty.

Regrettably, it transpired that the young lady in question was, by then, seriously hooked up to a rather more steady paramour – but being the nice person she was, she suggested I might like to meet her (and him) at the Young Conservatives Garden Party, being held on the Saturday afternoon that very weekend – and yes, it would be OK to bring a few friends with me. A rash gesture, as it transpired. Came the day and, as was our wont in those heady days, those of us who had opted in for an afternoon's fun and frolics among the nice folks (especially girls, it was fervently anticipated) of the YCs of Bath set about making proper preparation, with an impromptu after-lunch session in the Mess Bar. Suitably fortified for the fray, all checks on the wallet and watch checklist done, we set off for the garden party in a suitable number of cars (the fear of getting caught drink-driving was, in the minds of the terminally irresponsible, somewhat less than it is now).

So, little troubled by such fears, we eventually wove our way to the field on the outskirts of the city, the lawn of some rich YC's Dad no doubt, a very large area of which had been cordoned off – presumably to exclude any undesirables, who might have formed an ambition to include themselves in the festivities. Beyond the entrance gap in the fence, which was guarded by several YC henchmen, we could see the usual amenities – beer tents, a horse-riding ring, an open space where many attractive young people were cavorting to a band and, interestingly, a pool, positioned not far from the entrance to the festival. After a couple of minutes spent adjusting alcohol-distorted focus, I observed that the aforementioned pool was fashioned from sheets of shaped, corrugated iron, fixed together to form a large circular tank about twenty feet or more in diameter, the sides of which were about four or so feet high, and the pool itself accessed by some wooden steps leading up to the rim.

We waited more or less politely in line, to be welcomed by my friend and her friend, and were duly admitted to the party. Unfortunately, at this point, one of our number, who was as relaxed as a newt, spied some attractive lady YCs splashing about in the pool (chaperoned, as was proper, by some of the male variety), and decided he could not wait to be formally introduced. Even more unfortunately, the liquid easing of tensions earlier in the bar had probably impaired his thought processes – such as they ever were – and, we concluded afterwards, he had assumed that the pool was sunk into the ground by at least a few feet to permit swimming – so, with no more ado, he began stripping off his outer clothes while climbing the steps....

It was really unfortunate that his assumptions were nowhere near the mark. The corrugated iron tank was actually sitting on the ground, and so deep enough to permit only genteel splashing around on one's tiptoes. The dull thud as his head came into contact with the solid bottom of the tank, sitting on the even more solid ground beneath it, could be plainly heard. Within seconds, he surfaced groggily among the horrified (but, for whatever reason best known to themselves, as yet unspoken - as is the way of the well-bred) paddlers, and they scattered to make way for him, as he staggered to the edge of the pool, announcing he was about to be sick. His prophecy was fulfilled, as he reached the edge and proceeded to decorate the outside of the corrugated sheeting in gay colours, reaching terminal velocity in milliseconds. We were escorted ignominiously from the field by the duty heavies, and told never to darken their field of dreams ever again.

That was the last time I ever spoke to my fair maid of Bath. And what of our hero? He was last heard of, having survived flying fast-jets, as the captain of very large airliners operating on behalf of an Asiatic Airline, and not a whit repentant.

February Memories

Back again to the Aden campaign of the early 60s and, once more, we were short of ammunition; this time it was a lack of three-inch rockets - nicknamed 'drains', because they resembled nothing more than a seven-foot length of three-inch cast-iron drainpipe. Just screw on the head, usually a 60 pound, General Purpose High Explosive one, and clip on the tail-fin ring, and – Voilà! You had your RP (or rocket) – and we were firing hundreds every day, from under the wings of our trusty Hunter FGA MK9 jets. In desperation, the RAF armament supply chain was stepping up its deliveries from stores all around the world, and the 'drains' varied considerably, depending upon which small firm had originally made a batch of parts. However, not all batches were made to the same tolerances, and so now we come to the chilling bit of our February horror story!

A load of RPs was delivered to our airfield, and the armourers immediately assembled them and trailered them up to our flight line. Only one snag! The latches which locked the rocket to the mounting rail or, if in tiers, to the rocket above, were discovered to be faulty, in that they would not lock. Thus, the RPs could be held in place by the slip-stream of the aircraft in flight but, if the aircraft decelerated hard, the rockets could slide forwards and fall off. So – orders came from Command "Continue to fly and fire the RPs from the suspect batch, (literally hundreds of them), but do not bring them home, ie: fire off, even if you cannot identify your target." So, off we went, in support of our ground troops who were, at that time I think, the Northumberland Fusiliers. They were taking a pasting up in the rocky and mountainous territory where the rebels held sway, so we were needed all day and every day to give them fire cover. I got into contact with my FAC (Forward Air Controller – usually an army officer trained by us, to call aircraft down onto targets which we could not see, until he illuminated them with coloured mortar smoke), and he sounded quite agitated, because he was in close contact with the rebels and his party was taking fire. None of this could be seen from the air, so it was quite tricky stuff – you had to believe in your FAC, and he in your ability to shoot straight.

Down the dive I went, with my full load of six RPs switched to 'salvo', listening to his directions, and then I sighted his purple smoke. Quick shift of bottom diamond (the gunsight aiming point for rockets) and FIRE! Nothing!

I pulled hard out of the dive, weighing heavy with my rockets still on, noting where the nearest rocky bits were, and went around again at full power, to reposition and get some bangs down on the ground to help my FAC. Again, nothing, so I called the next section in to replace mine, and climbed up to sort the problem out. Nothing I could do would fire my rockets and, bearing in mind the warning not to bring them back to base, I tried airbrake and flap selections, to decelerate hard and shake the rockets off. No luck - so there I was, with six big sticks under my wings, all initiated by me by having pressed the R/P button, and threatening to come off if I landed hard or used my drag-chute.

I trundled home, with my wingman giving me a close look-over but finding nothing amiss. I told him to land first, in case I made a mess of the runway, then informed air traffic control of the situation, and what might possibly happen on touch-down. Into the circuit, more gently than normal, and then around finals, trying to feel the aircraft with its extra landing weight. I touched down as smoothly as I could, and allowed the aircraft to run out, without the shock deceleration of the drag-chute. Then, as I began braking, I noticed in the corner of my right eye a moving object. Suddenly, I realized that one or more of my RPs had detached from the rails and, in a flash, I saw one of them hit the runway, and break up as it bounced behind me. Still trying to stop, I waited for the bang! But nothing came, and I managed to stop and turn off the runway, to be met by our armourers, who took away the remaining four rockets – very gingerly indeed!

Fortunately, the armament officer managed to identify the batch of dangerous latches and isolated them, and we did not have a repeat of this problem. Perhaps the two that fell off would not have exploded, but I don't like to think of a fourteen-pound explosive charge being chucked down a runway at one hundred and fifty miles per hour! Needless to say, ATC were distinctly dis-chuffed, because the wayward rockets managed to destroy about a dozen runway lights and scatter pieces of live rocket motor all over the middle of the runway. Ah well! It was February after all!

'T'was Christmas Eve

The work was done the Flight shut down, and Boulmer set for sleep,
The North was gripped in thick'ning snow, the stuff was ten feet deep.

The shift was in the land of nod, dreaming of Christmas turkey,
And a few days off, spent with their mates, but only if they were lurky.
When suddenly they were rudely woke, from slumber inno..cent
The shout came down from RCC "A Lossie cab is bent!"

Bad tidings of the very worst, for Lossie must be relieved,
They now had only a dozen cabs, or so it was believed.
But woe! a thousand thousand woes! Our cabs were also knackered,
The trusty crew, some over fifty! were completely Christmas-crackered.

What could be done to help our friends? We were completely stuck,
 It seemed that,,barring miracles, Lossie were out of luck.
The youngest of the shift then spoke, and this is what he said:
"I've seen this sledge at t'back of t'shed, wi' this bloke all dressed in red."

He wasn't wrong , the guy was there, wearing a great big frown.
"I've really blown it this year, kids, my sleigh has broken down."
"Don't worry," said the shift boss, "Mate, we'll see you straight and true,
The lads will fix your bloomin' sledge and feed the reindeer too!"

And this they did, they greased those rails, they overhauled the steering,
They double-checked the servo jacks, and planetary gearing.
The sleigh just gleamed when they were through, Santa was overcome,
"Can I do aught for you," he said, "When my night's work is done?"

"Well yes, you can," the chief replied (without wishing to sound bossy),
"When you've made the children's dreams come true, you can leave your sledge
at Lossie."

And lo! It happened as they asked, and everyone was happy.
So thank you, A Flight engineers, down to the very last chappy.

Editor's Note:
The references in this ode to Boulmer and Lossiemouth may become clearer in the context of the first paragraph of Story 63: "'Oly Highland".

The Green Mountain

As if the excitement of operations from Aden wasn't enough for us 8 Squadron tyros with our trusty Venoms, in the late 1950s, political developments further afield in Arabia claimed our attention. There was trouble a thousand miles or so to the north east in Oman, and the British were being asked for help. Nothing has changed, you might say, for in the world of the 21st century the British are still working jointly with others in helping to deal with other people's conflicts. But, in 1957 – 1959, the support for Omani conflict was a purely British/Omani national affair; and, coming not long after Suez, the action was kept rather quiet from the world. So what led Aden's 8 Squadron Venoms to be based and operate from what was RAF Sharjah, so that they could fly to the Jebel Akhdar (The Green Mountain), delivering 60lb rockets and 20 mm cannon on targets atop this rocky 6,000ft-plus operating area? We were to find that this was activity not without its challenges! But operational detachments away from Aden seemed, at the time, as just an added dimension to our trade of armed operational flying. Only afterwards could one fully reflect on what it had all been about.

Britain's relationship with Oman was close and longstanding. There had been a trade treaty with the East India Company in 1646. Then, in 1798, there was an agreement whereby the ruler, then just the Sultan of Muscat, would take the British side in international affairs, in return for protection from outside interference, by other foreign powers seeking to extend their influence over his patch. Located at the crossroads of Europe, Africa and Asia, Oman was a country with a proud history as a seafaring nation. As well as ancient coastal ports and interior deserts, it had distinctive geography. In the north of the country, and unusually for Arabia, there extended a range of mountainous hills and valleys. In the contrasting south, there were areas where the monsoon created a summer climate of vegetation and abundant agriculture. As a nation and as a people, Oman was a very special part of Arabia. Its features and history gave it a rich cultural heritage. Omani/British relationships had, with mutual benefit, been strengthened over the years, and Britain found itself increasingly involved in Omani affairs. But, in the 1950s, Oman was still a truly medieval Islamic State, shuttered against all progress under the aegis of its traditional and autocratic ruler Sultan Said bin Taimur. The pervading anti-colonial, anti-British climate of the Middle East at the time provided fertile ground for outside-inspired disaffection, leading to internal unrest, and to what became the Jebel Akhdar Campaign.

Northern Oman's Jebel Akhdar (the Green Mountain) is part of a mountainous range rising, at its highest point, to 10,000 feet, and having a cultivated plateau at 6,000 feet, with several small villages in and around it. The range runs south-east, from the desert fringes of what is now the territory of the United Arab Emirates towards Oman's eastern plains and desert. In 1958, in this northern part of Oman, well-trained and well-armed insurgents had fled from earlier defeats by Omani and British forces, and were now encamped upon the Jebel. Offensive strikes, by Venoms with rockets and guns, were aimed at making life so unpleasant for them that they would surrender.

The first part of the Jebel Akhdar Campaign in mid-1957 had been fought around the valleys and villages of the Jebel. After a setback in early 1958, the British-led Sultan's Land Forces had quickly been strengthened and augmented, and British armoured cars had been sent up from Aden. With airborne fire support, these combined forces had overcome the opposition and restored control, but the rebel leaders, with a sizeable force of their followers, had escaped. In the stronghold of the Jebel, they were still well-armed and well-led, determined to find ways of challenging Sultan Said bin Taimur and the rightful Government. For the Jebel campaign, 8 Squadron operated from Sharjah, situated along the northern sea-facing curve of the Arabian Peninsula, and west of the Straits of Hormuz, that critical waterway through which much of the world's oil was carried. Sharjah is now a developed country of the United Arab Emirates; there are skyscrapers, and even a cricket ground where Test Matches are held. If, at that time, you were to head south-west along the rough desert road in one of those sporty Land Rovers now appearing everywhere, you would come to Dubai, which, with its creek, was just a fishing village, where craftsmen with ancient skills made handsome dhows.

At Sharjah, there was a rudimentary desert airfield, not ideal for Venoms or military operations. It did, however, boast an impressive fort, one section of which was used as Air Traffic Control and included a comms centre, where Signals could be transmitted and received. "Signals" were our standard method of operational and administrative communication with Aden, and with the RAF

Persian Gulf HQ in Bahrain. The only alternative airfield, Masirah, had a runway surface unsuited to the Venom's high pressure tyres. The surface at Sharjah
was rolled sand, with two strips, one for take-off and the other for landing. At
night, for take-off on a dawn strike, or for return to Sharjah in the dark after
dusk sorties to the Jebel, the strips were lit with simple flares. There were no
diversions; the only fuel calculation needed during a mission was enough fuel to
get back to Sharjah. Our missions were about 1 hour 40 minutes: 30 minutes
to the Jebel, 40 minutes in the operating area, and 30 minutes return. In order
to deliver an old 60lb rocket accurately and effectively, you ideally needed a 300
dive and a release range of about 600 yards. This was fine on the range back in
Aden but, in thinner air at 6,000 feet, with hills all around you, it was more
challenging, especially when arriving at the Jebel with lots of fuel. For the unwary, there could be interesting close-up views of the ground!

My last detachment at Sharjah was at the conclusion of the campaign which,
for several months, had been on-and-off, with only the occasional Venom presence. On a Saturday night in the RAF Khormaksar mess bar, in late November
1958, orders came to position four Venoms at Sharjah the following day, as
more purposeful operations to eject the rebels from the Jebel were about to start.
As duty flight commander, with the Squadron Engineering Officer, NCOs and
pilots, I spent until the early hours getting suitable aircraft, pilots and groundcrew organised into a workable operational unit. By Sunday evening, we were
established at Sharjah ready for tasking. We learned that units of the Special Air
Service (SAS) had been brought to Oman for an assault which would end the
rebellion. During this conclusion of the Jebel campaign, most of our harassing
sorties were by day but, towards the end, several were flown at dusk or dawn.
The dusk sorties spoilt the late evening for the rebels, who were probably thinking of a peaceful night. For the Venoms, their return and landing back in the
dark at Sharjah, on the sand runway lit by simple flares, was all part of the rich
experience. The dawn sorties were especially effective – rockets into their caves,
as the rebels were waking up, scratching themselves and attending to the needs
of nature, followed by gun attacks as they scattered. Understandably, this sort of
thing made a difficult start to their day.

After reconnaissance and probing attacks throughout December, in early
January the SAS eventually successfully scaled the 6,000ft mountain at night.

Venom strikes at dawn supported their final push to the top, where they overcame the opposition. Venoms were also in support of the rest of the action,
until the rebels surrendered – or in some cases decided to escape. An Omani
Government minister arrived at the Jebel by helicopter, signifying the winning
of the war for the Sultan of Oman. Throughout the Jebel Akhdar campaign, 8
Squadron Venoms had flown 1,315 operational sorties, and fired 3,800 rockets
and 271,000 rounds of ammunition. When it was all over, we went back to
Aden and Khormaksar, where our normal trade of armed low-level operations
continued - over what, in succeeding Hunter days, became known as The Radfan, and over the many other areas of the Western Aden Protectorate where
airborne firepower, as a threat or for real, was in those days called upon to help
keep the peace.

Credit: Les Phipps

Twister

It was normal practice with the "Posters" that a second tour (for an Equipment Officer) would be unaccompanied, overseas, and usually on Air Movements. Escaping a posting to RAF Gan with some relief, I found myself as a DAMO (Duty Air Movements Officer) at RAF Muharraq in 1971 where, once acclimatised, we worked hard and played hard – very hard. The Labour Government of the day had recently announced the withdrawal and closure of most of our overseas bases, both to save money and to focus more on European affairs. As there would be a huge amount of equipment and stores to be shipped back home, we used every opportunity to take up any spare payload on all flights westbound to the UK.

On this particular day on shift, I was asked by the Transport Operations controller if we could accept three VC10s, which were inbound, empty, to the UK, having delivered relief aid to Dakha in Bangladesh, following another flood disaster. All the aircraft were configured in side-guidance, which enabled the rapid loading and securing of standard NATO pallets, so really quick and easy, thought I; fill your boots, and impress the Boss and the rest of the squadron. Each VC10 was on a 90-minute turn-round time, and at 90 minute intervals, so the loads should be a breeze. "Yes," was my answer, followed by a quick call to the Cargo Shed, to task them with building up to 20 NATO pallets of stores and equipment, all netted up, weighed, manifested and ready to roll. Not too difficult, nothing to leave for the next shift, shower and to the bar – easy, and bask in the glory of another 'D' Shift triumph.

The first VC10 duly arrived on time. It was refuelled, the side freight-door was opened, and the pallets were rolled into the cabin from the Condec transfer loader and secured. The freight-door was then closed, and it was then just a matter of completing the trim-sheet and the aircraft was ready to roll. As she taxied out, the second VC10 landed right on schedule. Same process, and all was in order. The third VC10 arrived early, and the VASF (Visiting Aircraft Servicing Flight), trying to be helpful, as we were still loading the second aircraft, opened the freight door for us, and started the refuelling. While this was progressing, the second aircraft load was completed, trim-sheet done, and she too taxied out for take-off. We were now really in the swing and, as soon as the refuelling of the third VC10 was completed, on went the six loaded and netted pallets. All that was left to do was to close the freight-door and walk back to the Load Control office to complete the trim-sheet.

Except, the freight door would not close and lock! It closed without a problem, but the door- locks would not locate in the fuselage frame, no matter how often we opened and closed the door. This fault was an obvious 'No-Go' snag, and it seemed that the best-laid plans and anticipated kudos would come to nothing. No-one in VASF could think why this had happened so, in desperation, I rang Britannia House in Manama, which was the transport aircrew transit hotel. I was now really beginning to panic, but eventually got hold of an Air Engineer. Having asked me to go through the order in which the turn-round had been done, he informed me that we had twisted the aircraft fuselage, as we had done the refuelling with the freight door open. This was a disaster, and I could see the Court Martial, and the VC10 having to be put in a jig to untwist the fuselage. It would cost millions of pounds, let alone my career. Was there no solution…?

I could almost see the Air Engineer's grin over the phone. He said we were to remove the over- wing escape hatches on both sides of the fuselage, have half the shift climb out and stand on one wing, and the other half of the shift do the same on the other wing. Then, close the freight door. Once closed, we were to hook up an aircraft tug and while slowly taxiing the VC-10 in figures of eight around the apron, put our arms round each other and jump up and down. Was he taking the proverbial? But, what choice did I have? I gathered the shift and VASF guys together, and briefed them on what was to be done. I cannot begin to describe the looks and comments that came my way, but all the chaps realised that we really were up the creek without a paddle, and no-one had a better idea.

And do you know what? After about the third circuit round the apron you could hear the locks locating one by one with a clunk, and all the corresponding green lights illuminated on the engineer's panel. I recall that word had spread, and that quite a crowd of personnel had gathered to watch the fun and games, and to shout out suitable comments and encouragement! Luckily, this rather vocal crowd did not include the Station Commander. Anyway, there was huge relief, much giggling but deadpan faces when the slip crew arrived to take the aircraft back to RAF Brize Norton. The story must have done the rounds within 10 Sqn because, for months afterwards, whenever we handled a VC10 in the freighter role, we were reminded by the Loadmaster of the order in which to carry out the turn-round activities.

Finally, someone out there does have photographs to prove that this tale really is true. So, if you are that person who had the camera and photographs, please get in touch!

The Devil's Blacksmith – Forging A Chain Of Events

Some days it's better to stay in bed, I thought, as I pressed the transmit button...
..."Pan, Pan, Pan, Scottish Centre this is Foxtrot Yankee Juliet 58, Buccaneer, 2 POB, 35 miles west of Tain range, with an engine failure... standby." Pity, the day had started so well...

Actually, that's not true. It started with a team b*llocking from our Detachment Commander (DetCo), the latest in a number of similar 'pep talks,' delivered after met brief and prior to getting the maps out to plan another Red Flag[1] work-up sortie around the Highlands. This was December 197*, and the weather everywhere north of Watford had been seasonally dreadful for the whole detachment so far. With the cabs out on the rain- and wind-swept line all day and all night, serviceability and sortie rate were suffering, and the Engineers were constantly soaked through and frozen, trying to keep us in business. We'd lost quite a few sorties, due to what the DetCo considered to be trivial excuses and/or LMF[2], and his phrase "Carry on like that and you won't be going to Vegas" was becoming a Junta[3] motto. We were looking forward to escaping to Las Vegas and Nellis AFB early in the New Year, but had to serve our time in purgatory – at RAF Lossiemouth – first. A small price to pay, we thought.

Given that my Man A (pilot) and I hadn't yet been on the Squadron for a year, were both first- tourists, and had flown together since Day One of the Operational Conversion Unit, we felt tremendously privileged, proud to be selected to go, and extremely vulnerable to being kicked off the trip if we screwed up in any way. We were determined not to let the side down, but I hadn't endeared myself to the DetCo and his mates by casting doubt on the ability of our newly-acquired air-to-air missiles to hit anything faster than the NAAFI wagon. Had this been in the crewroom, I might've got away with it, but my unguarded comments were made in the bar, within earshot of the F4 Phantom squadron "Red Air", who were

---

[1] Red Flag: An advanced aerial combat training exercise, hosted at Nellis Air Force Base, Nevada and Eielson Air Force Base Alaska. Its purpose is to train aircrew from the United States and other NATO countries. In a typical Red Flag exercise, Blue Forces (friendly) engage Red Forces (hostile) in realistic combat situations.
[2] LMF: Lack of Moral Fibre.
[3] Junta: Slang for the most junior members of a Squadron.

representing the enemy for our training. I was, to coin a phrase, in danger of not "going to Vegas." No pressure, then. I think it was at about this point that I ought to have, if I'd had the experience, heard the first blow of hammer on anvil, and the Devil's Blacksmith forging a Chain of Events… clink… clink.

It was a typically 'orrible day. The rain was falling sideways, from low stratus that kept the world in gloomy twilight. This seemed to be the default condition here in Ex-RN Land. I recall hearing, for the first time but not the last, that The Highlands had 2 seasons – 9 months of winter and 3 months of p*ss-poor skiing – but, with the detachment almost over and the pace ramping up, there was a lot of press-on-itis in the air. And on the ground, too. There was the feeling amongst some of the less experienced of us – that is, Man A and me – that, if we upset anyone else, we might be in line to get left at home when the transport left for the USA next month; we couldn't afford to get noticed. Clink. We were flying as No2 of the second 4-ship, with nothing more difficult to do than "stick, search and report" but, given the conditions outside the rain-streaked window, this was going to be quite a challenge in itself. We noticed quite a few of our more-respected colleagues exchanging worried glances, and there was the occasional muttered comment along lines that the Royal Navy would consider mutinous but, at the end of the sortie brief, there were no dissenting voices to be heard. Not in public, anyway, and certainly not from me. Clink.

We left the line-hut with yet more encouragement from the DetCo slamming into the back of the door behind us. Staggering sideways against the gale, we did the customary contra-rotating aircraft walkround, but with somewhat less-than-usual attention to puddles of oil, fuel drips and sundry other leaks, due to an inability to distinguish them from the rest of the wetness around. The lineys[4] were sheltering in the wheel wells, and clearly morale had taken a hit that morning. They'd had a visit from the DetCo too, it seemed. Time to get in, shut the lid and go. Let's get it over with. Clink.

Starting the Bucc was always a bit of a palaver, since it required a Palouste air starter – a machine like a giant vacuum cleaner set to "blow" – to get the engines turning fast enough to become self-sustaining. With only 3 working Paloustes,

---

[4] Lineys: An affectionate name for the line mechanics (Airmen) who prepare the aircraft for flight.

and eight aircraft starting up, Man A and I were somewhat towards the back of the queue, and sat quietly waiting for our turn. Needless to say, by the time 'our' Palouste was being wheeled in front of us, it'd run out of fuel, and a bowser was summoned. Realising the delay this would generate, we got the attention of the crew chief; this wasn't easy, as he was huddled under his waterproof hood like a Hobbit, and not inclined to come out. We suggested just getting one of the shortly-to-become surplus Paloustes from the end of the line. The call for the bowser was cancelled, and the other Palouste hooked to the tractor; it almost made it to us before it shuddered to a halt. Chiefie pointed to it, and gave us that cut-throat sign that never means good news. It wasn't going well. We were now late. So late, in fact, that we'd missed the check-in, and the leader of the first formation was taxying. This was going to be the fastest start we'd ever done....clink.

We get the second engine going as the rest of the gang begin to line up on the runway nearly a mile away, and our taxy out is like a scene from the Wacky Races, as we struggle to get everything sorted out. Almost on top of things now, when there's a groan of despair from Man A. "Starboard oil pressure 'doll's eye' shows LOW." A swift debate follows and, as soon as we can, we give the engine a burst of extra noise. "Now it's cross-hatched" – not bad, not good, but somewhere in- between. An improvement, but not the "HIGH" indication we'd really prefer - in fact, are required to have before take-off. We line up just as No3 disappears into the murk, leaving a black smoke trail in his wake – so he's late too, then. Up with the throttles, check the gauges, oil pressure still cross-hatched. We both know what we'll have to face if we abort and take the aircraft back. The lineys 4 will ground-run it and probably find nothing wrong, and we'll maybe "not be going to Vegas." Clink. I suggest that it might be a "sticky doll's eye- give it a tap." Tap delivered, and I see through my window into the front cockpit that nothing's changed. "When I said tap it, I meant TAP it". Two well-aimed punches later, and the offending indicator has flicked to HIGH, and we're breathing a big sigh of relief as we race off in pursuit of the others. Clink.

As predicted, the weather is awful. We're about six or seven minutes behind the formation, and going flat out to catch up. However, since they're obviously late too, we aren't going to achieve much by just flogging the donkeys to greater efforts. About 45 miles behind at the planned speed, we need to cut a corner or two to make up the gap. Unfortunately, the track has been planned to avoid the low cloud by threading through the valleys, and this will make shortcuts hard to find. Visibility is down to three or four miles in the rain and scud, and we're belting along at an illegal speed and height, to try to close the distance without going into the murk above us. This is most uncomfortable. The straight-ish wings of the Buccaneer give a very hard high-speed ride in turbulence, and the cockpit soundproofing is non-existent. Despite the intercom, communication is by shouting. With R/T silence almost The Law, we daren't pipe up and ask if the plan still holds, we just have to trust that it does, and that everyone's where they're supposed to be. We hatch a Plan B to take a valley that offers a corner-cut, and the chance to intercept the gaggle as it turns over the Minch to go north. A quick bit of mental arithmetic, and we set off on our new course. We're in the "ultra" low flying area now, so down at 100 feet and almost picking our way between the firebreaks in the pine forests at just shy of 500 knots. Hair-raising stuff! Despite the promise it showed at first glance though, our chosen valley turns out to be a dead end. A box canyon. Nowhere to go but up, and we leave it to the very last second to do so, with the G hitting +6 straight away. I know we're very close to the granite, and find myself trying to suck the seat cushion inside me to make us thinner and save a few inches. No, really, that's what it felt like. I swear I see the radio-altimeter needle bounce off the bottom stop as we clear the invisible ridge, swathed in cloud. Phew! That was a bit close but press on - gotta catch The Team. Clink.

Being above cloud isn't a problem, provided you don't need to be below it, or there's somebody on the ground with a radar to see you safely through without hitting a hard bit. Normally we'd fly to an area that had ATC radar cover and use them to help but, up here in Moon Country[5], there's no help to be had. Except our onboard radar. Now, this wasn't ever an approved technique but Man A and I had practised it sometimes under benign conditions; so, when I announced that I had a sea-loch painting clearly ahead, he was confident enough in my radar-reading abilities to go down on my calls. We popped out of the stratus at about 400 feet over the water, with mountains on both sides, pointing west. No time to congratulate ourselves (??) because, at the same moment, we saw the tail of No4 disappearing northbound behind a headland, Stage Right. Not only that, but a

---

[5] Moon Country: Slang for that featureless area of northern Scotland.

couple of miles behind him were two F4s, unseen and just about to shoot! They obviously hadn't expected to see us arriving from their 4 o'clock, with a perfect intercept geometry. We called a warning on the radio, and slid effortlessly behind the rearmost Phantom with an exuberant "Fox2 Kill, F4 back man in the Minch!" Our (my) much-maligned Sidewinder had proved useful after all. The F4s reacted as if their backsides had been slapped – which they had been – and they immediately racked on the bank in a right-hand turn – perfect. We slid across the circle and "shot" the leader with our now non-existent missile, then reversed left to catch up with our gang. They had, predictably, disappeared. The fighters hadn't though.

Clearly my Expert Opinion on the usefulness or otherwise of our new missile was shared by the fighter chaps, because they either weren't playing 'kill removal' or had ignored our max-range shot, and had turned around to chase us. Now the Buccaneer was not a dogfighter and, even if we'd still had our heat-seeking missile, it was going to be bugger-all use with the Red Air rapidly closing from astern. All we could do was employ the Usual Tactic, which was to get as low as possible, as fast as possible, and hope to wipe the opposition off on the scenery. And we did our best. This was gloves-off and no-quarter, as they hadn't played by The Rules. We found another sea-loch running east, and ducked and weaved between the rocks, water and cloud, with the two Bandits on our tail desperately trying to get a shot on film. This was really exciting stuff, the wings were slamming through turbulent air with a sound like hammers hitting the airframe, and the noise was deafening. The physical buffeting and shaking had me cracking my helmet visor on the canopy, as we jinked and bunted our way up the valley, hemmed in by cliffs and cloud, and our speed creating a huge pressure-wave around us. The lead F4 was now occasionally visible through our self-built cloud and very close in the mirrors when – slam – I was thrown forward in my loosened straps (the better to see behind), as the aircraft seemed to lose 100 knots in an instant. I thought for a moment that Man A had tried the trick of popping out the Bucc's enormous air-brake to force our attacker to 'fly right by', to use that Top Gun expression. Then it all got much noisier.

I pushed myself off the blast screen and, as I regained an even keel, was aware that the attention-getters were flashing, and the 'clangers' were going off. The aircraft was yawing mightily to the left, and there seemed to be a lot of dust flying about. None of this was Good News. I shouted to Man A for an update on our status, as they say nowadays, but I couldn't make myself heard over the din for a second or two, so I peered through the blast screen between our seats to see a lot of red lights on the warning panel, and more appearing all the time. This looks bad, thought I, and got busy with the radio as Man A took the aircraft away from the ground and back into the clouds. "Port engine's failed," was all I got before I put the call out.

Up at Safety Altitude[6], we sorted ourselves out. The port engine had wound down, but the cause wasn't immediately obvious, so a process of investigation began, with me reading the Emergency Drills from the Flight Reference Cards. It wasn't many seconds before there was a groan from Man A: "FNA valve. Sh*t!" For those unfamiliar with the Buccaneer fuel system, the fuel tanks were divided into Master and Slave areas, and the FNA valves could be closed to switch off the flow between them. The large Tonka-Toy switches to do this were at the front of the cockpit, below the Oil Pressure Doll's Eye… When Man A had been pummelling the instrument panel to fix our earlier snag, he'd inadvertently caught one of these switches with the cuff of his glove, and hadn't noticed that he'd turned it off. Clink. We'd been so busy trying to cope with the weather and all the rest after take-off, neither of us had noticed that the engine was rapidly running itself out of fuel. Clink, clink.

We returned to base in a miserable mood. There was no possibility of getting away with it. If I hadn't put out the emergency call so early, perhaps we could've restarted the engine and carried on….if the weather had been better, we'd have done more fuel checks… if the blast screen hadn't been covered in greasy handprints, maybe I'd have seen the fuel gauges more clearly… if the doll's eye hadn't been sticky… We beat ourselves up with the What-Ifs all the way back, but none of this was going to make a jot of difference to the outcome. Both of us could see our ticket to the USA being flushed down the lavatory, closely followed by us. It took a lot of concentration and discipline to gather our wits together and complete the rest of the transit without making more mistakes, and we taxied onto the parking ramp in gloomy silence. The liney marshalled us to a stop, and our earlier-than-expected arrival had clearly caused a stir in the line hut. Engineers,

---

[6] Safety Altitude: An altitude that provides at least 500 feet clearance above obstacle along a particular route that a pilot might fly.

previously battened down against the weather, were now looking very interested in us. Our marshaller was pointing excitedly towards the left wing, apparently at the engine. "OK, matey" I thought "no need to rub it in – we know it isn't running". We shut down, and the crew ladders appeared immediately, closely followed by the Chiefie's head at the canopy rail. "Well done, sir. That must've been an albatross you hit. Took out the engine and half the wing…." What? Confused, we turned to look back over the wing, to see a large panel that ought to be over the wing-fold hinge bent up at 90 degrees, exposing a gaping hole, fringed with feathers, blood and guts. Invisible from the cockpit, it was this that had caused the stir as we parked. We looked at each other and cursed again. We had a perfect excuse for what'd happened…"Heard a big bang, possible birdstrike and engine damage…shut down as a precaution…safe recovery in marginal weather….where's my medal?…" but we both knew we couldn't use it.

The outcome? Honesty paid off, and we kept our appointments at Nellis, although temporarily assigned a different crew member until we'd learnt our respective lessons. With hindsight, and time, would we have fibbed and covered up the incident? A more experienced crew would've sorted out the fuel switches and restarted the engine, but we were unsure of the implications of doing that so we didn't. We might've got away with the Birdstrike Story if we'd been brave or stupid enough…. What we did do was go over to the adjoining hangar, seek out the F4 crews who'd chased us, and demand they show us their films. Unfortunately, according to them, the Photo Section had "lost them". Yeah, right!... No film, no kill. Buccaneer one, Phantoms nil. Result!

And, from everyone else's point of view, that was all that seemed to matter.

Credit: Pedro Aragão

The Torrey Canyon

Life's tapestry of memories, as we all learned quite early on when in Light Blue, was about change. Interwoven was not merely the constancy of that change, but its random unpredictability too. In more senses than one, a flying life is played out and needs to be 'taken on the wing'.

In the mid-1960s, the Torrey Canyon was classed as a large super-tanker, over 974 feet long, with a 125-foot beam and 68.7-foot draught, and with her carrying capacity already doubled, from its original 60,000 tons of crude oil to up to 120,000. As a result of steering confusions, a navigational error, stemming from the use of small-scale charts, and being equipped only with Loran[1] rather than the more accurate Decca Navigator[2], she struck Pollard's Rock, on the Seven Stones reef, at considerable speed, on 18th March 1967, while attempting a shorter route into Milford Haven. Sadly, a member of the Dutch salvage team was killed during the unsuccessful effort to re-float the vessel. By 26th March, eight days later, the combined interaction between the surging sea and the structural damage, resulting from the Torrey Canyon's 17 knots impact into the Seven Stones Reef, had broken the tanker's back. The environmental threat to neighbouring shore and marine life was now bound to be dramatic. Two large spillages, probably totalling 50,000 tons, would eventually escape in two, separate directions - the first one drifting off towards the northern coast of France and Guernsey, the second staying more local, to pollute the western end of Cornwall.

Whitehall decided that setting light to the oil, to burn it off in situ, should limit the degree of this catastrophe. Once the vessel started to break up, and detergent had been deployed from RN vessels, the decision was taken by Prime Minister Harold Wilson to try and burn off as much oil as possible. Fleet Air Arm Buccaneers from RAF Lossiemouth bombed the vessel on Tuesday 28th March 1967, and RAF Hunters from RAF Chivenor were tasked to drop aviation fuel to keep the conflagration going, but met with limited success, partly due to high tides at that time. Foam booms were used in an attempt to contain the spread of the

---

[1] Loran: LOng RAnge Navigation (aid).
[2] Decca Navigator: A hyperbolic radio navigation system.

oil, but also proved inadequate in the rough seas. After further attacks by RNAS
Yeovilton's Sea Vixens and RAF Brawdy's Buccaneers, and some timely words in
a Defence Minister's ear from Senior Air Staff Officer (SASO) No 38 Group, it
was decided to try napalm to set the oil alight. This information was passed to me
much later by Air Vice Marshal Peter Latham CB AFC, who had been that SASO,
and remembered the sequence of events. No 1(F) Squadron was given the task of
dropping the napalm.

On the morning of 29th March, after the squadron armourers had worked
hard all night, and with the West Raynham Station Commander, Gp Capt Ba-
sil Lock AFC, actually manning the Ops Desk (!), No 1(F) Squadron launched
three aircraft for the first napalm attacks . This three-ship formation consisted
of our OC, Sqn Ldr G 'Spike' Jones, accompanied by Flt Lt Brian Walton, our
Squadron Pilot Attack Instructor, and myself, then OC "B" Flight. Because of the
high political sensitivity of anything to do with napalm coming anywhere near
the civilian population, we were not just briefed, but ordered from on high, to fly
straight out from West Raynham after take-off, by the shortest route to the sea,
some 13 nautical miles to the north east. Then we were to fly a long clockwise
route, around and beyond the coast of East Anglia and all of Southern England.
This extra care thus avoided any over-flight of the mainland, apart from in those
first two minutes twenty seconds after 'wheels roll'; we were always over the sea,
right round Plymouth and Land's End to the Scillies, and even on up to Chivenor
after release of the napalm. Well before we arrived at the Scillies, we were in touch
with, and cleared into the operational area by the RN controller on board the
radar picket, the Battle-class destroyer, HMS Barrosa (D68). The 230-gallon drop
tanks on each inboard pylon of our Hunter FGA9 aircraft, gave us the 'legs' to fly
this 1hr 30minute sortie, including our onward flight into RAF Chivenor, where
we landed, refuelled and turned round, before flying back to West Raynham, but
this time by the short direct route. During this turn-round, we were treated to the
fine spectacle of our Boss, Spike Jones, drily seeming to reverse-interview his press
interviewer on what had transpired over the Seven Stones Reef off the Scillies.

The weather that day was particularly good for the whole of this round-
Southern-Britain operation. Each aircraft was armed with two 100-gallon napalm tanks on the outboard wing pylons, and we had been briefed not to hit
the ship, but to drop close alongside the long ship's structure. A further concern

was that the only available fuses had been in store for several years - these were of Swedish manufacture, and were already well beyond their recommended shelf-life. The Boss's attack failed to ignite the surface oil, but Brian Walton's drop as No 2 created a hugely impressive chimney fireball, which forced me to stand off and abort my first run until the smoke had stabilised. I re-attacked, and dropped my napalm just after I had entered this somewhat fiery smoke. It was only many years later that I realised that, from the length of the oil slick and the standard low-level skip-bombing speed of 420 knots, one can calculate that I was in that thick, grey-black, fiery smoke for no more than six-tenths of a second; this was confirmed by Brian's G45 camera film record of the smoke, within seconds of my attack. Nevertheless, as a result of the deep imprints jabbed so sharply into my memory-box from the sheer uniqueness of that experience, I remember several extremely distinct, split-second thought iterations and actions in that tiny span of time.

The prelude was the level-flight line-up and run-in, senses well alerted but very much in straightforward VMC[3], with splendid visibility and wall-to-wall sunshine. Taking good care now to adjust to the standard 420 knots release speed, and monitoring all those well-rehearsed, nap-of-the-earth, visual cues exactly at 50 feet ASL[4], the final approach proceeded smoothly – the sea was only choppy over the reef. Then, in that split-second between entering that smoke and crud to emerging from it again, I was almost too fully aware that: my aircraft was in the thick black smoke, I could see absolutely nothing, but knew that I was at only 50 feet; with my brain's automatic pilot 'in cloud' reflex, I must (and did) go straight onto instruments; there must be no delay, and I must 'pickle off' (explosively re-lease my pair of napalm outboard tanks) immediately or I will be too late. . . .

As I pressed the 'pickle' button on the stick-top, instantly there was a mas-sive, shuddering thump - certainly excessive, if one was deep in thick smoke at 50 feet! In common with virtually all of the Hunter force, I had never had to use the Mk 9's Explosive Release Mechanisms before; these were in the two small fairings protruding in a narrow hump on the top of each outer wing, which activated the downward firing of the fused outboard tanks, completely filled with napalm.

---

[3] VMC: Visual Meteorological Conditions.
[4] ASL: Above Sea Level.

Shock, Horror! – with a ruddy great bang like that on both wings, shaking both me and the airframe in that Stygian darkness, mightily different from banging the tanks off in the clear at altitude, I assumed that I had hit the mast in the smoke. At that very instant, I glimpsed, so close to my starboard wingtip, a narrow, 8-foot-diameter, yellowy-sheathed, vertical tunnel of the reddest hell-fire, its spurting flames and debris all accelerating upwards, illuminating the black smoke's gloom. I was thinking that I'd need to be mighty quick to eject and escape this disintegrating airframe at 50 feet in all that crud – I must pull …. back and up . . . . But, before I could respond and initiate that safety-first pull up, my canopy had burst out safely into the full, now almost blinding, sparkle-burst of brilliant sunshine and bright blue sky above me, the dark greenish-blue water still safely below … and my trusty Hunter still all in one piece but 'sans outboards' – without the 100 gallon ERM napalm drop tanks.

Further attacks on the stricken ship were required in the afternoon, including the employment of rockets to open up the ship's oil compartments. A further pair of Hunters was tasked under HMS Barrosa's control at 1500 hours, and three more joined in five minutes later. The following afternoon, six aircraft dropped a further 12 drop tanks full of napalm. Overall the operation was not a massive success, but these Torrey Canyon attacks were certainly the more fun side of a very real tragedy – it was, after all, an extremely large and static target which wasn't firing back!

Wikipedia reports the impact of the Torrey Canyon disaster as follows: "Some 50 miles (80 km) of French, and 120 miles (190 km) of Cornish coast were contaminated. Around 15,000 sea birds were killed, along with huge numbers of marine organisms, before the 270 square miles (700 sq km) slick dispersed. Much damage was caused by the heavy use of so-called detergents to break up the slick; these were first-generation variants of products originally formulated to clean surfaces in ships' engine-rooms, with no concern over the toxicity of their components; many observers believed that they were officially referred to as 'detergents', rather than the more accurate 'solvent-emulsifiers', to encourage comparison with much more benign domestic cleaning products. Some 42 vessels sprayed over 10,000 tons of these dispersants onto the floating oil, and they were also deployed against oil stranded on beaches. In Cornwall, they were often misused - for example, by emptying entire 45-gallon drums over the cliff-top to 'treat' inaccessible coves, or by pouring a steady stream from a low-hovering helicopter. On the heavily-oiled beach at Sennen Cove, dispersant poured from drums was 'ploughed' into the sand by bulldozers over a period of several days, burying the oil so effectively that it could still be found a year or more later. It is probable that the general resistance to the proper use of later-generation, much-improved oil-spill dispersants arose as a result of this operation."

Credit: Mike Freer

Credit: Al Pollock

The Tale Of The Shark In The Bath

At the end of our shift cycle in RAF Muharraq, we were blessed with two-and-a-half days off to catch up with sleep and relax, before the next shift began. When this rest period coincided with a weekend, we tried to arrange some activity for the whole shift, to enrich the team spirit and to get the chaps away from the base facilities and the NAAFI. A firm favourite was to charter a dhow, spend the morning shark-fishing over some aged offshore wrecks, and then run the dhow up to the beach, somewhere on the southern half of the island of Bahrain. We would then swim, drink beer and have a BBQ, before sailing back in the evening, after a fun and relaxed day out.

On this particular trip, we actually managed to catch a young shark, about five feet in length and with a good bit of meat on it. So, we thought it would be a good idea to take the specimen back to the Mess, where we could enjoy fresh shark steaks. The day ended a little later than normal and, when we got back to the Mess, we discovered that Chef and his staff had finished for the day. So, what were we going to do with the shark to keep it fresh? Easy, fill a bath with cold water, and place said shark in the bath until the morning, when we could carry it to the kitchens to be prepared for the evening dinner. Job done, have a shower and change and retire to the bar, happy after a good day out.

Now, in Muharraq, we had a resident detachment of Argosy aircraft from RAF Benson, and the crews did a six-week rotation. They were called ARDET, and the crews were, in the main, of a mature nature, had their own corner of the bar, and kept very much to themselves. Sometime later that evening, the door to the bar crashed open, and a very agitated ARDET member burst in and announced that he had discovered a shark in a bath. He was treated to a large whisky, and the windup commenced. Seeing what was about to develop, I and my Number 2 crept out of the bar, and ran across to the accommodation block, where we removed the shark and hid it behind the building, covered with a towel. Back to the bar, where the unfortunate crew member was getting even more agitated, and angry that no-one would believe him. "Show us," was the cry, and so a procession wandered across the sand to the accommodation block, drinks in hand. Our ARDET member threw open the door to the bathroom, to be confronted by an empty bath. The look on his face was indescribable, especially when he then checked all the baths and found no sign of the said culprit shark.

"Too much sun" was the consensus of opinion but, with a couple more drinks, medicinal of course, theatrical sympathy and an early night for the unfortunate recipient of our prank, a suitable recovery should be possible. The shark was returned to a cold bath for the night, and was delivered to the kitchen very early the following morning. There was some mention of the fracas at lunch, but nothing more was said, although faked sympathetic looks abounded. Come dinner, I forget what the poor chap ordered for his main course, but he was duly served with the pick of the very best shark steak! I am unable to describe the language and laughter that abounded for the rest of the evening but we did notice that, thereafter, every now and again, the ARDET guys invited us to their corner of the bar, and even offered us seats when they were tasked to fly a desert trainer. So, when you next order a shark steak, just ponder for a moment where it might have been stored!

Decision Time

Back in the late seventies, I was flying various incarnations of the venerable Canberra; a twin-engined light bomber, originating from just after WWII. In service, by then, for some thirty years, the cockpit layout bore little resemblance to more modern aircraft. Over time, bits had been added (or subtracted), to the extent that I doubt if any two of our fleet were internally identical. This wasn't a major problem, but it did add to the learning curve of pilots who were new to the squadron. Of much greater significance was the fact that the original Canberra airframe had been designed with propellers as the means of propulsion. This meant that the jet engines were mounted quite far out on the wings, so, in the event of one failing, the aircraft became extremely reluctant to fly in a straight line.

Asymmetric flight (as it is known) is controlled by using rudder to keep the aircraft in balance. So, every time you change the thrust of your remaining engine, you have to adjust the amount of rudder deflection, and every time your speed changes, you have to alter it too. That is fine, providing that you don't end up in the situation where you need more power to maintain speed, but the rudder is already at maximum deflection. This is known as running out of rudder authority, which the Canberra could do quite easily.

As a consequence of this, Canberra pilots spent much of their training time flying around on one engine. Take-off and landing are the most critical phases of flight anyway, without the added problem of rudder authority, so there was a laid-down requirement for us to carry out regular engine failure after take-off (EFATO) drills and asymmetric landings. These were usually flown in the T4 variant, which squeezed two pilots, side by side, into the cockpit, and were conducted under the watchful gaze of the squadron QFI. An asymmetric approach to land in a Canberra presented you with the challenge of deciding, at 600 feet on finals, whether or not you were going to get the thing on the ground in one piece. That was because, in the event of deciding at 600 feet to overshoot, you kept going downhill in order to gently increase speed sufficiently to acquire enough rudder authority to cope with full power on the live engine. Also, as the ground loomed ever closer, power to the live engine had to be increased gradually, because the RR Avon engine would accelerate very quickly if you simply shoved the throttle lever into the corner, and make it very difficult to stay in balanced flight.

Speaking of the RR Avon – it was, in fact, a robust and reliable engine that performed with distinction in a number of post-war aircraft, the Hunter and Lightning in particular. Unfortunately, the design of the engine intake on the Canberra did introduce some limitations. For example, if you had to descend through a cloud layer that was likely to cause icing, the engines had to be set at a fixed RPM and left alone, as any adjustment in power, with ice present around the engine intake, could result in a surge[1] or flame-out[2]. Taking off in a crosswind also required a special procedure, as the engines could surge as you went up to full power. The drill required you to line up on the downwind side of the runway, with the aircraft pointing 30° off line towards the wind. You then ran up to full power, released the brakes and steered the aircraft back onto the centreline as you accelerated.

Returning to the question of an EFATO, a particular problem with the E15 variant of the Canberra was that it carried a bigger fuel load than its stablemates, was therefore heavier, and needed more power. This was solved by fitting uprated engines, but no additional changes were made to the airframe. Consequently, in the event of an engine failure, it ran out of rudder authority at a higher speed, because you needed greater airflow over the rudder to counteract the increased thrust of the more powerful engine. This manifested itself in a particularly challenging situation on take-off where, immediately after getting airborne, a heavy E15 was not going fast enough for the pilot to control an engine failure and maintain maximum power on the remaining engine. The safety speed, as it was known, was some 10 - 15 knots above lift-off speed which, in a max-weight aircraft, seemed to take an age to achieve. There were various views amongst the pilots about what one might do in this event and, in many ways, we weren't helped by the fact that someone, in the past, had lost an engine at the critical moment but managed to save the aircraft. It was never clear whether there was any expectation that others would attempt to do the same, but my view was very clear. Before take-off in a heavy E15, I would brief my navigator thus: "In the event of an engine failure after lift-off and before safety speed, I

---

[1] Surge: Disruption of airflow inside the engine causing a loss of thrust.
[2] Flame-out: Jet engines rely on a continuous combustion process to produce thrust. When this stops the engine is deemed to have suffered a flame-out.

will close both throttles to try and maintain level flight and simultaneously call EJECT, EJECT. I do not expect you to acknowledge my call, just go."

After a short time on the squadron, I also developed the habit of conducting a final scan of engine instruments on the take-off roll, just before EMBS[3]. The two lines of dials were next to each other in a vertical display, so it was easy to see a discrepancy in either RPM or JPT[4], which might alert you to a potential problem. This wasn't a laid-down requirement but, nevertheless, I always did it, regardless of which variant of the Canberra I was flying. I had been on the squadron for about a year when, one morning, my nav and I strapped into a max weight E15, and set off to commit aviation. It was a bright and clear morning, with absolutely no wind to assist us, so I knew that the take-off roll would be longer than usual. Gently up to full power, and off we trundled, slowly accelerating down the runway. Everything was going fine until, just before EMBS, I glanced across at the engine instruments, to see one JPT above the maximum permitted, and still increasing. I called "Aborting", and closed the throttles, while my nav informed Air Traffic. We eventually ground to a halt just before the piano-keys[5] at the far end of the runway, and shut down the aircraft, taking care to starve the engines by closing the LP cocks[6]. The Avon had a habit of dribbling a small amount of excess fuel at shutdown, if you followed the normal drill which, in the Canberra, meant it would drip perilously close to the undercarriage. Very hot brakes and aviation gasoline do not mix well!

We vacated the aircraft where it stood and, after the customary discussion with the fire crew, who were very fast to react, and the Station Commander, who quickly satisfied himself that all was well, we returned to the squadron. About half an hour later, I was debriefing the Boss when our SEngO appeared, and confirmed that the top temperature controller on that engine was not working. Had we continued with the take-off, the JPT would have carried on rising, and the engine could easily have expired before we reached safety speed.

---

[3] EMBS: Emergency Maximum Brake Speed.
[4] JPT: Jet Pipe Temperature.
[5] Piano-keys: Black and white alternating stripes resembling the keys of a piano that designate the threshold of a runway.
[6] LP cocks: Low pressure valves that control fuel to the engines.

Calling Rover

Long before RAF Kinloss ceased to be operational in July 2011, we would detach there for up to two weeks at a time, whilst operating out to the west on the Hebridean ranges. Those were great days, often accompanied by some mischief, when in the company of imaginative squadron members away from the watchful eye of the squadron back at our base at RAF St Mawgan. We stayed in the Kinloss Officers' Mess, and many will remember it as being quite large and on three floors. We would usually be put on the third floor, occupying a complete wing together and thus 'out of the way'. After a day's flying, a game of squash and a shower, we would usually end up in the bar. There was a very keen and loyal receptionist called Charlie, whose ruddy face, staccato speech and strong accent were always a pleasure to encounter. He was a short, proud and wiry Glaswegian, who took his job seriously and was often on duty.

In those days, it was somewhat unusual to see a dog in an RAF Officers' Mess, but suggestion can be quite convincing to the point of believing, even though nobody has actually seen anything. One evening, as we left the bar to return to our rooms upstairs, Charlie gave us a friendly wave. As we made our way down the corridor, I let out my attempt at a dog bark, just for fun, then another. Charlie quickly responded and shouted "Is that a dog?" We confirmed that it was, and we gestured in the direction of the dining room, where the "dog" had headed. Charlie, evidently outraged by this intrusion and keen to sort it out, ran to look for the hound, peering under the tables and over the chairs. As he reached the far end of the room, we barked again, and pointed out the door shouting "There he goes!" Charlie quickly doubled back, and followed us as we started climbing the stairs, barking as we went. If you are familiar with the Kinloss mess, you'll know that there is a set of stairs in each wing, so it was easy to infer the direction of the dog by "throwing one's bark" as it were. "There he goes!" we shouted again, pointing to the stairs at the far end of the first-floor corridor. Charlie, in hot pursuit, and now totally convinced it was a Golden Retriever, ran along the corridor as we climbed the next flight of stairs; then we barked along the corridor on the next floor, as Charlie appeared somewhat flushed and breathless at the other end. Well, that was enough hilarity for one evening, as we were on the verge of inebriated laughter; we left Charlie wandering the corridors and retired for the night.

For some hours earlier that day, Kinloss had been subjected to a Taceval[1], and the "dog" episode had been a welcome light break. As we were effectively visitors, we weren't subject to the Taceval but, during the night, regular broadcasts reminding us that it was still in force, precluded any decent sleep. In the early hours, a few of us wearily gathered in the corridor of our wing and, eyeing the solitary speaker hanging from the ceiling, wondered if there was any way of disabling it. After some mutterings and fruitless suggestions, I went back to my room. Some minutes later, there was a huge bang, and after that the broadcasts magically ceased. There was a strong rumour that a .45 revolver had something to do with this, as next morning there was a hole in the speaker grille and, at the back, there were some strands of copper wire as taut as a guitar string, which disappeared into the ceiling at a shallow angle, with bits of plaster and wooden speaker cabinet on the carpet.

Although we managed to get back to sleep, we were a tad weary arriving at work the next morning. Fortunately, the range called our detachment hut and said that, as the wind was out of limits, we would not be launching that day. So, the boys drank coffee, read magazines and tried to find things to occupy themselves. We operated Canberra TT18s, basically B2s converted to the target training role, by adding equipment which enabled a target to be towed several miles behind. Our operations on the range allowed various military units to practise firing live Rapier and Blowpipe missiles at the target, using the Mk1 eyeball. It sounds dangerous in theory, but strict safety regulations ensured that there were no mishaps! Our transit to the range was usually flown at medium level but, if the weather was good and we had enough fuel left after our time there, we would return at low level, and it was always a memorable route back over the Isle of Skye and the Western Highlands of Scotland, weaving through fantastic valleys and admiring the brutal splendour of some of the highest Munros.

Today, however, this was not to be; the Taceval was still going strong, and the messages kept on coming over the Tannoy. And no, we didn't try to silence the speaker but, with the events still fresh in our minds from the previous evening, someone came up with an idea. I rang the guardroom and, putting on as official a voice as I could, announced to the corporal who answered "This is Squadron

---

[1] Taceval - Tactical evaluation of NATO declared units by NATO staff.

Leader Rover. I would like to speak to the duty sergeant please". When this gentleman came to the phone, I announced "Exercise, Exercise, Exercise. Exercise Loud Bark is now in force. Acknowledge." He duly acknowledged, and then followed a short pause, after which he asked "Could you tell me what to do with this message Sir?" I replied, "Do what you think fit, Sergeant." "Very well sir!" he said. I could almost see him standing to attention. I put the phone down, and we all cackled with laughter, put the kettle on again, and made ourselves comfortable for what was probably going to be a long day. Some minutes had passed when, over the station Tannoy, came "Exercise, Exercise, Exercise. Exercise Operation Long Bark is now in force. I say again…" etc. We looked at each other, eyes wide in excited disbelief, and almost fell to the floor with laughter. This was an unexpected bonus, and the message was regularly repeated for at least a couple of hours until, presumably, someone on the Taceval team put a stop to it. I'd seen the reaction to a Taceval broadcast like this before, and could imagine people all over the station frantically searching paperwork for this non-existent operation, whilst desperately trying to maintain the impression of cool professionalism. With the Taceval team observing somewhere in the background, I expect that there were many who felt distinctly uncomfortable. Even the Taceval team must have been caught out by this unexpected turn of events.

Later that evening, after the exercise had finished, I passed Charlie on reception; he asked about the dog, since he was disappointed that he had been unable to catch it. I said that it had been seen earlier that day, chasing a rabbit down the main runway until someone shot it with a Very pistol[2]. Surprisingly, Charlie seemed satisfied with the answer, and I went on to join a packed bar. Standing nearby was a Wing Commander, so I asked him how the Taceval had gone. "Very well" he replied. I said that we'd heard the broadcast of exercise Long Bark being tannoyed, and wanted to know what it was about. "Oh, it's an NBC[3] exercise" he said. Really? Could there have actually been an exercise called that? Could he have been making it up? Nah.

---

[2] Very pistol - Named after Edward Wilson Very (1847–1910), an American naval officer who developed and popularized a single-shot breech-loading snub-nosed pistol that fired flares.

[3] NBC – Nuclear, Biological and Chemical.

Never Drink On The Forecast

Attitudes to alcohol have certainly changed over the years and for the better. However, in the 80s, when this tale occurred, drinking and driving was an everyday occurrence, and drinking and flying was not uncommon on detachment. I'm not condoning it, just reporting it as a fact of life during those times. And, unsurprisingly, it could still land the unwary in a bit of bother.

It is always a pleasure to see your Lineys[1] keenly awaiting your arrival in dispersal, all bright- eyed and bushy-tailed, eager to hear of your most recent exploits of derring-do. The dispersal is always a hive of activity, with people and vehicles everywhere. However, it is less usual to see the Station Commander's car there; even less so to see said Station Commander waiting... beside your Lineys... accompanied by OC Operations, and none other than OC Plod (RAF Police) and a couple of his heavies, all in No1 uniform! This was the unnerving sight that Bob (my pilot) and I beheld on our arrival back at RAF Lossiemouth, post a very successful series of Sidewinder firings on Aberporth Range. What, you might ask, could be the reason for this grossly over-ranked see-in crew? Well, let me take you back seven days or so.

Credit: Gordon Niven

We were just completing the Qualified Weapons Instructor (QWI) Course and, as a grand finale, we had been allocated a couple of AIM-9G Sidewinder air-to-air missiles to fire against a Jindivik[2] on Aberporth Range - the first AIM-9G firings from a Buccaneer. The forecast for the week was extremely poor to begin with, but more promising as the week progressed. We landed at RAF Valley, in Anglesey, from a high-level transit, and went straight into arrival briefings et al at ST-CAAME (Strike Command Air-to-Air Missile Establishment). The programme for the first full day was a bit of mooching around Low Flying Area 7, a bit of weaponry, and impromptu scrapping with anything airborne (given our legendary

---

[1] Lineys: An affectionate name for the line mechanics (Airmen) who prepare the aircraft for flight.
[2] Jindivik: A remotely-piloted aircraft towing either a flare pack or a radar decoy.

manoeuvrability, this entailed running away as fast as possible in as straight a line as possible, but still top sport). Bob and I were programmed to lead a pair at 'crack of sparrows' (very early!) on a couple of simulated attack profiles (SAPs), and a first run attack (FRA) to drop a practice bomb at Pembrey Range, absolutely run-of-the-mill stuff. However, the forecast was for appalling weather, and you would have got better-than-even odds that the day would be a complete scrub. Hey ho! We were staying in the Trearddur Bay Hotel, our none-too-shabby digs for the week, so off to the bar for a few beers, dinner and an early night. The firings were still part of the course; we were still students; we could still get CHOPPED!!! Well, when did anyone go on detachment and on the first night have a couple of beers, dinner and an early night? Hmmm! And anyway, the aforementioned 'harry crappers' weather was already on the horizon. A quick peek outside as the bar extension was being negotiated, just to be sure. Yep, just as expected. Full blown westerly, plagues of frogs, the lot, marvellous. I could hardly see my hand in front of my face, it must be bad! Back to the bar.

Alarm ringing, alarm ringing, ALARM RINGING, I wish it would stop ringing, it's making my head hurt – even more than it was. HOLY S***, breakfast, plan, SAPs, FRA at Pembrey, and I feel like *&^&%**!!! Ah, but the weather. God, THE WEATHER! Rapid movement off the bed, followed very rapidly by a much slooooower movement towards the window. Pull back the curtains and... relief flooding through every nerve, every sinew, and every severely-damaged brain cell. The weather was still harry crappers, everything was dripping with moisture, the cloud very firmly attached to the deck. Hallelujah!

A bit of breakfast, a very quiet word with Bob; he is feeling every bit as shabby as me. "Don't worry mate", have you looked outside yet?" "No," was his reply. It was too bright – even with his sunnies on. Met brief confirmed that, indeed, everything was dripping with moisture, and the cloud was firmly stuck to the deck. There is a GOD. However, curiously, our Chief Instructor announced that we would be flying, and that we had better get our act together sharpish, take-off time was fast approaching. Incredulous looks between Bob and me..... followed by horrified looks between Bob and me. They're just winding us up. Hahahaha! They're just winding us up – surely? But we'd better go through the motions... which led us to briefing, out-briefing and then, horror of horrors, walking to our jets. Dumbfounded, we were actually going to get airborne with everything dripping with moisture, and the cloud firmly stuck to the deck and, to cap it all, our senses were still in a thick fog of their own from the previous night's libations.

I don't recall if we actually made any of the SAPs, we were up and down like the proverbial, in and out of low level, dodging the harry crappers, but miraculously, by the time we got to the south coast of Wales, the weather had improved sufficiently, and Pembrey cleared us in Hot[3]. Pembrey weapon patterns were great for wee aeroplanes like the Hawk, and no doubt the Gnat before that, even the legendary Hunter but, for the mighty Buccaneer, there was only one thing to do. Out over the bay, hang a right past the headland, and smash on through for an FRA to depart. Weapon switches checked, checked and checked again. No way were we going Dry[4], or have a 'switch pigs' on this one, not with half the QWI Staff following closely behind. Coast in, range boundary just ahead, one dayglo marker, two, oh and there's a white van parked by the fence with a couple of blokes watching:

"Off HOT!" What?????

"'Bob! We've just coasted in!"

"2 GO DRY," came the strangled cry from the Range Controller.

It would appear that the 'fog' was affecting more than just our cockpit, as our QWI Staff 'Mates' were heading for the wrong county, never mind the wrong weapons release point!

For clarity, every weapons range has a danger area, within which all targets are contained, with sufficient distance between target and boundary to ensure public safety AT ALL TIMES. Around each target, a Hazard Impact Area is established to ensure the safety of range personnel. Along the designated Line-of-Attack (LOA), and within the Range Danger Area for each target, there is a line of 3 evenly-spaced Day-Glo lead-in markers. So, there was never any danger to members of the public, and range staff would not be permitted to work along the LOA in use.

"Bob?"

"Definitely the target, White Target, DH (direct hit) for sure."

I had no reason to doubt him, he was almost a fully qualified Weapons Instructor. Maybe we had missed seeing a lead-in marker, after all, all things considered...

---

[3] Hot: Involving the expenditure of practice ordnance.
[4] Dry: Involving no expenditure of ordnance.

Range Controller: "Lead no spot!". (No weapon drop observed).

Gulp!

The transit back to 'Vallee Boyo' was uneventful, as the Judas weather was now clearing nicely. We were met in the Ops room by a stern, if nervous-looking OC 237[5], informing us that Pembrey were preparing to signal Strike Command about a bomb release outside the Hazard Impact Area, and needed a statement from the crew. We were to call them straight away.

First things first; Range Orders. The QWI course was useful in a number of ways, not least for being able to quote the number of rivets featuring in the ballistic and retard tail of our trusty 1000lb bombs. Equally useful was being able to quote Range Orders in your sleep. Find the relevant page, pick up the phone and dial. Stay cool, stay calm, this is no time to ruffle feathers - unnecessarily. "Yes, I was the Nav in the lead jet; yes, you have our names, ranks and service numbers correct; yes, we did drop on that LOA, on that target, at that time. Yes, I understand it is a serious, a very serious, matter (it was a very serious matter and no joking about it). Just one thing before you go, though. Can you tell me the actual colours of the lead-in markers and target on that LOA? Dayglo, dayglo, dayglo and white. Yes, that is what Range Orders say also. Might we ask you to send a chap out to confirm that is what is actually on the ground? Why? Oh just to be absolutely sure, it's not quite how we remember it (albeit through the various fogs)."

A short time later, Pembrey came back a little less abrasively, to inform us that the last lead-in marker was not dayglo, as stated in Range Orders, but white – just like the target. Ah, a bit of an impasse then. Mitigating circumstances? It would be embarrassing all round if ALL the facts came out in the signal to Strike Command, as would only be right. So, Pembrey agreed to paint the last lead-in marker dayglo, and we promised not to bomb it again; I thought it would be imprudent to ask if we had got a direct hit though. It turned out that the chaps in the white van were contractors, on their way to complete said paint job! Nuff said, back to the business at hand of firing our Sidewinders, PHEW!

The rest of the week went extremely well, two DHs on the Jindi flares for us and our course mates, the launch of our missile captured perfectly by our chase Buccaneer. And so, back to Lossie to prepare for a week of drinking, sorry driving

---

[5] OC 237: 237 OCU was the Buccaneer Conversion Unit.

round MOD trials sites and associated contractors. The flying programme for our return was posted the night before; a straight transit back, each stude flying with a Staff 'mate.' Except that, on the day, the crews were changed, so that Bob and I flew together and were sent on ahead of the other aircraft; odd; disquieting! And so there we were, taxying in to a very high-ranking reception committee. We smiled weakly at the assembled group, and strode off towards the Line Hut to sign the jet back in. Well, what else does one do after shutting down?

We were intercepted by the group, and challenged as to whether we were indeed the crew flying on this particular day, in this aeroplane and releasing a practice bomb on Pembrey - outside the Hazard Impact Area, albeit inside the Range Danger Area. Serious charges - yes we were. We were placed under close arrest, our ID cards were taken from us, and we were driven to the Officers' Mess, placed in separate rooms - minus our boot laces so we couldn't hang ourselves – and given a Police Sergeant guard.

A few hours contemplation is generally a good thing from time to time, just to put life into perspective. It's not such a good thing when you have the prospect of a Court Martial, and a dishonourable discharge with no pension, looming. Literally a few hours had passed, when I heard Bob shouting down the corridor; more bad news? A knock at my door revealed our QWI Instructor (and none-too innocent pilot of our No2 on that fateful day) with a huge grin on his face.

"You can go now, it's just a spoof."

Just a spoof! - ha f***** ha! A beer in the Bothy, with you b*****s, you must be joking! Subconsciously, I noted it was my turn to let off steam. On reflection, I can now see the Police Guard struggling to keep a straight face – git. Bob and I entered the Bothy, to find every man and his dog in there, to toast the jolly jape. However, I have never stared into the top of a full glass of beer for so long in my life. I was still going over the events of that near fateful day.

When you consider the implications, there is one clear lesson: NEVER DRINK ON THE FORECAST, particularly if you're a Stude on a course, and you could still get chopped! I am pleased to report that attitudes to mixing alcohol and flying (or driving) improved markedly over the following years, and am absolutely sure this sort of irresponsible and reckless behaviour could not happen in the RAF today...

Carry A Map!

The summer of 1980 was the first year the Hawk flew with the Royal Air Force Aerobatic Team – RAFAT – and expectations for the new aircraft were high. As the display season progressed, the team was still coming to terms with the increased range that the Hawk gave over the Gnat. Added pressure to perform arose from a collision between one of the aircraft and a yacht mast, off the coast at Brighton earlier in the month. This meant that, whilst waiting for the medics to declare the pilot fit after his ejection and swim, RAFAT could display only 8 jets. The team had a repertoire of 3 interchangeable types of display, dictated by cloudbase and visibility - Full, Rolling or Flat.

One summer Saturday morning, the team departed RAF Kemble for an arrival display at RAF Greenham Common, near Newbury, where the International Air Tattoo (IAT) was then being held and, as the cloud base was below 1,500 feet, a 'Flat' display was performed. At the end of the display, the recovery to Kemble was abandoned, because the airfield was in fog, and all 8 aircraft diverted to RAF Brize Norton. After a refuel and re-smoke[1], the 8 aircraft departed Brize Norton for an arrival display at RAF Wyton. Once again, because of the low cloudbase, this had to be a 'Flat' show. After landing at Wyton to refuel and re-smoke, the team departed for the final display of the day at St Neots, which was nearby. Joy of joys, a 'Full' display was flown, prior to a landing back at Wyton for the night.

Sunday was a beautiful warm sunny day, and the first flight for the team was a transit from Wyton to RAF Leeming in Yorkshire. Once there, and after refuelling, a 'Full' display was performed at Burnley, on the other side of the Pennines, before a return to land at Leeming. Then the fun began. We briefed for a transit from Leeming, to perform another display at IAT Greenham Common; this was to be followed by a landing at Kemble. Red 10 (the Team manager and Display commentator) was briefed to depart 30 minutes earlier, to land at Greenham Common and provide the ground commentary for IAT. As the team of 8 aircraft taxied out at Leeming, Red 4 suffered a hydraulic failure, and so all aircraft returned to dispersal. Since time was now critical, and the spare aircraft was at

---

[1] Re-smoke: The onboard system that produces coloured smoke was replenished.

Greenham Common, Red 1 – the team leader - had a moment of inspiration, and issued instructions over the radio. Red 4 left his unserviceable aircraft and got into the back seat of Red 8's Hawk, which then departed immediately for Greenham Common. The weather was beautiful and, although neither Red 4 nor Red 8 had a map (our normal terms of reference were to follow the Boss), they found Greenham Common easily, by flying south down the A1 to Stamford, then along the A43 past Northampton to Bicester, and from there past Oxford towards Newbury along the A34 – just like driving a car!

On arrival, Red 4 de-planed and mounted the spare aircraft, still unrefuelled, which had been brought in a little earlier by Red 10. Then he and Red 8 got airborne and met the rest of the team, who were still in transit from Leeming. The team, now with 6 aircraft, had waited for 10 minutes on the ground at Leeming, and so the RV[2] was roughly overhead the USAF Base at Upper Heyford. A small amount of diplomacy by Red 1 was needed, to persuade the USAF that we could use their airspace to join up; it was a Sunday afternoon, after all! We then performed a Full arrival display at Greenham Common IAT, with all 8 aircraft, just 10 minutes behind schedule. At the end of the display, 6 aircraft recovered to Kemble, whilst Reds 4 and 8 landed again at Greenham Common - the idea being primarily to collect Red 10 and his back-seater but, more importantly, to refuel, as the low state lights in both Hawks had been on for some time. The next day, Wing Commander RAFAT flew to Leeming, to collect the now repaired Red 4 jet and, by Wednesday, the team were back on the display circuit – but, thereafter, all pilots had to carry route maps.

Credit: MoD

A Far Eastern Experience

Reproduced from his book 'Rhapsody in Blue', by kind permission of the author,
Graham Williams, and Fonthill Media Ltd

It was Autumn 1961, and I had been an instructor at 229 Operational Conversion Unit, based at RAF Chivenor and flying Hunters, for nearly a year. We had started with Mk 4s, and we had just re-equipped with Mk6s, there being a plethora of such aircraft around since the Sandy's cuts of 1957 had just about had their full effect, and the front-line fighter squadrons of the RAF had been decimated. Duncan Sandys, then the Minister of Defence, had predicted, with great prescience, that the day of the manned fighter had finished, and that henceforth missiles were the answer to everything. I was grateful and lucky to still have a job flying fighters, so I was not in a position to complain; and Chivenor was a pretty good place to be in those days, even though the Mess was just a series of Nissen huts, and the art of keeping a coke stove going in one's room required some practice and skill. However I did have a unique place on the squadron; I was the only bachelor.

So, when the Boss walked in one morning, and said that he had to provide two pilots to ferry aircraft to Tengah, I do not recall being given very much choice in the matter; it was a case of who was going to volunteer to go with me. After some hesitation, Tony Park said he would, somewhat reluctantly, accompany me, to make sure I did not get into too much trouble. The task was to take the last two aircraft to 20 Sqn, who were in the process of reforming in the Far East, as the squadron did not have enough pilots to ferry all of their aircraft. One was a Mk 9 aircraft, and the other was a TMk7, their two-seat trainer. There were a couple of extra twists to this arrangement. Firstly, the right hand seat of the T7 was to be filled by a staff officer from Fighter Command, who "wanted to come along for the experience" – which was code for a good wheeze to escape the office for a couple of weeks, and get in a few rounds of golf in Singapore – and the other twist was that the Fleet Air Arm (FAA) wanted to take advantage of the flight, and add a Hunter T8 to the formation. The T7 and the T8 were virtually identical, except for cockpit instrumentation, and they had no navigation aids except DME, a device which gave you the range to a beacon, assuming that there was such a thing en route, and that you could actually get it to lock on. With 4 x 100 gallon drop-tanks, the 2-seaters had a range of about 1000 nautical miles. The Mk 9 had DME and a radio compass, and came with 2 x 230 gallon and 2 x 100 gallon drop tanks, giving it a range of about 1400 nautical miles.

Tony and I moved to St Athan in South Wales to prepare for this epic journey, and started to collect all the necessary maps and get the various diplomatic clearances. St Athan was a Maintenance Unit (MU), where new aircraft were stored and prepared, although I had to go and collect the Mk 7 from RAF Kemble. I remember it well because, when the day dawned, it was blowing a gale, 40 knots straight across the runway at Kemble; this was way outside the crosswind limit of the Vampire T11, in which the St Athan resident MU test pilot, Yank Jankiewicz, was going to take me. I demurred, but Yank insisted that it was not a problem, and that limits were not written for pilots of his ability. So, we went; and he carried out one of the hairiest landings I have ever experienced in a Vampire, about 20 knots faster than normal, and on one wheel for half of the landing run. But he kept it on the runway, and I collected our T7, XF310.

Then there was the question of who was going to fly the T8. In those days, all the FAA delivery and ferry flights were done by a bunch of civilian contract pilots, based at Rochester. The problem was that they were all quite aged, and used to delivering aircraft as singletons; hence, they had not flown in formation for years, nor it seemed did they want to. So, their Chief Pilot turned up with this somewhat reluctant volunteer in tow who, it seemed, was the youngest guy on the outfit, and the one who had the most recent experience of formation. His name was Keith. He was, I was led to believe, ex-RAF and had been at Chivenor himself, albeit on Spitfires. He had certainly had a fairly chequered flying career, which included delivering Spitfires to a nascent Israeli Air Force in 1948, under the leadership of a lady whose name I recall as Jackie Moggridge. From what little he said, it had been a fairly hair-raising trip. But it did not alter the fact that it was a good many years since he had flown formation.

Eventually, we had all the aircraft and pilots, including our passenger from Fighter Command, safely gathered at St Athan. We were already a few days behind schedule, a fact that was going to colour some of my subsequent decisions. Nevertheless, I decided that it was necessary to test Keith's prowess at close formation, even though that would put us further behind. We did a couple of trips, and we were encouraged and surprised to find that he coped fairly well. The aircraft were ready, we had all the maps and charts we needed and, we thought, the diplomatic clearances. The route was planned to be UK – Orange (France) – Luqa (Malta) – El Adem (Libya) – Nicosia (Cyprus) – Diyarbakir (Eastern Turkey) – Teheran – Sharjah – Karachi – Delhi – Calcutta – Rangoon – Bangkok – Butterworth (Penang) – Tengah (Singapore); a testing little trip, to put it mildly. For some bureaucratic reason, HM Customs would not allow us to depart the UK from St Athan, so we had to go to RAF Lyneham on October 23rd, and spend the night there, before finally launching off on the 24th. On the 24th, the weather was abysmal at Lyneham, although it was said to be clear at Orange, our first destination in the South of France. I was still a little concerned about Keith, but decided to go anyway. We had to climb through 35,000ft of cloud, and I was relieved to find him still on my wing when we lurched out of the cloud at FL 350, and we made Orange all in one piece and in time for a leisurely dinner.

I decided that we would try and get to Nicosia the following day. The first leg to Malta was uneventful, and normally the shorter range of the two-seat Hunters would have meant that we would have to stop and refuel at El Adem. However, when we looked at the forecast winds and did all our calculations, I reckoned that we could make Nicosia in one hop. If it looked as though we were going to be short of fuel, we could always divert from abeam El Adem; and, for once, the forecast winds met our expectations, and we made Nicosia in one hop, but not exactly flush with fuel.

It was at Nicosia that we had our first very negative experience. In those days – and it's probably still the same now – Transport Command crews had absolute priority on all accommodation en route. 'Captain Speaking', having travelled down the route in his very shiny Britannia or Comet, dressed immaculately in his best blue, having food delivered to him on demand, and being served coffee on the hour every hour, was so exhausted when he arrived at his destination that he had to have air-conditioned accommodation, so that he could get his eight hours beauty-sleep. On the other hand, single-seat ferry crews, who had been on the go all day, had done all their own servicing and refuelling, would have been lucky if they had got a cup of coffee at all, and probably had not had anything to eat, arrived at their destination absolutely knackered, having done two or three legs in one day, only to find that the transport crews had taken all the decent accommodation. Such was the situation when we arrived at Nicosia; the Movements Officer regretted to tell us that there was nothing available for us, and offered us a tent for the night, at which stage I decided to deploy our secret weapon. I had had my doubts about the virtue of having a Wing Commander as a passenger; however, when I told the Movements Officer that he would have to explain the situation to our VIP passenger, and then introduced him to the Wing Commander, suddenly accommodation became available. I just knew there was a reason for having him along.

That night in the bar, someone told us that we could make some easy money by selling whisky in Teheran. We were even told that, if we went to the back door of the German Hotel in Teheran, they would give us a good price for it. So, without really thinking about it, we bought ten bottles of whisky to take with us. We had planned to night-stop in Teheran in any case, but first we had to go to Diyarbakir in Turkey which, in those days, was not exactly the centre of the universe. On the following morning, the weather looked pretty fair, although there was extensive cloud cover forecast over Turkey. There was a rule that said you could not go if there was more than 50% cloud cover, because the Russians had a habit of bending the radio compass beacon, so that you ended up over their territory; but I was beginning to get concerned that we were getting even further behind schedule, so I decided to go.

The forecast was correct and, almost as soon as we got over Turkey, we lost complete sight of the ground, and we had to rely on dead-reckoning navigation, as we knew the beacons were unreliable - almost as unreliable as our navigation! I let down on the estimated time; fortunately, the cloud base was quite high, as there are some significant mountains in that area. But there was no sign of Diyarbakir. After some time, we did manage to make contact with Air Traffic Control, but the controller could not understand our problem, ie that we were at least uncertain of position, if not actually lost. The 2-seat Hunters were running very short of fuel, although Tony, in his Mk 9 with an extra 260 gallons, helpfully mentioned that he did not have a problem. I was just about to climb out and head for Adana, when suddenly I saw the airfield in the next valley. To say that I was somewhat relieved is probably a slight understatement; but our problems did not end there. ATC suddenly informed us that the runway was closed, as there were sheep or goats all over the place. We ended up landing on the taxiway.

I left Tony and Keith to do the refuelling, and was taken off to some hut in the middle of the airfield, where I understood that I could put in a flight plan for the next leg to Teheran. No one seemed to speak English and when, in a fit of pique, I tried to leave, it was made very clear to me that I was not going anywhere; even I understood the threat of a couple of rifles in my chest. After a short wait, a United States Air Force exchange officer arrived, with an interpreter in tow, and explained that we had arrived in Turkey without the benefit of diplomatic clearance. This appeared to be regarded as an original sin, and there was a weight of opinion that seemed to wish to put us in the slammer. Fortunately, the USAF officer managed to dissuade them from this course of action, and somehow we were allowed to continue. I have never thanked that man, but I was extremely grateful to him. He appeared to have the mother and father of punishment postings; he was the USAF representative on a wing of Turkish Air Force F84s which were, at the time, grounded for lack of spares (so he told me). No one spoke English, there were few facilities, and Diyarbakir was in the middle of nowhere. I have no idea what he had done to deserve it, but it must have been pretty serious. Without further ado, we got the hell out of Diyarbakir, and had a pretty uneventful trip to Teheran.

Teheran was a fairly lively city in those days, even though there appeared to be a surfeit of the military on the streets, keeping control, and we were accommodated in a hotel downtown. The first requirement was to find the German Hotel and offload the ten bottles of Scotch. Wandering around the city, with the Scotch wrapped in a map, was not something to be recommended, when there seemed to be a distinct possibility of being stopped by one of the many patrols, and asked to explain what we were doing. In fact, it almost turned into high farce as, when trying to avoid such a patrol, we managed to drop a bottle in the street, just as we had located the hotel. Fortunately, they did not take any notice and, after some discussion, the hotel took the remaining 9 bottles of Scotch off our hands. We concluded that the life of a smuggler was not for us, and vowed never to get suckered in ever again.

The following morning, we left Teheran with some sense of relief, and headed for Sharjah, in what was then the Trucial States and is now the UAE. Political sensitivities demanded that we flight-planned to Bahrain, and then diverted in mid-flight to Sharjah, because Iran had some sort of conflicting territorial claim. We refuelled at Sharjah, and had intended to go on to Karachi, but suddenly the canopy of my T7 started playing up, and would not close. We had a copy of what was referred to as the 'Vol 1', a sort of Haynes technical manual for the aircraft, but this did not throw much light on the problem. Sharjah in those days was very different to the modern city of today. It just consisted of a fort, an airfield, and a few buildings for the RAF facilities. The accommodation for transients was, once again, tents. The runway was just 'murram' - basically oiled sand, levelled and rolled. When the surface got a bit rough, they just moved the runway to a fresh bit, and then repaired the old one. The base was commanded by a Squadron Leader, with about 30 men. It took about an hour or more, by Landrover along the beach, to get to Dubai; and, when you got there, there was not much apart from the Soukh and the Creek; no hotels or restaurants, and very little electricity. Today, of course, it takes about seven or eight minutes along an eight-lane highway. So, we were stuck, and not quite sure how we were going to rectify the problem; that was until an electrician on the base heard of our plight and volunteered to take a look. He knew something about Hunters and, within a very short time, identified the problem as a blown fuse, which he replaced, and once again we were ready to go; but we had lost another day on our schedule.

Sharjah to Karachi was not a particularly long leg, but we had a major un-serviceability en route. Keith lost a fuel pump in the T8, and we had to talk him through the necessary procedure to deal with it. It had become increasingly clear, as we had progressed, that he did not have a great knowledge of, or familiarity with, his aircraft, and that we would have to nurse him along. At that stage, we only knew the half of it, as will become clear later on. However, we landed at Karachi without any further problem, but there was one procedure that we had to carry out which was for ever a source of mystery to me. We had to keep the canopies closed taxying in and then, under the watchful eye of some official, discharge an insecticide inside the cockpit and sit there for a minute or two, just to ensure that we had not imported any nasty bugs. Apart from the fact that we nearly suffocated, I could not for the life of me imagine what bug we could bring with us that they had not already got. We were finally cleared to open the canopies, and we then went to clear customs. We had refreshed our store of Scotch by this time – but only for personal consumption – so I declared it to the customs official and, taking no chances, told him that I would be happy to leave it in bond and collect it on the way out. His only comment was, "Why? Don't you want to drink while you're in Karachi?" So I took it with me, which was just as well, because we were about to fall even further behind our schedule.

We were accommodated in the Speedbird Hotel, just outside the airfield. This was run by BOAC, and was primarily for the benefit of slip crews from BOAC and Qantas; it could also take a full load of passengers, when necessary. It was a pretty high-class hotel, but they were not particularly familiar with RAF single-seat aircrew and, as we were aircraft captains, we were treated as BOAC captains – individuals just about akin to God – and signed all our bar chits as such; it certainly got us wonderful service. That first night, as were having a drink on the verandah, we were treated to a locust storm which was impressive, to put it mildly. We met a whole bunch of Qantas crews, who seemed determined to enjoy themselves; however, our more immediate problem was what to do about the fuel pump on the Hunter T8. Out came the 'Vol 1' again and, miracle of miracles, it did describe roughly what we had to do to change the pump. So, first thing the following morning, Tony and I decided to examine the problem, as Keith seemed to have opted out. The first thing we had to do was to defuel the aircraft. We borrowed a fuel bowser, and successfully completed that operation. Then we had to take out the unserviceable fuel pump from the bottom of the front fuel tank, which we did. I found the reference number of the pump, and sent off signals to Aden and to Singapore (the nearest RAF bases likely to have Hunter spares), asking for a spare pump. Then we sat back to wait. That evening the Qantas crews took pity on us, and invited us to a party. My main memory of this was having breakfast at 6 o'clock the following morning with one of the 707 Qantas crews, having not been to bed, at which point the co-pilot had an argument with the flight engineer and they went out on the balcony to settle it in the old-fashioned way. Then, just as we said that it was time to go to bed, the 707 Captain appeared, immaculate in his uniform, and announced that the crew coach was picking them up in 5 minutes, to take them out to the aircraft for the leg to London. I am told that things are not quite like that nowadays.

To our surprise, not just one but two fuel pumps appeared within 24 hours. The next exercise was to fit one to the aircraft; but, when I compared the new one with the item that I had taken off the aircraft, it was only half the size. The reason very quickly became apparent: I had taken the pump out of the fuel tank, but I had also taken the base plate off the bottom of the tank, an item that is normally never touched from the time the aircraft is built to its demise. What I really needed was a new seal, before I put it back. We gave the problem some thought, and decided that we just could not wait for a new seal. I went to the BOAC hangar, and borrowed a large tube of Bostik, put the new pump in the base plate, coated the old seal liberally with the Bostik, and reassembled the whole thing, tightening all the nuts up as hard as possible. Having connected everything, we then refuelled the aircraft, and sat for some time underneath it, to see whether it was going to leak. Amazingly enough it did not, and we were once again ready to roll.

The next leg, from Karachi to Delhi, was reasonably straightforward, apart from the fact that our landing at Delhi coincided with that of the Indian Prime Minister, Nehru. Nevertheless, after being stuck on the taxi track for half an hour, we managed to get refuelled and back in the air for another straightforward leg to Calcutta. There we found a Canberra crew waiting for us, to act as a weather escort for the next couple of legs. It was the time of the ITCZ (Inter-Tropical Convergence Zone), when the weather can be particularly unpleasant, mainly due to the build-up of cumulo-nimbus clouds and thunderstorms. Because of our delay in Karachi, the Canberra crew had been waiting for 3 or 4 days. They were particularly unhappy because, although they had been put in one of the most expensive hotels in Calcutta, they had been restricted by the management as to what they could eat and drink in the restaurant. We were put into the same hotel and, feigning complete ignorance, invited them to join us for dinner; we proceeded to have a rather magnificent and enjoyable evening. I have often wondered what happened to the bill, as I signed a chit for some horrendous amount, and was convinced that it would somehow find its way back to me. I am glad to say that it never did because, if it had, I would almost certainly have had to declare bankruptcy. The Canberra crew said that they would take off an hour before us the following morning, so that they could pass the weather and winds back to us. We never heard from them or saw them again.

By now, we were well behind our schedule and, in order to try and make up some time, I decided that we would almost certainly bypass our next route stop at Rangoon, and go straight to Bangkok. Fortunately, we had to fly just about overhead Rangoon, so that we could leave the final decision to then, once we had found out what the wind and the weather were at the other end and, more importantly, see if we had enough fuel to make it. As usual, Tony was sitting fat, dumb and happy in his Mk 9, with more fuel than he knew what to do with. It was Keith and I who would have the worry - although Keith did not seem to be unduly concerned; ignorance is sometimes bliss. Fortunately, the weather was absolutely gin-clear, and remained so as we passed overhead Rangoon. We tried calling the Canberra, without any luck but, fortuitously, a BOAC 707 picked up our calls, and asked us what the problem was. I explained what we were doing, and that we needed the wind and weather at Bangkok for the go/no go decision. He then proceeded to act as our shepherd for the remainder of that leg. The weather was clear at Bangkok, and we arrived with just a few minutes fuel remaining. I was never able to thank that BOAC crew, but they really performed a sterling service for us that day.

We had had very little support from the RAF along the route, but the Air Attache in Bangkok seemed determined to make up for it. He met us, and made sure that we got to our hotel, spent some of the evening with us, and introduced us to a guy who was celebrating the birth of a son with his pal, and asked us to join him. Keith had declined the invitation, and went off on his own. The name of our host escapes me, but I seem to recall that he was related, somewhat ironically, to Duncan Sandys. All I can remember of the evening is that we seemed to go all over Bangkok, ending up in some so-called teahouse drinking Saki. All we wanted to do was go to bed, as we had to be in the crew coach at 0500 in the morning; the only way to achieve this was to drink the Saki as quickly as possible, which was not really the smartest idea that I have ever had. No sooner had I got my head on the pillow when the alarm went off, and I dragged myself out of bed, washed, shaved, dressed and packed in the usual ten minutes. We were all waiting in the crew coach, but Keith had not appeared. I asked Tony to go back and see if he could find him; five minutes later he returned saying that Keith was just coming. He also mentioned quietly to me that, when he had got to his room, Keith was slugging back a very large glass of Scotch. Throughout the trip, his behaviour had been somewhat erratic, almost as though he was on some other planet. Suddenly all became clear. Sadly, Keith had a serious drink problem, just what one needed on a trip like this. However, it was Saturday morning, and we only had one more leg to do, or at most two if we stopped at Butterworth. So, we pressed on to the airport and the aircraft.

There were several important factors to consider at this stage. Firstly, the weather: whilst the ITCZ had not yet moved this far north, we were going to have to fly through it to get to Tengah. Secondly, would we have enough fuel to get to

Tengah in one hop without having to refuel at Butterworth? And, lastly, we were running short of starter cartridges for the 2-seat Hunters, so we could not afford to have more than one shut-down/restart. The weather looked pretty good, the winds were such that it looked as though we could easily reach Tengah in one hop, so we started up. After we started, it was clear that Keith had some sort of problem, in that he could not get his radio to work. After sitting there for some time trying to sort it out, it became obvious that we were going to have to shut down. Reluctantly I gave the chop signal, and we all closed down. I went across to Keith to find out what the problem was, only to find that it was his lack of familiarity with the aircraft systems that had caused the radio problem. At that stage, I decided that we were going to go nowhere that day, as it was plain to me that Keith was not really with us. Alan Jenkins was a bit upset, as he had arranged to play golf on Sunday morning with friends in Singapore, and he wanted to press on. But I then found out that our only possible diversion airfield, Butterworth, was closed, which made our further delay inevitable.

Once again, the Air Attache came to the rescue, and made sure that we were entertained. He had what seemed to us the perfect existence; he was accredited to 3 or 4 countries surrounding Thailand, and had his own personal twin-engined aircraft, a Devon, to get around in. His wife said she acted as the air hostess whilst her husband flew around, and he had a crew chief for the aircraft on his staff. He took us out to an island in the middle of some lake, where we had some outstanding shellfish. On Sunday morning, he insisted that we joined him to go to what he described as 'No 2 Mess.' It turned out that this was the house of the crew chief and his administrative SNCO, who were perfect, if reluctant, hosts, as it was before noon on a Sunday. All in all, a weekend in Bangkok was an experience not to be missed. This was before Vietnam had seriously escalated, and the American influence was minimal. It was, relatively speaking, uncrowded, and traffic was not the problem it is today. Our hotel was an interesting experience; located on the outskirts of town, it appeared to be a quite normal and well-appointed establishment. However, after about 8 o'clock in the evening, the dining room turned into one of the darkest night clubs I have ever been in, so dark that it was impossible to read the check. Just as well, really, as we never did discover who paid it.

Monday morning, and we were all in fairly good shape and ready to complete the trip. Even Keith looked fairly healthy and with it for a change. We only had three starter cartridges for the two aircraft (Tony's aircraft had a different starter system), so I briefed that, if one of us failed to start, I would get out and fit the spare cartridge, so that we did not have to close down whichever aircraft had started. Fortunately, we all started first time, and away we went. Even the ITCZ was fairly inactive and, apart from a slightly unpleasant ten minutes at one stage, we were not troubled by the weather. Only one incident marred the final leg. We were flying a very loose formation, and I looked round from time to time, to make sure everyone was there. Then I looked and there was only one aircraft besides mine; Keith was missing. Tony had not seen him and, despite many calls on the radio, there was absolute silence. I could not imagine how I was going to explain losing an aircraft; at best, it was somewhat careless, at worst it was gross negligence. I had just about given up when Keith came up on the radio, and apologised because he had fallen asleep and dropped about two miles astern. I was so relieved that I could not be bothered to get angry with him. We landed at Tengah without any further incidents.

One of the first things I did was to tell the 20 Sqn engineer what we had done to the Hunter T8's fuel tank and booster pump. He was horrified. The trip had taken us 18 days, and was an experience I would not have missed for all the world. What did we learn? Firstly, travelling with Qantas could be an interesting experience in those days. Secondly, before you take a spanner to an aircraft, make sure you know what you are doing. Thirdly, Canberra crews are not particularly reliable, but BOAC crews are fine. And lastly, the post of Air Attache in Bangkok was something to which every fighter pilot should aspire.

Credit: RAF

Ready, Aim, Fire

Commanding RAF Wittering in the early 1980s was an exciting prospect. I had previously commanded 233 Operational Conversion Unit (OCU), and knew No 1(F) Sqn well. The Hunter Wing (45 and 58 Squadrons) had disbanded, but No 5 Wing, RAF Regiment, comprising 2 operational Regiment Field Squadrons, 15 and 51, and the Armament Support Unit, were also on strength. Then along came a war in the South Atlantic; this is well documented elsewhere. Having dealt with our Station support for 1 (F) Squadron, and a Royal Visit to mark an RAF Regiment anniversary, life quietened down for a while. However, one incident provided a little more excitement than I might have hoped for. As part of my maintenance of Harrier flying currency, one day I went to Holbeach Range with Tony Harper. We did initial individual dry runs (non-firing attacks), to satisfy the Range Safety Officer's criteria, and then went 'Hot' (live-firing). I think it was on my first or second hot pass.

Off target, I simultaneously pulled 6G and rolled hard right, to reach the height for the downwind part of the circuit pattern. During this manoeuvre, all hell broke loose; for a very brief moment, while I was pulling and rolling, I assumed misbehaviour by the liquid oxygen (LOX) system was the problem, and that I would sort it out once downwind. Stratification in the pressurised oxygen tank often gave spurious warnings. The audio warning was absolutely deafening, giving a stunning performance. Unfortunately, I had firmly arranged my glasses, and tucked them well into my helmet, for optimum vision outside the cockpit, and this was neither the time nor place for any readjustment! Unable to read the tiny warning captions, I was unclear whether my LOX theory was correct. However, the presence of a second light could only mean that the fire extinguisher button was also illuminated, meaning that the caption also said FIRE. As I had slight difficulty seeing clearly which was the noise-cancelling button and which the fire light, I poked both in very quick succession: peace at last. The fire light stayed on. I had a quick glance at the hydraulic gauges, and all seemed well. I called Tony about my problem; he said, "drop the tanks," which I did immediately. He then said he could see no smoke or signs of fire. By now, I had hopefully begun to think it might be a spurious fire warning light. We chatted about possible diversions, RAF Marham being marginally closer than Wittering. I chose Wittering, because it offered access to 'good Harrier advice' should I need it. Throughout, Tony was very helpful, and his calming influence did a great deal to bring my pulse rate down 'off the ceiling'! Indeed, in terms of pulse rate, I am sure it was higher at Holbeach than it had been after I'd glanced off a few pine trees in a Swift in Germany; at least I had not damaged the Harrier. I later had my eyes checked, and some minor changes made to the glasses, and thenceforth positioned them properly.

I left Wittering earlier than I had hoped or expected, to take over as Air Commander in the Falklands. However, I did manage to get back later; when I became Inspector of Flight Safety, one of the requirements was staying current on a frontline aircraft. Given the workload, and the somewhat unpredictable nature inherent in the appointment, I realised it would be difficult to have enough time to gain and maintain proper operational currency. I asked the then Station Commander, Peter Millar, if I could be checked out on the Harrier again, and get at least enough flying to keep basically current. He kindly agreed. I explained my problem to Steve Jennings, OC 233 OCU, and asked him and his guys to treat me as a Flying Officer, which they did. For example, when I went for my Instrument Rating Test, I mucked up my 10,000 feet level off. I asked the Instrument Rating Examiner, Roger Moore, if we could treat the remainder of the flight as a practice. He said, "I am glad you asked that, sir, because you have just failed!" I felt reassured a close eye was being kept.

I greatly appreciated this, and I treasured the tankard they presented to me, inscribed:

Air Commodore Pat King (Honorary Flying Officer)

Credit: Rob Schleiffert

RVSM And The Brick

At the end of many years of undetected crime in regular service, I was spared the heartburn of having to look for a proper job by the advent of a wizard wheeze called Full-Time Reserve Service (FTRS). Securing a post under this scheme required one to persuade (by bribe or blandishment) a Binnsworth desk officer that one was fit and qualified to undertake the duties of one of the posts for which he was invariably undermanned. It also provided the opportunity, in my case sadly squandered, to demonstrate that one could be a better flight lieutenant the second time around. So started an idyllic 6½ years on 100 Squadron at RAF Leeming, flying the venerable, but much-loved, Hawk TMk1.

Although my day job was as a Qualified Pilot Nav Instructor (QPNI) on the Navigator Training Unit (NTU), I was occasionally invited (when they were desperate) to appear as a guest act on A&B Flight, who did the front-line support and aggressor work. So it was that, on a May morning in 2007, I and my mate Al departed Leeming, bound for Akrotiri, where we would provide support for 29 Squadron, the Typhoon Operational Conversion Unit. The first leg was planned to Orange, in the South of France, for a refuelling stop, thence to Luqa in Malta, night-stop, and on to Cyprus. The forecast included some headwinds, and fuel was going to be a bit tight. The Hawk, although not the most powerful beast in our inventory, would, given sufficient time and distance, climb to a very respectable cruising altitude in the high 30s, where it would float on the fumes. Then, as the fuel reduced, it would edge up to the low 40s, where our only companions were generally the bizjets.

The trouble was that, in between terra firma and desired cruising altitude, there was a wide band of airspace known, by the set of rules which governed it, as RVSM (Reduced Vertical Separation Minima), in which only suitably-equipped aircraft could operate, the requirement being the ability to transmit an accurate altitude to Air Traffic Control. The Hawk was not so equipped; it didn't normally matter, and we usually managed to blag our way through; some people had even been known to deploy the odd 'micro-porky': "Of course we'll be at altitude by the FIR[1] boundary," or some such. On this particular morning, no amount of

---

[1] FIR: Flight Information Region.

blagging was going to persuade French air traffic to let us into their airspace, unless we were already above RVSM or remaining below it. We didn't have the time to climb above it, so we had to stay below, until the controller was able to divert us from an airway and allow us to climb in free airspace. By this time, the damage had been done, precious fuel wasted, and the combination of higher-than-forecast headwinds and worsening weather at Orange meant that we would not arrive there with the required diversion fuel. So, we made an early decision to go to our nominated flight plan diversion, Lyon-Saint-Exupéry. Notwithstanding the flight plan, Lyon were a tad reluctant to accept us, until we made our situation clear to them, and we were reluctant to descend until they did. The result was a screaming last-minute death-dive, and an arrival on the ILS[2] in a clatter of bits, with Al grimly clinging on to my wing. The recovery could be the subject of a separate saga; suffice to say that we made it, and rolled out on the southerly runway, which is over 13000 feet long. Not only did we not need the brakes, we had to use most of our remaining fuel to reach the nearest exit!

Our parking slots, in the airport's leper colony, were not too far away, and surprisingly quickly, with the assistance of the ground staff – probably because they wanted to get rid of us – we were fuelled and ready to go. The downside of the nearby parking slots was the 3-mile taxy to the take-off end of the runway, which took about as long as the subsequent short hop to Orange. There we landed on a runway a mere 8000 feet long, but the parking ramp this time was some distance away. We parked the jets, prepared them for refuelling, and strolled off toward the Visiting Aircraft Section, where we hoped to beg a cup of coffee. At that point, we heard a soft pop, followed by a sighing sound, and turned to see one of the jets leaning over at a funny angle, the cause being readily identifiable as a flat starboard tyre. It was Al's jet, but I was wise not to laugh; ten seconds later, there was an empathetic pop and sigh, and my cab leaned gently in the other direction. We were now in a spot of bother, and our humour was not helped by a flight of 4 Mirage 2000s taxying past, their pilots clearly amused at what they saw. We technically had one-aircraft's-worth of serviceable wheels, but no means of transferring one to the other, so we were both stuck. There was nothing for it but to telephone Leeming, and request assistance. I'd like to say how sympathetic to our plight the

---

[2] ILS: Instrument Landing System.

shift manager was – I really would. However, his temper rapidly improved at the prospect of leading a road party down to the South of France, and we rapidly came up with a plan, although it would be a couple of days before they could arrive.

How to pass the time? Tragically, there was no suitable accommodation on base, so we had to slum it downtown. Marvelling at the utility of our newly-acquired 'company' credit cards, we were able to hire a car, so that we would be on call, and not reliant on taxis to and from the air base. We paid the daily duty visit to the ramp but, other than checking to see whether the tyres had miraculously re-inflated overnight, there was little we could do but wait. Time spent on reconnaissance is, they say, seldom wasted, so the surplus daylight hours were spent reconnoitring the local area, taking in such venues as Le Pont D'Avignon, and the quaint hilltop village of Chateauneuf-du-Pape – can't remember why. In the evening, we had ample time to consider our situation, as we attacked the confit de canard, and a drop of the local wallop, at our pavement table in the square, overlooking the Roman amphitheatre. It didn't take the brains of an Archbishop to figure out that the cause of the deflations was the blow-out of the fusible plugs in the wheels, designed to prevent an over-pressure, and that this had doubtless been caused by a build-up of heat. But why? – we had done no heavy braking. An after-action review of our day provided the answer. The Hawk T1, unlike its newer counterpart, is not equipped with nosewheel steering, and directional control on the ground is maintained by differential braking. The ambient temperature at both Lyon and Orange had been quite high, and the taxy, both out to the runway at Lyon and back to the ramp at Orange, had been long. In between, we had packed the wheels away in a nice warm undercarriage bay, where they could maintain their temperature, following which they distributed their accumulated heat to the rest of the wheel assembly – et voilà!

The engineers duly arrived, with four new wheels – they didn't have a lot of faith in us – spent a convivial evening in our company, and saw us off to Malta the next morning. They did not start for home until we had safely departed Luqa for Akrotiri – I think they pictured themselves on a ferry from Marseille to Valletta. They had, however, brought us a present. Each month, the ground-crew awarded a prize to the Squadron aviator adjudged to have committed that period's most heinous crime. This prestigious trophy was a brick – a very smart, emblazoned brick, but a brick nonetheless. In May 2007, there were joint winners. Harsh, but fair!

Both Feet In It

It was the autumn of 1967 and, after eighteen months at Cranwell, we had finally started our basic flying training. In those days there was no pre-grading course and not a propeller in sight – straight into Exercise 1, flying the Jet Provost. The JP was a sturdy little beast (thank goodness), with side-by-side seating for the instructor and student. In our fleet, it came in two guises, the Mark 4 with 2250 lbs of thrust, and the Mark 3 with just 1750 lbs. Both were powered by versions of the Rolls Royce Goblin, but the difference in performance was marked. Whereas the Mk4 was quite sporty, the Mk3 felt distinctly less urgent, and consequently gained the description "constant thrust – variable noise."

As a result, we embryonic aviators tended to fly the same Mark during the initial phase leading up to our first solo, and the crewroom buzzed with excitement as the days passed, and we all crept closer and closer to that important milestone. A first solo, for us, consisted of nothing more complicated than taking off, flying a circuit and landing; but, with less than 10 hours total flying experience I, along with nearly all my mates, viewed this as a pretty big deal. However, I was one of the students flying the Mk4, and I was finding it a bit of a handful on finals. As you approach to land, your rate of descent is controlled by power, and your speed by changing pitch via the control column. I initially found this challenging because, while every other aspect of my circuit work was fine, the responsiveness of the engine was catching me out on finals. I was devoting so much (of my limited) brain capacity to maintaining the rate of descent that my speed control was suffering as a result. Inevitably, as my frustration increased, I became more erratic, and I could sense that my instructor was running out of ideas.

The answer to my problem came in an innovative and unexpected way. It was late morning, and I was one of many sitting in the crewroom, enjoying a coffee before the next session of circuit bashing. A couple of friends had just gone solo, and others expected to later that day, so the pressure was mounting. Enter my instructor, who marched up to me and sternly demanded that I remove my flying boots and socks. As the crewroom fell silent I meekly obeyed, wondering if this was a part of some strange ritual. Producing a marker pen with a flourish, he proceeded to write '105 knots' (the JP's approach speed) in large letters across both of my feet. Then, without a further word, he left and soon everyone, including me, was laughing loudly at my self-inflicted predicament.

I went solo the next day.

Phantom Scramble 1976

"Leuchars and Northern IAF - alert one Phantom. " With that rasping and tinny message, coming over the "squawk " box from a distant operations centre, ringing in our ears, and the sound of klaxons and sirens urging us on, my navigator and I fled the comfort of the crewroom and ran to our waiting F4 in the hangarette. As we settled into our seats, there was a frenzy of activity around the aircraft, as safety pins were removed, and other vital tasks were performed to bring to readiness a fully-armed F4, in order to meet a potential inbound, airborne threat. With the canopies closed, I started both engines, and was aware of the hangar doors opening and the eerie encroachment of the 'haar,' or Scottish fog, swirling into our hitherto warm and comfortable world. A brief nod, a wave of the hands and a thumbs-up to the groundcrew saw us taxying into the dark exterior, and being instantly wrapped in the haar's wet and clammy embrace. Our business was to the North...

It had all started earlier in the day, a very warm one in the summer of 1976, when my navigator and I checked into the Interceptor Alert Force (IAF) compound at RAF Leuchars. My navigator," J," was a friend and colleague from a previous squadron, and was both very experienced and very able. I was enjoying my second F4 tour, was responsible for air-to-air-refuelling training on the squadron, and was also its Instrument Rating Examiner (IRE); the skills of both appointments would be sorely tested before the ensuing night was out. We settled into a familiar routine, having thoroughly checked the aircraft and prepared for what we hoped would be a quiet duty. However, there were some differences this time, particularly with the configuration of the aircraft. The squadron was due to fly to Malta the following week, to practise air-to-air firing, and carried a SUU-23 cannon on the centreline station instead of a fuel tank. This was an unusual fit, and we had been made aware of the performance differences, which were mainly less fuel but also increased weight and drag; all units involved in IAF were aware of these operational differences.

As the afternoon turned into evening, the temperature dropped and, as forecast, the haar started to form and creep in from the coast, not far away. We were on NORMAL alert but it was soon obvious that we should declare NO PRACTICE LAUNCHES, as this could result in the IAF aircraft being diverted on return, with all the logistical and operational implications that this would involve. We both now felt that an even more peaceful night was possible. The fog became thicker; J and I discussed the situation with the authorising officers in the chain of command, and subsequently declared MANDATORY LAUNCH ONLY. This was a very restrictive state, and required specific authority from senior sources, due to the potential risks involved to the aircraft and crew. Our peaceful night now seemed secure. There was another reason for my desire to stay put: my wife was just about at full term with our second, as yet unnamed, child, and I was naturally reluctant to incur unnecessary risks. No pressure, then...

"Leuchars Operations and Northern IAF, this is SOC (Sector Operations Centre), we have one "bogey" at North Cape". This message over our squawk box was unexpected and a tad unwelcome, as it meant that the Norwegians were tracking a Russian aircraft (quite likely a "Bear"), and that it would be equally highly likely to require identification. However, with all the meagre authority that I could muster, I reminded the operations centre that we were on MANDATORY LAUNCH ONLY. The reply was swift..." Roger. Standby." I can't remember the time lapse, but we were then informed: "IAF, you will be launched."

As J and I taxied the short distance to the runway, I was making rapid calculations as to the extent of the fog and the visibility required for a safe take-off. Meteorological visibility... that given to us by Air Traffic Control... differs from RVR (Runway Visual Range), and it is often the case that a cockpit view is different again. We both felt that there were "sufficient" runway lights for take-off, and that we were happy to go. However, the runway lights did pass by with worrying rapidity, and I was relieved when I left the bright orange glow of our fog-enhanced reheats behind as we left the runway. As we passed 200 feet in the climb, we emerged from the fog; we were now under a brilliant star-lit canopy, and were vectored north by the SOC for our intercept. The transit towards the Iceland/Faroes gap was uneventful and, although the details of the events now to be described have, after four decades, been dimmed somewhat, it is important to record that there were no gaps in operational performance by any agencies. However, from my perspective, the view from the cockpit remains clear.

It soon became obvious that we were operating at the extremes of controlling range for the intercept, and J was working hard to locate our target. Then, out of the ether, came a terse voice giving vital clues. Wary of possible erroneous and misleading information from our potential target, J investigated and finally located our bogey. During the search, we were both crucially aware of our reduced fuel state, and were making continuous calculations for our safe return, particularly as we did not know the location of our refuelling tanker aircraft. Suffice to say that we managed to identify the Russian "Bear" aircraft, and turned immediately for home. Despite our best calculations and planning, with the best available figures, our fuel consumption was higher than expected, due to the gun on the centreline, and it is an understatement to say that we were anxious to locate the tanker. We were not in radio contact with our controlling agency, and we started to search with our own excellent radar. Then I heard a low but clear curse from the rear cockpit and... "We've just lost our radar." Without the radar, we would not be able to see the ground in mapping mode but, more importantly, would lose a vital aid in locating the tanker. By then, we were in radio contact with the tanker, but were unable to establish positive positions, even though we had inertial navigation guidance. Then, for a second time that night, a mysterious voice gave us a very approximate range and bearing – this time for a rendezvous with the tanker. It was the only transmission that we received. We needed more than that, and resorted to the third source of information, the air-to-air TACAN, which gave a very accurate range, if nothing else. No joy... We were now scraping the barrel, and the tanker captain asked us to transmit, in order to achieve a DF bearing between us, but this also failed to work. During this tense period, J was calculating distances to home base and possible diversions, as our fuel state was becoming marginal. Remote and rarely used diversions were then being considered, along with the extreme possibility of jettisoning all our stores - 8 missiles, a gun and 2 wing tanks - in the event that we were unable to refuel. At this point, the tanker captain played his last card. He would use a flare gun to fire a green Very[1] flare to give his location. We heard the countdown and waited, scanning the horizon like a treeful of owls. Suddenly, in the eastern sky, a twinkling green star appeared, and then another and another. Joy, dear reader, was unbounded, but Fate was destined to have a final input, just to make sure that we didn't relax too much.

---

[1] Very: The Very Pistol was named after Edward Wilson Very (1847–1910), an American naval officer who developed and popularized a single-shot, breech-loading snub-nosed pistol that fired flares.

After some excellent intercept geometry between the tanker navigators and J, I eventually settled behind the centreline hose of the tanker. It was essential to achieve a no-damage first-time contact, and it was now my turn to perform well. The amber 'approach' light was illuminated on the HDU (Hose Drum Unit), indicating clearance to make contact. It was a no-nonsense approach; the probe hit the centre of the basket first time, and I pushed forward to activate the green light and much needed fuel transfer. In any refuelling situation, a red light on the HDU could illuminate, indicating an immediate and unquestioning withdrawal from the basket. In many years of tanker operations, I had never seen one – nor had any of my colleagues on the squadron – until that night! My left hand twitched on the throttles, but remained resolutely stationary as all the "training" circuit breakers in my head popped. A strangled radio call of "Maintain contact, maintain contact" was received, but I didn't need confirmation and had no intention of breaking contact, as all other indications were normal. The words "Fuel flows" soon afterwards elicited a whoop of delight from the rear seat, as I guess that J had been holding his breath for some time. We filled to full, anticipating bad weather at base, bade a grateful farewell to the tanker, and set course for Leuchars.

It is a truth, universally accepted, that Fate will always try to play a last card, and so it was that night. Fog (or haar in this case) is a fickle beast, and gaps can appear, allowing visual criteria to be established with the runway, even though the weather can be, strictly speaking, below limits. I therefore decided to make an approach but, at decision height, was forced to initiate the expected overshoot, and we sought sanctuary in the waiting arms of our Master Diversion Airfield at RAF Leeming in Yorkshire. We managed to return to base the next day, when the haar had lifted sufficiently and, after debriefing, I drove directly to the hospital to which my wife had by now been taken. In the early hours of the following morning, she was safely delivered of a boy. I remembered the story of Robert Bruce, the one-time crowned king of Scotland, and the tenacity of the spider in the cave in which he was hiding. The spider struggled six times to overcome problems, but eventually succeeded and inspired the king. Feeling an empathy with this story, perhaps it was no surprise that we named our son... Bruce, of course.

And Finally...
Some Words of Aviation Wisdom

There are many sayings associated with aviation, and these are some of our favourites:

- If the wings are travelling faster than the fuselage you are in a helicopter.

- If the switch is red or dusty, don't touch it.

- The only time you can have too much fuel is when you're on fire.

- The accident category "Birdstrike" does not include situations where the bird was still in its nest.

- When one engine fails on a two-engine aircraft you always have enough power left to get you to the scene of the crash.

- When a flight is proceeding incredibly well, something has been forgotten.

- The three best things in life are a good landing, a good orgasm, and, a good bowel movement. A night carrier landing is one of the few opportunities in life where you get to experience all three at the same time.

- You know that you have landed wheels up when it takes full power to taxi to the pan.

- As a pilot, one of two bad things can happen to you and one of them will certainly happen:
  a. One day you will walk out to the aircraft knowing that it is your last flight.
  b. One day you will walk out to the aircraft not knowing that it is your last flight.

- There are certain aircraft sounds that can only be heard at night and over the ocean. Most of them are scary.

- Son, you're going to have to make up your mind about growing up and becoming a pilot. You can't do both.

- The aircraft has a propeller to keep the pilot cool whilst flying. If you don't believe that, try stopping it and see how much the pilot sweats.

- Indecision is the key to flexibility.

- Anyone who flies his whole life within the envelope deserves to be posted home.

- It is better to be down here wishing that you were up there, than up there wishing you were down here.

- Flying a Lightning is like peeling a banana with one hand.

- You can only tie the record for a low fly-by.

- To err is human, to forgive divine; neither of which is MOD policy.

- Never share a cockpit with someone braver than you.

- If the enemy is in range, so are you./It is generally inadvisable to eject directly over the area you just bombed/Tracers work both ways.

- There are 3 simple rules for consistently making a smooth landing, sadly no one knows what they are.

- Gravity never loses, the best you can hope for is a draw.

And now, just to demonstrate that the breveted Master race don't have it all their own way:

Here are some actual maintenance complaints submitted by pilots (marked with a P) and the solutions recorded (marked with an S) by maintenance engineers.

P: Left inside main tire almost needs replacement.
S: Almost replaced left inside main tire.

P: Test flight OK, except auto-land very rough.
S: Auto-land not installed on this aircraft.

P: Something loose in cockpit.
S: Something tightened in cockpit.

P: Dead bugs on windshield.
S: Live bugs on back-order.

P: Autopilot in altitude-hold mode produces a 200 feet per minute descent.
S: Cannot reproduce problem on ground.

P: Evidence of leak on right main landing gear.
S: Evidence removed.

P: #2 Propeller seeping prop fluid.
S: #2 Propeller seepage normal – #1 #3 and #4 propellers lack normal seepage

P: DME volume unbelievably loud.
S: DME volume set to more believable level.

P: Friction locks cause throttle levers to stick.
S: That's what they're for.

P: IFF inoperative.
S: IFF always inoperative in OFF mode.

P: Suspected crack in windshield.
S: Suspect you're right.

P: Number 3 engine missing.
S: Engine found on right wing after brief search.

P: Aircraft handles funny.
S: Aircraft warned to straighten up, fly right, and be serious.

P: Target radar hums.
S: Reprogrammed target radar with lyrics.

P: Mouse in cockpit.
S: Cat installed.

P: Noise coming from under instrument panel. Sounds like a midget pounding on something with a hammer.
S: Took hammer away from midget.

The Final Landing – The Overriding Military Maxim:

"If you can't take a joke you shouldn't have joined."

Panavia Tornado F3
(Bagotville Beat-Up, Page 11)

Credit: MoD

Bristol Blenheim
(Chute and Shoot, Page 119)

Credit: Airwolfhound/Wikipedia

Grob Astir
(Into The Black, Page 120)

Credit: Aleksandr Markin

Gloster Meteor NF14
(25(F) Squadron In Cyprus, Page 179)

Credit: Alan Wilson

Gloster Meteor T7
(A Discretionary Commendation, Page 186)

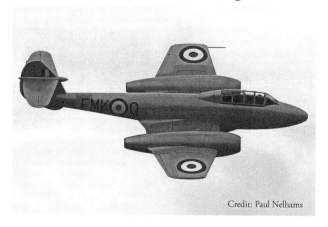

Credit: Paul Nelhams

Avro Lincoln
(But Modesty Forbids, Page 274)

Credit: Ken Hodge

Boeing B-29A Washington B.1
(But Modesty Forbids, Page 274)

Credit: RuthAS/Wikipedia

English Electric Lightning
(You Go Left, I'll Go Right, Page 278)

Credit: Mike Freer

Westland Wessex HC2
(Cable, Page 301)

Credit: Anthony Noble

English Electric Canberra E15
(Decision Time, Page 340)

Credit: Mike Freer

Vickers VC10 C1
(Twister, Page 324)

Credit: RuthAS/Wikipedia

100 Squadron Brick Mk 1
(RVSM And The Brick, Page 366)

Credit: Dim Jones

At the time of going to press the first two books in the "Out of Blue" series are still available through the Royal Air Force Benevolent Fund website:

www.shop.rafbf.org